TOUR
de
FARCE

By the same author

My Farce From my Elbow
Farce About Face

TOUR
de
FARCE

---

*A TALE OF TOURING THEATRES
AND STROLLING PLAYERS
(FROM THESPIS TO BRANAGH)*

IN FIVE ACTS

(WITH A CURTAIN RAISER, FOUR
INTERLUDES AND AN AFTER-PIECE)

BY

BRIAN RIX

WITH ADDITIONAL SCENES BY JONATHAN RIX
AND DECOR BY DAVID DRUMMOND

Hodder & Stoughton
LONDON SYDNEY AUCKLAND

British Library Cataloguing in Publication Data

Rix, Brian
  Tour de Farce: Tale of Touring Theatres
  and Strolling Players (from Thespis to
  Branagh)
  I. Title
  792 028092

ISBN 0-340-52265-8

Published by Hodder and Stoughton,
a division of Hodder and Stoughton Ltd,
Mill Road, Dunton Green, Sevenoaks, Kent TN13 2YA.
Editorial Office: 47 Bedford Square, London WC1B 3DP.

Photoset by Rowland Phototypesetting Ltd,
Bury St Edmunds, Suffolk

Printed in Great Britain by St Edmundsbury Press Ltd,
Bury St Edmunds, Suffolk

PRODUCTION CREDITS

I would like to acknowledge the following, who have been especially helpful in the production of this book. The many others to whom I owe a debt of gratitude appear in the Curtain Calls at the end.

JONATHAN RIX My younger son. A part-time schoolmaster, to make ends meet, he is becoming increasingly successful as a writer – and deservedly so. He has undertaken much of the research for this book (with the help of Kay Hutchings at the Garrick Club library), and he has so skilfully copied my writing style (such as it is) that I am quite unable to tell where he stops and I begin. Oh – and vice versa . . .

DAVID DRUMMOND A bibliopole and sometime strolling player. As you will discover, he once worked for me as an actor, which must have speeded his desire to achieve success elsewhere. This he has done by running the most remarkable shop containing memorabilia, juvenilia, books and ephemera of the performing arts at 11 Cecil Court, off St Martin's Lane in the heart of London's West End. He has provided all the pictures for this book, many of which you can see if you visit 'Pleasures of Past Times'. You should. It is indeed a pleasure.

DAVID F. CHESHIRE A theatre historian and journalist. As Information Officer of the Theatres Trust in London, the body set up in 1976 to 'safeguard the nation's theatres', he has been an invaluable and tireless source of information – which is understandable, considering his job. He himself is the author of several books, the last one, in 1989, being the definitive work – *Portrait of Ellen Terry*. Whenever David was out of the office, I was also helped by the Trust's director, John Earl. I only wish I knew as much about the theatre as these two gentlemen. I envy them.

CHARLES VANCE An actor-manager, he has toured more than 150 productions, many by Agatha Christie, and in over half he has been either an actor or a director or both. For several years he was President of the Theatrical Management Association (TMA) and currently serves as Chairman of the Standing Advisory Committee on Local Authorities and the Theatre (SACLAT) and is Vice-Chairman of the Theatres Advisory Council. No wonder he is a walking theatrical encyclopaedia.

RENÉE STEPHAM A theatre-booking agent. There is much about her in the story, so please read on.

OUR SPONSORS

Dedicated to the Tudors, who labelled us rogues and vagabonds, the Puritans, who closed us down and the Conservative MP, Mr Terry Dicks (Hayes and Harlington) who would, if he had the chance. 'Arty-farty people' indeed!!

BRIAN RIX,
WIMBLEDON COMMON, LONDON
APRIL 1992

SYNOPSIS OF SCENES
over 2,500 years . . . and still running

*Farce was introduced as a term in the English theatre
around 1660 to denote short entertainments which
'stuffed' the evening. Hence the title of this book –
and the chapter headings which follow*

CURTAIN RAISER
'*Is Your Honeymoon Really Necessary?*'   3
(E. V. TIDMARSH, DUKE OF YORK'S, 1944)
Scene-setting

ACT I
SCENE I   '*Outrageous Fortune*'   8
(BEN TRAVERS, WINTER GARDEN, 1947)
From Ancient Greece to Victorian Britain

SCENE II   '*See How They Run*'   29
(PHILIP KING, COMEDY, 1945)
The great actor-managers

INTERLUDE
'*On Monday Next . . .*'   39
(PHILIP KING, COMEDY, 1949)
The repertory movement

ACT II
SCENE I   '*Worm's Eye View*'   42
(R. F. DELDERFIELD, WHITEHALL, 1945)
Middle years for Donald Wolfit but . . .

SCENE II   '*The Happiest Days of Your Life*'   56
(JOHN DIGHTON, APOLLO, 1948)
. . . for me?

INTERLUDE
'*Loot*'   73
(JOE ORTON, ROYAL COURT THEATRE, 1975)
Two seriously rich touring circuits

ACT III
'*The Better 'Ole*'   86
(BRUCE BAIRNSFATHER AND ARTHUR ELIOT, OXFORD, 1917)
Second World War No. 1 dates

INTERLUDE
'*As Long As They're Happy*'   117
(VERNON SYLVAINE, GARRICK, 1953)
ENSA and CEMA

ACT IV
'*Reluctant Heroes*'   123
(COLIN MORRIS, WHITEHALL, 1950)
Another actor-manager struggles on to the green
(cf. greengage)

INTERLUDE
'*Hobson's Choice*'   171
(HAROLD BRIGHOUSE, APOLLO, 1916)
Or, more accurately, mine

ACT V
'*Out of Order*'   179
(RAY COONEY, SHAFTESBURY, 1990)
Thirty more assorted theatres in this tour de farce

AFTER-PIECE
'*Will Any Gentleman?*'   237
(VERNON SYLVAINE, STRAND, 1950)
A new breed of actor-manager

CURTAIN CALLS
The Players, from Burbage to Branagh, with further
production credits   245

ACKNOWLEDGMENTS   271

DATE SHEET   273

INDEX   287

INDEX OF TOURING
THEATRES VISITED

Prince of Wales Theatre,
    Cardiff   56
Pavilion, Torquay   58
Theatre Royal, Exeter   60
New Coliseum Theatre, Harrow   64
Arts Theatre of Cambridge   66
New Theatre, Hull   68, 142
Opera House, Manchester   87
Palace Theatre, Manchester   87
Tameside Theatre, Ashton-
    under-Lyne   92
Royal Court Theatre, Liverpool   93
Grand Theatre and Opera House,
    Leeds   95
Theatre Royal, Glasgow   99
King's Theatre, Glasgow   99
King's Theatre, Edinburgh   102
Royal Lyceum Theatre,
    Edinburgh   102
His Majesty's Theatre, Aberdeen 104
Theatre Royal, Newcastle-upon-
    Tyne   106
Tyne Theatre and Opera House,
    Newcastle-upon-Tyne   106
Theatre Royal, Nottingham   110
Grand Theatre and Opera House,
    Croydon   113
Ashcroft Theatre, Croydon   113
White Rock Pavilion, Hastings   127
Wimbledon Theatre   131
Dolphin Theatre, Brighton   133
Theatre Royal, Brighton   133
Winter Gardens Pavilion,
    Blackpool   136
Grand Theatre, Blackpool   137
Palace Theatre, Plymouth   139
Theatre Royal, Plymouth   139
King's Theatre, Southsea   144
Theatre Royal, Birmingham   147
Alexandra Theatre, Birmingham 147

Hippodrome, Birmingham   147
Embassy Theatre, Peterborough 151
Key Theatre, Peterborough   151
Theatre Royal, Bath   153
Little Theatre, Bournemouth   157
Grand Theatre, Swansea   159
Palace Pier Theatre, Brighton   162
Theatre Royal, Norwich   163
Victoria Pavilion, Ilfracombe   166
Royal Opera House, Leicester   168
Hippodrome, Golders Green 44, 179
Streatham Hill Theatre   179–180
Empire Theatre, Chiswick   180
Empire Theatre, Hackney   180
Empire Theatre, Wood Green   180
Richmond Theatre, Richmond-
    upon-Thames   181
Garrick Theatre, Southport   183
Hippodrome, Coventry   186
Playhouse, Weston-super-Mare 188
Futurist, Scarborough   190
Princess Theatre, Torquay   192
Forum, Billingham   193
Gordon Craig Theatre,
    Stevenage   193
Wyvern Theatre, Swindon   193
New Theatre (now Apollo
    Theatre), Oxford   196
Hippodrome, Bristol   198
Theatre Royal, Hanley   200
Devonshire Park Theatre,
    Eastbourne   202
Congress, Eastbourne   202
Pavilion, Bournemouth   204
New Theatre, Cardiff   205
Empire, Sunderland   208
Civic Theatre, Darlington   211
Theatre Royal, York   214
Alhambra Theatre, Bradford   215
Lyceum Theatre, Sheffield   217

Grand Theatre, Wolverhampton 219
Theatre Royal, Bury St
    Edmunds   221
Royal Shakespeare Theatre,
    Stratford-upon-Avon   225
Festival Theatre, Malvern   227

Palace Theatre, Westcliff-on-Sea 229
Grand Opera House, Belfast   230
Opera House, Cork   230
Olympia, Dublin   230
Gaiety Theatre, Dublin   230

With fleeting visits to even more theatres as we journey along – and the appearance of numerous actors, many of whom take their bow, in chronological order, in the Curtain Calls between pages 245 and 272.

CURTAIN RAISER

CLOCKWISE FROM TOP Ellen Terry and Henry Irving;
Charles Wyndham, Sybil Thorndike, Irene Vanbrugh,
Edith Evans and John Martin Harvey.

'Is Your Honeymoon
Really Necessary?'

Once upon a time, not so long ago, the great and the good in the theatrical profession were quite used to packing their bags and going on tour. Not always trekking round this country, of course, but often on highly rewarding trips to the Colonies – Australia, South Africa and that lost colonial outpost, America. Names like Sir Henry Irving, Sir Charles Wyndham, Sir John Martin-Harvey, Sir Johnston Forbes-Robertson and Sir Frank Benson emerge from the past, whilst – on the distaff side – Dames Ellen Terry, Sybil Thorndike, Irene Vanbrugh and Edith Evans could occasionally be spotted on a Sunday morning train call at Crewe or, more salubriously, aboard a transatlantic liner. In those days, it was no disgrace to be on the road, for it was seen as a particularly lucrative method of topping up the coffers to pay the creditors and the income tax. Furthermore, because there was no television and only rudimentary cinema, it enabled a huge theatre-going audience to keep in touch with its favourites. In 1912 there were no less than twenty Touring Circuits listed in the *Stage Year Book* ('where and to whom to write for engagements'), including the renowned Moss Empires and the, then, still separate Stoll Tours. The great conglomerate of Stoll Moss was yet to come. Howard and Wyndham, although very active in Scotland and the North, were not even mentioned. In the 1920s there were nearly 250 touring companies constantly threading their way through the country, giving their all in such diverse venues as the Alexandra, Widnes and the Alexandra, Birmingham; the Theatre Royal, Barnsley and the Theatre Royal, Bath. Dirty dressing-rooms and even dirtier digs were the lot of thousands of touring thespians in those days, quite apart from filthy trains. No wonder golf, poker and adultery were so popular . . .

All this frenzied activity lessened with the onset of the talkies and came to an end after the Second World War. To begin with, television was here to stay and fewer actors wished to leave the fleshpots of London, with all the ancillary opportunities of films, television and voice-overs. In addition, running two homes, with a mortgage to pay in London and rent to pay

3

on tour, was hardly a prudent financial exercise, even if it did mean a change of scenery and sleeping partners. What is more, no one seemed willing or able to undertake the task so staunchly pursued by Sir Frank Benson and Sir Donald Wolfit – that of bringing Shakespeare (and other classics) to the widest possible audience in the provinces. And can you wonder at it? Hermione Gingold's bitchy remark was enough to put the mokkers on any likely successor: 'Olivier is a tour de force. Wolfit is forced to tour.' At least, it is purported that Miss Gingold was responsible for that acid comment. Actually, it was written for her by Alan Melville as part of a sketch with Henry Kendall in *Sweetest and Lowest* at the Ambassador's Theatre in 1946. Some ascribe the remark to Kenneth Tynan. They are wrong. One thing is certain, though. Ken did put the boot in firmly and finally, as far as Wolfit was concerned, with his 1953 *Evening Standard* notice for *The Wandering Jew* at the King's Theatre, Hammersmith:

> Where, then, is Mr Wolfit's spiritual home? My answer is nowhere in particular: he is a nomad, part of the great (albeit dead) tradition of the strolling player, who would erect his stage in a tavern yard and unravel his rhetoric to the winds. Mr Wolfit is not an indoor actor at all. Theatres cramp him. He would be happiest, I feel, in a large field.

Would you want to tour after that? In fact, would you want to act at all, after that? I doubt it; and it is clear that such knocks affected Donald deeply and he never, really, took up full-time touring again, even though he was knighted for his efforts in that direction. No other actor-managers, of note, appeared on the scene to present the 'classics' on the road for many years. Until 1972, in fact, when – albeit fleetingly – Ian McKellen became a founder-member of the Actors' Company, along with Edward Petherbridge; and, some time later still, Sir Anthony Quayle launched his Compass Company, now led by Tim Pigott-Smith. Michael Pennington (with director, Michael Bogdanov) started the English Shakespeare Company and Kenneth Branagh his Renaissance group, thus enabling these splendid actors to be seen to great advantage in great plays. Of course, other renowned touring companies existed, or exist: the late Peter Bridge with his glossy revivals, cast with fading film stars; Duncan Weldon with Triumph Theatre Productions; Toby Robertson and Prospect Theatre Company, out of which grew the Cambridge Theatre Company, headed, originally, by Richard Cotterell and followed by Robert Lang, Jonathan Lynn and Bill Pryde – but in all such cases these companies were (or are) run by directors or producers who could (or can) buzz off home when the show's on the road. All except Robert Lang, that is. He went back to being an actor.

But touring for touring's sake, or as a positive career move, remained an anathema for the majority of actors, both well known or otherwise. Indeed, in his 1989 autobiography, *I Must Be In There Somewhere*, Joss Ackland has written:

There was only one problem: non-existent audiences. We played to empty houses throughout Britain. Most people thought *The Dresser* was a piece of furniture! It was this show that convinced me that TV had really made its mark, and good, live theatre was dead in the provinces . . . In most towns we followed an Agatha Christie play, which in the West End had come off almost before it opened, yet on tour it played to full houses everywhere.

From a personal point of view, there is considerable irony in Joss's comments. Not only was he emptying the touring theatres with *The Dresser*, loosely based by Ronald Harwood on a Donald Wolfit tour of *King Lear*, which is where I began my acting career, but his comment that only Agatha Christie seemed to fill provincial theatres also applied to me for, over the years from the mid-50s to the mid-70s, I only had to appear in a touring theatre with one of the Whitehall or Garrick farces, for house records to fall like flies into my lap. And yet I hated it. Not the records, or the audiences or the appreciation, but the touring. Being away from home. 'Train versions' – cutting all corners on Saturday nights – so you could dash off home, perhaps driving hundreds of miles, for a truncated weekend, before slogging round the country to yet another venue the following Monday, with all the loneliness and boredom and sense of point-lessness which accompanied the whole operation. Who cared if you were the best in Bradford or a wow in Wolverhampton? Perhaps your backers or your bank manager, but certainly not your wife and children. You couldn't wait to get back to the West End and the repetition, night after night, of the same play you had just toured, or the same play you would eventually have to tour again. At least you would see something more of your family then. Well, that was the theory, but one of the remarks which returns to haunt me, as the years rush by and memories fade, is retold by my children, now long grown up and with families of their own: 'Ssh, Daddy's sleeping' was apparently whispered to them, afternoon after after-noon, when they returned from school and I was known to be resting before continuing my nightly stint at the Whitehall or Garrick theatres, or 'Ssh, Daddy's sleeping' as they girded their loins to go to school the following morning. I must have been one helluva dynamic dad. But at least they could peek in and see me snoring on the sofa or drowsing on the bed, and know that I existed. When I was on tour, I was just a disembodied voice on the phone. And that went on, with minor alterations as children grew up and left home, for over thirty years. Twelve thousand six hundred and sixty-nine performances in all, spread over one thousand four hundred and fifty-six weeks; one thousand and seventy-three in London, the rest – three hundred and eighty-three weeks – on tour or in repertory. With rehearsals, that is nearly eight years away from my genial hearth. Can you wonder I got sick of it all?

And I am not the only one, by a long chalk. Others have done it, too, and would agree with me. Others would not.

What is more – it has been going on for centuries . . .

The lights fade and come up on Act I.

William Kempe, the original performer of Dogberry in *Much Ado About Nothing*. (Woodcut, dated 1600.)

ACT I

SCENE I
'Outrageous Fortune'

It was all that Greek poet's fault, really. If Thespis hadn't had the bright idea of shoving actors into his plays, as distinct from the chorus and its leader, then pushing them round the countryside on a cart as the original Number One tour, life on the road might never have been invented. Furthermore, to make matters worse, he won the first ever drama award in 534BC, and this gave him, and his successors, the strange delusion that it was all worthwhile. It was some little time, however, before the habit spread to perfidious Albion.

Eventually, though – like the plague – it arrived on these shores, where the earliest performances involved ritualised dancing and singing, as well as demonstrating the unquenchable human desire for storytelling. On the other hand, I haven't found any landlady stories dating back to this time, nor any reference to digs – other than latterday archaeological ones – so I think we can safely assume that there was very little touring along Thespian lines . . .

The Romans, who *were* on a tour of a kind, I suppose, built some auditoria in Britain, but their theatre was largely about controlling the masses, through popular entertainment. Unlike the Greeks they held theatre in low regard, and mixed spectacle with drama. You only need to go to the theatre at St Albans to see this mixture in action. At the front of the stage is a slot from which a wooden shutter was raised to hide the stage between acts. This 'curtain' was partially to increase the element of dramatic surprise, but more to do with protecting the audience from the wild animals used in the performances. St Albans, it would seem, had the first safety curtain in Britain, but I still wouldn't have wanted to sit in the front of the stalls. This type of theatre has, of course, not lasted – except in circuses – and the Roman influence is most felt through the Code of Theodisius made in AD435 which banned Sunday performances and is still causing problems for theatre managers, Equity and the Musicians' Union to this very day – never mind the Lord's Day Observance Society.

The Roman theatres had all closed by the sixth century, and the dramatic form was left to itinerant wanderers and developing church ritual. The wanderlust of the performer has been evident since recorded time, and throughout the Dark Ages scholars and bards moved about the country educating and entertaining, joining in festivities, raising the tone of debate, reporting news and events and, because of this, found themselves held in high regard. On the other hand, the church ceremonial took much from the traditional folk festivals which, in turn, were usually connected with the yearly agricultural cycle, as well as long-forgotten pagan rituals, illustrating – even in those days – that if you can't beat 'em, join 'em. So, despite the occasional wandering minstrels, most drama was home produced and performed, with its basis in Biblical stories, traditional tales, local folklore and athletic events, such as Morris dancing or Jack-in-the-Green.

The performances must usually have been in the open air, and there are even sites from pre-AD1000 which can be considered as 'theatrical venues'. The 'stone benches' to be seen at the Earthen Round of St Just near Land's End, and the tiered grass banks of the Piran Round at Perranporth are but two – whilst the Penrith Round in Cumbria, known as King Arthur's Round Table, would have held as many as 10,000 people. In Scotland there were play fields attached to several burghs (including those at Aberdeen, Dundee, Edinburgh and Perth) and these sites can only have been for public gatherings, which might well have included the performance of some long-forgotten dramas.

Most communities in Anglo-Saxon England would also have given pride of place to the Gleeman. He was the community's singer and storyteller and, despite disappearing with the arrival of the Normans, he, and his like, seem to have been much respected. Maybe that's why the Normans got rid of them, and it was centuries before the acting profession regained the level of respect accorded to those early performers – if, indeed, it ever has.

It is from around the time of the first millennium that we start to have concrete evidence concerning actual performances, mainly through the development of ecclesiastical drama, where the dramatic Christian story began to be performed as part of the ceremony. Chanting developed into song, and then written texts or 'tropes' were added when the religious orders realised how effectively these got the message across to the illiterate and non-Latin-speaking plebs. As that was the majority of the Great Anglo-Saxon Public, this early form of PR would have gladdened the heart of many a modern advertising agent – hyperbole heaped on pleonasm – in the true spirit of the television commercials, and Chaucer was not slow to dramatise this. In the Miller's Tale he describes the parish clerk, Joly Absolon – an enthusiastic amateur taking part in such biblical events – thus:

> Sometime to show his lightness and maistrie
> He plieth Herode on a skaffold hie.

Right, I guarantee that is my last Chaucerian quote for I, too, find him somewhat difficult to follow, without the academic guidance of Professor Neville Coghill to clear the air.

Inevitably, with performances in the vernacular, a secular influence began to be felt, and in AD1210 there was a Papal Edict which banned the clergy from performing plays in public. The idea of every vicar being a frustrated actor would seem to have some historic credence. I wonder what they did with their props and costumes? Probably kept them hidden away until the Feast of Fools. This was a New Year's celebration at which the low-ranking clerics were put in charge of the high ranking, and everyone seems to have had a swinging time. But even this simple knees-up fell out of favour by the fourteenth century, and eventually the Church lost interest in the development of drama altogether, and set about trying to take the fun out of it instead. It's somewhat ironic that, having reintroduced the dramatic form, the Church should then spend so much time trying to suppress it, but since many saw entertainment as the Devil's work, what else could they be expected to do? Having said that, it is possible to find churches paying for performances of plays as late as AD1499, and in AD1504 a church shelling out 1s. 3d. for mending the 'garment of Jesus' and painting the Cross.

Nevertheless, the Mystery Plays had developed out of the Church's ceremonial tropes, and by the 1300s their production had been taken over by the local guilds. Few of these plays remain with us today and they are of course known by the places in which it's thought they were produced – Chester, Coventry, Wakefield, York. The players in these productions were often paid for their work, but it's quite clear there were Number One and Number Two dates, even then. 'God' in Coventry was rewarded with the munificent sum of 3s. 6d., whereas 'God' in Hull was fobbed off with a measly 10d. If the performers weren't paid, at least they were fed at the parish's expense, and a late example of this, from Leicester in AD1525, shows that breakfast for the 'apostles and others' consisted of half a calf, three calves' heads, two plucks and a gallon or two of ale. I'll warrant there were a few heavy performances that day.

It was during the Middle Ages, too, that the pageant became popular, surviving well into Elizabethan times and still echoed in today's civic pageants and marches. 'Pageant' was originally the name for the movable stage on which the processional religious productions were shown (now the 'float'), and these had a top and bottom section, with the lower half not only representing Hell but also acting as the dressing-room. The analogy is apt; it is reassuring to know some things never change.

Each pageant had a pageant master who was in charge of rehearsals;

this involved the reciting of lines until the cast had learned them but, even then, most productions of this time would have included an 'ordinary' or 'roaming' prompter, who wandered around whispering the lines to anyone in trouble. There are times in every actor's life when an 'ordinary' would have been a dream come true. Towards the end of the fifth year of *Worm's Eye View* at the Whitehall, Ronnie Shiner, Jack Hobbs and 'Taffy' Davies dried up in the middle of a scene. The prompt came and no one took it. Again it came and again silence. A third time came the disembodied prompt. Ronnie looked at the corner.

'We know the bloody line,' he rasped, 'but who the hell says it?'

In spite of the Church's antipathy and the growth of amateur interest, the travelling performers were well established by the 1300s, though their role as educators had mostly gone. The joglars had made their way over from France, specialising in feats of balancing, and itinerant players were already setting up their booths as they travelled from place to place. The minstrels and goliards, who had developed from the itinerant scholars and bards of the Dark Ages, were still on the go, too. They wandered, from the eleventh to the fourteenth centuries, cheering up Church festivities, lending weight to Church dramas, entertaining bored pilgrims and adding a touch of wisdom and escapism to both marketplace and nobleman's home.

Of course these touring artists did not have the same transport problems we have today, since they pulled their props behind them. It must have been an horrific lifestyle. Not only was their progress open to the elements every step of the way, but they could not even be certain of a welcome when they arrived at the next town. It was a long time before things got better. As late as 1812 we find that the great Edmund Kean was walking from Exeter to Dorchester in search of work, and that in the process his eldest son Howard died from exhaustion. The privations these people suffered bring new meaning to the idea of being stage struck, and certainly make you appreciate the standards set by the Equity Contract for Tours and Seasons, which first saw the light of day in the 1930s.

By AD1469 these wanderers were settled enough to form into guilds; many were employed by wealthy and powerful households or by town corporations and, by the time Henry VIII had come to the throne, it was becoming an established practice for nobles to keep groups of actors on their books, as well as bands of musicians, jugglers and tumblers. By 1482 both the Earl of Essex and the Duke of Gloucester had their own players, and these were but two among many. There were also a number of boys' companies, who were able to add a little light and shade to plays because they were better at women's parts than the all-men companies. We can also be pretty certain that the boys cost less to run.

The members of these companies were expected to do other jobs too.

The actor was the tailor, or stable boy, or other menial. There was still little distinction, therefore, between the amateur and the professional, though obviously the strolling players did little except act. Some of the best examples of this pro/am crossover were seen in the university towns and colleges. By AD1500 these had a regular programme of morality tales, allegories, mumming and liturgical plays, and often professional troupes would be called in to help with their production.

In many instances, these strolling players wore the badge and livery of their 'master' and carried a letter of recommendation, but even this was no guarantee of a licence and it was usually necessary to get the mayor's permission before performing. One way was to send the most respectably dressed member of the company into town ahead of the rest, to apply for the licence, whilst the remainder of his disreputable-looking colleagues sneaked in under cover of darkness. If the company was 'unlicensed' it was even more likely to be hauled up before the local beak, and the players were seen much as gypsies are today, treated with a general disregard which categorised them as rogues and vagabonds. Indeed, there are a number of instances when the actors received a paltry sum in order to 'ridde the Towne of them'. No such luck in my time. It was always 'no play, no pay' and, until fairly recently, no holidays or time off sick, either.

The interest of the Court in theatrical events was obviously a great stimulus to the development of the professional actor. 'The Court Interluders' were established in 1493, and by 1503 they were accompanying Princess Margaret to Edinburgh where they performed a morality tale at her wedding to James IV. There were ten members of the company, and wages for the trip varied from £2 4s. 5d. to £6 13s. 4d. each. These were fairly respectable sums for the times but the actors still had to undertake two jobs for the price of one.

As with most things in this period, though, the rules were about to change.

With Henry's unification of Church and State, the desire and ability to control plays, with their religious and social importance, increased. Anything that helped the Catholic cause had to be suppressed and, in 1517, the Sergeant of the Warden of the Cinque Ports ordered the Barons of the towns not to allow the performance of the 'Passion of Christ' until they had the King's permission, which was not easy to obtain – as this letter from 1532 demonstrates:

> Whereas we understand by certain report of the late evil and seditious rising in our ancient city of York, at the acting of a religious interlude of St Thomas The Apostle, made in the same City on the 23rd of August now last past; and whereas we have been credibly informed that the said rising was owing to the seditious conduct of certain Papists who

WILLIAM SOMMERS.

Jester to King Henry the Eighth.

Pub.d by I.Caulfield. 1820.

took a part in preparing for the said interlude, we will and require you that from henceforward ye do your utmost to prevent and hinder any such commotion in future, and for this ye have my warrant for apprehending and putting in prison any Papists who shall, in performing interludes which are founded on any portion of the Old or New Testament, say or make use of any language which may tend to excite those who are beholding the same to any breach of the peace.

In 1543 Henry even put his worries into a legal framework and introduced an Act forbidding plays that meddled with religious doctrine. The Act was repealed in 1547 by Edward VI's government. Since Edward was only ten at the time, it's unlikely he had particularly strong feelings on the issue, but his Royal Proclamation of 1551, requiring all professional acting companies to have a licence, was the first in a long line of legislation that led to the ideas of 'legitimate' and 'non-legitimate' theatre.

In spite of all difficulties, however, by the mid-to-late sixteenth century we are beginning to see the growth of established and 'respected' groups of players: the Duke of Norfolk's Men were touring in 1556, Lord Dudley's Players in 1560, the Queen's Players in 1561. Most of the companies were on the road when they were not required by their master or at Court and, in 1574, the Earl of Leicester's Men performed at Stratford-upon-Avon in one of the Guild Halls. It is possible that the future bard himself could have been attending at the tender age of ten. Like so many theatrical 'greats' who followed, the visit of one of these touring companies was often the spark which lit the fire. Could that spark have been lit in young Will in 1574? He probably rushed off home to write something decent.

It was this upsurge of drama nationally, and centred on the Court, which brought out the depth of talent that marks the Elizabethan era. Of course the pay was still not great. A touring company could receive anything from 5s. to 20s. for performing, but only a star-studded cast from a big-name patron would reach the dizzy 20s. heights. Whatever the payment, passing the hat round was an essential supplement (as it can be, sometimes, in this day and age), and even those actors based mainly in London could still only expect around 5s. a week. Out of this they had to buy their own costumes and props. Mind you, when I went into my first rep job with the White Rose Players in Harrogate in 1942, I received £8 per week and my contract called for me to provide one evening suit (tails or dinner jacket), one business suit, one sports jacket and trousers, one dressing-gown and all make-up, except wigs. Index-linked, wouldn't you say, over the centuries?

Because of the irregularity of productions outside London, it was rare for there to be any formal theatre building, and such performances as took place were usually in the open air (in fields, market squares, on bridges – anywhere offering a space – hence Tynan's cruel remark about Wolfit), or in stables, barns and inns, where the yards often had galleries running round every storey – as in the latterday R S C Swan Theatre at Stratford. The town hall was frequently used as well and, in Leicester, the hooks and pulleys which had held the Elizabethan curtain could still be seen as late as 1865.

There was, of course, another factor which made touring a hazardous occupation, and that was the grisly habit of plagues sweeping the country. At such times, not only was the desire for theatre and the size of audience severely cut, so too was the welcome given to strangers. Many companies had to split up during these pestilential times. The only dubious advantage for the provinces was that during periods of high danger the Court retired from London to some convenient watering place, but that cost someone, somewhere, money. Of course the Court usually left London in the summer anyway, whatever was going on in the rat-flea-ridden-world, and visited various castles and houses at the hosts' expense. In 1572, for example, Elizabeth I took a house party of 400 on tour with her. When she got to Warwick Castle, where special accommodation had been built, the Earl and his family had to move out and stay with friends. These summer jaunts would bring a good deal of employment with them, but since they often passed through quickly, this was only a brief flurry of work. In fact, Elizabeth booked a return date to Warwick in 1575 and was entertained at Kenilworth by the Coventry Hock Tuesday Show, and by the Earl of Leicester's Men, one year after she'd granted that company its patent. This isn't to say that Elizabeth was exactly the actors' best friend. It was in 1572 that the first Act for the Punishment of Rogues and Vagabonds was passed – to be followed by one 141 years later, during the reign of Queen Anne, in which 'Common Players of Interludes' were again deemed to be dishonest wanderers.

Strangely enough, though, it was during Elizabeth I's reign that the quality of work began to improve. The examples of the earlier plays we know tend to mix morality and history, whilst jumping rapidly between broad slapstick and messy tragedy. It was the appearance of writers like Marlowe, Shakespeare, Lyly and Kyd which really got things going. The language became more powerful and the settings more meaningful. The theatre was for everyone, and names were becoming known. When the King's Men went to Barnstaple in 1605 (and again in 1607) they received 20s. for one show. This was by far the highest amount ever paid by the Barnstaple corporation, and emphasises what a draw was this one night stand. Not only was Shakespeare still writing for the company, but its main attraction was Richard Burbage, the first in the immortal line of leading Shakespearian actors. I imagine Barnstaple would pay a bit more than 20s. this time round, but knowing some local authorities' support for the arts, you never can tell.

Tours abroad began around the turn of the seventeenth century. The

Earl of Leicester's Company toured Holland as early as 1585–6, and in that latter year also appeared at the Danish Court at Elsinore. On the other hand, Ben Jonson went to the Netherlands so he could become a soldier, not a playwright – but then Jonson was a man ever in search of a scrap – and in 1598, a year after he'd returned to England, aged twenty-six, he killed a fellow actor, Gabriel Spencer, in a duel. It's hardly surprising that his plays were always landing him in jail . . .

Probably the best reason for going abroad in the seventeenth century was the baleful influence of the Puritans. These righteous and indignant people might have had their hearts in the right places but they managed to make life a misery for actors. James I, on the other hand, was very enthusiastic about the theatre. In 1615 he saw a satirical play about lawyers in Cambridge, and he enjoyed it so much that he went back the next week – comps on both occasions, I'll be bound. During his reign, and those of his sons, the role of theatre continued much as it had for the last fifty years. Companies made reputations, actors toured. Things weren't that different – even if James couldn't resist the temptation, from time to time, to suppress plays he didn't like – particularly if they were written by Ben Jonson. But kings don't last for ever; Charles I and the Civil War were coming round the corner and actors fought on both sides, but it would seem that most were with the King. They knew which side their bread was buttered – and Cromwell was distinctly mean with dairy produce.

With the Commonwealth came the banning of theatre, and although puppet shows, bear-baiting and a few other activities were exempt, there was little room for manoeuvre. The only safe venues were in the homes of nobles and in some schools, but that was all. Players like Robert Cox toured fairs and inns throughout the country, presenting drolls and burlesques mixed up with rope dancing and conjuring, in the hope of avoiding the ban. But it was a risky business, and many were arrested.

It wasn't until the Restoration in 1660 that visible life came back into the theatre – along with the word 'farce', which literally meant 'stuffing' and was used to describe all the bits and pieces surrounding the main five-act drama. It was the comic after-piece which gradually gave farce its modern meaning; Garrick was very keen on these, to show his versatility, and wrote several. The curtain raiser followed a similar pattern. The most important change, though, was that women now had a role to play: Anne Bracegirdle, Elizabeth Barry and Nell Gwynn are probably the three best-known names to have come down to us, and their scandals have come along with them. Anne Bracegirdle was the motive for a murder, when a Captain Hill killed a man called William Mountford, whom Hill thought was his rival for Anne's affections; but, except on this occasion, she raised many a laugh by being a splendid comedienne. Elizabeth Barry became better and better as an actress, but she never married. The fact that she was so desired, successful and yet unattached, makes it hardly surprising that she was the subject of much scandalous gossip, whilst Nell Gwynn is, of course, famous for her kingly connections and her oranges, rather than for her undoubted charm and popularity as an actress, particularly in prologues and epilogues.

The arrival of women meant, of course, the demise of boy players in the female leads – players who had been seen all over the country – like Richard Sharpe, who ran up a bill for 41s. 10d. for stockings with Condell (one of the men responsible for the publication of Shakespeare), and Edward Kynaston, one of the last boy players, whom 'ladies of fashion' liked to take for drives in their carriages after the show, while he was still in his petticoats, and for whom Charles II had to wait whilst he was shaved for the part of a tragedy queen. By the end of the seventeenth century the boy player was all but finished (with the notable exception of the child prodigy, Master Betty, who flickered into fame nearly 150 years later in men's roles) and the woman player was established. This does not mean that men stopped dressing as women, of course. I remember an incident, similar to the Ned Kynaston tale, which I witnessed in France in the 1950s when Bambi, a famous 'drag' star of the times, was out driving with 'ladies of fashion' in his full slap, much to the vicarious pleasure of all and sundry – particularly as his escorts were probably drag queens, too. But he did look absolutely ravishing – even in bright Mediterranean sunlight – as did his companions, whether male, hermaphrodite or female – I know not what.

With the return of the monarchy, back came the idea of favoured companies, and the issuing of patents to theatres by Charles II further split the acting profession into 'legitimate' and 'illegitimate' performers – which meant that only Patent Theatres could officially present five-act tragedies and comedies with music. This division was not helped by the Puritan undercurrent which still ran through the country, and by 1737 the Licensing Act abolished the right of provincial companies to act for hire, gain or reward, and once more actors were classed as rogues and vagabonds. Other changes came with the Restoration, too. Sets and costumes started to take on far more significance, and from 1660 to the middle of the eighteenth century there was a good deal of characterisation expressed in clothing and make-up. The hero would have a plume of feathers in his helmet, and the rogue would wear a black wig. The use of sets affected the writing too, since it was no longer necessary to have such descriptive, scene-setting speeches. One of the factors which made Shakespeare's plays so poetic had gone and the audiences could now come out 'humming the scenery'. These two changes also made life harder for the touring company. Once audiences have tasted developments they like, they won't settle for less and the strolling companies now had to supply sets and costumes, and those who couldn't fell into a different class. This was not an overnight process of course, but it was one which would take on greater and greater significance as the urban population increased, as transport and communication improved, as the concept of 'legitimate' theatre took hold, and as more comfortable theatres began to be built. Bath was among the first in 1705, followed by those in Birmingham, Bristol, Doncaster, Brighton, Liverpool, Norwich, York, Edinburgh, Glasgow, Margate, North Shields – the list goes on . . .

The stage of this period was higher than the pit, which could be covered, so that a large dance floor was created. Also, the boxes were level with the stage. One of the best examples of this Georgian interior can be seen at Richmond, Yorkshire, where most features are still in place, despite having a wine cellar built under the theatre in 1850 and then having it taken out again in 1962. I know a number of actors who would have liked to work in such close proximity to this kind of cellar (and preferably in it), as in days of yore, when dressing-rooms and hell were synonymous in the pageants. Hell would then have been a little more bearable, particularly if the wine was of vintage quality; or even if it wasn't. Not too many actors I know turn down the odd glass or two of plonk.

Indeed, throughout the years there have been a number of thespians brought down by the demon drink – probably the most extreme example being the Bath Players who became known as the 'Brandy Company', and were kicked out of their Somerset base because of it. They had to move to Exeter, but this didn't change things – they still 'had not got the words'. Actors from towns like Launceston had to be drafted in to make up the numbers. In the end, most of the Bath Players died of drink, setting an example followed, unhappily, by many a famous actor to this very day. I could tell you a tale or two, I'll warrant – but here is one to be going on with . . .

I was trying to engage a well-known actor, Basil Radford, for my tour of *Reluctant Heroes* in 1950. His agent, a Mr Vere Barker, suggested that we meet in the back bar of the Café Royal, off Regent Street, one freezing February Monday morn. Vere Barker was a partner in Connies, a very successful theatrical agency in those days, and his partner was Connie herself, a Mrs Constance Chapman. When I arrived at midday, there was Vere with his client, Basil Radford, and Basil well into his third or fourth large Scotch. There, also, was Connie, well into her third or fourth large gin, awaiting a client of hers. Uproar outside in the street and Connie's client arrived: Robert Newton, bibulously loud and booming good-naturedly to all concerned, dressed in a string vest, pyjama bottoms, slippers and an old sports jacket, unbuttoned to show that he had not tied his pyjama cord too securely, revealing to the world at large that there was much, indeed, to reveal. I was but a young, callow, actor-manager, new to the London scene, with its grand theatrical names and their agents – but the barman, and any other drinkers who could stand the din and the sight, appeared to be totally unmoved. Apparently, such goings-on were a regular feature of the day's events and would continue until Robert was poured into a taxi at closing time, to sleep it off until the evening session. But it killed him in the end – just like the 'Brandy Company' – and I suppose it killed Basil, too. *Mutatis mutandis* . . .

Back in the eighteenth century, financial considerations were often to the fore when new theatres were built, and not all of them were particularly safe. There were a number of productions which had to be stopped while the gallery, or some other part of the theatre, was propped up, as the structure could be seen swaying about. (When I was in an amateur production of *Quiet Week-End* for my mother in the Parish Hall, Hornsea in 1940, the gallery had to be emptied during the last performance, for it was visibly descending towards the floor under the weight of its visitors. The audience accepted this near disaster without the slightest surprise – after all, it was a very *old* Parish Hall. The galleryites stood quietly at the back of the stalls and the performance continued. Not a laugh was missed.) Quite a few companies had to switch venues quickly, and of course fire was an ever-present risk along with collapsing sets and furnishings. The developing eighteenth-century obsession for machinery did not make life easier either, and actors had to act around the devices rather than having them fitted to their needs. There were other theatres so large that people wouldn't go because they were so cold, and fires had to be burned in the pit. The old pitches were still around as well of course, as this description of a Yorkshire market-town venue demonstrates:

> A long, low ramshackle building, with a partition open at the top, running down the centre. On one side of this partition was the theatre, on the other side were a number of pens and stalls where unsold cattle were kept on market days . . . I shall never forget the smell which greeted us on entering this filthy den.

Mind you, I've known a pong like that, actually, when the sewer pump broke in the middle of a matinée at the Whitehall Theatre. (Most London theatres have these under the stage – which is generally below ground level – and require such self-activating drainage assistance.) Everyone, actors and audience alike, was engulfed by a noxious miasma, but two of us on stage were engulfed by laughter, too – for the line 'there was a nasty stink in Whitehall this afternoon' had just been delivered by Dennis Ramsden to me, as the smell hit the stage. Our uncontrollable (and unforgivable) giggles had to be seen to be believed.

From the 1720s onward companies began to be known by the main town on their circuits, rather than by the name of their patron. Following the Restoration, these companies struggled to establish their own territories

– towns and villages where they could rely on custom and their own pre-eminence – but this did not come easily. Rivalry was still common enough and was to do with the size of the audience – ratings, as in modern-day television. In fact, the theatre was not altogether dissimilar to an evening's viewing. It was the custom of the times to have very full bills, which meant that people felt they were getting value for money, allowing them to come either early or late, yet still see a complete piece. It also meant the actors did not have to rely on just one play for the success or failure of the entertainment. The shows usually ran from seven p.m. to midnight, and audiences could come in for half price towards the end.

A typical Norwich bill from 1727 offered: 'An Excellent Play called *Dido and Aeneas*; a Harlequinade, *The Pye-Dancer*; an acrobatic turn and a "moving Wax-work" of Edward IV, Jane Shore and the Princes in the Tower.' The main piece of the evening would have been a standard favourite. During the 1741 season the *Norwich Gazette* advertised a number of plays we would still recognise today, including four by Shakespeare (*Hamlet*, *Henry IV*, *As You Like It*, and *Twelfth Night*), and five more recent hits (Rowe's *Tamerlane*, Congreve's *Double Dealer*, Cibber's *Love's Last Shift*, Addison's *Cato*, and the ever-present *Beggar's Opera* by John Gay). On second thoughts, I'm not so sure you would recognise them today, after all. Acting styles were very different and a certain Dr Bowdler was about to do his dirty work – which he saw as exactly the opposite.

London hits were soon performed in the provinces. *The Beggar's Opera*, for example, was presented by the Bath Company of Comedians in the same year as it appeared at Lincoln's Inn Fields, 1728, and with the same manager, John Rich. It is a *Beggar's Opera* playbill from around this period which supplies me with one of my favourite announcements: 'Mr Radford will perform his ability, which is the last time he proposes to do it in Publick.' Whatever it was he proposed to do, it certainly didn't make him a London star. One can only assume his ability was singularly small. Mr Radford was one of those many actors who made their names in the provinces and the provinces alone and, as far as I am aware, was no relation to the Basil Radford I later engaged in the back bar of the Café Royal . . .

Of course, there were numerous companies roaming about, which had neither decent venues nor enviable reputations. A Mr Jones led a company round South Wales in 1741. He set out with six players, but during the tour the numbers diminished and at one point he was performing Farquhar's *Beaux' Stratagem* with a cast of three. This need to eradicate characters, to double up, to compress plays, to simplify and improvise sets and props, was one that had been going on for many years, and was to carry on for many more. These 'country versions' were necessitated to a great degree by the fact that the actors were semi-literate, and that whole texts were still relatively rare, whilst money was in short supply for such fripperies as furniture. In one 'production' Desdemona had to lie on a bed made from a plank and two chairs, and as Othello leant towards her the whole thing collapsed, he landed on top of her, and the audience had hysterics. I would have put it in every night from then on . . .

An Act was passed, in 1788, that gave the Justices the power to license plays for sixty days at a time. This provided a greater degree of stability for the actors, and allowed full-length productions outside the patent houses, as well as ensuring that the companies based mainly in one town – the stock companies – could develop their repertoire and their theatres, and make more reliable plans. Many were already established on this basis but at last they were within the law. It made it easier for the big names to go on tour in the summer season, moving from town to town, making brief appearances at local theatres, and giving the provinces the chance to keep up with the London scene. It also meant that talented newcomers in the provinces were able to take over in the capital and could attempt to establish a reputation for themselves, and for those who stayed out of town there was the chance of being spotted, and to learn at the feet of the 'masters'.

When the young William Macready had to perform with Sarah Siddons in Newcastle in 1812, he was so nervous in her presence that she had to prompt him on his first line but, then, the visiting stars in those days were never ones to waste time on rehearsals. This was not necessarily because they felt it was beneath them, but generally because the time a star could spend in any one place depended on how much they were being paid. Travelling was the main problem. A great old actor-laddie is reputed to have arrived just in time at one of these venues and enquired of the manager, 'Where is the stage and what is the play?'

In 1829 Edmund Kean was due to appear in Croydon, doing two plays on two nights. One of these was *The Iron Chest*, and in it, as Wilford, was the young actor Edward Stirling. This was how Stirling remembered Kean's only rehearsal. Present were Kean, Stirling, and that was it.

STIRLING What do you wish me to do?
KEAN   Why, in the library scene, sink gradually on your right knee, with your back to the audience. When I place my hand on your head to curse, mind you keep your eyes fixed on mine.
STIRLING Is that all, sir?
KEAN   Yes – do whatever else you like after that; it will be all the same to me.

Not much of an opportunity to learn there.

In the 1820s Samuel Phelps was with Kean at York. Kean was playing Shylock. This is how Phelps remembered it:

He didn't come to rehearsal, and although Lee, his secretary, rehearsed carefully enough, I did not know where to find Kean at night, for he crossed here, there, and everywhere, and prowled about like a caged tiger. I never took my eyes off him. I dodged him up and down, crossed when he crossed, took up my cues, and got on pretty fairly, till he thoroughly flabbergasted me by hissing, 'Get out of my focus! Blast you! Get out of my focus!'

But the 'star system' brought in the audiences, and with the stock companies establishing themselves in the towns, and theatres being built, there was a more stable breeding-ground for actors, and success bred success. This continued up until the 1820s and 30s when there were forty-nine companies on the road, and about two hundred companies spread around the country – including those that performed only a few weeks in the year. Below them were still the 'penny gaffs' – generally found in the poorer districts – where indifferent performers dealt somewhat over-enthusiastically with a surfeit of melodrama and often the standard was so awful the gaffs became known as 'blood-tubs'. Then there were the 'fit-up' companies, the one-night-standers who would appear in almost every district, in the small towns and villages which were not large enough to warrant a permanent theatre of their own.

Stock companies always had plays in hand and could give them at the drop of a hat. The players had to know all the plays, and learned their lines from cue scripts, which only gave them the last words spoken by the previous character and then their response. This led to actors assessing the importance of their part by how many 'sides' they had. (Even in my day there were cue scripts, which H. M. Tennent's used to send out during the war to struggling rep actors from their prestigious West End productions. I remember them with fear and trembling. Imagine trying to learn a virtual three-hander from such abominations. I had to, with *Design For Living*!) Rehearsals were scanty and mainly consisted of checking the words and setting one or two stage positions, which basically meant not upstaging the actors higher up in the performance pecking order. Most stock companies had twelve main players, and added to these utility players and occasional extras, whilst serving as a training ground for young hopefuls, many of whom paid a premium for learning their craft. In 1820 the Theatre Royal, Hull had a company of thirty including twelve women whilst, further up the coast, Scarborough had a regular twenty members. But the pecking order was still there, and, borrowing from Harvey Crane's excellent book *Playbill*, here it is:

1 The star – who would travel from stock to stock
2 The leading man
3 The heavy

4 First old man
5 Second old man
6 Comedian
7 Light comedian
8 Low comedian
9 The villain
10 Juvenile
11 The walking gentleman
12 The walking lady

It is particularly interesting to me that the low comedian is so far down the list. He performed the roles now associated with farce and the music hall, and suggests why these particular forms are still held in low esteem by many a lofty critic. Edmund Kean suffered in the early days because provincial managers felt he was the perfect Harlequin. He was, but he wanted to be the perfect leading man instead. The managers did not see this – they'd typecast him because he was distinctly short in stature. In 1807, however, he rejoined Samuel Jerrold on his southeast circuit based around Sheerness. Kean was to play the lead; at last he could be a great hero. The opening night came and Kean entered, as Alexander the Great, and immediately a shout went up from one of the boxes: 'Alexander the Great indeed! It should be Alexander the Little.'

Kean halted the audience laughter with one of his stares, and proudly announced, 'Yes – with a great soul.' Hardly the soul of wit, either, but it will have to do.

Such audience intervention was nothing unusual – in fact it was rather mild. It is only in the twentieth century that a sacrosanct quiet has become the norm in theatres. Prior to this, actors and audience were in nearly non-stop dialogue. People would shout out, offer advice to characters, start arguments with neighbours, throw things from the gallery into the pit – as well as at the actors – and generally behave more in the style of modern-day football fans. In 1826 Prince Puckler-Muskau described it all like this:

The most striking thing to a foreigner in English theatres is the unheard of coarseness and brutality of the audiences. The consequence of this is that the higher and more civilised classes go only to the Italian opera, and very rarely visit their national theatre. English freedom here degenerates into the rudest licence, and it is not uncommon in the most affecting part of a tragedy . . . to hear some coarse expression shouted from the galleries in a stentor voice. This is followed, according to the taste of the bystanders, either by loud laughter and approbation, or by the castigation and expulsion of the offender . . .

Incidentally, I have been present when there was such a loud interruption from the front that the curtain had to be rung down, followed by the 'expulsion of the offender'. It was during the war, in 1942, and I was in the dress circle of the Aldwych seeing *The Watch on the Rhine*, by Lillian Hellman, and on stage were Anton Walbrook, Diana Wynyard, Athene Seyler and Charles Goldner, who was playing the part of a blackmailing Romanian. Athene Seyler made some comment about his country being 'more a profession than a nation', whereupon a man in the stalls shouted out that he objected, for he *was* a Romanian. The true-blue Brit sitting next to him shouted, 'In that case you're a bloody enemy,' took a swing and laid our Baltic chum out. Chaos! And the curtain was lowered whilst the two protagonists (one comatose) were ejected. After a suitable pause, for the shock to subside, Miss Seyler appeared between the front-of-house tabs and enquired if we wished the play to continue. She received a mighty chorus of 'Yes' by way of affirmation, so she bowed deeply and retired. The curtain rose, to find the four actors frozen in the positions they were in before the fracas. Like so many sleeping beauties they came to life, and *The Watch on the Rhine* proceeded. It was all jolly exciting, I can tell you. The interruption, I mean. Perhaps we should encourage audience participation to be revived.

Mind you, the audiences were not just random in their abuse, and the actors were forced to respond. It was not uncommon for the audience to call so loudly for a popular actor that scenes were cut, and their favourite brought on early, to a huge ovation. A notorious theatre for this kind of mayhem was the Dock in Devonport. The audience loved winding the actors up. One man in particular was a favourite target. Mr Hayne was the company's tragedian, and on this occasion he felt it necessary to deliver Othello's speech to the Senate like this:

> Most potent, grave and reverend Signiors,
> My very noble and approved good master,
> [I'll tell you what young fellows; I'll have every one of you in custody before you are aware of it]
> That I have taken away this old man's daughter,
> It is most true . . .
> [That young woman with the blue ribbons is as bad as any of you!]

And so on.

It was at the Dock that a totally unrepeatable rejoinder came from a member of the audience. As the hero held the dead heroine in his arms, raised his eyes to heaven, and asked what he should do with her – he was told in no uncertain terms by a drunken sailor. Furthermore, he was advised to do it whilst she was still warm.

The Dock audience also managed to come up with two other memorable pieces of theatricality. Once during *Othello*, when the Moor is murdering Desdemona, another Jolly Jack Tar jumped on stage with cutlass drawn and told the actor to unhand the woman. The actor did just that and then ran off stage and out of the theatre, refusing to return. I can't say I blame him. On another occasion, during a particularly dramatic shipwreck scene, yet a third member of the Senior Service scrambled over the heads and shoulders of the audience screaming, 'Man overboard!' and proceeded to rescue the poor actor-manager who was playing Don Juan, despite considerable resistance. And was it that same actor-manager (and was it at that same Dock theatre), who announced at the curtain call that next week he would portray the Moody Dane, and his wife the tragic Ophelia? Came a voice from the audience (yet a fourth sailor, or a chorus of the first three?): 'Your wife's an ugly old whore,' followed by the rejoinder: 'Be that as it may, next week she will portray Ophelia.'

Such audience behaviour was a baptism by fire, and it meant that either you learned quickly or you went under. The stock and touring companies were the only places in which actors could practise their art and, apart from the occasional amateur phenomenon, everyone went through this same process. Squire Bancroft played 346 parts in numerous provincial companies over a five-year period, while Henry Irving managed 428 characters in three years on the circuit – meaning he studied nearly three new roles a week – and these were full-length plays, not half-hour T V 'soaps'. Of course, this often resulted in half-remembered lines and characters, improvised scenes, and bits of other plays appearing where they shouldn't. The audience were not afraid to point these blunders out, and once the actors had made their delicate apology, the play could continue. I should imagine there was often more pleasure taken in spotting mistakes than in enjoying the performances themselves.

The financial remuneration for all of this varied considerably from one place to another, but certain comparisons can be made. From the early years, until the mid 1700s, earnings were distributed through the share system. Once the expenses had been dealt with, the money was shared between the actors. This very reasonable-sounding method was distorted by the manager taking extra 'dead' shares for extraneous expenses, and thus it became open to all kinds of abuse. Throughout history, managers have disappeared leaving the actors to deal with the bills. It happened to me, indirectly, as late as 1979 – and I am sure it will to others, in spite of all Equity's efforts. There are *still* rogues and vagabonds about.

By the mid eighteenth century, salaries were beginning to be phased in, but these were barely sufficient, and if business was bad the actors were always the first to be asked to take a cut in pay. Wages varied greatly from place to place and according to the status of the company and the performer. A strolling player could expect less than 6s. a week, whereas a middle-order actor, with a reasonable company, could expect £2 or so.

(Two hundred years later, the minimum salary for touring was still only £3 per week.) Of course, for the stars anything was possible. A popular provincial actor could make up to £500 a year, whereas someone like Gustavus Brooke could return from the United States in 1853, £20,000 the richer. The idea of increased pay for big names was one that really became established in the early 1800s. Players like the Kembles and Garrick had earned good money but there had not been the disparity between them and the lesser-known players which was to become the Victorian norm. The stars of the 1820s had begun to earn in a night what they would have earned in a week at the start of the century: William Charles Macready, Tyrone Power, Charles Young, Mrs Jordan, were all capable of earning £100–£150 a week; indeed, in 1819 Macready was getting £50 a night in Brighton – two and a half times more than I received for a *week*, 131 years later, in the same town.

While the big names were making money, the lesser lights were not. These mere mortals were still relying on the benefit system, as they had done for centuries, to help make ends meet. This system meant that all profits went to a particular actor from one performance, after expenses had been met, but the beneficiary was still expected to pay set charges for his or her own benefit. Props, publicity, hospitality – and any extras – all had to come out of the actor's pocket. Often the size of the charges and the moderate popularity of a performer meant the actor could actually lose money through a benefit. Cricketers are the only 'entertainers' who continue to profit from this system. Actors have become too grand for such handouts – unless in dire straits, and then the money floods in, as do the crocodile tears.

Peter Paterson, a man who left the acting profession after earning £3 6s. 6d. for three months' work in the booths, asked this question in his 1864 book *Glimpses of Real Life*:

> Who but one haunted by a restless burning desire for dramatic distinction would welcome years of poverty, privation, sickness of soul and body, a constant sense of self-imposed beggary, and an internal reproach for frequent acts of meanness not to be avoided, and even dishonesty, which may not be shunned?

The answer to that question was often 'those who were born of players themselves'. Not that their parents always wanted them to join the business. Macready said he'd 'sooner see a son of mine coffin'd at my feet than that he should take to acting and the stage', whilst Nell Gwynn ensured that her son was created the Duke of St Albans, which puts her ahead of Dorothy Jordan, whose eldest son – by the Duke of Clarence – was merely created the Earl of Munster. Mind you, many actresses dragged themselves up – if not by their boot straps, then by their nightdresses – for in the two hundred years from 1722 to 1945, forty-seven actresses married peers, including one royal duke, eight ordinary ones, three marquesses, seventeen earls, four viscounts and sixteen barons. I have no record of what happened to all their issue, but I know that some did, indeed, go back into the theatre. A grave disappointment to all, I'll be bound.

Many companies came mainly from one family. In the 1840s the Lincoln Circuit was run by Mr and Mrs Robertson. They had seventeen children, including Madge Kendal, and obviously wouldn't have had much trouble with casting. Roger Kemble was another man whose children toured with him, the eldest being Sarah Siddons, but this didn't always ease financial problems as one would expect. On one occasion admittance to their performance was 'contingent on the purchase of packets of tooth powder'. Of course, Roger Kemble's company was not just a family one, and one of the most colourful actors to work with him was George Cooke, a man with a great love of the grape. One night at Liverpool he was particularly pie-eyed and the audience were calling for an apology. George Cooke took his time focusing and then let fly: 'Apology from me! From George Frederick Cooke! Take it from this remark – there's not a brick in your infernal town which is not cemented by the blood of a slave.'

I shouldn't imagine that helped the sale of tooth powder too much.

Public criticism of the morals, of the theatre world and its performers, was still commonplace. Scandal surrounded many lowly actresses who married above their station, and actors who drank and brawled still upset the audiences' feelings, but it was not the actors' behaviour which caused the slump in provincial audiences from the 1830s to 1860s. The theatre was to some degree stagnating, and it was not until the latter half of the nineteenth century that things began to show change. This stagnation and the changes that came about can be traced to a number of events. First, the star system had spoiled the audiences, and they became less interested in seeing their local actors. Second, prior to the 1843 Theatres Act, the minor theatres – debarred from legitimate drama – had developed the populist melodramas and burlettas, and thus alienated their upper-class audiences. Then this same Act removed limits on the length of the season, and so stock companies could spend the whole of a year in one town, whilst the advent of the railways meant entire companies were able to travel up from the London theatres. Last – but not least – the prim and proper Victorians wanted morally virtuous productions with bigger and better sets. The end result was the demise of the stock companies, their circuits, most of the booths, the growth of the touring actor-managers, and the development of the music hall. This was not, of course, an overnight transformation, and some stock companies did manage to struggle through to the 1890s, though they did not have to cope with the legal restraints which were used against the travelling booths – never mind the threat of double bookings. At the Walsall Whitsun Fair in 1849, Wombwell's Menagerie tried to bully an acting troupe off a desirable patch. The actors drove the menagerie away by attacking the cages, full of terrified wild animals, with picks and crowbars. I've seen patrons scrapping over seats at West End smash hits – but this is ridiculous!

So what took the place of the stock companies? The actor-managers, of course – awaiting your pleasure, and their cue, in the next scene. Please join them . . .

Rapid fade to black and lights up on Act I, Scene II.

SCENE II
'See How They Run'

As the locally based stock companies began to lose their bloom, the London-based actor-managers and national touring companies stepped out from the wings. In 1871 there were twelve touring companies on the road, and by 1901 there were 143, and no stock companies. The companies travelled from town to town on the trains; they moved weekly from theatre to theatre, not restrained by circuits, able to visit the whole country in one tour if they so wished. Sometimes the dates were not big enough to sustain a company for a whole week, and the custom of 'split weeks' came about, when smaller companies would, in fact, split a week with another company, spending only three nights in any one venue. In his early days, Donald Wolfit played dates in this fashion, but by the time I was with him he was long past such small venues. Indeed, my touring days with the old boy cannot have been too dissimilar to those of the actors working in the companies of Irving, Benson, Greet, Tree, Forbes-Robertson, Barrett and all the rest, and there is something rather pleasurable in this continuation.

It was left to the amateur companies to fulfil the needs of many an aspiring local performer, so much so that by 1957 there were 30,000 groups reckoned to be putting on at least one production a year. Amateur companies have been going for hundreds of years, of course. Names such as Robert Elliston, David Garrick, Henry Irving, Nigel Playfair, Edward Terry, Herbert Tree, Frederick Robson, Lilian Braithwaite, Charles Wyndham, Lewis Casson and Michael Redgrave all began in amateur theatricals of one kind or another – the list goes on and on, and includes me. I used to tour in the early 1930s around Hull with my brother and sisters in my mother's company, 'Mrs Fanny Rix and Her Bright Young Things', and we went down a storm in such illustrious parish hall venues as Seaton, Atwick, Gembling, Leven, Rise, Driffield and Sigglesthorne, in the East Riding of Yorkshire. Samuel Phelps also began as an amateur, in a company where people paid to play a particular part – 30s. covered Othello or Macbeth, 15s. gave you the Thane of Fife, and Malcolm was a snip at 7s. Nowadays we talk about the hidden subsidy, the work put in by hundreds of aspiring actors for little or no pay. They are rightly annoyed with their lack of financial support, but they are to a degree merely carrying on a theatrical tradition.

The development of theatres continued throughout the nineteenth century, and the facilities and special effects were greatly improved. The Theatre Royal, Ipswich introduced the 'ghost glide' in 1858 because it was essential to the production of Boucicault's *The Corsican Brothers*, where the ghost had to rise up before the audience, like so much ectoplasm, and float in front of their very eyes. The machinery – a narrow sloping cut with a wheeled platform mounted in it, on which the actor stood and appeared to emerge from the depths as it was pulled across the stage – was not removed until 1877. And so it went on, bigger and better effects, train crashes, earthquakes, raging fires, until at the start of the twentieth century even naval battles were being staged in tanks that held up to 100,000 gallons of water – built by Frank Matcham at the Hippodromes in London and Bristol. With all this activity on stage it became necessary to hide the forthcoming spectacle from the audiences and from 1881 the front-of-house tabs – short for tableau curtain – were regularly employed, following their introduction and use by Irving.

Along with the on-stage 'improvements', there were the front-of-house changes, too. The upper-middle-classes were being enticed back by comfier seats, the moral righteousness of the productions, and the better 'class' of actor. Of course, backstage, things were still dreadful. At times it was cold and damp, at other times the heat was stifling. It was reported in 1860 that the dressing-rooms at the Liverpool Amphitheatre and Theatre Royal were 'the veriest dogholes', had dangerous and inadequate lighting, and were full of 'noisome smells'.

The introduction of gas didn't make things any easier either. Fire had always been a hazard with the wick lamps and the wax candles, but with gas it was even worse. In Glasgow the Queen Street Theatre burned down in 1829, the City in 1845 (the same year it was built), the Adelphi in 1848, the Dunlop Street Theatre in 1863 and the Theatre Royal in 1879. Worse still, not only did the theatres catch fire but so did the performers, particularly dancers. Gas had another drawback too, for it meant that the auditorium became stuffy and smelly, so much so that some people would only turn up for matinées or at the beginning of the week. It also meant actors developed dreadfully sore throats. In the days before smoking was banned in theatres, a similar result was created by tobacco smoke, which sometimes cast such a haze that it was like acting in a mist. When the Whitehall Theatre auditorium was cleaned before the run of *Dry Rot* in 1954, everyone thought the proscenium arch was painted gold, but they were wrong, for as the scrubbing took place it was found to be actually painted in silver, and the 'gold' had been nicotine tar from countless fags lit up since the theatre had opened in 1930. The Whitehall was the first West End theatre to adopt a 'no smoking' policy. The proscenium arch was going to stay silver from that day on . . . and it has.

The actor-manager is a role that goes back to the start of the theatre, and will continue as long as people wish to be in charge of their own lives. From the middle of the nineteenth century onwards, these theatrical hybrids grew in significance and became the central focus for theatre in the provinces. Their companies were able to take legitimate drama on the road by using the burgeoning communications network and it meant that someone like Frank Benson could spend nearly all his career on tour, and still stand a chance of a knighthood at the end of it. The rise in stature of the actor, so long awaited, was at last coming about, even if it was still mainly at the top end of the profession.

The man most associated with these developments is, of course, Henry Irving, who made his professional stage debut at the Lyceum Theatre, Sunderland, in 1856, and gave his last performance at Bradford in 1905. He spent ten years touring before he achieved success in the capital, and every year after that, whilst at the Lyceum, would take his company on a summer tour, either in Britain or America. The first decade included two and a half years in Edinburgh, a few months at the Theatre Royal, Glasgow, plus the Theatre Royals of Manchester, Oxford, Liverpool, Newcastle-upon-Tyne, and so on. Just to prove the vagaries of his profession, when Irving played the Queen's Theatre, Dublin in 1860 he was booed, hissed and attacked, by audiences upset at the sacking of one of their favourite actors. Irving kept going . . . Good thing too. In 1895 he became the profession's first knight – but not before he had been black-balled at the Garrick Club. As the saying goes, you can't win 'em all – although *he* did, in the end. There was a huge fuss, and he was admitted at the second attempt.

Artistes were not just performing legitimate drama of course. From the 1820s on, light and comic opera was toured the length and breadth of the country, and people like W. S. Penley continued this tradition for many years. He later became a household name as the first *Charley's Aunt*, although prior to this he had come to the attention of the London audience in a rather unusual way. Penley took over from Beerbohm Tree as the hapless Rev. Robert Spalding in the forerunner of modern English farce, *The Private Secretary*, and established himself as a West End favourite. There was a spate of sentimental comedies too. Henry Esmond was one of the men who exploited this form most, touring with his wife Eva Moore in plays that he had written, and became one of the few actor-writer-managers.

A great deal of money could be made from touring. John Laurence Toole, who for twenty-six years ran the stock company at the Charing

Cross Theatre, always took his company on tour in the summer, and he earned a fortune. When he died in 1906 he left £79,984 behind him. Whereas a static audience and heavy competition restricted earnings in London, travel expenses and cheaper provincial prices were the barriers to profit on tour. There was a simple solution for the touring actor-manager: he sent out more companies. At one time Ben Greet had ten companies working both here and in America (like Benson, he was knighted, too), and Benson usually had three on the go. Both these men relied on Shakespeare to attract their audiences, so it's hardly surprising that Sir Johnston Forbes-Robertson was able to make more money out of *Hamlet* than from any other of his productions. If only the Bard was around to collect his royalties he would make Sir Andrew Lloyd-Webber look like a non-starter.

From 1875 (when Irving announced the provincial earnings to the Royal General Theatrical Fund) to the outbreak of war in 1914, actors' earnings could range from 25s. to £175 a week, and this figure did not change much during this period. By the turn of the century the top earners were better off than they had been at the end of the star system in the 1830s, and so were actors who could get stable work with a touring company. The London-based actor-managers were, of course, somewhat of a clique and a law unto themselves. They were awarded their knighthoods, joined the same clubs and were generally quite pleased with themselves. It is all the more remarkable, then, that these were the people responsible for establishing an actors' union and the funds for actors in distress. In fact it is almost unique in trade union history for the initiative to come from the top. The new union was inevitably too London oriented, and so the Provincial Actors' Union was formed in Manchester in 1907; the two combined the next year but soon folded. It was not until 1929 that the British Actors' Equity Association was born. None the less, things were getting better for the players. They had more secure contracts, a lighter workload and they now had props, costumes and travel expenses paid for them. It was becoming possible to claim middle-class status and even to call on the services of agents. Actors had become employers. (Agents, by the way, began to appear in the 1820s, though as far back as the 1500s the actor William Bird was working as an agent for other actors. As an actor-manager at the Whitehall and Garrick Theatres, I never had an agent, but I wish I'd thought of *being* one – just like Mr Bird!)

There was also a change in the upbringing of many actors. With the increased wealth brought about by the star system, the children of actors had begun to be sent to the public schools, and people from the educated classes came to see the theatre as a place where a living could be earned. In line with the Victorian outlook on life, these middle-class thespians wanted to dignify their profession. Not that things were always that easy for them. Samuel Phelps' daughter was expelled from her school when it was discovered that her father was an actor. The fact that he was the first to run Sadler's Wells Theatre as the home of good Shakespearian productions mattered not one jot or tittle.

As always there was another level below those earning an acceptable wage. Throughout the nineteenth century the penny gaffs flourished (although 'flourish' is hardly the right word) in most cities and towns, and after giving several performances in a night the actors could expect to take home 10d. to 1s. 2d. for their labours. Their working conditions were dreadful and it is hardly surprising that they fought over the stage food just as stock actors had fought over wax candles. It is impossible to know how many actors worked in the gaffs but it probably ran into hundreds, if not thousands. Statistics available from 1841 to 1891 indicate that at least two-thirds of all actors and half of all actresses worked outside London, and while in 1881 there were 4,565 actors on the census, by 1911 there were 18,247. This later figure not only suggests the newfound popularity of the profession, but also the number of companies and theatres crying out for talent.

Of course, actors don't just want money, they want applause, and the provinces provided this too. After John Laurence Toole retired, he was invited to the opening night of the New Grand in Margate, only to be greeted with a huge ovation as he took his seat. Bram Stoker, who worked for many years as Henry Irving's manager (and also wrote *Dracula*), remembered the great man in Dublin being carried back shoulder-high from the theatre to his hotel – a somewhat different reception to the one he received in 1860. Such adulation was soon to become the territory of the film star and the pop singer, but before these *nouveaux riches* took over, the matinée idols ruled the roost. Actors like Gerald du Maurier, Owen Nares, Godfrey Tearle and Lewis Waller brought in middle-class women in their droves. Lewis Waller even had a fan club known as the KOWS – the 'Keen on Waller Society'. It seems at odds with our present-day vision of Victorian and Edwardian womanhood, but the majority must have been desperate for something to make their lives a little more interesting, just like pop fans of today. It was Waller who, on the night of Queen Victoria's death, entered his dressing-room weeping, 'She's dead . . . she's dead . . . the receipts are bound to drop.'

Waller, like so many of his generation, worked for Frank Benson, who was probably the best loved and most respected of the actor-managers on the touring circuits. His was not a glamorous career. When Sir George Alexander suggested Benson for his knighthood, the people at the Lord Chamberlain's office knew nothing about him. When it came to the investiture itself no one had brought a sword, and one had to be borrowed from a military outfitters next door, but at least he had the singular honour of being knighted in the theatre – by King George V – in a box during the Shakespeare Tercentenary Celebrations at the Theatre Royal, Drury Lane in 1916. But Benson was not destined to make huge sums. As his manager Harold Neilson said, 'When Benson dies he will be followed to the grave by five thousand creditors, all of whom will shed a tear because they cannot lend him a bit more.' He produced thirty-five of Shakespeare's plays, giving numerous performances to children as well as adults, believing he could take the Bard to the people. He was also a great believer in sport; his productions were famous for their fight scenes, and when Oscar Asche (the author of *Chu Chin Chow*) arrived from Australia he only secured a job with Benson after giving numerous assurances that he was a first-class wicket-keeper. Well, as a cricket lover, that makes sense to me – and is at least a change from that other story of Benson's advert in the *Stage*: 'Wanted, leg-break bowler and opening bat, able to play Laertes.'

Companies still toured – much as companies had done for centuries – but there were significant changes. To begin with, the majority only presented one play from night to night. Sir Johnston Forbes-Robertson was even heard shouting, before he entered as the mysterious, Messiah-like stranger in *The Passing of the Third-Floor Back*: 'Christ! Will they never let me give up this bloody part!' The audiences were changing too and had developed a sense of decorum; they had started to queue, and sometimes even interruptions were frowned upon. Sir Charles Hawtrey had introduced the idea of seat numbers on tickets, and Sir John Martin-Harvey was making late-comers wait until the end of the act. This all fitted the pattern of the Victorian world, and was reflected in the type of theatre they wanted to enjoy. Wilson Barrett toured another righteous piece, *The Sign of the Cross*, first shown at a theatre he ran – the Grand, Leeds – in 1895, and he went on to make a fortune with it. Clergymen even gave sermons on its virtues. I'm not quite sure what virtues they found in a tale of a slave girl converting a Roman patrician to Christianity, so that both of them ended up being fed to the lions, but it was just the kind of thing to pack the house out. Rather like some evangelists on American TV, their moral message and moral behaviour often seem to be slightly confused – but the audiences love it.

The desire to uplift the spirit was reflected in the popularity of Shakespeare too. In 1890 this notice appeared in the *Shields Daily News*:

A few friends in North Shields of Mr Edmund Tearle decided to present an illuminated address testifying amongst other things their appreciation of the efforts he had made in seeking to raise the tone of the stage and to encourage the performance of what might be termed legitimate drama which is only too often abandoned at the present time for sensational trash . . .

WILSON BARRETT   104.D.

Whether touring Shakespeare, sensational trash, or *Peter Pan*, nearly all actors' lives had been changed by rail travel. The railways had become very much a part of their background, and performed the function that the inns had done for centuries.

At Normanton Junction in 1907 the Benson company, the Compton company and the Tearle company were waiting for their connecting trains along with several other groups. Whitford Kane, a young out-of-work actor, arranged to meet some old friends there; they introduced him to one of the actor-managers present or, rather, one of the few actress-managers – Mrs Bandmann-Palmer – who escorted the tyro to her carriage, interviewed him and took him on. In my young day, it was the back bar of the Café Royal where that sort of thing happened.

The railways also gave the big names a chance to flaunt their importance. Lena Ashwell remembered working with Sir George Alexander in the 1890s: 'When these great actors went on the road the company travelled in a special train with the name of the manager and the names of the occupants of each carriage printed in large type and pasted on the windows.' Wilson Barrett always had special guards for the skips (the wardrobe and property baskets), and because he insisted 'that an actress should maintain an air of reserve and aloofness', he would hire separate compartments. Of course the lower down the scale the company the poorer the travel arrangements. This was balanced by the establishment of the Music Hall Artistes' Railway Association in 1897, which meant members could get a twenty-five per cent discount on the cost of tickets. Just like our Senior Citizens' Rail Cards today. Except we get a third off. There are advantages to the Welfare State, after all.

The music hall had filled the popular gap left by the changes in theatrical restructuring, being the form of entertainment to which the plebs were welcome, but which had numerous lofty critics. Even so, there was money to be made (Dan Leno at his peak was earning £20,000 a year), so many actors worked the halls when they weren't touring with a legitimate company. Since they could take home £20–£30 a week by doing turns at different venues, it is hardly surprising that so many switched or varied their allegiance. What is more surprising, considering the attitudes of the upper classes to such establishments, is that a number of big theatre names also made appearances in music halls. Sir Herbert Tree toured the provinces playing Svengali in a condensed version of his smash hit *Trilby*, and wasn't even put off by a call-boy enjoining him to ''Urry up 'erbert.' Sir Cedric Hardwicke was another big name who played the halls, touring one-act plays after the First World War.

During that war, the actors rallied round. Sir Herbert Tree toured the United States playing the patriotic Colonel Newcombe; Sir John Martin-Harvey was particularly keen on giving war lectures, singing patriotic songs and delivering 'Shakespeare's War Cry', and Lena Ashwell helped found the Women's Emergency Corps and then took the first concert parties to France.

From the middle of 1915 the actors were performing regularly to the troops. Many of them were fighting, too. Cedric Hardwicke was one of the last officers out of France, and Frank Benson won the Croix de Guerre as an ambulance driver.

At home there were difficult moments, though they were not as dangerous. The 1917 entertainments tax put up ticket prices so much that initially business was reduced by up to thirty per cent. The theatres had to close at ten thirty p.m. to save fuel, and travel restrictions limited touring but, as always in war, people wanted entertainment and so the theatres, especially in London, were packed. The entertainments tax, introduced for the First World War only, lasted for forty years – followed by SET and VAT. Once a commodity has come within the grasp of the Treasury, it hardly ever escapes from its toils.

The First World War can be seen as a watershed in so many ways. Not only was much talent lost, but after it came the film and radio boom. The generation of actor-managers, out on tour, was coming to an end, and the growth of the provincial repertory movement was about to begin. If you would like to know more of this, please read your programme notes in the forthcoming Interlude.

In this brief history we have travelled over a thousand-year period (2,500 if you count Thespis), and still we have the strolling players, existing more comfortably perhaps, but – as ever – struggling to earn a living and having to create their own audiences and sometimes – like the extraordinary Century Theatre 'Blue Box' near Keswick – their own venues as well. Even after the onslaught of film, television, radio, sport and all the rest, the simplest and most powerful way of getting your ideas across to others is to gather a group of like-minded people together and head out on the road, with all the inconvenience, boredom, learning, hysterical experiences and broken marriages which that will entail. Who knows – if your ideas are commercial enough, you may even make some money. Long may it be so.

But I wouldn't do it again. EVER . . .

Quick curtain.

A caricature of Beerbohm Tree watching a rehearsal from the Gallery.

INTERLUDE
'On Monday Next . . .'

The impetus for the repertory movement came pre-war, when Annie Horniman formed her company in Ireland in 1904 at the Abbey Theatre, Dublin before moving to the Gaiety Theatre, Manchester in 1908. In 1909 Alfred Wareing opened the Glasgow Rep and in 1918 the Huddersfield Rep; in 1911 repertory came to Liverpool, with its heyday at the Playhouse during the reign of William Armstrong, which lasted from 1922 to 1941, when it closed for a time because of bombing. In 1913 it was Birmingham's turn, under Barry Jackson. There was J. B. Fagan's Oxford Playhouse, A. R. Whatmore's Hull Rep, Terence Gray's Festival Theatre, Cambridge, with its intended lack of proscenium, props and scenery, the Peacocks' White Rose Players at the Grand Opera House, Harrogate (which I later joined) – and many more.

Within a few years there were over a hundred reps established around the country, some of them with a permanent base, others operating as small touring companies. Companies such as Jevan Brandon-Thomas's in Scotland and the North were setting a very high standard without big names, although he finally settled in two homes – the Lyceum, Edinburgh and the Theatre Royal, Glasgow from 1933 to 1938, whilst Alfred Denville had no less than twenty repertory companies operating, as well as sending out over 150 companies on tour. Terence Byron had a further six companies playing the North of England, and a little later Harry Hanson came on the scene with his Court Players, operating in about a dozen theatres, including those at Leeds, Sheffield, Peterborough, Nottingham and – wait for it – Penge. He also sent companies out on tour, in conjunction with George Black Jnr. Harry was nothing if not camp. He used to wear toupees to match the season – blond for spring, red for autumn etc. – but once, during the Second World War he appeared in a snow-white creation. When this was remarked upon, Harry was ready: 'I was in bed during this raid, quivering, my dear, but quivering. My toupee was on its block, ready for the morn – all brushed, brown and burnished – when this bomb landed next door. Before my very eyes, my dear, my beautiful toop turned white.' Once, at the end of a season at the Theatre Royal, Leeds, the Court Players presented *Rebecca*. Now, Rebecca never appears, but at the end of the last performance Harry came on to make a thank-you speech, to be greeted by a stentorian Yorkshire shout from the gods: 'Who's this, then? Rebecca?' I never had the pleasure of meeting Harry Hanson, but he once did me a great favour, forfeiting his season at the Spa Theatre, Bridlington so that my winter season, which had been a struggle, could continue in that town during the holiday months. This favour became even more valuable, for it was whilst at the Spa that I came across *Reluctant Heroes* – the play which was to launch me on my Whitehall farce career. I owe Mr Hanson a lot – although I don't suppose he ever knew.

The repertory system once again increased the actor's workload. A day in the life of an actor in the 1934 Northampton Company went something like this: a rehearsal of *Bulldog Drummond*, a matinée of *Jack and the Beanstalk* (with a certain chap called Errol Flynn as Prince Donzil), two evening performances of *Sweet Lavender*, and finally a broadcast of *The Dear Departed*. And somewhere in amongst that they'd have been learning their lines for the next play too and, if Errol Flynn was anything to go by, finding time to hop into bed with the leading lady, or the pretty young juvenile (or both), as well.

Those companies which didn't do anything too experimental or intellectual usually did best, and kept going longest. Apart from repertory, there was a market for popular plays at reasonable prices and many smaller managements snapped up the provincial rights of London hits and sent them out on tour. There were even touring 'names', who were regularly seen on the road, recreating the parts established by their better-known peers, whilst Shakespeare seemed to be in the hands of two actor-managers, Robert Atkins and Donald Wolfit. But there were problems. If you weren't 'in' with the Howard and Wyndham circuit, dates were not easy to come by. Many of the more unfashionable theatres had been bought up for cinemas or as investments. Venues had landlords with little interest in artistic matters; often they were sub-let to other landlords, so inevitably rents rose, and the managements had to look to smaller casts and simpler productions. As always, it was the actor and actress who suffered . . . 'twas ever thus.

Act II beginners, please.

ACT II

SCENE I
'Worm's Eye View'

'What did you do in the last war, Daddy?' is a question easily answered by many an actor. 'I went on tour,' is the reply. Not because you fancied touring, but simply because life in the theatrical provinces was infinitely richer than it had been for many, many years – ever since the advent of the cinema, in fact. This resurgence was caused by the closing of the West End theatres by the government; or by the Blitz; or by the necessity to be seen to be 'doing your bit' through the medium of E N S A (Entertainments National Service Association, translated by the rude soldiery into 'Every Night Something Awful'); or through the parsimonious financial backing of C E M A (the Council for the Encouragement of Music and Arts). How the Establishment viewed these two organisations can easily be judged by the accolades bestowed by a grateful nation on their founders. Basil Dean, a highly respected, albeit tough, theatre director had really started a rudimentary E N S A in the First World War as the Entertainment Branch of the Navy and Army Canteen Board. For this, he had been awarded the M B E, but was now elevated to C B E for all the sterling work he had put into the Board's successor, E N S A. On the other hand, John Maynard Keynes who, incidentally, founded the Arts Theatre, Cambridge as well as C E M A, was made a Peer of the Realm. But then, C E M A did go on to become the Arts Council of Great Britain, with Lord Keynes as its first Chairman. His Lordship also told us how to control our wayward economy. We are still trying . . .

If you were lucky, however, you could stand up for King and Country through the good offices of H. M. Tennent Ltd, by far and away the most prestigious of West End theatre managements, who, in normal times, wouldn't have been seen dead out in the sticks, except for the usual pre-West End warm-up. H. M. Tennent's conversion to the great unwashed in the provinces began when Hugh 'Binkie' Beaumont, the managing director of the company, led a deputation of powerful theatrical folk, including Basil Dean, to Number Ten, to argue a case for reopening the theatres, which had all been closed at the outbreak of war. With the valuable assistance of the King's former secretary, Lord Wigram, their prayer was swiftly answered, and theatres were allowed to open in the provinces, thought to be safer than the West End. Half a sixpence is better than half a penny, so immediately Mr Beaumont seized his opportunity and launched the production of *The Importance of Being Earnest*, starring John Gielgud and Edith Evans, at the Golders Green Hippodrome, where it was allowed to run to packed houses, for it was considered a sufficiently safe distance away from the West End. Were we really naïve enough to believe the German bombing would be as accurate as all that? But there we are. That was the absurd official interpretation put upon the word 'provinces'. Mind you, *The Importance* really did visit the theatres far away from London as well. And what a cast! Apart from Sir John and Dame Edith (their titles came later), Dames Peggy Ashcroft, Margaret Rutherford and Gwen Ffrangcon-Davies (so did theirs), George Howe and Jack Hawkins were all to be seen, at prices which ranged from 3s. to 8s. 6d. For those of you who do not understand old money, I can assure you that such a cast, at those prices, was well worth any nearby bombs which might happen to fall on your city.

'Binkie' Beaumont also launched other tours as well (the actors received £10 per week and, if you were big enough, a cut of the takings) including Noël Coward's *Design for Living*. What they made of that *ménage à trois* in Brum, where the tour was launched, we shall never know – but Birmingham, too, was considered a safe area, so 'art' was suddenly being thrust upon the embattled populace, whether they liked it or not. Many of them liked it. As to what constituted a safe area, we had an awful lot to learn. The reality of indiscriminate bombing, plus V1s and V2s was still to come.

Fortunately, the appetite of the theatre-going public was voracious. Everybody seemed to want to be entertained and the most unlikely productions drew audiences in the provinces which, for sheer size and enthusiasm, are unlikely to be repeated. Many of the plays were good middle-of-the-road comedies though, for both the West End and the provincial theatres have rarely deviated from that general preference. *Dear Octopus*, *On Approval* and *Rebecca* were three plays toured by H. M. Tennent, and you can hardly call those avant-garde. Nor, for sheer whimsicality, could you ever beat J. M. Barrie's *Dear Brutus* – but that was revived, with John Gielgud in the lead and Muriel Pavlow as his make-believe, dream daughter, and the production was both a success in the West End and on tour. However, it did play a certain number of performances to the troops, as part of the tour, and their comments – barely printable – must have made heckling sound like child's play. I wish I'd been there.

Of course, many an actor (and actress) fought for King and Country in the conventional way, and a number were highly decorated for their service. However, others were exempted, for a variety of reasons, from the hurly-burly of killing Germans or Japanese. You were either too young or too old for military service, unfit for military service or what was euphemistically known as 'temperamentally unsuited for military service'. The great and the good even arose above those categories, and were released from the services (like Olivier and Richardson) or exempted, simply because they were capable of keeping up morale to unprecedented heights. Or, rather, that was the theory.

Such an actor-manager was Donald Wolfit.

With hindsight, I suppose it is possible to see Wolfit's career as a form of wish-fulfilment. In the preface to his mid-50s autobiography, *First Interval*, Donald wrote: 'It is the story of a theatre which, in the form I knew it as a boy, has now largely disappeared.' He then attempted to re-create that form of theatre over many years, playing number one, two and three dates, as well as 'fit-up' theatres – E N S A being the wartime equivalent – and he enthusiastically toured those dates, too. Much of this dedication to bringing the classics to the 'masses' may well have sprung from his early days with the Charles Doran Shakespearean Company, but as another theatrical knight, Sir Ralph Richardson, began with the same touring company, it cannot be said that this was infectious – for Sir Ralph in no way chose the same path as Sir Donald. It was almost as if Wolfit resolved to make those catty remarks of Miss Gingold and Mr Tynan into his epitaph, but to a fairly casual observer like myself – coming from an out-of-town, non-theatrical background – I am pretty certain this was not so. He just found himself hoist by his own petard, as I was in due course, determined to be an actor-manager and having to go to unimaginable lengths to keep his company afloat. When he found himself in an 'inferior' position, that of being an employee, he chafed at the bit and made life difficult for all concerned.

A classic case to illustrate this is Wolfit's behaviour at the Old Vic in 1951. Tyrone Guthrie was the newly appointed director of the theatre and he engaged Donald for four productions – *Tamburlaine the Great*, *The Clandestine Marriage*, *King Lear* and *Timon of Athens*.

The whole sorry mess lasted less than four months, even though Wolfit received some of the best notices of his life for his Tamburlaine and his Lord Ogleby. Ostensibly, the two men had fallen out over Wolfit's behaviour on-stage after *Tamburlaine* had moved from Waterloo Road to Stratford-upon-Avon. Wolfit had apparently begun to resort to many an old actor-manager's tricks – up-staging, moving whilst other actors spoke, jumping in before they had finished their lines and giving them copious notes at the end of the performance (or even during the performance, with many a glowering look) – so much so that they complained to the director himself, Tyrone Guthrie. The result was a backstage confrontation of

TOP Donald Wolfit warming up for his row with
Tyrone Guthrie as Tamberlaine the Great. LEFT, the
author warming up for all of his ten lines as
Curan the courtier in *King Lear*. RIGHT, the programme
to prove it all happened.

monumental proportions, with Wolfit eventually seizing on a very slight excuse to claim breach of contract, immediately handing in his notice. On leaving the company he launched into a virulent attack on the governors of the Old Vic and their alleged misuse of public money. Not many members of the profession supported him in his views, but I believe they were genuinely held political beliefs, reinforced by his treatment during the war by C E M A, and expressed most forcibly in his autobiography:

> Up to now the Council for the Encouragement of Music and the Arts had been of some trifling assistance in the matter of finance, in all some few hundred pounds. The chairman was concerned more and more with great affairs of state and was leaving the conduct of the newly formed Council very much to the secretariat. My progress as a presenter of the plays of Shakespeare, not only in London for successive seasons, but in the provincial cities and towns, had been watched with great interest. The fact that I had managed to keep my head above water in the most difficult times that ever beset an actor-manager was subject matter for both congratulation and recrimination. We had now reached the high noon of bureaucratic interference, our liberties were ebbing away under a mass of forms and restrictions. Under the guise of Encouragement, the Arts were now to be formed, or even forced, into a precise pattern by a group of people who wished to dictate and had a subsidy in their hands.
>
> It was suggested that I should apply for a grant-in-aid to cover me against loss on the autumn tour of 1942, which in fact had already been booked by the theatre managements who had expressed complete satisfaction with my previous visits, now extending over a period of five years.
>
> In a long correspondence it finally became clear that the conditions attached to this guarantee were quite unacceptable. I was to be asked to surrender certain key dates on the tour so that the Old Vic company, which was now beginning to raise its head in the recesses of Lancashire, should be able to visit these cities in my stead.

Can you wonder there were ructions when Wolfit joined the Old Vic company some eight years later? Especially when I remind you that the director of the Old Vic during its sojourn at the aptly named Victoria Theatre in the 'recesses of Lancashire', Burnley to boot, was none other than that gaunt giant of the classical theatre, the yet-to-be-knighted (like Sir Donald) Tyrone Guthrie – the very man who had received C E M A's benison in preference to the outraged actor-manager.

Wolfit completed that particularly biting attack on C E M A by writing: 'I was now to undertake the greatest task of all, the addition of *King Lear* to the repertoire.' Not altogether surprisingly, he did not see fit to mention that a certain young actor was about to join his company, with absolutely no professional experience at all. That callow youth was me. And the date? 3rd August, 1942.

(Until I appeared in *Dry Rot* at the Lyric Theatre, Shaftesbury Avenue during the autumn of 1988 and the beginning of 1989 – my short-lived return to the boards after seven years as secretary-general of MENCAP – I was always under the impression that Wolfit rehearsed at the Duke of Wellington pub in Great Windmill Street, which houses the Lyric's stage door, hard by the Windmill 'We Never Closed' Theatre. Indeed, I made a point of this in the first part of my autobiography, *My Farce from my Elbow*. But I was wrong. Forty-six years later, almost to the day, I discovered it was the Duke of Argyll in Brewer Street – but what's in a name? Well, two names to be precise.)

Rehearsal rooms are all the same. Damp in winter, unbearably hot in summer, especially a warm August, and the first-floor accommodation at the Duke of Argyll in Brewer Street was no different. So, sweating with nerves and the effects of London humidity, I attended my first read-through, all for £3 a week. At least, that was what I was getting for the actual performances on tour. God knows how much less it was for rehearsal, assuming we got anything at all. Nothing changes. Small-part actors are still underpaid. In fact, it is actors themselves who are the greatest source of subsidy for the theatre. You only have to look at the numbers out of work at any one time, and then consider their often inadequate salaries when they finally do find employment, to realise this. But when it's your first job, as it was mine, you never think of things like that. The world is a wonderful place, even if you have only three lines to speak, the bombs are keeping you awake at night and you are the lowest of the low – an acting ASM. In other words, a general dogsbody just happy to be kicked from time to time, as this betokens recognition. Mind you, when you are a young, reasonably presentable, dark-haired, male ASM you are inclined to get recognition of a different kind – but in these days of sexual liberation there is no point in going into that. Just let it be noted that I removed all heavy hands, which descended on my thighs from time to time, with increasing confidence and rapidity as the months wore on. Eventually, when my heterosexual proclivities were recognised, they stopped descending altogether. Oh, and by the way, for the uninitiated, ASM stands for Assistant Stage Manager and the acting bit is not like being an acting unpaid lance-corporal, but merely indicates you play as cast – carrying spears and the like – not gracing the boards with your presence in some memorable supporting role.

I was amazed at everybody's apparent confidence. There was the great man himself, Donald Wolfit – 'Sir', to the likes of me – being greeted like some old friend by quite a number of the actors, as was his leading lady (not yet his wife), Rosalind Iden. There was his producer (they called directors producers in those days), Nugent Monck (definitely heavy-handed), blocking out *King Lear* with amazing facility and precision, and there was I, clutching my *Complete Works of William Shakespeare* wishing I had the same insouciance as everybody else. It did not take me long to realise that, underneath, all actors are a seething mass of doubts and uncertainties at the first rehearsals of any production, but in those far-off days I was distinctly damp behind the ears and thought I was the only one. Rather like the young actor who was on a fortnight's trial at rehearsal (you could be in those days) and worried that he wasn't going to hang on to his job. He had just finished spouting his one and only speech, when he suddenly saw the manager of the company approaching the director, with a note in his hand, and pointing in his direction. He broke into a cold sweat with fear, especially when the director called him over. 'My God, this is it,' he thought, as the director handed him the piece of paper, 'it's my notice.' Glancing at it, he burst into hysterical laughter. 'Great news, everyone,' he yelled. 'It's only my mother – she's dead.'

After three weeks of rehearsal – yes, three weeks only for a repertoire of four plays, *King Lear, Hamlet, A Midsummer Night's Dream* and *Twelfth Night*, we were off to our first date – the Prince of Wales Theatre, Cardiff. Many people considered that Wolfit only engaged inexperienced young actors like me (he did, but there was a war on), or actors who were well past their sell-by dates (also true, but they already knew the lines and didn't bump into the furniture) and that he did not rehearse for long enough. Well, you have to remember he was an actor-manager with precious few resources (he had recently lost his 'trifling' C E M A grant) and he was only adding one new play (O N L Y! – it was *King Lear*) to a well-tried-and-tested stockpile of productions, with actors who had been with him on and off for a number of years, and generally in the same Shakespearian calendar. Somehow we managed to make Cardiff in some degree of good order, with a Sunday get-in and set-up, followed by a lighting rehearsal, a dress rehearsal and a first night on the Monday, all quite impossible in today's thinking. But even the Sunday get-in was unusual in those days, for all travel had to be made by rail and Sunday trains were even worse than they are today, if such a thing is possible. But we had four lots of scenery to hang and prepare, four lots of lighting plots to be arranged (you toured your own hired spot bars and acting-area lights as well, plus temporary Strand Electric control boards), four lots of props to be sorted out, four lots of costumes to be laid out and hung up in the wardrobe and one lot of actors to be ready for that Monday first night when the curtain went up at a wartime six thirty p.m., half an hour later than in London. As you can see, there was indeed lots to do. No wonder we did not have time to read the papers. On the very day we were getting-in, one of the last major cavalry charges of the Second World War took place. Six hundred Italian soldiers galloped on horseback against two thousand Russians, who had machine-guns and mortars at their disposal. With flashing sabres, the Italians put the Russians to flight and thus took their place in history. Also taking their place in history, in a less heroic mould, were twenty men arraigned in the Abergavenny Court for improper conduct, mainly in the back row of a cinema which was showing *Third Finger Left Hand* (with Myrna Loy). You can imagine the sniggers which that piece of information encouraged. We all read about that, you'll notice. Not unnaturally, for it was in the *News of the World*. Mind you, with two older members of our cast who had done time for choirboys, who were we to laugh?

It was no wonder, too, that Wolfit was exhausted for, although Nugent Monck was officially the producer of *Lear*, Donald was gradually taking over command, so much so that the programme credit now read: 'The play produced by Donald Wolfit who wishes to acknowledge the expert collaboration of W. Nugent Monck, Founder of the Maddermarket Theatre, Norwich.' Within a few weeks Mr Monck was no more, having been frozen out, and you only had to mention his name for Wolfit to allow you to change any stage direction given to you by the original producer.

It must have been a combination of all those factors which made Wolfit disappointed with his own performance on that opening night, quite apart from the weather. He wrote:

> Curiously enough it was a sultry and thundery weekend and very oppressive, I remember. The storm broke about half an hour before the mimic storm in the play, so that it seemed as if my first assault on the part was carried out in a perpetual roll of real and theatrical claps and reverberations. Despite the warm and enthusiastic reception the generous theatre-goers of Cardiff gave my first attempt I was disappointed and knew I had failed . . . Physically, I was exhausted, but not mentally or spiritually. I spent the night in study.

I spent the night snoring loudly in my first-ever theatrical digs, for I was exhausted too – trying to drown out the real thunder, during the performance, with a tiny, tinny thunder-sheet. The part of Curan, a courtier, with all of ten lines to speak at the beginning of Act 2, Scene 1, hardly necessitates such nocturnal meditation as undertaken by my boss.

Wolfit was happier with his second night's performance, so we were now into the normal business of touring. Of course, there were still the other plays to rehearse, dress-rehearse and put into the repertoire, but the Becher's Brook of *King Lear* had been surmounted and there was now the chance to look around and find out what an actor's life, especially on tour, was like. I will begin at the beginning and start with those most famous of institutions – theatrical digs. I bet you thought this book would be all about such places. Well, you would have been wrong. However, such illustrious establishments do have their position in theatrical heraldry, so here goes . . .

My digs in Cardiff were quite reasonable I suppose. A huge double bed, with the obligatory po underneath and an outside privy at the bottom of the garden. Well, you couldn't call it a garden exactly; more a small back yard with a rickety old shed, from which swung a wooden half door, creaking on one rusty hinge, acting as an inadequate shield for the earth closet within. Hardly conducive to nocturnal wanderings, especially as there was no street lighting (due to the black-out) to light your desperate way, should you be caught short in the middle of the night. All very basic, but at least my landlady did not hang up that famous old notice: THERE IS A CHAMBER POT UNDER THE BED. IF USED DURING THE NIGHT DO NOT REPLACE, AS THE STEAM RUSTS THE SPRINGS.

I also made the mistake of telling my landlady that I thought her Welsh rarebit was delicious, at a brief meal I had on that first Sunday night, before returning to the theatre to continue the get-in and setting-up. I should have known better. She had managed to get hold of a pound or two of mousetrap from somewhere off the ration, and I had incessant meals of soggy cheese on soggy toast from then on, until the train call a week later. That should have taught me to keep my stupid mouth shut – but it didn't.

For the uninitiated, I had better explain about a train call. On a Sunday, all the actors were herded together at the station (I say 'were' because nowadays the majority travel by car) and bundled into dirty, freezing third class carriages which had labels gummed on the windows naming the company within, in an effort to keep out *hoi polloi*. The scenery travelled free in accompanying luggage vans and starving actors dashed out at stations to grab cups of cold buffet tea and rock-hard Spam sandwiches, as they wended their way – very slowly – from one town to another. Veteran variety pro, the late Sandy Powell, used to tell a lovely story, which concerned both digs and trains. He had spent an uncomfortable week resisting the advances of an amorous landlady whilst appearing in Scarborough. Much relieved, he left for the train call on the Sunday but, to his horror, found he had to rush back to his digs for his ticket, which he had forgotten. As he tore into the house through the back door, he was somewhat startled to see his landlady, stark naked on the kitchen table and straddled above her, also starkers, the local stage manager from the very theatre in which Sandy had just finished playing. The landlady might have been short of clothes but she was pretty long on 'chutzpah'. 'Oh, Mr Powell,' she said with becoming modesty, 'you will think I'm a flirt.'

It will not have taken a discerning reader long to note that the general drift of landlady stories is much the same. Sexual activity and bowel movements seem to predominate, with horrendous harridans, disgusting dirt and foul food bringing up the rear. You see, you cannot write an innocent line like that, without some double meaning becoming evident. I will therefore confine myself to one or two more tales and then, I promise you, the rest is silence.

My old friend Leslie Crowther belongs to the bowel brigade. Once, he too was in digs with an outside loo, and a thoughtful landlady had provided him with a torch – unlike mine – to help him negotiate the black-out in Cardiff. As is usual in such stories, Leslie was taken short after midnight and, grabbing his torch, made his uncertain way to a couple of outside loos, which were back to back. Suddenly a window was flung open and there framed in the window, lit by the pitiless glare of a forty-watt bulb, was his landlady. 'Mr Crowther,' she yelled, 'are you going to the lavatory?' Leslie explained that he was. 'Well, don't go in that one, luv. It's next door's and we're not speaking.'

I, on the other hand, support the harridan and dirt cohort. In my first autobiography I told a sad story about Bastien and Blackpool. I had better explain that Bastien was our labrador, and I was now married to Elspet Gray (and I still am, after more than forty years, in spite of all that touring); the year was 1950 and we were on a seemingly endless tour of *Reluctant Heroes*, and trying to find a London home. One of our early dates in March was Blackpool. That in itself is enough to warn you that all was not well with our planning. I mean, who ever heard of a play doing business in Blackpool in March? We even arrived in a snowstorm . . .

Bastien was now huge, and for most of the tour he had been suffering from a disease called hard pad. One conventional vet said he would have to be destroyed – so we took him to a vet who believed in homoeopathic treatment. Each day Bastien was given various pills and potions, fed on a diet of fish and clad in a little green woollen jacket. He survived, but not before he had been sick over Elspet and me in the car during an intercity journey (even our friends wouldn't come near us for a time after that – a pretty kettle of fish, indeed!) and had caused tumult by twice tearing open pillowcases when left alone in our bedroom because he was too ill to be taken to the theatre.

The first time he did this was in Blackpool. The landlady was a truly ghastly creature who terrified us all and rationed her hot baths as though the war was still on. 'ONE bath per week EACH' read the notice, hard by 'God Bless This House'. 'ONE bath per week EACH. No more than FIVE inches must be run. 6d. extra PER BATH. DO NOT use the bath before permission has been obtained. Vim is provided at no extra charge. LEAVE THE BATH AS YOU WOULD EXPECT TO FIND IT.' So, you paid your sixpence, entered the freezing cold bathroom, to be confronted by a chipped, stained bath and a geyser which could have doubled for a Wurlitzer organ. You turned on an assortment of taps, the mighty machine groaned and wheezed into life and out came a dribble of tepid, rusty water. F I V E inches? You couldn't get in T H R E E before the damned water was stone cold anyway. It's the only time I've tried to bath in cold iron filings. At least my behind was scoured clean by bits of chipped enamel and old, residual Vim.

By this, you will gather that we were somewhat in awe of our gorgon landlady. She'd looked askance when we'd taken Bastien along, but we persuaded her that his green jacket and need for smelly fish made him quiet and docile and really he was just a lovable lap-dog. Grudgingly she admitted us and him, with dire warnings of immediate ejection if so much as one dog hair mucked up her already filthy house. We meekly concurred, and Bastien was duly installed with his bed made in our large suitcase, and off we went to the theatre.

On our return for our joyless supper, we first looked upstairs to check on Bastien. Horror upon horror. As we entered the room, feathers floated and billowed up from all corners. Bastien greeted us wildly, certain that he'd done a good job, the threshing of his tail adding to the chaos already abounding. We slammed the door, all thoughts of our cold cod and chips downstairs forgotten, and spent the entire night catching and collecting feathers, then stuffing them back into the torn pillowcase. Sisyphus had it easy, compared to us. At least boulders roll towards ground level. Feathers have altogether different flights of fancy.

As dawn came up over Blackpool's cheerless, treeless streets, we were completing our Sisyphean task. Elspet was reinforced in her belief that Bastien should go, for she'd tried to give him away shortly after I had presented him to her as a Christmas present, the year we were married in 1949. Our large puppy's Christmas offerings, spread generously around our flat in Bridlington (we were in rep there) did N O T enhance the Christmas spirit, and my gift was spurned. However, I sulked so much, hinting darkly that our marriage might well be in jeopardy, that he was returned to the fold. Fourteen years later, in spite of Bastien, Blackpool and other vicissitudes, we were still together and Elspet lovingly held poor old Bastien's head as he was put to sleep.

And now a word from our president, Ronnie Corbett. Or, rather, a past president (like me) of the Lord's Taverners, the cricketing charity which published a book in 1987 called *Theatrical Digs*:

It seems very appropriate to me that the proceeds of a book on theatrical digs should go to charity, because, in the days when such establishments played an important part in my life, I found that one of the most important qualities needed in judging one's digs was charity. Also faith and hope. Not to mention mercy.

It also seems appropriate that they should be called 'digs'. Nobody is quite clear about the derivation of the word, but I believe we cannot overlook the archaeological connection. There is an obvious link. Indeed, I understand that modern science has now evolved a system of carbon dating the encrustations on sauce bottles to determine whether the premises were originally established in the neolithic or palaeolithic eras – although there has been no breakthrough yet in the research to discover why some landladies fell into the pterodactyl class, while others favoured the tyrannosaurus rex. However, this is mere historical background. Let us move on to theatrical digs as I knew them . . .

. . . My experience of digs goes back a good few years. They say that distance lends enchantment to the view . . . but, of course, the young are resilient. I don't remember suffering all that much at the time. In fact, to tell the truth, those digs to me, as a beginner in the business, were all I could ask for. (Also, all I could afford.) They were really a second home to me. They're where I learned my trade. They made a man of me. And do you think I'd have swapped them for the bridal suite at the Ritz? Are you kidding? I'd have swapped them for a decently built dog-kennel.

And what's more, I did. (Gaiety, Bootle.)

Finally, to round off these fond reminiscences, I would like to pay tribute to possibly the best-known landlady in the business, or rather – to be accurate – the best-known landlord, Basil Hartley, who runs bedsits at 'Novello House' in Leeds. His late mother began taking in theatrical 'guests' over fifty years ago, in a house called 'Vaudeville'. She then joined forces with her son, they put two houses together and 'Novello House' and 'Villa Novello' came into being. Not altogether surprisingly, they were named after Ivor Novello himself who had stayed there, when he was appearing at the Grand Theatre, Leeds in *King's Rhapsody* – his last tour before he died in 1951. A white grand piano still stands in the lounge, once played by Ivor, but since then dozens of artistes, known and unknown, have tickled the ivories so lovingly caressed by the master. Oh dear, I am beginning to sound like an Ivor Novello script. It is definitely time to fill in the visitors' book with some suitable remark ('my bad back is almost better after a week on your bed and board') and set out on the road again. After all, it has its attractions. When one old actor was asked if he ever thought Hamlet had slept with Ophelia, he considered for a moment and then said, with a certain degree of nostalgia: 'On tour, yes. In the West End, never!'

I have described how the get-in took place at the Prince of Wales, Cardiff in 1942. Nowadays very little seems to have changed, except that with road transport superseding the railways, it just works a little more efficiently, that's all – with the bigger productions enjoying the luxury of a Sunday get-in, even though this costs a great deal more in double time. In Wolfit's era, however (and before that), the Sunday get-in was practically unknown. Only those at the beginning of a tour, like ours, could have the scenery dispatched by rail in time to be moved in on the Sabbath. The rest scrambled in on a Monday. In those days, too, you have to remember that local road haulage was generally horse-drawn, so your precious sets and lighting and costumes and props were often subjected to additional hazards from the elements before an inadequate tarpaulin could be thrown over them, as they wended their way from the station goods yard along the back streets to the theatre, where once again they were likely to be drenched as they were manhandled out of the wagons, through the dock doors, into the scene dock, at the back of the stage. No wonder so many backcloths, depicting some magnificent silvan scene, looked like well-used crumpled bedsheets when finally suspended and lit, generally with a suspicious-looking water stain in a most awkward place. Probably on the figleaf, covering Cupid's tiny parts.

Of course, the get-in was an altogether slower business than the get-out. Ground plans had to be consulted, lighting equipment positioned, scenery hung and cleated together with care, otherwise it could fall on the actors and cause physical damage. It did once at the end of *Hamlet*, as Wolfit stepped through the curtain to take his bow, when a tormentor (one of the two wing pieces downstage by the proscenium arch, both stage left and right) collapsed and Wolfit was only saved from a nasty accident by a quick-thinking stagehand who caught the eighteen-foot flat rather like a Rugby player making a mark. Actually, this near miss took place on a Saturday night, just before the get-out itself. By then, everything that could be uncleated *was* uncleated, backings no longer in view had been struck, props not wanted again, already packed in the skips – as were the costumes in the wardrobe. Once, when we were touring *Suspect* for E N S A, the suspect herself had to wield an axe at the final curtain, whilst laughing crazily throughout. On the night in question, an over-zealous A S M had packed the axe, leaving a completely bewildered audience surveying an actress doing her best to mime her final moment of madness. If the axe had been handy, I think she would have used it on any stage manager in sight.

All these props, costumes and scenery, plus the actors' luggage, travelled for nothing, provided there were enough third class railway tickets purchased for the company. It was only after Beeching had his go at British Rail that such perks were stopped. By then, though, most scenery had started to be moved by road and the actors, too, had acquired cars, so mileage allowances took the place of free tickets, and the train call, as we knew it, disappeared. Yet it was the railways that made modern-day touring a reality, and there are still many actors who travel by train. They prefer the comfort of letting someone else do the driving, even if it means they don't see much of their homes at the weekend. On the other hand, they avoid nervous breakdowns and ulcers worrying about the road ahead being blocked, or a sudden fog descending, or a snowstorm developing, or the car breaking down – which can still make driving to reach your theatre on time for a Monday night such a nailbiting experience. I know. I've chewed mine down to the elbows on many occasions. Oh, incidentally, the next time you see a container van in a lay-by, generally with the name G. H. Lucking & Sons on the side, you will know it contains the sets and the props and the wardrobe for some touring production. But don't worry at its apparent loneliness. It hasn't been hijacked. It's merely waiting for the relay driver to come and pick it up with his cab, before moving it on to some other get-in.

And so the touring theatre plays; and having played, moves on . . .

Slow fade to black and lights up on Act II, Scene II.

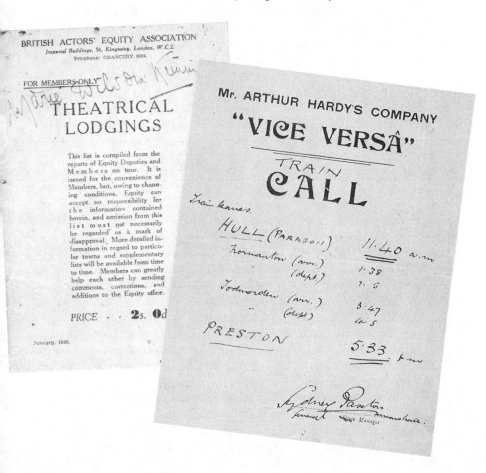

SCENE II
'The Happiest Days of Your Life'

PRINCE OF WALES THEATRE
Cardiff

When I entered the stage door of the Prince of Wales for the first time, I at last recognised the difference between a proper theatre and the Parish Hall, or the Floral Hall, Hornsea where I did my early amateur acting in plays produced by my mother. It was the stairs. In Hornsea the dressing-rooms were just behind or under the stage, with one room for the men and one for the women and a loo tucked coyly in between. Here, in a professional theatre, the loos were still in short supply but the dressing-rooms burgeoned on every floor, from stage level to the height of the fly tower. And there was only one way of moving from room to room and floor to floor.

Stairs!

No luxury like a lift had ever been contemplated. As an actor it was your job to get on stage on time, without the benefit of a call-boy or a p.a. system, and the amount of stairs you needed to negotiate had to be part of your time-and-motion calculations. If you were an assistant stage manager, however, you were not only allotted a dressing-room at the top of the building (at a height which would have put an eagle's eyrie to shame) but you found yourself constantly dashing up and down the stairs taking hand props to those lucky actors who were senior to you. In my case this meant literally everyone. Only the wardrobe mistress was treated with the same contempt as me. Her steam-filled hovel was usually next door to mine – and she had the costumes for no less than four productions to clean, press and deliver to those backstage. Furthermore, she was generally on her own, unless any dressers were hired for the week. At least in Cardiff there were a few fellow serfs crammed into the same room I occupied, even though they were all superior to me by virtue of having been employed at least once before in their lives. But none of this caused any unhappiness at the time. I was just so pleased to be employed in the one job I had secretly coveted since I was a child – in fact, ever since I had become jealous of Freddie Bartholomew when he appeared in the title role of the Hollywood version of *David Copperfield*. Over the years this jealousy had been converted into a desire to become an actor, but before I managed to achieve this I went through the charade of contemplating becoming a doctor, or going into my father's business of shipowning and broking. I was saved by the Second World War which provided the perfect excuse not to do either. I volunteered for air-crew, was put on deferred service and immediately auditioned for Donald Wolfit when he was on tour in Hull with his production of Constance Cox's *David Garrick*. I never regretted that decision, for being an actor – and subsequently an actor-manager – has stood me in good stead ever since. Even during my years as Secretary-General of MENCAP. It is amazing how a familiar face – which was mine – can open doors or have letters and telephone calls answered. But all that was a long way off in that wartime August of 1942.

The POW began as the Theatre Royal in November 1878, became the Playhouse in 1920 when it was reopened after the First World War by a group of local businessmen, and was finally named the Prince of Wales in 1935 when Prince Littler (no relation) became the managing director. By then, of course, Mr Littler was well on his way to being the boss of many theatres, through the Stoll Moss Empire (if you will pardon the pun) and the Howard and Wyndham Group, but his battle to keep this particular theatre open was finally lost in 1957. It was the Theatre Club which kept it going in 1958, but alas they lost that battle, too (but not before we visited it on our pre-London tour of *Simple Spymen*), and those ghastly late-night films you can now receive on closed-circuit telly in hotel bedrooms became the order of the day.

I am glad to report that Cardiff soon found soft porn pretty dull, but the Council decided to put all its eggs into the New Theatre basket, and now the old Prince has been changed into an amusement centre. And it seems it will never be re-established as a theatre. The shades of Sir Henry Irving and the Kendals – Madge and William – not forgetting Sir Donald Wolfit and many others, will no doubt haunt the new centre, desperately trying to find their follow spots. I mention the Kendals here deliberately. Of course they did play the original Theatre Royal, and there remains to this day the story of one night, in Cardiff, when William tried to insist on his marital rights. Madge, a somewhat domineering figure, totally obsessed with the financial arrangements of running the company, was just not interested. Poor old hen-pecked William kept on pressing the point, however, and Madge finally, and grudgingly, agreed. 'Oh, all right,' she grumbled, 'get on with it, but pass me tonight's returns first.'

THE PAVILION
Torquay

Cardiff to Torquay is no distance at all, as the crow flies. Unfortunately, we were not our scavenging feathered friends. Well, scavenging we might have been, from time to time, but we were definitely very leaden footed when it came to flying – particularly on a Sunday wartime train call. By the time we had crawled to Gloucester, changed trains and crawled to Torquay, most of our day of rest had been *put* to rest. There was just time to clock into our digs before darkness fell – even with the emergency double-summer-daylight-saving-time – and absolutely no time to visit the theatre to get on with any work. That all started the next morning, at the crack of dawn, when the get-in got under way.

The get-in was much easier than Cardiff because the stage of The Pavilion was not exactly built to house grand opera and we only had room to mount two productions, *King Lear* and *Twelfth Night*, so the rest of the scenery, costumes and props were thankfully left behind at the railway sidings under a system known as demurrage. (In the short time I worked in my father's shipping office I had learnt that demurrage meant the amount which was payable to a shipowner by a charterer for failure to load or discharge a ship within the time allowed. Until I arrived in Torquay, I had no idea that the same rules applied to theatrical scenery. However, I believe the rates were fairly generous and still made the whole method of transporting theatricals financially viable. I dread to think what those rates would be today.)

According to the leaflet prepared by the Torbay Civic Society, 'The Pavilion at Torquay is an excellent example of English seaside architecture, built when the English seaside was in its heyday (1912), and because it was built at the edge of the sea and not at the end of a pier it is exciting as a building.'

All very true, but the place was intended for music, not drama, and was hardly conducive to allowing a full appreciation of Wolfit's *Lear*, although it could be said to be better matched to the Illyrian delights of *Twelfth Night*. The audience was seated in a large semi-circle, separated from the stage by a vast orchestra pit big enough to house the Torquay Municipal Orchestra in all its glory, and did its best to follow Shakespeare's greatest tragedy from seats which did not always allow a full vision of the stage and with the disturbing noise of surf crashing on the beach to interrupt their appreciation of the dialogue. Mind you, it certainly added to the effects in the storm scene. In Cardiff it was a thunderstorm; in Torquay it was the English Channel. No wonder Wolfit hired a boat one day, and ordered me and another A S M to row him out to sea. I think he had Canute-like schemes to control the waves which were disturbing his evening performances. In the event, he failed, the tide turned, the boat began to take in water – and it was only by dint of frantic baling and rowing that we ever made it to the shore again. No wonder old Donald was so exhausted that night. When it came to carrying Iris Russell (Cordelia) on to the stage at the end of the play, he almost dropped her. Muscle fatigue had, it seemed, taken its toll. Never had Sir John Gielgud's exhortation to an aspiring Lear been more apposite. 'Make sure you cast a light Cordelia,' Sir John advised. For once, Mr Wolfit would have agreed.

After this visit attempts were made to turn The Pavilion into a conventional theatre as well as a concert hall. A rising platform was installed in the orchestra pit, which filled in the gap at the front of the stalls when the orchestra was not in residence, and the stage was at last within hailing distance of the seating. But, in spite of such ingenuity, The Pavilion remained patently unsuitable for any dramatic entertainment. I know. I played there again in 1950 with the pre-London tour of *Reluctant Heroes*. Thirty-eight years earlier, the borough engineer, Major Garrett, who acted as the architect to the project, had been instructed to build a concert hall, and a concert hall it remained.

Eventually, however, The Pavilion achieved a somewhat ignominious end. The heating failed, due to neglect, and in 1977 it was closed. A White Knight, in the shape of private enterprise, was at hand and two years later it was restored to become a skating rink and leisure centre. No great loss as far as we thespians are concerned and at least this 'much-loved landmark' is providing entertainment as was intended, although the likes of Basil Cameron, Sir Thomas Beecham and Sir Edward Elgar will never mount the conductor's podium again. And to think it originally cost only £16,942 4s. and 4d. to build. They knew a thing or two about 'brass' in those days. Even in faraway Devon.

THEATRE ROYAL
Exeter

The sad litany of closed-down or demolished theatres goes on. Wolfit seems to have had a penchant for picking houses that were doomed to go dark. Mind you, his venues were mainly Number Two theatres which could simply not stand up to the overwhelming appeal of post-war television. Obviously, Wolfit was not to know this and his proud boast that his was 'the company that has presented more than 600 performances of works of the National Dramatist in London and all the principal cities of the British Isles since the outbreak of war' still held water, even though you may doubt that Torquay and Harrow (our next venue) qualify as 'principal cities'. The fact is that out of our fourteen-week tour, six theatres are no longer open to the public as theatres and two of these have been demolished.

The Theatre Royal, Exeter, opened in 1889, after a tragic fire destroyed its predecessor on Monday 5th September, 1887 during which 188 people watching the performance from the gallery were burnt to death. The architect of the original theatre was the well-known Mr C. J. Phipps but, in spite of his expertise and reputation he only allowed for one exit to the gallery and during the fire the bodies just piled up at that door. Shades of football-ground disasters a century later at Bradford and Hillsborough; or even the Underground fire at King's Cross. Indeed, an account in *The Times*, two days after the theatre was destroyed, makes familiar reading – even allowing for the change in journalistic style:

> A disaster unparalleled in the history of the English stage attended the burning down of the New Theatre Royal, Exeter on Monday night. The building was erected only last year . . . Placards which still remain on the walls announced the fact that Mr G. R. Sims' well-known play *The Romany Rye* would be produced for the first time in Exeter on Monday night . . . At nine o'clock there was the usual influx into the popular parts of the house of those who are theatrically known as 'half-timers' and then the pit was crammed. The fourth act opened success-

fully. About ten minutes past ten there was a hitch. Mr Powell was at the time – a remarkable coincidence – speaking of an 'interference in the business'; the drop scene at the same moment fell heavily; there was a loud titter among the audience, who had not the remotest idea of the impending disaster, and it was expected that the curtain would in a moment again 'ring up'. The conductor remarked 'There's something up,' and was about to fill the interval with a selection of music. The curtain at that moment slightly waved, and as it had not gone completely down the persons who were in the first two rows of the stalls caught a glimpse of the floor of the stage. Almost immediately after there was a cry of 'Fire!' raised from the body of the auditorium. A terrible panic ensued; the people rose from their seats 'en masse' and a general rush for the doors was made . . . The curtain only momentarily concealed the fire, and soon flames darted forth from the stage. The people in the pit, stalls and upper circle got out comparatively easily and quietly. In the gallery, however, which was the most crowded part of the house, a fearful panic occurred. Women shrieked and swooned; men half mad with excitement rushed and stumbled over the prostrate bodies, while in the only means of exit a block ensued. In a very short time the interior of the building was converted into a furnace.

Outside, the sight was a pitiable one. People appeared on the balcony over the front entrance, wringing their hands and crying for help, and the scene nearest the gallery windows was simply beyond description. The struggle for life at this time must have been terrible. The rescuers stated that bodies on the steps and in the passages to the gallery were crushed, charred, bleeding and mingled in fearful confusion with the falling wreckage. The throng in the balconies increased and some could not be restrained from leaping into the roadway. Among the missing are two 'fly men'. It is thought that they were unable to escape from the flies where they were at work, and where the fire is supposed to have originated.

That would account for the 'drop scene' falling heavily, I suppose. But worse was to come . . .

On 8th September the *London Evening News* reported, under the head-line SHOCKING SCENES AT FUNERAL:

Here and there, there were women, red-eyed and sobbing, but a few seemed to have collected together as they would to see a Punch and Judy show. They had come out sightseeing, and they meant to see at any cost . . . Loose women carried lapdogs, bottles of gin, luncheon baskets and children. Men smoked their pipes. Such a procession as there was consisted principally of a jostling crowd. Many, however, as if anxious for a front seat, took a short cut across the graves, and raced as if they were following the hunt. The behaviour at the graves was scandalous, and largely consisted of spectators pulling one another down the mound of wet red clay, which others formed into pellets, with which they pelted one another. The appearance of the coffins was disgraceful. Many of them were hardly screwed down at all and shreds of half-roasted flesh, charred bones and clothes were hanging out in fringes. Even the rough crowd noticed this, and made vulgar comments thereon . . . There were only seven graves in all, and into these were hustled and bumped sixteen coffins. The whole sight was sickening.

Not surprisingly, the fire regulations for theatres were changed after this tragedy. Before then it was common practice for the gallery to be completely cut off from the rest of the theatre but rules were introduced to give alternative access and egress to the upper circle. The dreadful loss of life in the Theatre Royal also cost C. J. Phipps his reputation. Up until then his output of theatre design had been phenomenal, but after the fire he was publicly blamed for planning a building with structural faults and inadequate safety precautions, even though the inquest on the victims had recorded a verdict of accidental death. It was years before Phipps regained his reputation, and even then it was due to another and even more famous theatre architect, Frank Matcham, who is responsible for so many of the splendid theatres which are still operating successfully today. Such was Frank Matcham's ability to build better and safer theatres, that he enhanced the reputation of the theatre architect, and Phipps was able to return to the fold. In the event, the rebuilt Theatre Royal was the first to be custom-built to meet the new regulations, but this did not save its future as a theatre. It was demolished in 1962, and replaced by an insurance office. No doubt that would have pleased the late Reverend Tremelling who came forward with this charming remark about that dreadful fire: 'Even to allow two or three people to place their lives in the hands of a few vain, drunken, ignorant, thoughtless stage players was a mistake.' *Don't* put your daughter on the stage, Mrs Worthington. You can see the sort of company she will keep.

Meanwhile, back at the ranch we young actors, far from being vain, drunken, ignorant or thoughtless, were behaving in an exemplary fashion towards the younger female members of the company who were facing a hazard of a different kind when they clambered into bed. Bed bugs . . .

All the fairies from *A Midsummer Night's Dream* were sharing the same digs and one morning, soon after our arrival in Exeter, Fairy Moth rushed round to where I was staying with several other members of the company, including Michael Blythe, who subsequently became a TV director with HTV.

It was clear that all was not well: 'Come quickly,' she sobbed. 'The landlady says we brought the beastly bugs with us and won't let us leave.'

Michael and I girded our loins and strode round purposefully to defend the honour of Fairies Peaseblossom, Cobweb and Mustardseed – not forgetting Moth, Anne Rogers, who went on to become an actress of some note. After a great deal of blustering, we succeeded in getting the girls out, but one of them, Fairy Peaseblossom – Tilsa Page – was known as Fairy Dettol thereafter, for she soaked herself in that pungent disinfectant for weeks in an effort to see that bed bugs never attacked again. She developed a dreadful skin rash instead . . .

48   EXETER. — *Theatre Royal.* — LL.

NEW COLISEUM THEATRE
Harrow

The New Coliseum was another of the unfortunate theatres fated to close, for it is now a supermarket. Harrow, in the suburbs of London (although the residents of that town would not care to hear their location described in such terms), is the home of the famous school on Harrow-on-the-Hill which may have fostered delusions of grandeur but, unlike Windsor, with its lovely Theatre Royal and Eton nearby, the local Harrovians have been unable to support a theatre for very long.

The Coliseum was built at the outbreak of the Second World War and was opened by Queen Mary, the Queen Mother, in May 1940 – just as Hitler conquered France and the British Army was preparing the evacuation at Dunkirk – and it never really recovered from that less than propitious beginning. Certainly Wolfit scarcely made the welkin ring, even though things were becoming somewhat brighter for us in the war. Indeed, the fact that we were now so close to London made us a little more conscious that there was a world outside the theatre, and a pretty nasty one at that. A certain General Montgomery had just repulsed a Rommel attack that was supposed to take the German forces to Cairo and the famous Battle of El Alamein was but six weeks away. In Russia the German forces had begun their unsuccessful attack on Stalingrad, which became one of the greatest defeats of all time for a German army, and we had just dropped our first two-ton 'block-busters' on Düsseldorf. But in the cavernous Coliseum, none of this good news was readily apparent, and there were a lot of empty seats to keep us all – and none more so than the proprietor, Alfred Denville, M P, J P – fairly gloomy.

Mr Denville was a remarkable man. Born to theatrical parents, he made his first stage appearance at the age of six weeks at the old Greenwich Theatre. Twenty-four years later, in 1900, he became an actor-manager, launched the Denville Stock Companies, a further twenty repertory companies and, over a period of time, more than 150 companies which went on the road. Eventually, though, he gave up much of this activity, went into politics and became Member of Parliament for the Central

64

Division of Newcastle-upon-Tyne, which he served from 1930 to 1945. He still found time to build the Coliseum, Harrow, though, and before that was the donor and founder of Denville Hall, a retirement home at Northwood in Middlesex for 'aged actors and actresses', which still flourishes today.

Three actors, with whom I worked, ended their days in Denville Hall. Naunton Wayne, famous for his cricket-mad duo with Basil Radford in Alfred Hitchcock's *Night Train to Munich*, was with me in the film *Nothing Barred*, written by John Chapman, and the Kenneth Horne comedy, *Sleeping Partnership* on television. Robertson Hare, known to all and sundry as 'Bunny', was the small, put-upon character in all the Aldwych farces in the 1920s, most written by Ben Travers, and went on to form a very funny partnership with Alfred Drayton in a number of Vernon Sylvaine farces. He, too, was in one of my films, *The Night We Got the Bird*, as well as one of my television productions and, like me, was known for losing his trousers pretty regularly on stage, and his 'Oh, calamity' was a by-word with the theatre-going public. Finally, Wally Patch. Wally and I were together, on and off, throughout the run of *Reluctant Heroes*, playing Sergeant Bell. It was a magnificent performance, but Wally had learned his voice production as a bookie on the racecourse, so it was not projected with an actor's expertise. The shouting Sgt 'Tinkerbell' was a great strain on his vocal cords – 'the "voce's" a bit on the ribs ternight, Guv,' he'd croak at me from time to time and, in the end, he could only manage six performances a week, with matinées off. But it was worth it. He was a lovely fella and, incidentally, 'voce' is not misspelt. That was Wally's posh, Italianate way of describing his voice.

So, those are but three of the actors, and actresses, who have reason to thank old Alfred Denville for his foresight in starting Denville Hall. In his spare time, he was also a Justice of the Peace and the author of several fairly unsuccessful plays. Not bad for someone who was born in a trunk. At least the lid was open.

THE ARTS THEATRE
of Cambridge

The theatre is billed as The Arts Theatre *of* Cambridge, so it is quite clear that is how the management wish it to be described. Perhaps that is because its founder was always referred to by his three names of John Maynard Keynes. It's odd that, isn't it? Some people are always given their full nomenclature: John Middleton Murry, for instance; or Mabel Lucy Attwell; or Nyree Dawn Porter, reputedly – and undeservedly – described by the late – and acerbic – Sir Noël Coward as 'the three worst actresses in England'. But there we are.

So, we arrived at The Arts Theatre of Cambridge on Monday 21st September, 1942 – or, rather, the company arrived but the majority of the scenery did not. Quite simply, there was too much of it for The Arts Theatre of Cambridge's small stage so it remained on demurrage at the railway station. Mind you, the non-arrival of scenery was nothing new to The Arts Theatre of Cambridge for, on another occasion the scenery left its previous theatre and failed to turn up at all. The management had gone bankrupt during the day and the set was duly impounded. At least that didn't happen to us. Wolfit always paid his way.

During our week in Cambridge, a rather odd thing did happen, though. One morning members of the company were told that a film was going to be shown to a number of Service Brass-hats. A screen was to be placed on the stage and assorted generals and admirals and air-marshals would be in the stalls. Members of the company were not permitted to watch this entertainment – if entertainment it was. However, one or two of us from the stage management managed to sneak up to the prompt corner, and catch a sideways glimpse of the film. It was most definitely not entertainment. The film was captured German propaganda material, showing the unscrupulous blitzkrieg in all its horror, conquering everything and everyone in its path. By now, of course, the mighty German army had suffered its first defeats, so it was a bit out of date, but it was pretty effective, all the same. You could see why the powers-that-be did not want us contaminated by such insidious material. Afterwards, I couldn't help wondering if the film had been captured at Dieppe, which we had raided only a few weeks before. But I should think the British and the Canadians, taking part in that assault, were far too busy to act as film distributors.

John Maynard Keynes built The Arts Theatre of Cambridge, but he must have been one of the last to undertake such an enterprise out of his own pocket – which is all the more laudable when you remember that he was then First Bursar of King's College, Cambridge, and almost certainly able to persuade others from the University to contribute. His interest in the arts – perhaps kindled by his marriage, in 1925, to the beguiling Russian ballerina, Lydia Lopokova – continued until his untimely death in 1946. When the theatre opened on 3rd February, 1936, Miss Lopokova's influence was evident, for it was the Sadler's Wells Ballet (later the Royal Ballet) which provided the first entertainment. Margot Fonteyn, Frederick Ashton, William Chappell and Robert Helpmann were all on stage for the gala opening – not bad for a small theatre, with just over 500 seats. Not exactly profitable, either, even in those halcyon days. Obviously, Lord Keynes, as he became, was more efficient as an economist with the nation's wealth than he was with his own. But you can see why the Cambridge Arts Theatre Trust, which owns The Arts Theatre of Cambridge, still puts Lord Keynes at the top of its letterhead. The trustees have every reason to be proud of him. Not to say, grateful. And that, I suppose, goes for us all.

NEW THEATRE
Hull

It seemed odd returning to the very theatre where – only a few short months before – I had auditioned for Donald Wolfit. Then I was an amateur actor stumbling through Hamlet's 'O, what a rogue and peasant slave am I', which I had learnt for my mother's amateur production of Philip King's first ever farce, *Without the Prince*. For Donald's delectation, I also declaimed Robert Service's poem 'Bessie's Boil', with which I had entertained the troops of the West Kent Regiment on the Sunday before my audition (again at my mother's behest), and the great man was so bemused (or so desperate to stop me), that I was offered my first professional contract forthwith. If you could call it professional, bearing in mind it was for the magnificent sum of £3 per week.

The difference between the amateur and the professional, though, is enormous, and I was only too aware of this as I approached the stage door of the New, clad in my newly acquired camel-hair coat (which took up all my savings and my clothes coupons, too), topped by a brown trilby hat, self-consciously turned down all the way round to make me look like an actor-laddie. My mother and father, who came to the first performance of *King Lear* on the Monday night, nearly died when they saw my camp regalia displayed at the end of the performance. Where was the 'normal' gangling youth who had left Hull, or – to be precise – Hornsea, such a short while ago? But they displayed a stiff upper lip, refused to comment and drove me back to my childhood home for the night. My father, being a shipowner, had a petrol ration of reasonable proportions and, provided he was returning home from work and only broke his journey, as opposed to diverting his journey, was able to stop off at such non-essential venues as the theatre. It was very convenient. Mind you, I had to be back at the theatre at ten o'clock the next morning to re-set for *A Midsummer Night's Dream* but, once again, my father's petrol ration came in handy and I swept up to the stage door with nauseating self-satisfaction. I was a smoker in those days, and my father used to send me a hundred 'Perfectos No. 2' every week as well, so you can see why my fellow artists looked upon me as being somewhat of a dilettante. Petrol and fags were never easy to come by in the war, and I seemed to acquire both with the minimum of trouble. But I still lived on that £3 a week, so I wasn't all bad.

Mind you, that £3 was about to be increased, to the incredible sum of £4 10s. During our stay in Hull, Wolfit enjoyed my parents' hospitality to lunch and this seemed to kindle in him a spark of human kindness towards one very junior member of his company – me. At the Thursday matinée of *A Midsummer Night's Dream* I achieved my first big laugh, and although Wolfit was pretty brusque about it afterwards, he realised it was an achievement, of sorts, and rewarded me accordingly.

Briefly, I had dropped my trousers, or rather my tights, on stage for the very first time in my professional career and the schoolgirls in front responded with a huge laugh. It was during the 'rude mechanicals' scene, and I had just recited: 'In this same interlude it doth befall, That I, one Snout by name, present a wall;' et cetera, et cetera, when my tights fell down, Pyramus and Thisbe corpsed, Bottom (in the shape of Wolfit) wondered what the hell was going on, and the audience were delighted. It was all a mistake, of course, for my tights were too big for me, my hands were occupied holding up the wall, and gravity played its natural part – but the business stayed in for the rest of the tour and, furthermore, stood me in good stead for many a year thereafter. Years later, when I was the subject of *This Is Your Life* for the first time, Wolfit said then he had always known that I would become a comic actor but, in truth, I think he was being wise after the event.

This is as good a time as any to pay tribute to Hull's fortitude during the war – a fortitude which is seldom mentioned, seldom recognised and generally forgotten. Over ninety-six per cent of Hull's housing suffered damage, of one sort or another, from bombing raids which took place on a regular basis, from the day the Nazis realised it was but a quick dash from northern Europe to north-east England. Yet there is hardly a mention of Hull's bravery in any history of the time and, during the war itself, complete anonymity reigned and Hull was never referred to by name – only as Humberside or the North-east. The people of Hull all felt belittled and bitter about this niggardly behaviour, even though we were assured it was for our own good. The Germans didn't take much notice, though. They still kept on bombing the place to hell . . .

The New Theatre was equipped to cope with these regular visits from our Aryan friends. The fiftieth anniversary programme notes:

Throughout the bleak wartime years, the show went on – with the bar reinforced as a bomb shelter, and the encouraging words in the programme, 'the theatre is a safer place than your own home!' At first, audiences were thin, but West End managements, suffering from the terrible effects of the Blitz, began to see the attractions of playing in slightly less hazardous venues. These ex-West End shows drew large audiences, even though, on the night of 7th/8th May, 1941, the scenic studios received a direct hit, demolishing the stage lantern, two auditorium doors, thc front row stalls, and all the props and costumes of the Sadler's Wells Opera Company!

At least by the time we arrived, sixteen months later, most of the damage had been patched up, but I am not so sure about the 'large audiences'. In fact, Peppino Santangelo, the managing director of the New, wrote this in his programme notes the week we were there:

ON SUPPORT

Theatrically, Hull is getting the time of its life. The public is obtaining the best possible entertainment available at any time. First class artists and companies appear on our Stage with clock-like regularity and yet, the same Hull Public, who ought to grasp this opportunity with both hands, is completely apathetic.

The Anglo-Polish ballet, constantly has played to £2,000 a week on Tour, but when it visits Hull its receipts drop to £400, and consequently, both they and we incur a substantial loss.

Do you think it is easy for me to secure first class companies at this rate? Do you think Noël Coward is encouraged to visit Hull? Why should he? Would you? Hull must make up its mind whether really it wants a first class theatre and wishes to remain a No. 1 date or sink into complacent mediocrity.

Dear old Peppino. Ever since I was a boy, he had been writing in a similar vein; cursing the very people who actually supported the theatre and completely missing those who stayed away in droves. But he never learned. He just went on, smouldering away, until he retired to Guernsey, where he became a senator. But the story – his story – of how the New Theatre came into being, is worth the telling . . .

The Hull Repertory Company was founded the year I was born, in 1924, and performed in a lecture hall that was eventually converted to the Little Theatre, and attracted a faithful following – my parents being among those with regular seats. Even so, the company was always short of funds and long on enthusiasm, presenting fortnightly productions, until Peppino Santangelo arrived. His flair and professionalism turned the venture around, audiences grew and Peppino waxed ambitious. He had plans approvcd to convert the adjoining Assembly Rooms into a theatre, which he felt his new audiences deserved, and the work went ahead, only to be halted, in 1939, by the outbreak of war. Pepe (as he was known) was not to be denied. He begged, borrowed and improvised (stole would have been too much, even for this ambitious man) and the theatre eventually opened to a packed house on 16th October, 1939, with Noël Gay's *Me and My Girl*, which had been forced out on the road by the closure of the London theatres.

Would that those packed houses had continued but, as you can see from the programme note on the week we were there, it was a struggle. Somehow, though, the New battled on, and the old Little Theatre next door was converted into the fire station, offering instant succour should any fire break out as a result of enemy action, arson or natural causes. But still the audiences stayed away, and in 1951 Peppino's company decided to sell. Because my father was my backer, and had been ever since I had become an actor-manager in 1947, and was still in business in Hull, Pepe went to see him and asked him if he was interested in purchasing the property. Knowing the average business enjoyed by the theatre, my father's reply was short and to the point, but he did remember to tell me. I agreed with my old man, but mentioned it to the owners of the Whitehall Theatre, where I was then ensconced, for they seemed to be interested in buying unlikely properties. To my surprise, they went ahead with the purchase and promptly regretted it for, although they retained Peppino Santangelo as the manager, things went from bad to worse. In an effort to counteract falling attendances, touring shows were only booked for half the year, and seasons of repertory filled in the rest of the time, but all to no avail, for business remained in the doldrums and, in 1958, Pepe retired to the Channel Isles.

It was then that the dreaded Bingo struck and the New looked to be lost for ever as a live theatre. In the nick of time, the U S Cavalry arrived, in the shape of the Hull City Council; their offer was accepted by the owners of the Whitehall, the Cooper family, and from then on the New has steadily increased its audiences and major refurbishments in 1968 and 1985 have made the theatre one of the most attractive on the touring circuit. But it was a close-run thing . . .

Slow curtain.

ROYAL LYCEUM THEATRE, EDINBURGH.

Proprietors and Managers,   - -   Messrs HOWARD & WYNDHAM.
Acting Manager and Secretary,   - - - - - -   Mr ARTHUR WESTON.

TO-NIGHT FRIDAY, 20th MARCH 1891.

Special Complimentary Benefit
TO
Mr J. B. HOWARD,
In commemoration of his completing TWENTY-FIVE YEARS both as Actor and Manager in the City of Edinburgh.

On this occasion will be performed the Play, Dramatised by CHARLES WEBB from Sir WALTER SCOTT's

LADY OF THE LAKE

RODERICK DHU ...	(Chief of the Clan "Vich Alpine")	MR J. B. HOWARD
KING JAMES V. OF SCOTLAND	{otherwise James Fitzjames, the} the Knight of Snowdoun	MR EDWARD O'NEIL
HERBERT } LUFFNESS } ...	Two Gentlemen of his Suite	{MR R. DE FONBLANQUE} ... MR J. ROYCE
JAMES BOTHWELL ...	(Earl of Douglas, an Outlawed Exile)	... MR F. DOUGLAS
MALCOLM GRÆME (a Young Chieftain, his Friend—Ward of the King)		MR W. SMITH
BRIAN ...	{The Weird Outcast Monk, supposed to be gifted} with supernatural power	MR H. MOXON
RED MURDOCH } MALISE }	Henchmen to Roderick Dhu	{MR DALTON ROBERTSON} ... MR J. DOBSON
NORMAN ...	... ... (a Young Bridegroom)	MR F. GAULD
ARCHIBALD } SANDIE }	Two Ghillies of Roderick's in attendance on Margaret	{ MR CAMPBELL MR CARLTON
YOUNG DUNCAN ...	... ... (of Duncraggan)	MR J. JONES
ALLAN BANE	{an Aged Minstrel, and faithful follower of the} House of Douglas	MR A. ALEXANDER
JOHN O'BRENT ...	(a Soldier of Fortune—with Song)	... MR T. WALKER
ROBIN HOOD	... ...	MR S. BARRINGTON
LITTLE JOHN	... ...	... MR T. BROWN
FRIAR TUCK	... ...	... MR WARDE
LADY MARGARET ...	(Mother of Roderick Dhu) ...	MISS BELLE CECIL
ELLEN DOUGLAS ...	(The Lady of the Lake)	MISS FLORENCE KINGSLEY
BLANCHE OF DEVON (a crazed and captive Lowland Maid)		MISS MAGGIE HUNT
THE WIDOW OF DUNCAN OF DUNCRAGGAN	... ...	MISS F. WRIGHT
MAID MARION	... ...	MISS M. KEITH
MATTIE ...	... ...	MISS GOODYEAR

Men-at-Arms, Highlanders, Peasants, Morris Dancers, Courtiers, &c., &c.
☞ **TERMINATING WITH THE THIRD ACT.**

To Conclude with the Screaming Irish Farce

HIS LAST LEGS

FELIX O'CALLAGHAN, ...	... MR J. B. HOWARD
RIVERS, ...	... MR A. ALEXANDER
CHARLES RIVERS, ...	... MR EDWARD O'NEIL
DR BANKS, ...	... MR H. MOXON
THOMAS, ...	MR GAULD
JOHN, ...	... MR J. DOBSON
MRS MONTAGUE, ...	... MRS HOWARD
JULIA, ...	MISS WINNIE MORGAN
BETTY, ...	... MISS B. CECIL
MRS BANKS, ...	MISS KEITH

A reproduction of the original silk programme produced for special
occasions such as this Complimentary Benefit for Mr J B Howard.
This proves that as an Irishman he *could* get away with playing a
Scotsman in Edinburgh.

INTERLUDE
'Loot'

HOWARD AND WYNDHAM
STOLL AND MOSS

Donald Wolfit now embarked on the Number One dates of his tour – six weeks at Howard and Wyndham theatres, one Moss' Empire (they always put in the apostrophe in those days), and one final stumer at the Grand Theatre and Opera House, Croydon – definitely *not* a Number One, for no one seemed to wish to take responsibility for this theatre, and there is no record of any owner on my programme. Not that it matters much, for the theatre has long disappeared and a much grander edifice in the shape of Fairfield Halls, including the Ashcroft Theatre, now graces the town and entertains the locals, and many others who come from further afield.

This interlude, then, would seem to be the place to tell the history of Howard and Wyndham Ltd (followed by Moss' Empires Ltd and Stoll Theatres Corporation Ltd), or the convoluted, and sometimes nepotistic, story of their influence on touring would be far from complete.

Their story begins in the last century when two actors – one from Ireland, J. B. Howard, and one from Scotland, F. W. P. Wyndham – came together to run the newly built Lyceum in Edinburgh, another theatre designed by C. J. Phipps and built for the incredible price of £17,000. The opening night was on 10th September, 1883 and the town was agog, for no less a personage than Henry Irving (still twelve years from his knighthood) was engaged to grace the boards with his London Lyceum Company, including the great Ellen Terry. This was not just for the first night, either, for Irving was appearing for all of two weeks, with a repertoire which included *Much Ado About Nothing*, *The Merchant of Venice*, *Hamlet* and *The Bells*. The excitement and clamour to buy seats was overwhelming, as was the hospitality and adulation accorded the two leading artists, Mr Irving and Miss Terry.

What a splendid consummation of the fledgling partnership between the two actors-turned-impresarios Howard and Wyndham, and it is not surprising that their years together created such a powerful team, that dominated the legitimate touring circuit for nearly a century. Moss

Empires and Stoll Theatres ruled the music-hall roost, but they, too, had much influence over the 'straight' theatre, and this must also be recorded.

The link between the two men, Howard and Wyndham, had been forged by Wyndham's father, R. H. Wyndham, who was a popular and successful actor-manager north of the border. He had run his own stock theatre, the Adelphi in Edinburgh, ever since he had left that city's Theatre Royal after it had been destroyed by two disastrous fires. (In keeping with the times, it was burnt down on two further occasions, before its demise at the end of the last war.) Anyway, old Wyndham decided that enough was enough, and handed over the reins to a younger member of the company, J. B. Howard, an Irishman with a good reputation and a penchant for playing Scots parts with an Irish accent. Such was his charm and ability, however, that the nationalistic Scottish audience didn't seem to mind, even when he played Rob Roy. Being a more typical Scot than some, though, Mr Wyndham, Sr wasn't totally philanthropic and he ensured that his young son, F. W. P. Wyndham, became a partner (albeit a junior one) in the enterprise. And thus the great theatrical company was formed and it soon prospered with the Lyceum Theatre as its flagship.

The Golden Jubilee Programme commemorating the founding of the Howard and Wyndham touring circuit – 1895 to 1945 – records the following:

1895 The Company was formed and incorporated on the 5th March to take over the interests of Mr J. B. Howard and Mr F. W. Wyndham, two of the most prominent acting Managers of that date. The Theatres taken over were:
> Royal Lyceum Theatre, Edinburgh.
> Theatre Royal, Edinburgh.
> Theatre Royal, Glasgow.
> Royalty Theatre, Glasgow (leased).

It was noted that Messrs Howard and Wyndham were Joint Managing Directors. But then comes a sombre postscript: 'Mr J. B. Howard, Joint Managing Director, died 10th May, 1895.' So the popular Irishman did not live long enough to see just how successful the company would become.

The Programme goes on:

1896 On 1st October 1896 the Tyne Theatre, Newcastle-on-Tyne, was leased for twenty-one years.
1900 The property adjoining the Theatre Royal at Cowcaddens Street, Glasgow, was acquired.

1901 The property adjoining the Theatre Royal at St James's Place, Edinburgh, was acquired.

1903 The property at West Port, Edinburgh, was acquired for Scenery and Property Stores.

1904 The King's Theatre, Glasgow, built during 1903/4, was opened on 12th September.

1906 The King's Theatre, Edinburgh, built during 1905/6 by the firm of W. S. Cruikshank & Son, of which firm the present Chairman and Managing Director was a partner, was opened in December 1906, and subsequently acquired by Howard and Wyndham Ltd.

Ah, but there is a little tale here, worth the telling. Cruikshank was an Edinburgh builder who had just completed the King's Theatre for a company that had gone bankrupt. He managed to get paid by doing a deal with Howard and Wyndham, whereby they acquired the theatre and in return the builder's son, A. Stewart Cruikshank, joined the board of their company. Stewart was very young at the time and had no previous experience of theatrical management, having been apprenticed to his father as a joiner. However, he worked hard at learning the business, and became managing director of the group when Fred W. Wyndham retired from that post in September 1928 and then chairman in February 1945. By then, Howard and Wyndham had become a massive conglomerate and yet another Cruikshank had joined the board, Stewart Cruikshank, Jnr. His father, who had lived up to his early trade and become a master joiner of theatre companies, was killed in a car accident in 1949, whereupon his son was promoted to managing director and a certain Prince Littler became the chairman. It was a very tight little group indeed, for Mr Littler was also Chairman and Managing Director of Stoll Theatres Corporation Ltd, Associated Theatre Properties (London) Ltd, Theatre Royal, Drury Lane Ltd, and chairman, only, of Moss' Empires Ltd. I will attempt to explain in words of one syllable, but it will not be easy and we have to go back to 1912 and Fred Wyndham himself . . .

In 1912 the company took over Robert Arthur Theatres Ltd, with theatres in Aberdeen, Dundee, Newcastle-upon-Tyne, Nottingham and two in Liverpool, the Shakespeare and the Royal Court. This meant Howard and Wyndham now controlled ten theatres, including five in England, and had doubled the company in less than twenty years. Not bad, for two jobbing actors whose early ambition had been to run the Lyceum in Edinburgh. But more was to come.

In 1931 the Opera House, Manchester was acquired; in 1932 a theatre employee with Moss' Empires Ltd, a Mr H. M. Tennent, resigned from that company and became the booking manager for Howard and Wyndham. One year later he took up the position as the manager of a new combination, Moss' Empires and Howard and Wyndham Tours Ltd.

Hugh ('Binkie') Beaumont joined him as joint manager, and so an association was formed that was to present 'important' plays in the West End and the provinces. In three short years this became the incredibly successful producing management, H. M. Tennent Ltd, with 'Binkie' at its head, for Harry Tennent was not long for this world, although the company he formed retains his name to this day. Of course, the ubiquitous Howard and Wyndham had a share interest in this company, too, as they had in the companies of many other well-known producing managers – Charles B. Cochran Ltd, Henry Sherek Ltd, Linnit and Dunfee Ltd, Daniel Mayer Co. Ltd and Bertie A. Meyer. The chase was on.

In 1942, 'furthering the expansion of the Company's interest, Mr A. Stewart Cruikshank and Mr Stewart Cruikshank, Junr joined the Board of the "Prince Littler Consolidated Trust Co. Ltd", that company acquiring control of the Stoll Group of Theatres.' So saith the Jubilee programme, with an air of pride. Father and son joined a further ten boards between them, and a year later saw them on the board of Associated Properties (London) Ltd, controlling the following West End Theatres: His Majesty's, Apollo, Phoenix, Adelphi, St James's, Aldwych, Lyric and Cambridge. A far cry from Edinburgh, when the progenitor of this family line, a master joiner and builder, only came into the business to raise the wind after some indigent client had gone bust.

The story is by no means finished, although I will not weary you with all its twists and turns, for I still have the Stoll Moss tale to tell. However, I must mention two other families who became involved in the Howard and Wyndham empire. First, the Beaumonts, through bricks and mortar, as well as marriage. John Beaumont controlled the Grand, Leeds and the Lyceum, Sheffield, booked his tours through Howard and Wyndham and had the good sense to marry A. Stewart Cruikshank's daughter, Dorothy – who was, of course, Stewart Jnr's sister. John Beaumont became a member of the board, as did his stepson, Elyot, who was still there, trying to book attractions for the theatres, when they finally ceased to exist as part of the Howard and Wyndham circuit. Second, the Donald family, who controlled most of the cinemas in Aberdeen, also acquired His Majesty's Theatre, in that granite city, and used the Howard and Wyndham booking facilities, through Harry Tennent and 'Binkie' Beaumont, to arrange their visiting touring companies. They also instituted a pleasant ritual for the actors. On Monday nights there was a posy of flowers for each of the ladies and a drink of your choice for everyone after the show. Twenty years later, a younger Donald, Peter, joined the board of Howard and Wyndham and he was at the helm when, almost twenty years after that, the company went public and was quoted on the stock exchange. He was still there, shortly afterwards, when things went horribly wrong and the public company had to dispose of all its theatrical assets. The majority were acquired by local authorities. Somewhat different from the great days

HOWARD & WYNDHAM
LIMITED

Chairman: **PRINCE LITTLER**
Managing Director: STEWART CRUIKSHANK

HOWARD AND WYNDHAM THEATRES

EDINBURGH	KING'S
EDINBURGH	LYCEUM
GLASGOW	KING'S
GLASGOW	ROYAL
MANCHESTER	OPERA HOUSE
NEWCASTLE	ROYAL
LIVERPOOL	ROYAL COURT

BOOKED IN CONJUNCTION

ABERDEEN	HIS MAJESTY'S
BLACKPOOL	GRAND and
	OPERA HOUSE
BOURNEMOUTH	PAVILION
*BRISTOL	HIPPODROME
CARDIFF	PRINCE OF WALES
*COVENTRY	HIPPODROME
*DERBY	HIPPODROME
LEEDS	GRAND
LEICESTER	OPERA HOUSE
*NORTHAMPTON	NEW
SHEFFIELD	LYCEUM

* ONCE NIGHTLY ONLY

HEAD OFFICE
9 GRAFTON STREET, LONDON, W.1

General Manager
P. J. P. DONALD

Business Manager
J. H. O'HARE, C.A.

Booking Manager
E. F. WOODS

Publicity Manager
G. A. SCOTT

Telephone: REGENT 2341-2
                     2508-9

Telegrams:
"Wyndhoward, Piccy
LONDON "

All Correspondence to the Managing Director

King's Theatre, Edinburgh

Lyceum Theatre, Edinburgh

King's Theatre, Glasgow

Theatre Royal, Glasgow

Opera Hovse, Manchester

Theatre Royal, Newcastle

Royal Court, Liverpool

when actor-managers like Donald Wolfit (and me) had to go cap in hand to obtain a booking and the Howard and Wyndham list of theatres surveyed the view from such commanding heights, as seen on the previous page.

Sir Oswald Stoll

Sir Edward Moss

SIR EDWARD MOSS (1854–1912)
SIR OSWALD STOLL (1866–1942)

Perhaps not always 'verray parfit gentle knights' (oops! sorry! Chaucer again), but at least Sir Edward and Sir Oswald were true to that great Victorian tradition – they were Empire Builders. However, their efforts brought more happiness to the masses than many an illustrious contemporary, subduing the natives in over a quarter of the globe, for *their* Empire was but a building (or a series of buildings) in the cities of Great Britain, and they never had to use force or coercion or fear to place their subjects in thrall. Quite simply, they performed this small miracle – and great service – by providing large quantities of music, laughter and entertainment. Like those other two impresarios, Howard and Wyndham, one (Sir Oswald) was conceived in Ireland, but born in Australia, and the other (Sir Edward), although born in Manchester, was brought up in Scotland, but there the tenuous similarity ends. Howard and Wyndham came together at the beginning of their managerial careers and concentrated on the 'legit' side of the theatre, while Sir Edward and Sir Oswald were already well down the path of success when they decided to pool their resources for the benefit of the popular music hall.

Both Stoll and Moss were brought up in the world of entertainment and, although the present-day billing lists Stoll first, it was not always so. Quite naturally, for Moss was the older by some twelve years. Born in Manchester, he was educated in Glasgow and then moved to Edinburgh, where his father made a small fortune by designing, building and exhibiting a panorama of the battles in the Franco–Prussian War of 1870. Why the good burghers of Edinburgh should be interested in such a faraway event defies reason, but interested they were and Mr Moss Sr prospered greatly. With these profits, father and son (Edward was involved as a stage manager) took over the Queen's Room at Greenock, which they turned into a music hall, and then went back to Edinburgh, where they opened the Gaiety in 1877 as a music hall. It was then that the one-syllable name, Moss, came into its own. The Gaiety was known as 'Moss's', and in my time only was the final 's' dropped.

Next, the Mosses took over an old wooden theatre at Leith and artists were expected to double at both their dates, Edinburgh and Leith, which meant many an out-of-breath singer or comic wheezing away at their first entrance – but such duplication was very common in those days. It was the only way the majority of the music-hall acts could make a living. The Theatre Royal, Sunderland was the next on the list of Moss theatres, followed by the reconstructed Gaiety at Newcastle-upon-Tyne.

Edward Moss had actually joined forces with another music-hall proprietor, Richard Thornton – who had once worked as a pit lad at St Hilda's Colliery and then gone on to run a penny gaff in his native South Shields – to start the Sunderland theatre and the two men went into partnership. They expanded rapidly, with a string of Empires springing up all over north of Watford. The first, in 1890, was the Empire in Newcastle, followed by those in Edinburgh, Birmingham, Sheffield, Liverpool, Hull and Leeds.

It was then a potential rival entered the scene – Oswald Stoll. Still only thirty-three years old, Stoll had achieved a great deal along the same lines as the forty-four-year-old Moss. He, too, came from a showbusiness background, for his mother had been a dancer with the Three Hardcastle Sisters in Dublin during the 1860s. She had married 'above her station', to a scion of the Grays of Enniskillen. The proverbial disinheritance took place for the young Roderick Gray but, none the less, he still found the will to sire two children, before emigrating to Australia, where Oswald joined the family as a newly born Antipodean. Alas, Roderick, now the father of three, soon returned to his maker, and Widow Gray, *née* Hardcastle, merely returned to Liverpool. There she met George Stoll, who did not seem to mind the idea of a ready-made family, for they married and Oswald took his stepfather's name. But now, instead of being an immigrant son of a highly respected Irish family, Oswald was subjected to the vagaries of a stepfather who ran a waxworks show, which became an animal entertainment and then the Parthenon Music Hall. No wonder the impressionable young lad was overwhelmed, especially when his stepfather, too, died and he virtually became his mother's partner in the running of the music hall. In fact, from then on until she joined her two late husbands, Mrs Stoll was always present in the box office on the first night whenever her son opened up a new theatre – but in her earlier years she was much more than a lucky charm.

Such artists as Vesta Tilley and George Robey appeared at the Parthenon, while it was rumoured that the great Dan Leno actually trod the green for a mere £5 for the week. Mrs Stoll must have had a great deal of Irish blarney to get away with that. But she did – and the business flourished. Oswald, being an ambitious young man, felt the need to expand beyond the boundaries of Liverpool and found that Wales was a fertile market. At the age of twenty-three, he and his mother bought

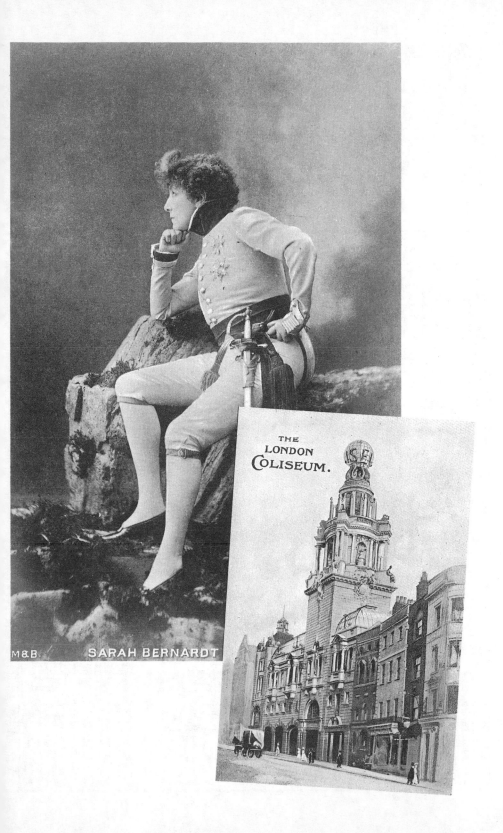

M&B. SARAH BERNARDT

THE
LONDON
COLISEUM.

MOSS' Empire
THEATRE NEWCASTLE

Proprietors: MOSS' EMPIRES, Ltd.
Chairman: PRINCE LITTLER   Managing Director: VAL PARNELL   Telephone: 24444 (3 Lines)
Manager: STANLEY C. MAY

WEEK OF **APRIL 12th** **6.15** TWICE NIGHTLY **8.30** USUAL EVENING PERFS. ON GOOD FRIDAY

1954

WAKEY! WAKEY!

THE GREAT RADIO BAND SHOW   VARIETY'S OUTSTANDING PERSONALITY

BILLY COTTON

AND HIS BAND

WITH
ALAN BREEZE
DOREEN STEPHENS
CLEM BERNARD

THE NEW STYLE FUNSTER

LESLIE RANDALL

A FOOL AMONG FRIENDS

KAZAN & KATZ
ON THE TRAMPOLINE

GEORGE MEATON
THE BIG NOISE

MORGAN & GRAY
DANCE TEAM

NENETTE MONGADORS & ANNE
HIGH SPEED JUGGLERS

NIXON & DIXON
COMEDY TEAM

AERIAL THRILLS

THE MONTONS

Levene's Hall in Cardiff and turned it into Stoll's first Empire. After a fairly barren period, the next Empire was opened in Swansea, followed by those in Newport, Leicester and Nottingham. The young Mr Stoll was on his way – not forgetting Mum sitting in the box office on each opening night.

Now the two youngish impresarios, Mr Moss and Mr Stoll, could well have locked antlers, for clearly their expansion and ambition had placed them on a collision course. But they had more sense than that, and settled on a friendly partnership. Together with Richard Thornton, they formed Moss' Empires Ltd and the company came into being in December 1899.

Soon Richard Thornton left the group to manage his own northern circuit, although this was run in conjunction with Moss', and his erstwhile partners decided upon conquering the capital, London. Although they could not originate an Empire in the capital, for the Empire in Leicester Square was already *in situ*, and had been for fifty years, they moved just up the road to Cranbourn Street and built the London Hippodrome. One year later, in 1901, Edward Moss was knighted. (His partner had to wait another eighteen years.) As a matter of interest, the Stoll Moss offices have, until recent times, been by the side of the Hippodrome, in Cranbourn Mansions and, to give you an idea of comparative prices, Howard and Wyndham built the Lyceum in Edinburgh, some seventeen years earlier, for £17,000; the Hippodrome in London cost £250,000. Mind you, it was one of architect Frank Matcham's biggest and best theatres, which he only went on to supersede with his design for the London Coliseum.

The Coliseum was also the biggest and best for its owner, Oswald Stoll. He resigned as the managing director of Moss' Empires Ltd (the chairman, Sir Edward, immediately took over in both capacities), struck out independently and built the theatre which was considered to be by far and away the best-equipped and most luxurious music hall in the country. This opened in December 1904 and, eight years later, the same team of owner Oswald Stoll, and architect Frank Matcham, created another wondrous theatre in the provinces – the Bristol Hippodrome – which stood comparison with its London counterpart. Furthermore, Oswald Stoll booked other than music-hall acts for this new venue and before the First World War the great Sarah Bernhardt graced its stage, following a season at that other prestigious Stoll venue, the Coliseum, London.

The two great conglomerates, Stoll and Moss, remained separate for many years, finally coming together again through the omniscient and omnipresent personality of Prince Littler. I have already listed his tentacle-like presence in the Howard and Wyndham world. He was no less of an octopus in that which had been the creation of Stoll and Moss.

This book is not intended to encompass the vast panorama of music-hall touring, nor to dwell on the many managerial ramifications in the West End of London, but it would be quite impossible to ignore one particular company which still bears the names of Sir Oswald and Sir Edward. I am referring, of course, to Stoll Moss Theatres Ltd, now controlling no fewer than twelve West End theatres, including four on Shaftesbury Avenue, as well as the London Palladium and the Theatre Royal, Drury Lane. The chairman, until his death, was Australian M. R. H. Holmes à Court – whose widow has now taken his place – the managing director being Roger Filer; there was a time when those positions were held by Sir Edward Moss and Sir Oswald Stoll. I wonder what they would make of it all now? Probably regret the passing of those great music-hall days and the disposal of their empires. But at least some of the great theatres still continue, either in private companies – the Apollo Leisure Group being the biggest – or in the public domain of local authorities, whilst the London Coliseum is to be acquired by the English National Opera. But never again will any of these own and control so many of our provincial houses as the once all-powerful Howard, Wyndham, Stoll and Moss. The Monopolies Commission might have something to say if they did.

Act III beginners, please.

ACT III

'The Better 'Ole'

OPERA HOUSE
Manchester
PALACE THEATRE
Manchester

On the day Stalin telegraphed to the defenders of Stalingrad, that it 'must not be taken by the enemy', Donald Wolfit's Company arrived at the Opera House, Manchester to take the city by storm with his increasingly confident *King Lear*. The Opera House itself had been captured by Howard and Wyndham some eleven years earlier, and was now considered to be of prime importance in their operational plans. Not that we were allowed to forget it either. 'What Manchester thinks today, London applauds tomorrow,' we were told with monotonous, and incorrect, regularity.

As it turned out, our Lancashire Old Moores were wrong. Donald's first attempt at the role in London was only politely received when it went to the now demolished St James's Theatre in London, some four months later – and the principal London critic, James Agate, was distinctly sniffy. I remember buying *The Sunday Times*, with the absurd idea that I would be noticed, and I was somewhat taken aback at the criticism I read, for I had expected raves for the great man. He did achieve those raves, of course, on his second attempt at the role in London, at the Scala Theatre in April 1943. Agate then wrote: 'I say deliberately that his performance on Wednesday was the greatest piece of Shakespearean acting I have seen since I have been privileged to write for *The Sunday Times*.' So Manchester was right, after all. Just a little bit out with their timing.

I had never before seen, or appeared in, such a vast theatre as the Opera House, with its 2,070 seats; it was quite overwhelming. Over the years, I was to appear there a number of times but it gradually lost its audience and, at one time, any touring play had to appear at the Rex Cinema in Wilmslow, if any business was to be forthcoming. The middle-class, well-to-do locals only had to walk out of their front doors to the cinema, whereas the twenty-minute journey to the huge echoing cavern, which was the Opera House when less than half-full, seemed to present an insurmountable obstacle. But in Wolfit's day, and with the public's insatiable

PROGRAMME

THE OPERA HOUSE
MANCHESTER

THE PALACE THEATRE, MANCHESTER.

desire for the theatre in wartime, all the seats were comfortably filled for our week of repertoire, even though Donald did achieve an unexpected laugh in the middle of *Hamlet*. By now, of course, he was a bit too old and certainly too overweight for the part. He had to strap on an all-enveloping pink corset, in an effort to control his increasing middle-aged spread. His make-up, too, was interesting. A base of Leichner No. 5, which transmitted a translucent jaundiced glow to his features, with Leichner No. 7 being used as a brown shading to paint in interesting hollows in otherwise healthy, ruddy-hued, somewhat-bucolic cheeks. At this particular performance, Wolfit had managed to buy a brand-new pair of black silk tights for his moody Dane and, desperate for a pee, tore at the front seam to make the necessary aperture, for he had no time for the more conventional method of lifting his doublet and lowering his hose. He returned to the stage and, as he reached the apposite soliloquy, 'O, that this too too sullied flesh would melt,' a veritable spider's web of white ladders appeared on his black tights, all aimed unerringly at his crotch. It would have been a perfect laugh for his Malvolio in *Twelfth Night*, but it seemed a teeny-weeny bit out of place for Hamlet. What worried Wolfit most, though, was the ruination of the irreplaceable silk tights. After all, there was a war on.

Strangely enough, I have never played the Palace at Manchester, which was the Opera House's great rival for many years, probably because the Palace concentrated more on musicals and music hall and my productions did not fall into this category. But it would be quite impossible to miss out a brief history of these two great theatres in a book such as this, for they have offered the Manchester theatre-going public, and the world of touring, so much over the years. The Palace was first on the scene, when the curtain went up on Whit Monday, 1891, on the ballet, *Cleopatra*. The managing director was the famous George Edwardes, and he chose to open with this 'cultural' attraction as a defence against the local non-conformist church's view that the Palace would be 'a happy hunting ground for immorality and an occasion for falling'. This body of 'Wesleyan' opinion also ensured that the magistrates refused to grant a licence to the theatre, so the opening night was 'dry'. However, Mr Edwardes had no less than 3,675 people to entertain at the Palace in those days (now it is a more manageable 2,000), so he included such music-hall stars as Marie Lloyd and Ben Nathan on the bill, and the place was packed. 'Gaiety George' continued this successful policy for some years, and many a famous artist appeared at the Palace in Oxford Street (Manchester, not London) including Dan Leno, Little Titch, Vesta Tilley and those three knights of the music hall: Harry Lauder, George Robey and Charles Chaplin.

The Palace's opponent, the Opera House, opened on Boxing Day, 1912, as the New Theatre. The production was *Kismet*, followed by *Ben Hur*, complete with chariot race. All manner of other productions took place there in those early years, including cinema, circuses and 'Tango Teas', but the New was struggling and the original company was wound up in 1914 and the theatre closed. It reopened as the New Queens a year later, and the tide began to turn with the success of the Beecham Opera Company. So successful was opera, in fact, that in 1920 the name of the theatre was again changed, to the Opera House, in tribute to Sir Thomas Beecham, and the name of his company was changed, also, to the British National Opera Company. In 1931, the Opera House became the flagship of Howard and Wyndham and many successful productions began life in Manchester, on their way to London. In fact, producers only needed a sell-out production at the Opera House, together with an equal success at two or three others of the H&W chain, for their costs to be completely recouped before they ever saw the lights of the West End. In the week following Wolfit, Ronald Squire and Isabel Jeans were there, in Somerset Maugham's *Home and Beauty*, and the two weeks after that saw Noël Coward in his *Play Parade* – with performances of *This Happy Breed*, *Present Laughter* and *Blithe Spirit*. Sybil Thorndike and Emlyn Williams were there in *The Corn is Green*, as were Leslie Banks and Constance Cummings in *Goodbye Mr Chips*. Once the war was over, under the benevolent eye of 'Tommy' Appleby (who was the spitting image of Tommy Trinder), the Opera House continued to flourish, with great names such as Edith Evans, John Gielgud, Peter Ustinov, Vivien Leigh, A. E. Matthews, Ralph Richardson, Margaret Leighton and Alec Guinness appearing on stage and ensuring that the 'House Full' boards were nearly always out.

Meanwhile, during the war all the favourite radio stars were appearing at the Palace. They included: Arthur Askey, Henry Hall, Joe Loss, Jimmy James, Ted Ray, Jack Warner, Tommy Trinder, Vic Oliver, Tessie O'Shea, Max Wall, Jimmy Jewell and Ben Warriss and Max Miller. Remember, there was as much glamour and excitement attached to their names as to many of our latterday television or film 'personalities' and the place flourished. Furthermore, Ivor Novello used to occupy the theatre for long stretches at a time, particularly with his musical *The Dancing Years*, which played for nearly six months in all, spread over a total of eight years, and from America came Laurel and Hardy and Danny Kaye. You can see why Moss Empires wished to become involved, and in 1959 the Palace was sold to them for just under a quarter of a million.

Then came the crisis for the two great houses. Attractive productions and crowd-pulling artists became harder and harder to find. It was clear that some action was imperative, and in 1977 both theatre managements declared they would have to close within six months unless a saviour could be found. In the case of the Palace, this was to be in the shape of a construction company, Norwest Holst, who provided the funds for the directors of the Palace Theatre Trust to purchase the building and start off the reconstruction fund. To this were added sizeable grants from the

Arts Council of Great Britain, the Manchester City Council and the Greater Manchester Council and, under the expert guidance of the newly appointed managing director of Manchester Theatres Ltd, Robert Scott, and the benevolent eye of the chairman of Norwest Holst and the Theatre Trust, Raymond Slater, the Palace was able to reopen, completely refurbished to the highest possible standards, on Sunday 22nd March, 1981 at a Royal Gala Performance, in the presence of the Prince of Wales and it has never looked back since.

For the Opera House, however, the road to recovery was considerably rockier. No immediate saviour was to be found and the place became a bingo hall. Probably the plushest one in the business, mark you, but still a bingo hall. *O tempora, O mores!* There had been a strong belief that the Opera House, being the 'legitimate' theatre, would be the one chosen to continue, but after careful investigation it was decided that the Palace was intrinsically the better bet for the future, and so the poor old Opera House became a somewhat blowzy old lady. But the story has a happy ending. Such was (and is) the success of the Palace, that it became clear there was a need for another 2,000-seat theatre in Manchester and so the same team who took over the Palace went to work on the Opera House. On Saturday 29th September, 1984, the newly appointed and decorated old lady of Quay Street opened her doors again to the theatre-going public with Harold Fielding's production of *Barnum* with Michael Crawford. Princess Anne was there on this occasion to see the Opera House well and truly relaunched and, like its sister theatre in Oxford Street it has never looked back. Maybe there is something in 'what Manchester thinks today' etc. after all . . .

Just to prove me completely and absolutely wrong, and to illustrate – yet again – what a fickle jade is the theatre, I wrote the above in July 1990. Less than six months later, on 20th December, the following story appeared in the *Stage*:

Manchester Theatres Ltd, the company which owns the city's Palace and Opera House venues, has been sold to the Apollo Leisure chain at a cost of almost £3.9 million . . . one consolation for the former owners is that Apollo has agreed to take responsibility for dealing with the £2.1 million debts run up by Manchester Theatres Ltd.

Vista Entertainments, the firm which took over control of Manchester Theatres last year, said this week it had decided to sell the two sites following six months of poor trading . . . Apollo already owns Manchester's largest site, the Manchester Apollo (the former Ardwick Hippodrome), and it now holds all but one of the theatres with a capacity of more than 2,000 seats.

It's a rum business – show business – isn't it? Happily I can report that under Apollo's management the theatres are again flourishing, Manchester has become the winner of the Arts Council Arts 2000 Drama Award, whilst Bob Scott – the original managing director of Manchester Theatres – is once more leading Manchester's attempt to house the Olympics.

Let's turn to the odd man out – a 2,000-seater *not* owned by Apollo in the Manchester area – Tameside.

SIR THOMAS BEECHAM.

TAMESIDE THEATRE
Ashton-under-Lyne

Ashton-under-Lyne is, of course, in the Manchester area, so I am going to take a leap in time and rush forward some thirty-four years, to 1976. Tameside was one of the last touring theatres I played in before my final stint at the Whitehall with *Fringe Benefits*. But then, I could never have been there with Wolfit for, from 1934 until it was leased by the Tameside Metropolitan Borough Council in 1975 from E M I to be turned back into a theatre, and then purchased in the early 80s to continue as such, it had been used as a cinema. It had started life as a theatre, though, in 1904, as part of the Broadhead Variety Circuit – with all the great names playing there at one time or another, including two who were eventually only seen in Ashton-under-Lyne on celluloid – Charlie Chaplin and Stan Laurel. There had been legitimate touring theatre in the area for many years. In the eighteenth century John Neville ran a company which toured 'second class' towns in Cheshire and Lancashire, including Preston, Ashton-under-Lyne, Oldham, Warrington and Bolton. My apologies to the good citizens of those stalwart places for the description is but a quote and in no way attributable to me. Anyway, it was on one of those tours that Mr Neville gave a Macbeth without a Macduff and even at his most stretched my boss, Donald Wolfit, never did that. There was a lot of doubling, of course, but at least someone always managed to get on in the appropriate costume, speaking mostly Shakespeare's lines. Mr Neville was also given to flights of fancy. One of his venues was but a room in a town hall. It was described as 'The Stalybridge Temple of the Muses'. Ken Tynan could have used that one too, in his catalogue of ancient venues.

Tameside Theatre never claimed such a high-falutin title for itself, even though – like its cousins in the heart of Manchester – it has a very large auditorium, with a capacity in excess of 1,800 seats. Obviously, small is not beautiful to our Mancunian friends, but let's hope the North-west can continue to support three such big theatres. Four, if you count the Manchester Apollo. If a job's worth doing, it's worth doing proper, that's what I always say. What do you always say?

Answers on a Donald McGill postcard, please.

ROYAL COURT THEATRE
Liverpool

The journey from Manchester to Liverpool was comparatively short, even in those wartime days. Unhappily, as it has turned out, the life of the Royal Court was also to be comparatively short – especially when put alongside its neighbours in the North-west, whose theatrical renaissance – albeit faltering from time to time – must seem like a dream to the theatre-goers of Liverpool.

But it wasn't always like that. 'The latest theatre built in this country', was the proud boast when the Royal Court opened its doors on 13th October, 1937 and, indeed, it *was* the latest, with its huge revolving stage, its palatial Number One dressing-room, its lift taking all *hoi polloi* such as me to the upper floors, its massive bars and entertainment facilities in the front-of-house. So you could see why the city was proud of it. But that pride did not last long and by Saturday 12th April, 1969 it closed its art deco doors for the first time.

Why am I so certain of the date? Well, I was appearing there on that day in the post-London tour of *Let Sleeping Wives Lie* and there was a great deal of hoo-hah going on, as you can imagine. When it came to the final performance on that Saturday night, I made an impassioned speech for the theatre's reopening and promised that, if it ever did, I would make every effort to present that first production. I missed out by one week only, but I was there again in October, on my way back to the Garrick Theatre with *She's Done It Again* and, once again, the place was packed. It beats me where all that enthusiasm went. The reopening was a splendid achievement on the part of the local council, led by Sir Harry Livermore, which had raised the necessary funds to take over the theatre from Howard and Wyndham, but it didn't last and when I next visited the town some six years later, it was clearly not long for this world – as a Number One touring venue, that is. Now it has been acquired by the same management which runs the famous 'Cavern' in Liverpool, but instead of the words of Shakespeare flying up, or the trousers of Brian Rix falling down, the air is rent with the din of a pop venue. But I suppose pop artists have brought more fame and fortune to Liverpool than the Royal Court ever did. Ah, me! I wonder what will happen when the lease runs out in the Year of Our Lord 2035? One thing is certain, though: I won't be around to worry about it.

Fortunately, theatre is far from dead in Liverpool. There are, of course, the two repertory theatres, the Everyman and the Playhouse, which still provide a wide variety of dramatic offerings (the local authority having been locked in a long-standing battle with the Arts Council over their share of funding), while the Empire is the venue for larger-scale productions.

The Empire began life as the New Prince of Wales in 1866, but became the Empire when it was acquired by Edward Moss in 1897 and rebuilt to the designs of the ubiquitous Frank Matcham. You will notice that the man from Liverpool, Oswald Stoll, did *not* originate an Empire in the city where his music-hall activities began, but he got in on the act when his amalgamation with Moss took place. The theatre was rebuilt again in 1923 and enlarged to seat 2,300 people. More recently, a three-million-pound modernisation scheme was completed and its new owners, the Apollo Leisure Group, boast it is 'a showpiece venue which provides comfort and a unique theatre atmosphere for both patrons and performers'. Maybe I shouldn't worry about that Royal Court lease, after all . . .

Royal Court Theater, LIVERPOOL

GRAND THEATRE
AND OPERA HOUSE
Leeds

Whenever I go to Leeds, I seem to be mistaken for someone else. Not every time, of course, but I'm sure you will forgive the hyperbole. The first time was when I was appearing with Donald Wolfit in October 1942. An old schoolfriend, David Stross, lived in Leeds and one afternoon when we had no matinée, I went up to see him at his parents' house and, stupidly, did not check to see if anyone was going to be at home. Nobody was, so I asked a passing neighbour if she knew anything about the family's movements. That is a pretty silly thing to do, at the best of times, but even more foolish in wartime. Before you could say 'Adolf Hitler', a police car arrived and two very large plain-clothes policemen got out. With the minimum of ceremony, I was bundled into the car and questioned as to my knowledge of Germany and as to where I had hidden my jemmy and all the other necessary house-breaking implements. It took a great deal of red-faced talking on my part to persuade them that I was but a humble member of Mr Wolfit's company, and that I had been looking up an old chum. Even then, they didn't believe me implicitly, until they drove me to the front-of-house of the Grand, compared my likeness with the Angus McBean 10″ × 8″ which was displayed in some out-of-the-way corner of the building and had a word with the company manager, Alexander Brownlow. I had started off by trying to contact an Old Scholar from Bootham (where we were educated) and ended up feeling like a very naughty schoolboy indeed. It was most unpleasant.

The second time I was not recognised was more recently, when I was secretary-general of MENCAP (the Royal Society for Mentally Handicapped Children and Adults). I had occasion to make a phone call to my sister Sheila (very much a leading light in that part of the world, because of playing 'Annie Sugden' in the TV soap, *Emmerdale*) from the Queen's Hotel. I approached the hall porter and craved some suitable coinage for the slot-machine, and saw him looking at me very closely. 'Excuse me,' he said, 'but aren't you George Cole?' 'No,' I replied, 'but we have been mistaken for each other in the past,' and, somewhat icily, snatched my money and attended to the phone box. As I finished my call, I turned to see our Yorkshire door-keeper friend still staring at me. 'I know,' he triumphed, 'weren't you Brian Rix?'

I have already described how the Leeds Grand and Opera House came into the hands of Howard and Wyndham, through the marriage of John Beaumont to Dorothy Cruikshank. John Beaumont started life before the mast, as an apprentice on board a three-masted, full-rigged windjammer but, as so often happens in these stories, theatre was in his blood. In fact, his mother, Ada Thorne, had been a leading lady with the great George Edwardes and, although she may have passed on her love of the green to her son, she did not bestow her histrionic talents. John hated acting, but loved management, both stage and front-of-house – a talent he had probably acquired from his father, Edward, who was already established as first the general manager and then the managing director of the Theatre and Opera House (Leeds) Ltd Company.

The Grand actually opened its arched portals on 18th November, 1878, backed and built by a group of local industrialists, whose company was to remain in possession for nearly one hundred years. Until, in fact, it was acquired, lock, stock and barrel, by the Leeds City Council in July 1973. Howard and Wyndham had been the virtual owners for one year prior to this, through a complex share deal with the original company, but they weren't around long enough to get their name plates engraved, never mind screwed on the doors. When constructed, the theatre was probably the finest of its size in Britain, and was the one-off masterpiece of architect George Corson. It had been built in the teeth of non-conformist fears about the 'insidious influence of theatrical entertainments', but a timely comment by Prince Albert, the Prince Consort, may have helped matters along somewhat, when he accompanied Queen Victoria to the opening of Leeds Town Hall a few years earlier. Hearing that the plans for a theatre were opposed, he commented that 'nothing is more calculated to promote culture and raise the tone of the people.' Luckily he made that remark to the then Lord Mayor, Sir Peter Fairbairn who, no doubt, passed the information on to his son, Sir Andrew Fairbairn, who used it to good effect as the first chairman of the Board of Directors. The Leeds worthies were able to 'erect a magnificent temple of drama for the West Riding' and, happily, the 'support of the best people' (as the audience was described) has continued, with ups and downs, ever since.

Those same worthies, however, were not willing or able to run the 'magnificent temple' themselves. A suitable hired hand could not be found, so they leased the theatre to a relatively young actor-manager, Wilson Barrett, who remained in charge for sixteen years. Mind you, one theatre was not enough for him and he also operated at the Theatre Royal in Hull, as well as the Court and eventually the Princess's Theatre, London. But by 1894 the Grand Board decided that they wished to take a more active part in running the show, so Wilson Barrett's lease was terminated and a managing director, John Hart, was appointed. Wilson Barrett was shattered, but five years later he took the Lyceum in London over from Sir Henry Irving, and five years later still was dead from cancer. He was fifty-eight.

John Hart had come to the attention of the Board as the manager of the Bradford Theatre Royal – the theatre which would house Irving's last performance – and introduced many changes. Pantomime now became a diehard Leeds tradition, electric lighting was installed, a new stage was built and many great names, both 'straight' and music hall, bestrode the stage of the Leeds Grand. It was then that Edward Beaumont, John's father, entered into the story. Like John Hart, Edward was associated with a neighbouring town's theatre, being general manager of the Lyceum, Sheffield. He became the general manager, also, of the Theatre Royal, Sheffield and, under John Hart, held the same position at the Grand, Leeds. The roads were a lot less busy in those days. Eventually Edward moved up to be the managing director of the Sheffield Theatres and, when John Hart retired, succeeded him at the Grand. Like his predecessor, he brought many outstanding productions to Leeds, and was a firm believer in 'keeping the stage free of vulgarity'. I wonder if that would have excluded me?

The name of John Beaumont, Edward's son, first appeared on the Grand programmes as the resident manager in April 1931, having followed in his father's footsteps as the manager of the Lyceum in Sheffield. In due course he mirrored his father exactly, becoming the managing director of the Lyceum in 1939 and of the Grand in 1943. His directorship with Howard and Wyndham came six years after that. In those days, the Lyceum was still attracting major tours but, in the event, was the first to go to the wall when it closed in the 1960s. It reopened in 1990 with a great deal of support from the local authorities and the EEC, plus public subscriptions, too, of course. The Leeds Grand, on the other hand, escaped closure and, although it could no longer be retained by the Beaumont family, it has remained open – having been purchased by the Leeds Corporation in 1974 – and extensively remodelled, particularly to house Opera North. This renovation cost the theatre dear, in historical terms, for all the complex and wonderful below-stage machinery was removed and such carelessness, some might say vandalism, destroyed for ever this irreplaceable nineteenth-century legacy. No more could a critic write as in the *Yorkshire Post* in May 1884: 'The mechanical arrangements in the earthquake scene are very striking. The earthquake flung down temples and palaces, marble columns and sculptured monuments in the chaos and havoc of destruction.' But at least the theatre has continued to function and that, many would argue, is worth the sacrifice of a few old artefacts. I am not one of such persuasion.

I am not one of Jewish persuasion either, but I own part of the Levi Eshkol Memorial Forest in Israel, and I have never even visited that country. Quite simply, I was appearing at the Grand in 1970 with *She's Done It Again*, and we (the company and I) were invited to a 'bit of a do' held by the J. N. F. Fourth Fellowship in Leeds. I remember drinking a lot of tea and eating far too many cream cakes at the time, and for our part in the proceedings we were presented with this certificate which states, quite simply, that Brian Rix and Members of the Company have had a row of trees planted in their name in this particular forest. I wonder what would happen if I visited the grove in question, waved my certificate and demanded to see the plaque. Somehow I think I would be disappointed – but I told you this little story to illustrate the unusual things actors have to do when they are on tour. After all, you can't spend every afternoon in bed, or enjoying the delights of the cinema, which you get into free, by the way, on showing your Equity card. You have to socialise occasionally, even if you put on a great deal of weight in the process. During the war, it was more grim and earnest, though. Not rows of trees, but comforts for the troops and others. The front of the Leeds programme carried this message:

The Grand Theatre
ADOPTED MINESWEEPER

We are still awaiting word from the Skipper as to where to forward our next parcel.

If anyone happens to have any wool to spare, we have plenty of willing workers waiting to knit it up.

The cold weather is coming, so please do your best to find some.

That must be how the phrase 'Hello, Sailor' began. All those matelots mincing around in angora cardigans and cerise-coloured socks. What a pretty thought.

THEATRE ROYAL
Glasgow
KING'S THEATRE
Glasgow

When we went North of the Border for the first time with Advance Players' Association Ltd, we were entering Howard and Wyndham territory, with a vengeance. In Glasgow and Edinburgh, they ran the lot! No wonder visiting managements found it difficult to negotiate competitive terms. But it was not until some years later that I became aware of such a monopoly. Mind you, the local authorities have now taken the place of H&W, but at least they've been rent in twain, behind their respective city boundaries. Unfortunately, my libido knew no boundaries at that time, either, as this quotation from my first autobiography, *My Farce from My Elbow* may prove:

> So on to Glasgow – and my first fight over a bird. I was shacked up with a girl in the company who was married. As her husband was shacked up with a girl elsewhere it seemed a perfectly reasonable quid pro quo. Unfortunately, a rather stuffy actor called Cecil Cross, who was sharing digs with us, didn't agree. He was very scathing about her morals and about my part in encouraging the lack of them, and we argued furiously about the rights and wrongs of adultery every night until dawn was coming up. Unfortunately, it was the only thing that was, for I'd then stagger into bed so exhausted that the adultery part was quite out of the question. This really brought new meaning to 'sleeping with a woman'.

The Theatre Royal was first built in 1867 as Bayliss' Coliseum, renamed the Theatre Royal two years later and then destroyed by fire. It was rebuilt twice more after fire, the first time in 1880 and then again in 1895. The architect, on both these last occasions was C. J. Phipps. It is said that this is the largest, and possibly the finest, theatre by Phipps to survive. In the mid-50s the theatre was taken over by Scottish Television, when they were granted their I T V franchise for the first time, and many people thought it would be lost as a theatre for ever. This was not to be, and it was magnificently restored in 1975 to all its former glory, but with 400 fewer seats, and the local authority assuming control. It is now used as a touring house but, more importantly perhaps, as a home for Scottish Opera.

Opera is no stranger to the Theatre Royal. When touring with his British National Opera in the 1920s, Sir Thomas Beecham was not best pleased when the audience applauded at the end of Act I of *La Bohème* before the music had stopped. He glowered at the offending miscreants and then delivered a stern lecture as to how to behave at the opera. The same happened at the end of Act III and he shouted that they were 'a load of bloody barbarians' and stomped out of the orchestra pit. It took a great deal of persuasion, by fellow artists and management alike, before he was willing to return for the final act. There is another story, too, about an overweening and overweight soprano in the production of *Tosca* to whom the stage crew took a dislike. They decided to wreak their vengeance by replacing the mattresses, on to which she was to jump from the battlements, with a trampoline. I imagine Sir Thomas was then convinced beyond all doubt that Scottish stagehands, particularly those in Glasgow, were worthy of far more descriptive epithets than 'bloody barbarians' as his leading lady bounced up and down like a yo-yo.

Over the years, I have toured on several occasions to that other 'legitimate' Glasgow theatre, the King's, when the Royal was in use by the television company. It, too, is a glorious theatre, reflecting the best of Frank Matcham's later manner, for it was built in 1904. Now, under the aegis of the local authority, it proves the perfect foil to the Theatre Royal with its mixture of touring plays, musicals, pantomime, summer shows and amateur productions. But when I was last there, in 1975, it was the only theatre available for the lot and the result was a complete sell-out for *A Bit Between the Teeth*, in which I 'starred', along with Jimmy Logan. We broke the theatre record that week. I like to think that was all down to me, but somehow I have the sneaking suspicion that a favourite Scottish son, like Jimmy, might have had something to do with our success, too. He even ran the Metropole in Glasgow at one time, and that was pretty popular as well. It is a week I will always remember, for my mother died on the Wednesday night and I had to hire a private plane to be with her in Hornsea Cottage Hospital, before returning to Glasgow in time for the show. My mother timed it to perfection. As the curtain rose at seven thirty, she breathed her last.

But mentioning my mother reminds me that I have not yet finished the full quote from my first autobiography, for she now becomes involved, in a totally innocent way, I hasten to add:

The row between Cecil and me continued on to the Sunday train call from Glasgow to Edinburgh – so much so that he called my girlfriend a whore. It all ended in a perfectory bout of fisticuffs and we both stepped off the train looking the worse for wear; to this day, I still have a small scar on the bridge of my nose to prove it really happened. To make matters trickier, my mother, together with a friend, decided to visit me in Edinburgh that week – with the result that I had to explain away the cut on my nose by saying I'd bumped into a wall in the black-out. This deception, plus staying with my mother, finally put paid to my relationship with the married lady and my possible trip to the divorce courts was avoided. Cecil Cross changed his name to Hugh Cross, continued as an actor, but became a very respected local politician with aspirations to become an M P.

He never achieved this for, like my mother, he is dead. But both of them were with me, guarding my morals, on my first visit to Edinburgh. It made it all rather boring, actually . . .

Jimmy Logan and the author busy breaking
that house record in Glasgow

KING'S THEATRE
Edinburgh
ROYAL LYCEUM THEATRE
Edinburgh

We seem to have dwelt a considerable time in Edinburgh, mainly, I suspect, because of the already recounted history of Howard and Wyndham, the Royal Lyceum Theatre and, when Stewart Cruikshank entered the lists, the King's Theatre. Nowadays, the Lyceum does not take part in the touring scene as much as in days of yore, but it is the home of one of Scotland's leading repertory companies, the Royal Lyceum Theatre Company. When it all began, however, in September 1883, the actor-manager making the curtain speech was, of course, Henry Irving – on tour. Ninety-two years later another actor-manager, also on tour, stepped forward to make a curtain speech – me. There was more than time separating us, though. Irving had just played Benedick in Shakespeare's *Much Ado About Nothing*, while I had just played Fogg in Michael Pertwee's *A Bit Between the Teeth*. What is more, I had lost my trousers, in so doing. You can be certain that Irving did not lose his.

My playing at the Lyceum was just a quirk in time, though. The pantomime was still occupying the King's and a few weeks of touring had been shoehorned into the Lyceum. I have never played there, before or since. On the other hand, I have trodden the boards at the King's on three different occasions, this first time with Donald Wolfit, and the week was a sell-out. It is interesting to read Wolfit's comments about the tour in general, and Scotland in particular, in his autobiography, *First Interval*:

> I played forty-two performances of *Lear* during this autumn tour before I ventured into London with the play. Once only did I attempt him twice on the same day but I found it to be an impossible task, and as I was, thank heaven, my own master in deciding how my performances should be distributed, and not under the dictates of some producer who has never experienced the fatigue of a leading role himself, I arranged to open the week with *King Lear* and play one other performance towards the end, preferably on the Saturday so that there would be the Sunday to rest my voice and recover my strength.

As I continued to add these great plays to my repertoire, I was aston-ished to find how rarely they had been presented in the provincial cities. Correspondence in the *Glasgow Herald* elicited the fact that Richard Crookback had not been seen in any of the city's theatres in full since Barry Sullivan in 1894. Benson had played a Colley Cibber shortened version (in Scotland) once in the interim before my visit in 1941. *King Lear* had been seen prior to my visit some fifteen years before; but in many of the large cities I played it had not been presented professionally for more than thirty years.

I do not have ready access to that correspondence in the *Glasgow Herald*, but I am certain Wolfit was correct. On one particular point, however, his memory played him false, though, in regard to his performances of *King Lear*. On that first ever tour of the production, he played the old king on six Saturdays out of a total of fourteen. What is more, he some-times played the role three times a week. No wonder he got through eight bottles of stout during a performance. I think I should have needed the round dozen . . .

And did you notice his passing shot at producers? Good old Donald! A veritable bulldog, wouldn't you say? Some might say a pit-bull terrier.

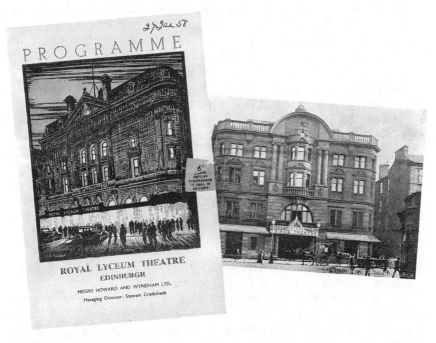

HIS MAJESTY'S THEATRE
Aberdeen

Wolfit never went to the granite city on 'my' tour; nor, I regret to report, have I ever played it since. I once spent forty-eight hours hanging around the railway station during my service in the R A F, waiting to catch a train which never seemed to leave Carlisle, but that is as near as I ever got to this impressive theatre. In view of the Donald family's interest in this property, as well as to their interests in Howard and Wyndham, and as we are in Scotland, I will pay some attention to it now.

Robert Arthur was the first owner of this splendid property, opened in 1906, and which is a further example of Frank Matcham's architectural genius. He designed over two hundred theatres, having learnt his art by leaving his native Newton Abbot for London, and joining the architectural practice of J. T. Robinson. Robinson was a splendid teacher who, among other theatres designed the Old Vic in 1871. He died quite young, aged forty-nine, but he had already sown the seeds of greatness in young Matcham, who went on to become the most famous theatre architect of all time. Furthermore, Frank had the good sense to marry the boss's daughter, and took over the practice when his father-in-law was finding out who really designed the Pearly Gates. To provide capital for Matcham's latest creation, Mr Arthur disposed of another Her Majesty's Theatre in Aberdeen, making it a condition of sale that the old theatre could never again bear the royal title, nor present opera, pantomime, melodrama or any stage play. The cunning fellow got away with this draconian covenant, and the erstwhile Her Majesty's became the mundane Tivoli. Coming from Dundee, Mr Arthur was determined to stamp his authority on Aberdeen, and he succeeded.

For the next twenty-five years, all the great names appeared at the new theatre, which had, perforce, changed sex from 'Her' to 'His'. Sir Henry Irving, Sir John Martin-Harvey, Dame Ellen Terry, Sir Johnston Forbes-Robertson, Sir George Robey and many others, titled or not, appeared at this far-flung outpost of the London Midland Scottish Railway. It was freezing cold in the carriages and not much warmer when you reached your destination. But the theatre had a large capacity, 1,800 seats, so the takings warmed the cockles of many an actor-manager's heart. They continued to provide fuel for the Robert Arthur Theatre Company, too, but by 1912 the company's financial troubles were becoming desperate. Arthur had over-reached himself by expanding too rapidly in the suburbs of London, where he could not compete with the larger groups of theatres and added to his woes, some said, by gambling. Vesta Tilley wrote: 'I believe he lost a fortune playing roulette at Monte Carlo. I frequently saw him at the tables there, and, knowing his reputation as one of the thriftiest of Scotchmen [sic], I wondered how he could possibly be fascinated by such a risky game.' The company staggered on for another few years, propped up by Howard and Wyndham, but in 1923 His Majesty's, Aberdeen was taken over by a rival manager – of the Tivoli, no less – Walter Gilbert. He survived for a further ten years, by which time the 'talkies' had had their wicked way, and Mr Gilbert wished he had never decided to go 'legit'. Help was at hand, in the shape of a city councillor, the owner of the Gondolier Dancing Academy as well as the majority of Aberdonian 'flea pits' – James Forrest Donald Esq. Councillor Donald immediately spent £10,000 on improving the theatre, a great sum of money in those days – especially for an Aberdonian – and on 14th August, 1933 His Majesty's Theatre reopened, complete with revolving stage (the only one North of the Border, a distinction still held to this day). Sadly, the councillor did not live long to reap the benefits of his investment. He died in 1934 and was succeeded by his two sons, James and Peter, and it was Peter who was at the helm of Howard and Wyndham when that company turned up its theatrical toes four decades later.

It is pleasant to report, however, that in spite of the theatre being acquired by the former Aberdeen Corporation in 1972, the Donald family still exert a beneficial influence over the theatre's affairs. The councillor's grandsons, James and Peter, are the respective director and manager of His Majesty's and it is their proud boast that this is virtually the only Civic Theatre in the country to show a profit. Which, for a late Aberdeen councillor and his Scottish grandsons, seems to be about par for the course.

THEATRE ROYAL
Newcastle-upon-Tyne
TYNE THEATRE AND OPERA HOUSE
Newcastle-upon-Tyne

After the comforts of staying with my mother in a private hotel in Edinburgh – comforts greatly appreciated in spite of being deprived of my casuistical connubial company – it was back to digs in Newcastle with a vengeance. The leading actors could stay in the Turk's Head, hard by the theatre's stage door, but for us lesser mortals, it was back to peeling wallpaper, outside loos, pos under the bed and the smell of stale cabbage everywhere. Furthermore, we were reaching the end of the tour, so rehearsals had long since ceased, understudy calls were desultory and time hung heavy on all hands. Having only limited means of transport, it was quite impossible to move out of Newcastle and see the glorious countryside but a stone's throw away, or explore the myriad castles and churches, including Hexham Abbey, which sprout like so many offshoots of the Roman Wall, from which those historic and beautiful buildings were often quarried. All that realisation had to wait, as far as I was concerned, until after the war when I was on tour with a car, and I was allowed to discover all the wondrous sights which surround the home of Newcastle Brown.

The original Theatre Royal, Newcastle opened in 1788, three years overdue and three times over budget, but even so, the whole total, including additional borrowing, was less than £9,000, and the town now had a playhouse, with Letters Patent granted by George III, of which it could be proud. A change from the strength of feeling against actors, expressed in the preamble to an Act of 1715 passed by Queen Anne, which described them as 'rogues, vagabonds, sturdy beggars and vagrants'. Those same miscreants now had a secure home and a licence to perform in the North-east. Many famous names took advantage of this, including members of the Kemble dynasty, as well as the Macreadys – father and son. It was the son, sporting the same name as his father – William Charles Macready – who went on to the greater fame and fortune, passing down the theatrical expression 'a Macready pause' to describe any actor who hangs around for an intolerably long time before speaking, purely for dramatic effect. He would get short shrift in farce, I can tell you.

The first Theatre Royal did not suffer the fate of so many of its contemporaries. It was not burnt down (although in 1823, the mistaken belief that a fire *had* started caused a panic and seven people died), quietly closing its doors in 1836. The whole operation moved from Moseley Street to Grey Street, but the new Theatre Royal *did* burn down in 1899 following a performance by Frank Benson of Shakespeare's *Macbeth*, adding fuel to the fire (if you will forgive the pun) which has always raged about the ill luck arising out of the Scottish play. 'This means ruin,' Benson is purported to have said and, indeed, he was not insured and lost about £5,000 – a great deal of money in those days. But he struggled on and achieved considerable success on the road, only to die in straitened circumstances some forty years later. Before that fire the Theatre Royal had faced another challenge from a rival playhouse, the Tyne Theatre and Opera House.

There is a pretty fiction, still abroad in Newcastle, about the origins of this theatre. It is told that it was designed as an Italianate opera house by local architect William Parnell. 'But,' say the sceptics, 'it would be quite impossible for an inexperienced designer like Mr Parnell to have performed such expert feats of theatrical architecture. He must have had help.' The story then conjectures that as Mr C. J. Phipps was in the town in 1867, to superintend the renovation of the Theatre Royal auditorium, he was importuned by Mr Parnell to lend a hand with the new opera house plans. It is even suggested that the master carpenter, William Day, who built the two theatre stages, may have been responsible for what can only be described as an early attempt at industrial espionage. All very mysterious. But the plot thickens . . .

The name of that great Italian patriot and master of revolutionary war, Giuseppe Garibaldi, may seem far removed from the Tyne Theatre and Opera House, but according to some Novocastrians (to give them their Roman nomenclature) the building was designed just to please him. It is even said that he attended one of the first performances in 1867, in the company of the builder (and proprietor of the *Newcastle Chronicle*) Mr Joseph Cowan. This seems extremely unlikely, as air travel 'twixt Rome and Newcastle was still unknown in those days (in spite of Leonardo da Vinci), and at the time of the theatre's opening Signor Garibaldi was rather busy preparing to enter papal territory – or he might even have been under arrest, for that was his fate around that time – which would probably have put all thoughts of first night appearances, or even telegrams, out of his mind.

It is true that Garibaldi knew Mr Cowan, and did indeed visit Newcastle in 1854, when he was presented with a sword and an illuminated address, but since that was thirteen years before the theatre's opening it seems unlikely that there was then much poring over putative plans for the new opera house. Again, the great man came back to England in 1864, but turned down Joseph Cowan's invitation to address public meetings in Newcastle, Glasgow and Birmingham, because he did not wish to embarrass or antagonise the British Government. Again, that was three years before the Tyne Theatre's opening. No luck this time, either.

However, it is possible to suppose that Signor Garibaldi once said to Mr Cowan that if he was ever building a theatre it would be jolly nice to think along the lines of an Italian opera house and, no doubt, that is precisely how Mr Cowan did think. Furthermore, the Newcastle builder made sure his son spoke fluent Italian, on the odd chance, possibly, that if Giuseppe ever did grace the Tyne Theatre and Opera House, he would never want for an interpreter. Unhappily, such a visit is not recorded. But it makes a jolly good yarn, all the same. Verdi would have been proud of it.

The two theatres went along, in anything but friendly rivalry, for a number of years, with the newly built Tyne being the more successful. At one time the lease of this theatre was held by Augustus Harris, the second head of the Harris dynasty to rule Drury Lane, and Covent Garden, Her Majesty's and the Olympia in London chucked in for good measure. Under Harris' management pantomime was king, with direct transfers from Drury Lane to the Tyne Theatre. Then along came the ubiquitous Howard and Wyndham who took out a lease on the Theatre Royal and transformed it into a success. Only for ten years though, as the theatre became more and more dilapidated and the proprietors refused to undertake any renovation, so H&W terminated their lease and promptly joined forces with the recently knighted Sir Augustus Harris at the Tyne. The Theatre Royal replied by offering the lease to Robert Arthur, who thereupon staged a new adaptation of Alexandre Dumas's *Denise* – by none other than the aforesaid Sir Augustus Harris. This is truly an excellent example of dog-eat-dog, although Mr Arthur must have resented paying the royalty cheque to his illustrious rival. But business improved again at the Theatre Royal, until the disastrous fire of 1899. Unlike Frank Benson, Robert Arthur was insured, Frank Matcham was engaged and the new Theatre Royal emerged. In fact, the new auditorium was only slightly larger than that of the rival Tyne, so the battle for supremacy continued.

Then came the crisis for Robert Arthur Theatres Ltd, and to cut his losses, Arthur had to seek an accommodation with Howard and Wyndham. At first this was a joint booking arrangement for both Newcastle houses, but in 1912 H&W assumed total control which continued with the Theatre Royal until 1972, when the Newcastle Corporation took over and rebuilt the theatre to the highest possible standards. They closed the theatre in 1986 and reopened with Charlton Heston in Robert Bolt's *A Man For All Seasons* on 11th January, 1988. Meanwhile, Stoll Theatres Corporation had leased the Tyne Theatre, with little effect, and in 1980

Theatre-Royal, Newcastle.

Last Week but one of the Company's performing here this Season.

THE FOURTH AND LAST NIGHT BUT ONE OF

MR and MRS

Charles Kemble's

ENGAGEMENT.

Thursday Evening, May 12, 1814,
Will be presented, the historical Drama of

Deaf and Dumb,

OR,

The Orphan Protected.

The Part of St. Alme, by Mr CHARLES KEMBLLE.

De L'Epee	Mr MUNRO	Pierre	Mr WILLIAMS
Darlemont	Mr FINN	Lopeza	Mr SKINNER
Franval	Mr STANLEY	Dominique	Mr LANCASTER
Dupree	Mr FAULKNER		

And the Part of Julio by Mrs CHARLES KEMBLE.

| | Claudine, Mrs MARA | | |
| Marianna | Mrs GARRICK | Madame Franval | Mrs SKINNER |

End of the Play, A NEW PAS SEUL, by Miss Parr.
A SAILOR'S HORNPIPE, by Mr Swan.

To conclude with the musical Farce of The

PRIZE;

OR,

2538.

Lenitive	Mr LANCASTER	Heartwell	Mr STANLEY
Label	Mr FAULKNER	Juba	Miss PARR
Caddy	Mr WILLIAMS		
	Mrs Caddy	Mrs MARA	

And the Part of Caroline (with the original Songs) by Mrs C. KEMBLE.

Last Night of Mr and Mrs C. KEMBLE's Engagement.
On Friday Evening, will be presented, Shakespeare's Play of The MERCHANT OF VENICE.
Shylock, Mr C. KEMBLE. Portia, Mrs C. KEMBLE. To which will be added, a Farce called The
DAY AFTER THE WEDDING. Colonel Freelove, Mr C. KEMBLE. Lady Freelove, Mrs C. KEMBLE.

Mr and Mrs CHAR............ BENEFIT, and positively the last Night of their performing
here this Season, will .... Comedy of The PROVOK'D HUS-
BAND. The Parts of ....

Theatre Royal, Newcastle.

the theatre was eventually rescued from dereliction by a group of amateur enthusiasts who created the Tyne Theatre and Opera Company Ltd, under the chairmanship of the greatest enthusiast of all, Jack Dixon. In my travels, I have been backstage twice at the Tyne Theatre. The first time I was shown the amazing Victorian stage machinery, which must be quite unique in any theatre in the world. Then, on Christmas Day 1985, a fire started and much of this precious heritage was lost. But, such is the determination of Jack Dixon and his friends, the machinery has been completely restored by present-day craftsmen and it is a credit to all concerned.

So, today the two theatres are still locked in friendly rivalry. For a time, the Tyne provided a home for the excellent regional rep – the Tyne Wear Theatre Company – and the Royal cruised along as a major touring house, receiving visits from the R S C among others. But in 1988 the repertory company upped sticks, changed its name to the Northern Stage Company and took up residence at the Newcastle Arts Centre. Once more, the Tyne Theatre and Opera House was thrown on its own resources. However, Jack Dixon and his merry men and women are a doughty bunch, and they have continued with their struggle for what they believe to be a unique theatre. They are quite right in their belief, and must take heart from the fact that the ghost of Garibaldi is right behind them – and if they can't use his chauvinistic techniques to good theatrical effect, they may as well shut up shop. I would hazard a guess, however, that they won't.

Finally, a story about the Royal Shakespeare Company on one of their annual jaunts to the land of Brown Ale, with the Scottish play on view. As the line was spoken:

> To-morrow, and to-morrow, and to-morrow,
> Creeps in this petty pace from day to day,

a Geordie voice rang out from the stalls:

> 'Booger 'ell! That'll be Saturday!'

And Saturday is the night of the train version and the get-out. It's time we touring actors packed our bags and moved on.

THEATRE ROYAL
Nottingham

Move on we did – 'Donald Wolfit and his Famous Company' made its way to our penultimate date and our first Moss' Empires theatre. It was in Nottingham that I saw that famous notice in the chorus dressing-room (where else would I be allocated?) which has passed into theatrical folklore: 'Ladies of the chorus are requested not to use the basin for purposes other than washing and the hand laundry of underwear. SITTING IN THE BASIN IS EXPRESSLY FORBIDDEN. By Order, George Black, Managing Director, Moss' Empires Ltd.'

Apparently, at some time past in a Moss' theatre, an unfortunate chorine decided to use the basin for other than its original purposes and brought it crashing to the floor, resulting in an injury that is too painful to contemplate. We men were more fortunate in this respect and smugly smirked at the notice as we turned on the cold-water tap to aid our concentration. It was at times such as these that we relished the useful difference between the sexes.

Incidentally, I must report a divergence of opinion here, or perhaps memories playing tricks. In his autobiography *Double Act* Michael Denison reports that the notice read: 'Standing in wash basins is strictly prohibited. Very serious accidents have happened to artistes when trying to remove "wet white". The basins collapsed and THE GIRLS WERE TERRIBLY LACERATED'; while David Conville states that it was the simple command 'DO NOT WASH YOUR FEET as it might break the basin.' I think I should point out that this demonstrates perfectly the 'rule of three'. An almost identical joke, regurgitated three times with, hopefully, a bigger reaction on each occasion. As long as the reaction is favourable, that is.

You will note the name of the managing director, George Black. His predecessors had once been Sir Edward Moss and Sir Oswald Stoll, and his successor was a man whose name was destined to go into the annals of television history – Val Parnell. It was *Val Parnell's Sunday Night at the London Palladium* and the incredibly popular game, 'Beat the Clock', which attracted viewers in huge numbers during the 1950s and 1960s and kept Tommy Trinder's name on everybody's lips long after the war, as well as making a star of Bruce Forsyth. It did me no harm either, for the Palladium popularity on I T V forced the B B C to examine its strait-laced policy for Sunday nights, and thus *Laughter from the Whitehall* was born, resulting in a contract for me to present and act in a series of farces that numbered nearly one hundred by the time the curtain came down seventeen years later.

Mind you, George Black himself was pretty adept at being a producer as well as managing Moss' Empires. His two sons, George and Alfred, also continued in a similar vein and were responsible for many a successful touring revue after the war, as well as smash hits in the West End such as *Piccadilly Hayride, Seagulls Over Sorrento* and *Take It From Us* (the highly popular stage version of the radio series *Take It From Here*). Eventually, though, they were seduced by the blandishments of television, joined the board of Tyne Tees Television and that, as far as the theatre was concerned, was that.

I will not weary readers again with my unfortunate experience of being 'off' during *King Lear* – because I was so busy watching the chorus girls next door at the Empire in *Chu Chin Chow* – for I have recounted this twice before in previous autobiographies. I have also told the story about *Reluctant Heroes* being chosen for the Whitehall in 1950, at a bad matinée, thanks to the enthusiastic support of a small gathering of Nottingham play-goers; while the fact that my first girlfriend came from Nottingham is so far in the mists of time as to be nearly commensurate with the Book of Genesis. I will simply move on to modern times, in the story of the Theatre Royal, via its early days – back to 1865, in fact.

The Theatre Royal was the second of the many theatres designed by C. J. Phipps, and his splendid colonnade of Corinthian columns still dominates the theatre square as you approach it from Market Street. The theatre itself was reconstructed in 1897 by Frank Matcham and again in 1977 by Renton Howard Wood Levin for Nottingham Corporation (who had acquired the theatre from Moss'). The Empire next door was demolished but in its place has risen a splendid concert hall, with parking for cars actually possible nearby – an unusual achievement in itself. It is altogether a magnificent endeavour on the part of the Corporation, at a time when the arts are often seriously underfunded and the need for financial restraint is on every bureaucrat's and politician's lips. But then, Nottinghamites have always been bright. Quite apart from providing my first ladylove and spotting the potential of *Reluctant Heroes*, they have recycled the legend of Robin Hood to such good effect that now the whole world believes in him, including the good councillors themselves. If they are not exactly robbing the rich, they are at least providing caviare to the general, which – contrary to custom – is greatly appreciated.

And so the week commencing Monday 16th November, 1942 drew to a close. We were one week from being out of work and, as the experience was to be new to me and I would be going home for a frugal Christmas anyway, I viewed it with equanimity – unlike many of the older actors who were with Wolfit. They knew only too well the horrors of missing a job because of a bad audition, or because of a previous contract just overlapping, or simply because of being considered unsuitable, often for months on end, for *any* job which was going begging. Like the poor old actor who had been out of work for over a year and finally landed the role of Long John Silver in *Treasure Island*. He realised that this was his chance to make his name, especially if he could emulate Bernard Miles and perform with a live parrot. He hunted round all the pet shops until he found the perfect one. 'Come back on Friday,' says the shopkeeper, 'I'll have him spruced up and ready for you.' 'No, I can't come on Friday,' says the desperate old man, 'I'm having my leg amputated.' You have to have been out of work for many a long month and year to appreciate that. But it is funny, I promise you. At least to us theatricals.

As is the story of another actor who had been 'resting' for yonks. He at last landed a job in repertoire at the National Theatre, with some pretty good supporting roles. 'It's bloody marvellous,' he enthused to a friend. 'Great to. be back in work again; great parts; great directors; great money; and you know the best thing of all? I've only got to give three performances a week.'

It's catching, you know. Here is a theatrical 'shaggy dog' story: three canine friends of man are being tested for their intelligence. Each, in turn, is presented with a pile of bones. The architect's dog arranges them in a neat cuneiform pattern; the accountant's dog opts for the plus and minus symbols – whilst the actor's dog eats all the bones, rogers the other two dogs and asks for the afternoon off.

Cave canem . . .

The Theatre Royal Nottingham in 1908.

GRAND THEATRE AND OPERA HOUSE
Croydon
ASHCROFT THEATRE
Croydon

The original Grand Theatre opened on 6th April, 1896 and closed on 18th April, 1959 when it was demolished. The phoenix which arose from the nearby ashes exactly three years later, in 1962, when the Fairfield Halls opened, was the Ashcroft Theatre, named after Croydon-born Dame Peggy. Although it is a small theatre, with under 800 seats, it gives the impression of being larger when you are playing there, because it has a stepped auditorium. I presented a season of farces at the Ashcroft, once, with Jimmy Thompson playing the roles I had created. It would be unfair to comment on the business we attracted, for Jimmy was ill for most of the season, and there was 'a consequent diminution of the box office takings'. At least, I think that was the phrase the Croydon Council, who own the Halls, chose to excuse the débâcle, but probably it was simply because most of the likely audience had gone away for the summer hols.

In the days when we called a spade a spade, or when we were just plain tactless – depending on your point of view – the capacity of the Ashcroft would have ensured it was classed as a Number Two date. In these homogeneous times, however, we refer to touring theatres as largescale, midscale or smallscale, and the Ashcroft is slap-bang in the middle. The old Grand, on the other hand, was definitely a Number Two theatre and I imagine Wolfit only took it because it enabled him to transport his entire company, plus the scenery and costumes, close-by to London where he was hoping to find a theatre to produce his *Lear*. As he wrote in *First Interval*:

With the tour over I searched for a London theatre. That fine dramatic critic, Beverley Baxter, had written a play which owing to lack of support had to be withdrawn from the St James's Theatre. I am not sure that Beverley Baxter is not a far better critic owing to the fact that he wrote a play which was a failure, and I wish he would now write one which proved a success. That would make him a better critic than ever. At any rate, the St James's fell vacant on the last week of 1942 for a period of six weeks and I went there with *The Romance of David Garrick*, to be followed by a two weeks' season of *King Lear* and *Twelfth Night*, both newly designed by Ernst Stern. This was the only occasion when I attempted to play Lear four times a week, and even though I alternated it with Malvolio it proved a severe strain.

I, too, was under a severe strain. With a lack of objectivity that was incomprehensible, other than the fact that I was cheap and available, Wolfit cast me as Sebastian, Rosalind Iden's twin brother. I couldn't be less like Rosalind (Lady Wolfit – as she became) if I tried. She had a pert, pretty nose, with wide cheekbones, large blue eyes and blonde hair. I had a Roman nose, with long angular features, small brown eyes (once described by an unkind friend as 'pissholes in the snow') and jet-black hair. We were *not* an ideal match. By the time I had shaded every hollow in sight, highlighted every worthwhile feature and donned my unspeakable blond wig, I looked like a tatty transvestite tart from one of the worst all-male variety shows that were then disgracing our music halls. I was not a happy choice, but I did my best. My mother and sister Sheila were in the audience at the St James's Theatre to see my painful first performance and when it was all over we repaired to Lyon's Corner House. 'I thought that sniff you gave on your opening line was very funny,' opined my sister. I had inherited that sniff from my mother's side of the family, so I knew she couldn't think of anything better to say. My mother, realising only too well where the sniff came from, maintained an embarrassed silence throughout. Well, I mean what else *was* there to say, other than 'kindly leave the stage'? But she didn't – and I didn't. In fact, after my disastrous first appearance in the West End, Donald Wolfit actually asked me to go on tour with him again and, like a fool, I accepted. After all, it was only for six weeks.

But those were six weeks I will always remember. It was an E N S A tour for our gallant lads and the play, horror upon horror, was *Twelfth Night* and, God help us, I was still Sebastian – it was enough to drive strong men to drink.

Well, if it didn't drive them to drink, it sometimes drove them out of the theatre, as I shall recount in the Interlude which follows, when I tell you a little bit about E N S A and C E M A. I hope you will find the telling instructive or, even, entertaining. Which is more than can be said for our version of *Twelfth Night* – my part in it, anyway.

Curtain

DEPARTMENT OF NATIONAL SERVICE ENTERTAINMENT

by arrangement with

THEATRES' WAR SERVICE COUNCIL

" THE WHITE ROSE PLAYERS "

from

THE OPERA HOUSE, HARROGATE

present

"SUSPECT"

by

EDWARD PERCY and REGINALD DENHAM

PROGRAMME - - - ONE PENNY

INTERLUDE
'As Long As They're Happy'

ENSA
(Entertainments National Service Association)
CEMA
(Council for the Encouragement of Music and Arts)

John Maynard Keynes began CEMA during the Second World War
to bring culture to the masses, and Basil Dean – recalling his similar
activities in the First World War – took on the responsibility of forming
the entertainments organisation to serve the armed forces. His head-
quarters were at the Theatre Royal, Drury Lane; NAAFI (the Navy,
Army and Air Force Institute) were the sponsors and ENSA (Entertainments National Service Association) was the end result. Sometimes with
good effect – sometimes not. I would suggest that *Twelfth Night* came into
the latter category.

Wolfit must have been living in a dream world, when he wrote the
following load of old malarkey in *First Interval*:

> Now at last the barriers were down at Drury Lane and in fear and
> trepidation ENSA consented to a tour of the garrison theatres in the
> Southern Command with a play by Shakespeare! We took the entire
> production of *Twelfth Night* from the St James's, company, costumes,
> and Stern's exquisite reversible screens, for a six weeks tour, playing in
> all some twenty camps. It was strenuous work. Based at hostels, we
> travelled to four and sometimes five camps in a week, returning at night
> to the luxury of ENSA beds which seemed to be made of teak.

So far, so good. But now the great man's memory somewhat clouded
o'er.

> These camp performances [Wolfit didn't mean that as a pun] were, as
> I had anticipated, a great success, and the audience were extremely well
> behaved. [He should have been wearing my wig. Never have I been
> barracked – another pun, I fear – so much in all my life.] With its

exquisite mixture of poetry and foolery *Twelfth Night* was an admirable choice.

Poppycock! It is truc that our audiences were grateful to be entertained, but it was the pretty young pages (our fairies from the *Dream*), pushing Ernst Stern's reversible screens about, who received the greatest attention. Whistles and whoops accompanied every appearance, while groans and raspberries provided the general background to the actors struggling through William Shakespeare's somewhat tenuous plot. As for me! Least said, soonest mended!

Donald did admit to one little local difficulty. That was when we played to some American troops at Tidworth. Within five minutes of our first night (we were there for *five*!) only the officers were left. All the rest were – noisily – gone. Wolfit was furious and let the Officer Commanding have an earful when we repaired to the Mess after the performance. I will let the great man conclude the story:

> The next evening was a complete contrast; not a murmur was heard – no restless feet, no applause or even laughter. It was as if we were playing behind thick plate glass. We were nonplussed and commented on it to the officer in charge afterwards. He expressed his delight that we had noticed it and confessed that Shakespeare was a new thing to him. 'But I just had a talk to the men this morning,' he said, 'and in case there was any further trouble tonight I had the military police parading the aisles with their revolvers out of their holsters.'

All absolutely true. I know. I was there. Never have I been so grateful for armed protection. But really I needed it everywhere on that tour.

I did do another six-week stint for E N S A some twelve months later, when I had moved to the White Rose Players at the Opera House in Harrogate, shortly before going into the R A F. But things were better then. To begin with, we were doing a modern play and a thriller – *Suspect* by Edward Percy and Reginald Denham. Even so, the following notice still appeared in the programme: 'Unrestrained coughing detracts from the enjoyment of the rest of the audience, and also makes the performance more difficult for the players. Will you do what you can to help? Thank you.' I would have needed more than such politesse in *Twelfth Night*, I can tell you.

Basically, though, E N S A concentrated on what has become known as 'light' entertainment, and thousands of variety artists, some good, some awful, toured the theatres of war to bring laughter and song to the assembled squaddies and erks and Jolly Jack Tars. Throughout the war, the great and the good did lend their talents to the noble enterprise, one of the last being Noël Coward, who consented to appear in a revue in 1944 with Bobby Howes, Josephine Baker and Geraldo's orchestra. One of the first plays to be toured, however, was by Coward. It was *Fumed Oak*, and the artists taking part were no less than John Gielgud and Beatrice Lillie. Laurence Olivier, Ralph Richardson and Sybil Thorndike did their stuff much later in a grand tour of *Arms and the Man, Peer Gynt* and *Richard III*, which included a performance for the British military personnel who were facing such a deeply distressing time, trying to lessen the horrors found in the unspeakable concentration camp at Belsen.

Other great names from the music-hall side were also present from time to time: Gracie Fields was one of the first in France, entertaining the BEF in 1939, but she was then particularly badly treated. When Italy entered the war in 1940 her husband, Monty Banks, was declared an enemy alien – even though he had lived away from Italy from the age of ten – and he and Gracie went to live in America, where Gracie continued to give concerts in aid of the British war effort. But she was still reviled at home, being included in such unattractive headlines – generally applied to British stars in Hollywood – as 'Gone With the Wind Up'. This was all very sad, but Gracie had the last laugh, when she became a Dame of the British Empire in her later years. Other artistes fared better in the war: George Formby, Vera Lynn, Max Miller all did Buggins's turn, while the last variety star to appear in India, as the Japanese war was ending, was Tommy Trinder. One of the dancers appearing in that show said it all about those times: 'I was happier than I ever believed it possible to be. I remember the huge, appreciative audiences in Algiers, Cairo, Bombay and Baghdad – places I never dreamed of seeing . . . I only wish ENSA could have gone on for ever.'

Ah, well! I must just have been in the wrong place, or the wrong play. Certainly the wrong part, that's for certain.

CEMA was originally formed to bring music and the arts to theatreless towns and, in particular, to areas which were heavily involved in the war effort in Wales and north-east England. Unlikely venues such as the Parish Hall, Amble, the Guest Hall, Alnwick Castle and the Pavilion Theatre at Rhyl were treated to performances by the inexhaustible Dame Sybil Thorndike and her husband Sir Lewis Casson, who seemed to span the yawning gulf 'twixt the red-nosed ENSA and the blue-stockinged CEMA with dextrous ease. As did other artists who came mainly from the Old Vic which, as we know, was now in the 'recesses of Lancashire'. As the war came to a close, CEMA metamorphosed into the Arts Council of Great Britain, which continued to send out smallscale tours to similar venues, with works such as Shakespeare's *As You Like It*, John Osborne's *Look Back in Anger* and Peter Shaffer's *Five Finger Exercise* – and an unlikely piece of casting with Jessie Matthews playing Louise Harrington, but very successful, nevertheless. Another piece of original thinking by the Drama Department of the Arts Council (whose deputy drama director,

Jean Bullwinkle, O B E, gave me this information – and she should know – she recently retired after serving for over forty years) was employing a tiro Ken Tynan as the Director of *Othello* for one of these smallscale tours. No doubt Sir Donald would have welcomed his success in directing. Then he would not have become such a viperish critic, as far as Wolfit was concerned. Who knows, he might have come to love Donald's barnstorming technique. Those E N S A, C E M A and early Arts Council tours were not above playing in such windswept places. Sometimes without the barn, too. You could certainly tear a passion to tatters in those days . . .

Act IV beginners, please.

Sybil Thorndike and Lewis Casson.

ACT IV

WHITE ROCK PAVILION
HASTINGS

Director of Entertainments: KENNETH F. DAY.   Telephone 1840.

Week Commencing MONDAY, 27th MARCH,
Evenings at 7-30.
Matinees: Wednesday and Saturday at 3 p.m.

RIX THEATRICAL PRODUCTIONS
present
DERMOT WALSH
(By permission of The J. Arthur Rank Organisation) in

RELUCTANT HEROES

A FARCE BY COLIN MORRIS
with
ELSPET GRAY

MARIE GERMAINE	JANET BUTLER
BRIAN RIX	LARRY NOBLE
ALLAN SCOTT	GEORGE RADFORD

COLIN MORRIS
and
WALLY PATCH

Directed by FRANK DERMODY.
PRIOR TO WEST END PRESENTATION

Admission — 4/9, 3/6, 2/6 reserved;
1/6 unreserved
(including tax).

Advance booking office open Weekdays 10 a.m. to 7-30 p.m.
Sundays 11 to to 12-30 and 3 to 5 p.m.

Cafe open every day   Licensed Lounges

Coates & Hall. Marshall Avenue. Bridlington

SCENE I
'Reluctant Heroes'

When I finished that ENSA tour of *Suspect* on 8th April, 1944 – using the jargon of the day – the Nazis were conducting brutal reprisals against the French Resistance in the Jura Mountains, Uncle Joe was driving the Krauts out of the Crimea, the Yanks were about to hit the Nips for six in New Guinea and our boys in blue had got their fingers out and were dropping mines in the Blue Danube, which was a jolly good show.

The war was entering its penultimate phase. D-Day was less than two months hence, the surrender of Germany just over twelve months away and the atom bombs on Hiroshima and Nagasaki a mere four months after that. It was a fine time to be called to the colours – but that is precisely what happened to me and, to be even more precise, on D-Day itself. But my deferred service, which had been extended by now to fifteen months, as opposed to the original ten, was spun out even further for, as our first troops hit the beaches of Normandy, I was being prepared for an operation on my antrums – a double nasal antrostomy, to give it its technical name – and my RAF service was put off for a further six weeks of convalescence. That operation really put paid to any chances I had of becoming a pilot and, after some fairly desultory basic training, I was grounded and offered the splendid option of becoming an ACH/GD or a Bevin Boy – in other words, a miner.

ACH/GD stood for Aircraft Hand/General Duties and as those duties could be confined to the ablutions or the cookhouse or that other well-known brick-built house, I decided that discretion was the better part of valour, and opted for the mines. But the curse of my long-suffering sinuses descended down the pit with me, too, and it wasn't long before I was experiencing exactly the same trouble that affected me a-flying – namely a burst ear drum. I was hauled up in front of a medical board for yet a further examination, and was ticked off for not drawing attention to my problem earlier. As my medical papers had been freely circulated between the RAF and the Ministry of Labour (responsible for Bevin Boys), this struck me as being singularly unfair, but said nothing, lest it affected my chances of getting out. And get out I did, but instead of being ahead of all the other young actors returning to the boards, I found myself back in the RAF as a medical orderly instructor, sporting two stripes and a pretty big chip on my shoulder at the unfairness of it all. Of course, it wasn't unfair at all, for I had to work my passage like everyone else, and it wasn't until October 1947 that I was finally demobbed – long after Dickie Attenborough and the like had grabbed all the best jobs going.

There was little point in knocking on those particular casting doors because they were all firmly shut, so I borrowed some money from my father and my uncle, added to that my own gratuity, and started life as an actor-manager. I followed the pattern set by Donald Wolfit so he must be held entirely to blame if you loathed the plays I eventually produced, or be congratulated if they gave you a bit of a giggle. At first I did not present farce, however, but repertory in Ilkley, Bridlington and Margate, and it was at Bridlington in 1949 that two very important strokes of good fortune occurred. In the first place, I met my wife, Elspet, and kept her within range by employing her as an A S M in Bridlington, and then by marrying her in the same year. You can't belt and brace more securely than that, although I also promoted her to be the leading juvenile in the company, just to make absolutely certain. Besides, as a young married couple, we needed the money.

The other important move I made in that year was stumbling across a play which I thought was the funniest I had ever read. I wondered why it had never been produced in the West End and became determined to take it there, at some time in the future, to make my fame and fortune. The play was *Reluctant Heroes*. It did make my fame and fortune – but it had to be toured first, and that is how we get back to basics . . .

The *Stage* advance notice on 23rd March, 1950 read as follows:

Reluctant Heroes

> Rix Theatrical Productions are sending out a short tour of this new farce by Colin Morris, opening at the White Rock Pavilion, Hastings, on Monday next. The cast includes Dermot Walsh, Wally Patch, Elspet Gray, Brian Rix, Larry Noble, Marie Germaine, Janet Butler, Allan Scott, George Radford and Colin Morris. John Cleaver is Stage Director and Production Manager is William E. Raynor. The farce is being directed by Frank Dermody.

It makes very simple and rather boring reading, doesn't it? But it was anything but simple or boring for me. I had never sent out a tour in my life before. In fact, I had only been on the road with Donald Wolfit for a total of fourteen weeks, and that in the very junior position of an acting

A S M. I couldn't count the twelve weeks I had spent on those E N S A tours, for they bore no relation whatsoever to their illustrious counterpart, the commercial tour, with all its attendant pitfalls and the distinct possibility of losing your shirt. I was, shall we say, an innocent at large; a lamb to the slaughter and very definitely wet behind the ears. Frankly, I was lucky to get away with it. But I did.

Booking the tour was the first hurdle, and to negotiate that you had to have a 'name'. But trying to cast a knockabout army farce with such a luminary was rather like asking Dame Peggy Ashcroft to take over in *A Little Bit of Fluff*. It was not easy. Agents were distinctly distant. In fact, it was quite a surprise if any of them condescended to do business with me at all and only one, Gordon Harbord, was positively helpful. The only snag was that his client list was definitely downmarket and we had to see an awful lot of actors before we could get a decent cast together, and one that still didn't include any actor of note. However, Rank film artist Dermot Walsh was being released from his contract, and he was quite glad to join – even though he came from the grand agency of Linnit and Dunfee – and Wally Patch would have killed to get the part of Sgt Bell, having recognised it as the chance of a lifetime. So, with those two names above the bill, I was able to start booking the tour. But you could hardly describe the venues as Number One dates.

When I say I was able to start booking the tour, I am speaking figuratively. I had to hunt around for a booking agent to do the job for me, because that was the normal practice in those days – particularly if you were an unknown management. Being in that category (and I was certainly qualified in that respect), also meant that the booking agent you were able to engage would not automatically be one out of the top drawer. So the dates my newly acquired booking agent, Leslie Bloom, was able to book for me were not exactly the cream of Howard and Wyndham, but I don't think he tried very hard. I mean, just look at the list. Remember we were starting in March, and note that four out of the six dates are at the seaside, during what could hardly be described as the height of the season: the White Rock Pavilion, Hastings; Wimbledon Theatre; the Dolphin Theatre, Brighton; the Alexandra Theatre, Stoke Newington; the Winter Gardens Pavilion, Blackpool and the Pavilion, Torquay. Of those, two are no longer used as theatres (the Winter Gardens Pavilion, Blackpool and the Pavilion, Torquay), and two are no longer with us (the Dolphin, Brighton and the Alexandra, Stoke Newington). The Dolphin was a tiny little theatre which nestled up to its bigger brother, the Theatre Royal, in Brighton. It was probably all right for amateur productions, which didn't have to worry too much about the weekly take, but for a professional company, even one like ours, the capacity of around £1,000 for eight performances was definitely cutting it a bit fine. I needed at least £500 a week to get out and, even though my share of the take was sixty-five per cent, I would have had to play to absolute capacity to make that possible. I *didn't* play to absolute capacity, so my father and uncle were very depressed. So, come to think of it, was I.

As for the Alexandra, Stoke Newington, it was the kiss of death. The manager asked me to pop along to see him the week before our engagement, and I duly obliged. I found the theatre bolted and barred, except for a couple of posters announcing that *Reluctant Heroes* would be there the following week, and a notice at the box office to say that they had gone to lunch. This in itself was a lie, as I soon found out, for all the staff had actually been laid off and the box office was very definitely closed at lunchtime, at dinnertime, at breakfast-time, or at any other time for that matter. The manager explained that the previous production to grace the Alexandra's boards, some two weeks earlier, had played to a grand total of £94 7s. 4d., including entertainments duty and, as the advance bookings for *Heroes* were in the region of £2 10s. 6d. it might be in everyone's interests if I withdrew. I didn't need any further prompting and agreed to cancel the contract forthwith. In those days you could behave in such a cavalier fashion, plunging your own cast (and yourself) out of work for one week, without further recourse. Nowadays, the world is a different place and 'weeks out', as they are known, are very strictly rationed indeed.

The remaining four weeks of that initial tour were all pretty dicey, too. We played in theatres with no real policy for plays at all. Wimbledon was a barn, or seemed to be, when half full; the Winter Gardens Pavilion, Blackpool was part of an even bigger barn, the Opera House, the Ballroom and the Pavilion, which made up a vast complex totally unsuitable for plays in the winter, even if playing to capacity – which it wasn't. Furthermore, it was freezing, with snow showers throughout the week and our already mentioned horrendous landlady to add to the joys of spring. We were very unhappy. The Pavilion, Torquay cheered us up a bit, for the audience did laugh 'uproariously', and even the vast space of the orchestra pit didn't seem to stop them. Mind you, they were very pleased to find that Wally Patch was born in Paignton and that his real name was Vinnicombe. It added a proprietorial air to the whole proceedings.

To pile Ossa on Pelion (or is it Pelion on Ossa?), our opening week at the White Rock Pavilion, Hastings, was nearly a financial disaster for me of a different kind – and the explanation of this enigmatic statement will help to clear up why Leslie Bloom only appeared to have booked us a six-week tour, in the first place, and why he would no longer continue to represent us, in the second place. Here goes . . .

WHITE ROCK PAVILION
Hastings

I must be fair to Leslie Bloom and explain that he had only booked a six-week tour because Wally Patch was under a previous contract to go on tour with another play called *The Magic Cupboard*, and he could only manage our short engagement. Of course, it was financial suicide for me to contemplate such a limited run, even though the whole production, including two sets (all built and mounted in Bridlington), cost a mere £1,000. But I was full of optimism and a Micawber-like belief that something (or someone) would turn up to enable me to continue after the initial period, and I pressed on regardless. Leslie Bloom should have pointed out the risk I was taking – but he didn't – so I took it.

His motives for letting me go ahead became apparent at the end of my first week at the White Rock Pavilion. I had signed a sharing contract with the theatre and was to receive the rather low figure of fifty-five per cent – the usual percentage being ten per cent higher. The money, however, was to go direct to Mr Bloom, who would deduct his booking fee – five per cent of our share – and pass on the balance to us. Unfortunately for him, I asked the Hastings Director of Entertainments, Kenneth Day, for an advance on the Friday in order to pay the salaries. This was normal practice which Leslie had obviously overlooked. Mr Day consulted his copy of the contract, and it was then that I saw that my share was *not* fifty-five per cent, but sixty-five per cent. Consternation! I hurriedly fetched my version of the agreement and close scrutiny soon revealed that Mr Bloom had used an eraser on mine, typed in the lower percentage and had planned to make off with the extra ten per cent, plus the booking fee, with me none the wiser. Multiplied by six, this became a reasonable sum, and it was now all too obvious why I had been encouraged to go ahead with such an economically unsound six-week tour.

Kenneth Day and I requested Mr Bloom's presence at the White Rock Pavilion offices as a matter of some urgency. Mr Bloom arrived, to be confronted by two angry and outraged managers waving unidentical contracts, who made it quite clear that he would no longer be allowed to represent either party in further negotiations of any kind and, what is more, his greed – not to say dishonesty – would be noised abroad. And so Leslie Bloom ceased to be a power in the land – as far as Number Two dates were concerned.

Of course, this was easier for Kenneth Day to do than it was for me. After all, he had Hastings to offer. I had an army farce, telling the tale of three recruits and a bullying sergeant, and in five weeks I would be without that very sergeant, Wally Patch. I was, you might say, up the creek without a paddle. But, true to theatrical tradition, there was a good fairy waiting in the wings. Her name? – Renée Stepham.

Actually, that wasn't her name. She was born Rachel Solomon, but just when she was about to leave Skinner's Girls' School in North London, to join a lawyer friend of the family as a secretary, it was pointed out that her name might cause a bit of a racial problem in the legal profession, and she was advised to change it. Now it so happened that Renée's grandfather, Jack Solomon, was a bookmaker in Tattersalls and also the unfortunate possessor of a club foot. His mates bestowed upon him the *nom de guerre* 'Step-ham', so Miss Solomon became Miss Stepham. Furthermore, her family used to call her Renée, not Rachel, so Renée Stepham was born. And flourished.

As a lawyer's secretary, Renée was involved in various bits of theatrical litigation and became known as a bright girl, interested in the business. In September 1939, the month war broke out, she was offered a job by Bernard (now Lord) Delfont, at the salary of £2 10s. per week, with the promise that 'as the business grows, you will grow with it.' Renée was with Bernie for just under nine years, and had started to act as a booking agent for both variety acts and a number of touring shows. She realised, however, that she was not going to grow as fast as she would have hoped, and so she found a backer, in the shape of John Beaumont from the Grand, Leeds and the Lyceum, Sheffield, who put £800 into her venture. He stipulated that he did not wish his interest to become known to his father-in-law (A. Stewart Cruikshank, the chairman and managing director of Howard and Wyndham Ltd), and agreed with Renée that she should book the most difficult theatre in the H&W chain – the Lyceum in Sheffield which John Beaumont found almost impossible to fill. Renée was so successful that Cruikshank responded by proposing that Renée should take over the bookings for the Grand at Leeds as well, whereupon John Beaumont took fright, recognising his power-base would be eroded, and Renée got nothing. However, Peppino Santangelo, from the New Theatre, Hull, realised that to have a hardworking booking agent in London might solve some of his problems and Renée became the New's sole booking representative. The Alexandra, Birmingham and the Grand, Wolverhampton followed suit, and Renée soon had a tiny circuit. Furthermore, Sir Peter Saunders (then plain Mr) came forward and offered the booking rights for the comedy *Fly Away Peter* and, eventually, *The Mousetrap*. Meanwhile a desperate young actor-manager, with only five lousy weeks left of a tour of *Reluctant Heroes*, was on the phone night and day to try and solicit help. That desperate young man was, of course, me.

Renée *did* come to my aid. Not without certain misgivings, for I did not present an easy package to sell, especially as I had no Sgt Bell to lead the company after Torquay. But desperation is the mother of invention, and even that seemingly insurmountable obstacle was soon overcome – by the sheer gall of persuading Basil Radford to take over the part of the ranting sergeant for a further six weeks until he made the film of *The Galloping Major*, when Wally Patch was free to return to the show. The only reason Basil agreed to do this was because his son, George, would have been out of work if he hadn't. George played the medical orderly in *Reluctant Heroes*.

So, the tour went on . . . and on . . . and on . . . for a further fourteen weeks on the road until the oasis of the Whitehall. And all of those fourteen weeks were somehow secured for us by Renée. Mind you, I can't say they were all Number Ones. In fact I'm not sure that any of them were, but we kept going and that was all that mattered. Incidentally, Miss Stepham is still going strong today, and over the years her client list has included the London Festival Ballet, the Ballet Rambert, the New D'Oyly Carte Company, Duncan Weldon and Triumph Theatre Productions, his erst-while partner, Paul Elliott and E&B Productions, Michael Codron, Cameron Mackintosh, Mark Furness, Bill Kenwright, Charles Vance, Lee Menzies et al. Oh, incidentally, Renée Stepham – Rachel Solomon – has never taken more than a one and a half per cent booking fee from her clients. And that, only recently. When she first started it was one per cent. Pretty generous for a girl who had to change her name because it was too Jewish.

But I must tell you about the White Rock Pavilion, Hastings.

It's a similar story, really, to the Pavilion, Torquay. Built in the 1920s, and opened by the then Prince of Wales on 6th April, 1927, it was intended as a home for the highly successful Hastings Municipal Orchestra, under its conductor Basil Cameron. The thought of using the building as a theatre never entered anyone's head during the design stage. When the nearby Gaiety Theatre became a cinema in 1932, the White Rock Pavilion had to become all things to all men, in spite of a wide platform, no stage equipment and an auditorium that put sound and acoustics at the head of its priorities and the ability to see the stage, in anything like comfort, at the bottom.

So, a portable proscenium was lashed up and the Fol-de-Rols moved in, with such names as Arthur Askey, Richard Murdoch, James Warner and Mona Washbourne, who was a pianist with the Fols. Miss Wash-bourne became an actress by joining the Harry Hanson Court Players who, in turn, moved into the Pavilion after the war to present seasons of rep. Other attractions were booked, too, such as out-of-season visits of *Reluctant Heroes* or *Worm's Eye View*, leaving the Court Players to join the luxury of the holiday-makers. Clearly, such a dog's dinner could not last.

In 1984 extensive alterations began to take place in the Pavilion, to improve the sight-lines, the seating, the access and the stage facilities. Hastings Council lavished a million pounds on the project, and now the town has a 1,179-seater worthy of presenting all manner of shows to an audience who can hear, see and appreciate what is being performed. It wasn't like that in March 1950, I can tell you . . .

Nor was it like that a century earlier when another venue in Hastings was on offer. This rejoiced in the name of the Theatre Royal, but it was actually a converted barn hung with canvas. When Fanny Kemble made her comeback by touring the provinces in 1847, she noted 'as far as I can see, *all* the theatres throughout the country are Theatres Royal.'

No longer in Hastings though. It is now the White Rock Theatre and even 'Pavilion' has been dropped. Times change – and theatre names change with them. Somehow, though, the traditional Theatre Royal sounds more dignified than something you could suck, with the words 'a present from Hastings' printed all the way through it.

WIMBLEDON THEATRE

I have passed some scurrilous comments on the first six dates of the *Reluctant Heroes* tour, so feel I had better be fair and give the theatres we visited some kind of hearing, even if the space allotted is rather short. After all, if a theatre is closed, with only a small chance of reopening, or has been demolished, there seems little point in singing its praises, for patrons will have been denied the opportunity of judging it for themselves.

Wimbledon, however, does not quite fall into this category for, although the theatre has been threatened many times with demolition and re-development, this fate now seems extremely unlikely because, apart from being classed as a Grade II listed building, it reopened in time for the 1991 pantomime season – having been refurbished for a vast sum of money, with the help of the local Merton Council, so it may yet reclaim its position as the Grand Old Lady of Wimbledon Broadway.

Wimbledon Theatre started life as a young maiden in 1910 when it was built at the behest of Edwardian showman and entrepreneur, J. B. Mulholland. He built two other out-of-town theatres – the Metropole, Camberwell Green and the King's Theatre, Hammersmith – but his pride and joy was the one nearest to the Wimbledon Lawn Tennis Club, styled as 'Surrey's Premier Theatre'. Many great names graced the stage in those early days, including Matheson Lang, Julia Neilson, Fred Terry and Ellaline Terris, with Gracie Fields, Sir Frank Benson and Robert Donat appearing in the 1920s. By the time of Mr Mulholland's death in 1925, Wimbledon Theatre had become one of the most successful touring dates in the country. This happy state of affairs, however, was not to last.

Repertory became the staple diet during the 1930s, with the Wilson Barrett and Jevan Brandon-Thomas Company, and after the war Peter Haddon took over this onerous task. But not before touring had been tried once again, and that is how I found myself there in April 1950. Although the theatre was still owned by the Trustees of J. B. Mulholland, it was leased to South-Western Theatrical Productions Ltd, whose joint managing directors were Bernard Delfont and Ben Kanter, and we all know how Bernie went on from strength to strength – after he had got rid of Wimbledon. Times were hard, though, and eventually the London Borough of Merton had to buy the theatre in 1965 simply to bale it out, and two years later it was renovated at a cost of some £80,000. Alas, and alack, this in itself was not enough to stave off trouble, and by 1980 the theatre again faced bankruptcy.

This time it was saved from the official receiver by the efforts of a newly appointed general manager, Michael Lyas, which may well have guaranteed its future. Forty years ago my future was anything but guaranteed. Four weeks to go, still no booking agent, no Sgt Bell, and no dates either. No wonder I viewed my impending trip to the late Prince Regent's watering hole with foreboding.

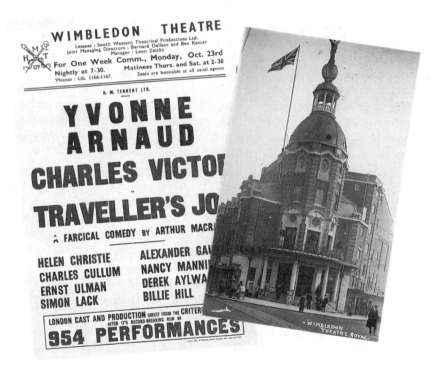

Wimbledon Theatre in Bernard Delfont and
Ben Kanter's time, and as it was just after
the theatre was opened in 1910.

DOLPHIN THEATRE
Brighton
THEATRE ROYAL
Brighton

The diminutive Dolphin, adjacent to the Theatre Royal whose lowly capacity I have already described, began life as the Court. It was acquired by the Theatre Royal Brighton Company in 1947 and its name was changed to the Dolphin. It always remained in the shadow of the larger theatre, though, and eventually became the Paris Cinema, showing those unmentionable foreign films. Now it is no more.

Its purchase was the idea of the company's managing director, J. Baxter Somerville. A camp and snobbish solicitor (well, he was snobbish to me, never even deigning to say 'hello' whenever I played Brighton!), J B, as he was called, entered the theatre in 1931 as the publicity director for the Greyhound Theatre, Croydon. He went from strength to strength, becoming the Press representative for the Greater London Players and the Little Theatre, Epsom – and if any reader has heard of either, I should be glad of further information for, not altogether surprisingly, I am singularly bereft of such. Nothing daunted, he eventually went back to Croydon, founded the Repertory Company there and also took out a lease on the Westminster Theatre. In 1935, he became the managing director of the Brighton Repertory Company, who were then performing at the Theatre Royal, and began his successful term of management, which ended in 1963 with his retirement. During his years in office, the Theatre Royal became one of the most sought-after pre-London dates for plays on their way to the West End, while the Dolphin remained the poor relation of the moneyed classes, who frequented the larger venue next door.

So, there we were, with the Alexandra, Stoke Newington already cancelled, two playing weeks left before the tour ground to a halt, negotiations proceeding to replace Wally Patch with Basil Radford, and a new booking manager, Renée Stepham, struggling to find anyone who would be willing to take us on spec. Not a happy situation, and one made worse by the superiority displayed to us lesser mortals by the neighbouring gods at the Theatre Royal who, in reality, had feet of clay like us, for they were none other than Ronnie Shiner, Bernard Lee, Gordon Jackson and Nigel Stock in *Seagulls Over Sorrento*. I am happy to report that both plays opened in the West End at roughly the same time. *Seagulls* at the Apollo Theatre and *Heroes* at the Whitehall. *They* ran for 1,551 performances; *we* ran for 1,610. Honour was served.

Of course, I was to play the Theatre Royal on a number of occasions as the years wore on and my fame was noised abroad. *One For The Pot*, *Chase Me Comrade!*, *Don't Just Lie There, Say Something!* and *A Bit Between the Teeth* were played immediately prior to London, while *Let Sleeping Wives Lie* was there after a two-year run at the Garrick, and we enjoyed full houses at all times. But things weren't quite as jolly in those chrysalis Dolphin days, if you will allow me such miscegenation.

The Theatre Royal began life in 1807, on land sold by the Prince Regent, with a production of *Hamlet* when Charles Kemble played the Moody Dane. Sarah Siddons and Edmund Kean also played there in the early days, and it was a popular venue. In 1866, the theatre was bought by one of its great managers, Henry Nye Chart, who enlarged it according to the designs of – none other than – C. J. Phipps. Mr Chart died, his widow, Ellen Elizabeth Nye Chart, replaced him and the theatre went from strength to strength. The greatest names in the theatrical world made the trip down south on the *Brighton Belle*, playing to ridiculously overcrowded houses. It is extraordinary to think that as many as 1,900 people squashed into the auditorium – an auditorium which today holds a mere 951 – to see artists such as Sir Henry Irving, Dame Madge Kendal and the notorious, if that is the word, Lillie Langtry. But remember, there were no cinema and television distractions in those days – and precious few fire regulations, either.

Mind you Mrs Nye Chart was not averse to a little overcrowding herself. A tale is told by historian James Harding that in the 1880s, at the end of the Christmas pantomime, Ellen Elizabeth popped on to take her customary annual bow. 'A large woman of handsome proportions, she always wore a low-cut dress, and always bowed very deeply.' That evening, a stagehand lurched on from the backstage bar, the Single Gulp, where he had been imbibing too freely, and 'when her bow was at its deepest' grasped what she had so generously revealed. 'Now,' he shouted, staggering back into the wings, a lifetime's ambition achieved, 'sack me!' Our historian does not record whether she did just that, or simply took him upstairs to her office, with its inevitable casting couch. We shall never know the outcome.

After J B's retirement, the theatre was run by Melville Gillam, who had come from the Connaught Theatre, Worthing and then, from 1971, until his death ten years later, the theatre became part of the Louis Michaels' group, which had theatre interests in Bournemouth, Bath, Richmond, Surrey and the Theatre Royal, Haymarket. Louis was also Duncan Weldon's partner in Triumph Theatre Productions. In 1984 the theatre changed hands again, and it is now owned by David Land, a well-known theatrical agent, who was involved in all the early works of Andrew Lloyd-Webber and Tim Rice. No wonder he can afford to run a privately owned, non-subsidised theatre. There aren't many of those around these days . . .

WINTER GARDENS PAVILION
Blackpool

When *Reluctant Heroes* was in Blackpool's unsuitable winter venue, the Pavilion was part of the Blackpool Tower Company Ltd, which owned the majority of the theatres, the ballrooms and the piers in the town of 'Albert and the Lion'. Two of their directors were Sir Harold and Bert Grime, who also owned the big local newspaper the *Evening Gazette*. Now, through marriage, I am connected *very* vaguely to the Grime family. So vaguely, in fact, that neither Sir Harold nor Bert would have known it – but Bert's daughter-in-law, Rosemary, had an uncle who was married to my mother's sister – and if you can work that out you are clearly cut out to be a genealogist. Such blatant nepotism, however, didn't make any difference to our rattling and echoing round that vast canyon that was the Winter Gardens complex. Yet in spite of that the *Evening Gazette* did give us a good notice, headed 'THIS IS GRAND FUN' – so perhaps the local critic knew of my family connection, after all.

Eventually, the Blackpool Tower Company sold out to EMI, now Thorn EMI. They disposed of their seaside assets to Trust House Forte who, in turn, disposed of them to First Leisure, chaired by Lord Delfont – and it was under his aegis that I last appeared at the Winter Gardens in 1987. Well, to be absolutely precise, it was actually under the aegis of the Conservative Party. I was in Blackpool to chair a fringe meeting of the 'Community Care Campaigners' who were touring the annual political party conferences to try and obtain more help and understanding for people with a mental handicap living in the community. I have to report that my last appearance at the Winter Gardens was more successful than my first. The Circle Bar was absolutely packed, which is more than can be said for the Pavilion thirty-seven years before.

GRAND THEATRE
Blackpool

Strangely enough, I have never played the Grand Theatre in Blackpool, although I have had a number of productions there on tour, including *Reluctant Heroes* itself, with John Slater playing Sgt Bell, while we were still running at the Whitehall, and *Diplomatic Baggage* in 1964, which was on its way to Wyndham's Theatre. As the Grand still continues to operate as a theatre, albeit no longer part of the old Blackpool Tower Company, I should describe it here.

The auditorium of this theatre, first revealed to the public in 1894, is credited as being one of Frank Matcham's finest creations. Despite being a Grade II listed building, this did not stop it coming under the threat of demolition in 1973 when Lord Delfont, or rather First Leisure PLC, sold the building to Littlewoods Stores. The Theatres Advisory Council then helped the Friends of the Grand Theatre to get the then Secretary of State for the Environment, Geoffrey Rippon, to instigate a public enquiry and, subsequently, to withdraw the planning permission. Lord Delfont, with good grace, bowed to the decision and made it possible for the Grand Theatre Trust (initiated by the Friends) to purchase the building, by accepting deferred payments over a period of ten years. The Grand was saved, and it is now recognised as one of the most successful touring venues in the United Kingdom. Rather a jolly little story, don't you think?

Meanwhile, back in 1950, the last of Leslie Bloom's bookings came in with the tide. Another out-of-season seaside venue, but as this was the Pavilion, Torquay, and as I have written about this already, in my days of innocence with Donald Wolfit, I will move on quietly to the dates proposed and promulgated by Miss Renée Stepham. Little did we know that we still had nearly four months to go before a West End theatre would offer us a safe haven. Miss Stepham was, of course, trying to make bricks without straw. Our Sgt Bell was all-important to the play and we had to offer her no less than three sergeants during the remainder of the tour. Basil Radford was unhappily miscast for six weeks; the author stepped up from a smaller role to play the part for a further seven; and Wally Patch returned for the final week of the tour, prior to our opening at the White-hall Theatre, in September. But Renée was game to the last and, although a number of the dates were not exactly out of the top drawer, she managed to keep us battling on (which accorded with an army farce) and we finally made it. But it was an exhausting business, I can tell you.

INTERIOR OF THE GRAND THEATRE.

PALACE THEATRE
Plymouth
THEATRE ROYAL
Plymouth

I must put these two theatres together for, although I have only played the Palace and it no longer exists as a touring venue, the new Theatre Royal has come within my purview in my capacity as chairman of the Arts Council Drama Panel. It is one of our most important clients, at the time of writing, although likely to be devolved to the local Regional Arts Board within the foreseeable future.

> Time goes, you say? Ah no!
> Alas, Time stays, *we* go.
> *The Paradox of Time*,
> HENRY AUSTIN DOBSON.

Drama has been practised in Devon and Cornwall since the thirteenth century, yet Plymouth's attitude towards its theatres has varied. The original Theatre Royal began as the Frankfort Gate Theatre in 1758, but after a visit by George III and his Queen to the theatre in the mid 1760s, the owners illegally changed its name to the 'Theatre Royal'. Around that time existed a rival to the ramshackle, misnamed 'Theatre Royal' – the Dock Theatre – and an attempt was made to open a third theatre, but this soon failed. However, the Dock Theatre was able to put one over the 'Theatre Royal', insofar as Sarah Siddons played there in 1785 immediately after her great triumph as Lady Macbeth at Drury Lane. The Dock battled on for a further hundred years, finally closing in 1899, although by then it had become a penny gaff, with any historical importance long gone.

The so-called 'Theatre Royal', however, had disappeared even earlier, and had been superseded in 1813 by an impressive complex of hotel, assembly rooms and the new, correctly named, Theatre Royal itself. However, like the Dock, it was not the easiest of venues to act in although iron spikes, built in front of the orchestra pit, helped to keep the audience off the stage. In spite of this deterrent, patrons did frequent the place and the theatre lasted, with varying fortunes, until it was finally demolished in 1937. Before then, though, a rival had come along to challenge the original Theatre Royal, in the shape of the Grand Theatre, which opened in 1889. The Grand was one of the only two West Country theatres ever to be visited by Cornwall's greatest theatrical son, Sir Henry Irving. However, it too lost its way and was demolished in 1963.

That left only the Palace Theatre for us to visit in 1950, and by then this was also on the skids. Built originally as the New Palace of Varieties in 1898, it was a very grand affair indeed with its adjacent hotel. When the complex was built it was the costliest investment, at £185,000, in any West Country building enterprise. All the variety 'greats' were seen there, including Dan Leno, George Robey and the incomparable Marie Lloyd. It is reported that it was at this venue the licensing authorities objected to her famous song, 'She Sits Among the Cabbages and Peas'. Miss Lloyd obligingly changed it to 'She Sits Among the Cabbages and Leaks'. History does not record what further action was taken.

Twice-nightly performances were normal at the Palace, because it was a variety house, and no attempt was made to change that for us. We just had to give five non-stop hours of *Reluctant Heroes* for six consecutive nights. Carrying cumbersome army equipment, on top of wearing heavy army greatcoats and battledress, reduced the three army recruits, played by Dermot Walsh, Larry Noble and myself, to absolute grease-spots. Especially as we were on-stage for the entire evening and had to cope with our new Sgt Bell, Basil Radford. And when I say 'cope', I am not exaggerating.

Basil was one of the kindest of men, and a very amusing actor, particularly in films. Unfortunately, he had one long-standing habit which clouded his memory when it came to remembering lines. On average, he got through a bottle of whisky a day, sometimes more, and had been doing this, so he said, since the end of the First World War, having developed the taste when he was a fighter pilot. Nerves made his whisky-drinking all the greater, with a disastrous effect on his recall mechanism, and this was the problem we faced for all twelve performances in Plymouth. We three recruits behaved like mad ventriloquists, feeding the Sergeant's lines to him and then responding to the very words we had just mouthed to poor, bemused Basil. It was horrendous and, unfortunately, noticed by both Press and public alike: 'Basil Radford, who has recently joined the cast, plays the lead as a blustering, barking sergeant. One could at times sense in his performance a struggle with this strenuous and exacting role.' So wrote the critic in the *Western Morning News*. He was only too right. As an actor-manager, with dreams of conquering London, I could see my ambitions going down the drain, along with those bottles of whisky which were being excreted as sweat and other bodily wastes by dear Basil. But the joke is he *did* keep us going, dries, fluffs and all, for a further six weeks, *and* with the audiences laughing, and this enabled Renée to continue booking the tour until our goal was achieved. We were not doomed, after all. I shall always be grateful.

On the other hand, the Palace, as a theatre, *was* doomed and by the 1960s the inevitable bingo had taken over. It struggled back with repertory from 1978 to 1982, but when the new Theatre Royal opened its doors in November 1982, the Palace became a disco called 'The Academy', and so it remains to this day. And it is unlikely to change because the Theatre Royal, together with its integral Drum studio space, serves Plymouth and the West Country well. Like so many of these projects it owes a great deal to one man – Ralph Morrell, the Chairman of the Board of Management and a leading councillor when the plans to build this superb new theatre were first mooted. A far cry from the elegy to the old Theatre Royal, penned by that well-known and highly respected critic from the West Country, J. C. Trewin:

> In its declining years the Theatre Royal added nothing to stage history. It was certainly a bad date for the profession . . . Nothing mattered in the arts except the things that were being currently talked of; hence the sudden swing to the talking films that by the mid-thirties left Plymouth culturally dead. Its nadir came when in quick succession, it lost the Repertory Theatre and the Royal. I'm afraid that not many people cared.

Thanks to Ralph Morrell and other enlightened Plymouth citizens, plus a splendid theatre team, originally led by Andrew Welch and Roger Redfarn, they care a lot more now. Even so, it still has its ups and downs – as do all theatres, it seems.

Marie Lloyd as she appeared at the Tivoli and Empress in Brixton.

NEW THEATRE
Hull
(PART II)

The headlines for the week following Plymouth could have been 'Local Boy Makes Good' or 'A Prophet Welcomed in His Own Country' – for we were back on my native heath – but they weren't. Actually, the *Hull Daily Mail* was rather better, from a box office point of view: '*Reluctant Heroes* a Parade of Priceless Clowning', whilst the notice went on to qualify this further: '. . . a packed house rocked in helpless laughter . . . here is Brian Rix in a part that, for sheer comedy, will surely prove a prizewinner . . .' Poor old Basil Radford wasn't even mentioned, which was a bit unfair, for his performance had improved by leaps and bounds over the weekend, when he had really made an effort to learn his lines on the Sunday. However, the *Yorkshire Post* did recognise the improvement by writing that 'his is a magnificent part played to the full'. That put new heart into Basil and, although he was so clearly miscast, he never again drove us to despair and distraction as he had done that first unforgettable week at the Palace. We lived to fight another day.

I have visited the New Theatre in Hull on a number of occasions over the years and I have always been warmly received. *Simple Spymen* opened there on its way to the Whitehall, on a wintry 17th February, 1958, and people dug themselves out of snow-drifts just to get there. It was like being back in the war. Because of the difficulties the audience had encountered in reaching the theatre, they were even more appreciative than they had been for *Reluctant Heroes*. The weather was still lousy when we were there nine years later, week commencing 27th February, 1967, on our way to the Garrick Theatre with *Stand By Your Bedouin*, but had improved by 28th April, 1969 when *Let Sleeping Wives Lie* was on offer. The audiences, and their reactions, remained good though, on both occasions – as they did for *She's Done It Again* on 28th September, 1970.

I was not to see the New again for another six years, when – this time on our way back to the Whitehall – our offering was *Fringe Benefits* and the date was 17th May, 1976. Never again would I set foot on the stage which had been constructed on the site of the old Assembly Rooms and was the dream of Peppino Santangelo, now long retired. You will recall Pepe, from my Wolfit days, as I am sure you will recall his somewhat militant style of writing. He was still around though on 15th May, 1950, which saw the opening night of *Heroes* in Hull, but this time there was a surprise in the Editorial column:

Dear Sir,

We may or may not always agree with the arguments or comments contained in your Editorials but we do appreciate the enthusiasm that prompts them and the onerous task of writing week after week and, apparently year after year, an article on the same subject – The Theatre. Keep it up – we look forward to them.

Yours faithfully,

(Mr) S. Spencer (and Friends).

Editor's Note – Thank you – I have waited some eighteen years for some kind person to say that!

Which all goes to prove you *can* bite the hand that feeds you. You can also be a local lad who makes good and is a prophet in his own country.

Here endeth the second lesson.

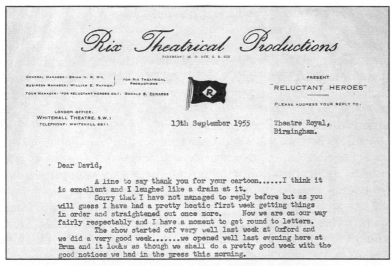

A letter from the tour manager Donald Edwards to David Drummond – still an actor – but showing an early talent for finding pleasures of past times.

KING'S THEATRE
Southsea

The inexhaustible Frank Matcham was at it again when he designed the King's, in 'Italian Renaissance' style, towards the end of his career in 1907. By the time we got there, forty-three years later, it could have done with a lick of paint – and it has hobbled along, never quite being in the first rank of touring dates, ever since. But for all that, it is a very pleasant, though somewhat large venue (1,760 seats) and in the summer months, which make up the tourist season in Southsea and nearby Portsmouth, it can play to good business. Ours, in May 1950, was so-so.

Nevertheless, Southsea's closeness to London has always, over the years, ensured a constant stream of leading actors and actresses to the theatre so that its record of attractions looks very impressive indeed. H. B. Irving, Sir Henry's son, was the first principal actor to grace its boards in September 1907 with a trilogy of his father's successes, *The Lyons Mail*, *The Bells* and *Charles I*, and on that opening night the Portsmouth Orpheus Society also made their presence felt by belting out the National Anthem before the performance began, and the audience joined in wholeheartedly. Stirring stuff, and altogether appropriate for the city harbouring Nelson's *Victory*.

Patriotism has never been in short supply in Pompey. Yes, I know Southsea and Portsmouth are really separate – but to a landlubber like me they seem as one. On the other hand, I do know that Gosport is a few miles away and its theatrical traditions go back many years. It was once part of the Reading circuit, housing a stock company run by a certain Mr Thornton – who was particularly popular with George III. I only hope he remembered his court etiquette when in the presence of the King, for Mr Thornton was particularly prone to on-stage losses of memory. One night in Gosport he forgot to hand over the letter which unravelled the plot of the particular piece he was playing, entitled *Isabella*, and died with it still clutched in his hot hand. After many hissed reminders he elegantly rose again: 'One thing I had forgot,' he proclaimed, 'through a multiplicity of business and the pressures arising therefrom – give this letter to my father; it will explain all.' Then he promptly died again.

Meanwhile, back in Southsea – or, more accurately, some time later in Southsea – Sir Frank Benson, Sir Herbert Beerbohm Tree, Wilson Barrett and Fred Terry were soon hot on HB's heels, while just over a decade after that, the famous Aldwych farces – the forerunners of mine at the Whitehall – often used the King's for their warm-up week before opening in their London home. 'Flying Matinées', with the London casts direct from their West End theatres, each for one special afternoon performance, were common in the early days, and allowed Hampshire audiences to see such artistes as the Vanbrugh sisters, Miss Violet and Dame Irene, Miss Sarah Bernhardt and Dame Ellen Terry. The latter Dame must have felt quite at home, for her grandfather used to keep a pub in Old Portsmouth called 'The Fortune of War', which again reminds us of what Portsmouth has meant to our naval tradition over the centuries. The city has never meant so much to our theatrical one, I fear, although it has tried very hard.

It all began in the mid-1850s when a certain Henry Rutley bought the Landport Hall in Portsmouth and renamed it the New Theatre Royal. His assistant at that time was J. W. Boughton who eventually took over the theatre in 1882. He immediately set about rebuilding it and engaged C. J. Phipps to design the alterations. At the same time he bought the land on which the old Prince's Theatre had stood (having recently been destroyed by fire), plus the plot next door, and kept this in escrow until he could afford to build his ideal theatre. Nine years later this came about, and Frank Matcham undertook the work on the new Prince's. Nine years later still, Mr Boughton engaged Mr Matcham once more, this time to renovate the Theatre Royal and four years after that the same couple, owner and architect, were at it again, designing and building the King's, Southsea.

Mr Boughton died in 1914, but his company – Portsmouth Theatres Ltd – continued to run the three theatres until the Prince's was 'destroyed by enemy action' in 1941. The Theatre Royal went over to bingo in 1959 (although I believe a few performances have been given since then on a thrust stage in front of the proscenium) and the King's was sold to its present management in 1964.

So, my first visit was under the old management and all my subsequent ones (a television series of Vernon Sylvaine farces, rewritten by Michael Pertwee, *Six of Rix*, on 31st May, 1971; *Don't Just Lie There, Say Something*, on its way to the Garrick, on 6th September, 1971; *A Bit Between the Teeth* on its post-London tour, on 10th March, 1975 and *Fringe Benefits*, on its way to the Whitehall, on 19th April, 1976) were under the new licensees. In my day, the King's was run by Commander Cooper and his charming wife, Joan – but now the Commander is no more, although Joan still runs it with the administrator, Ivor Barnes. Joan was herself an actress, and that is probably why all we theatricals were particularly well treated when we visited the King's. There's nothing like a little practical experience to teach you the facts of life when it comes to touring, and Joan Cooper has never forgotten that. Nor have (to be sung to the tune of 'Uncle Tom Cobley') Rex Harrison, Cicely Courtneidge, Evelyn Laye, Noël Coward, Vanessa Redgrave, Dotty Tutin, Sybil Thorndike, old uncle Lewis Casson and all, old uncle Lewis Casson and all . . . (end of song – resume normal speech). Knights, Dames and Commanders of the Order of the British Empire they may be (or have been), but they recognised a good gaff when they saw one.

After Southsea, it was a jolly little trip to South Wales and the Prince of Wales Theatre, Cardiff, but as I have already done justice to this venue, can we take it as read, please, and move on to our next date? Thank you.

Kings Theatre, Southsea

THEATRE ROYAL *Birmingham*
and, while we are at it, the
ALEXANDRA THEATRE *Birmingham*
not forgetting the
BIRMINGHAM HIPPODROME

At the turn of the century there were eleven theatres entertaining the Brum general public. Apart from the three in the title they were the Prince of Wales, the Temperance Hall, the Empire, the Curzon Hall, the London Museum Concert Hall, the New Grand Theatre, the Metropole and the Imperial Theatre. The famous Rep hadn't yet opened. Now (apart from the Rep) only three are still standing: the Alex, the Hippo and, in a totally different guise, the London Museum Concert Hall. Mind you, the latter is used to change. William Coutts reopened the theatre in 1896 and renamed it Coutts Theatre after himself. He then, however, lost his licence and went on to build the Lyceum Theatre, which was the forerunner of the Alexandra of today. After that the ex-Coutts theatre became, in succession, the Bull Ring Cinema, a fruit warehouse, a restaurant, a nightclub and a karate centre. You will gather that it might well be considered lost, as a place of dramatic entertainment, although a certain amount of histrionic ability does go with a really effective karate chop. But I digress . . .

When *Reluctant Heroes* visited the Theatre Royal in the week commencing Monday 5th June, 1950, the place was still owned by Moss' Empires Ltd (with Prince Littler as the chairman and Val Parnell as the managing director) and the city was sweltering in a heatwave. So were we, in our army uniforms, and the pretty sparse audience's reaction was pretty muted, to say the least. In spite of these shortcomings, however, it was this week which, provided the spark which ignited the charge which propelled us on, to live in the house, which Edward Stone built – the Whitehall Theatre. The unlikely pyrotechnist was none other than a manufacturer of nuts and bolts from Wolverhampton, by the name of H. J. Barlow who, for some obscure reason, had offered his money and management to put on R. F. Delderfield's *Worm's Eye View* at the Whitehall, then in its fifth 'Fantastic' year. I reasoned that the *Worm* must be running somewhat out of steam (for Ronnie Shiner had left the cast to go into *Seagulls Over Sorrento* and Basil Lord, good as he was, could not be classed as a stupendous 'draw' like Ronnie), and so I invited Mr Barlow to view *Heroes* as a possible successor. Mr Barlow came, saw and, in spite of the heat, was conquered – but, all to no avail, for he had already decided to leave the Whitehall and move his production over to the Comedy Theatre. He could do nothing for us. However, he did have the good grace to enthuse about us to the owners of the Whitehall, who ignored his advice and took in another play instead. This, thank God, was a disaster, and so the Whitehall eventually approached us and that is how we came to open at that theatre on 12th September, 1950, exactly three months after that dehydrating débâcle in Birmingham. Nuts and bolts may have been Mr Barlow's living, but he was pretty prescient as a producer, too.

Six years after that all-important date, the curtain fell at the Theatre Royal for the last time. The building was then sold and demolished and a Woolworth's store was built on the site that had housed a theatre for over 180 years. But in these acquisitive days it's easier to sell cheap goods than it is cheap seats, even though – according to Jonathan Swift – ''tis as cheap sitting as standing'.

All my subsequent visits to Birmingham, theatrically that is, were to the Alexandra Theatre, for so long the home of the Salberg family. I used to love going there, for business was marvellous, Derek Salberg was a splendid host and the audience's reaction was wonderful. So much so, that in his autobiography, *My Love Affair With a Theatre*, Derek wrote: 'Early in 1967 Brian Rix again packed the theatre, this time with *Stand By Your Bedouin*. Indeed, only once, on that occasion with a double bill, did he ever fail to draw capacity houses, for although, whenever his farces were announced, many regular patrons cancelled, they were always replaced by a considerably bigger number.' I'm not complaining. Bottoms on seats is what it's all about, and there were 1,367 posteriors at every performance when I was there, give or take the odd double-booking, or the extra lot standing. No wonder I liked the place.

Altogether I played at the Alex on seven occasions, and if you want to know when, a complete record of all the tours in which I was involved over the years appears as an appendix to this book, together with a few other details, which you might find of interest – if you are so minded. But for now, I must concentrate on the story of the Alexandra itself. I have already started the ball rolling by mentioning William Coutts and how he built the theatre, as the Lyceum, in 1901.

Mr Coutts' attempts to promote melodrama at the theatre proved to be a disaster and, a little over a year after the Lyceum had opened, it was up for sale and bought for a mere pittance – £4,450 to be precise – by a Mr Lester Collingwood, who promptly changed the name to the Alexandra in honour of the Queen. Described as a 'flamboyant' personality, he sported a magnificent moustache under which was suspended a huge cigar, dropping ash on a large expanse of waistcoat offset by the inevitable gold watch and chain. Lower still were immaculate trousers which, it is said, were quite often removed in pursuit of frequent amorous adventures. In his spare time, Mr Collingwood managed the theatre and was particularly successful

Clockwise from top left: Ben Jonson and a dramatic performance in the theatre of his day; outside the Theatre Drury Lane c. 1660; a performance of John Grouse and Mother Goose in Covent Garden c. 1805.

Clockwise from top left: John Philip Kemble as Rolla in Sheridan's *Pizarro* and his niece Fanny as Isabella in *The Fatal Marriage;* Richard III as played by Edmund Kean and George Cooke; Samuel Phelps as King John.

Clockwise from top left:
Gustavus Brooke as
Richard III; Frank Benson as
Coriolanus; a caricature of
Johnston Forbes-Robertson
confers with Hamlet's creator.

Types of playgoers – from the gallery to the stalls (according to artists of the time).

Marriages made in Heaven?
Top left: David Garrick and his wife; *top right:* Madge and William Kendal; *centre:*
Nina de Silva and John Martin-Harvey; *bottom:* Rosalind Iden and Donald Wolift.

Theatre Knights.
Clockwise from top left: John Gielgud;
Michael Redgrave; Alec Guinness; Ralph
Richardson; Brian Rix; Laurence Olivier
and Charles Wyndham.

Theatre Dames.
Clockwise from top left: Flora Robson;
Genevieve Ward; Gwen Ffrangcon Davies;
Wendy Hiller; Peggy Ashcroft; Sybil
Thorndike and Edith Evans.

Top: the week before Basil Radford took over in the tour of *Reluctant Heroes.* In a pub, naturally! *Left to right:* Wally Patch, George Radford, the author, Elspet Gray, Basil Radford, Larry Nobel, the Landlord and in front, Alan Scott. *Left:* the beginning of the Whitehall run of *Reluctant Heroes.* Neon lighting wasn't allowed until 1953 – a legacy from the war. *Right:* the souvenir programme cover for *Dry Rot* at the Whitehall in 1954.

with his pantomimes – he occasionally graced the boards himself by appearing as the moustachioed villain in melodrama. All was going splendidly, until Lester's penchant for the ladies proved his undoing. On his way to 'audition' an actress in Sheffield, his car collided with a milk float, and he was killed. Quite an original way to go, really, especially as he was one of the first fatalities to occur because of the motor car and quite definitely the first to be killed by a milk float.

Along came Leon Salberg, together with his brothers-in-law, Joshua and Julius Thomas, who purchased the theatre from the Executors. Leon was in charge and, in spite of having no previous theatrical experience, he turned out to have great theatrical flair. The Alexandra prospered, although after the First World War it settled into Number Two theatre status, having found it hard to compete for the Number One touring attractions which were being booked into the nearby Theatre Royal and Prince of Wales. Pantomime still flourished at the Alex, though, and in 1927 Leon Salberg decided to fill in the rest of the year with repertory. This policy continued with great success from then until 1974, when rep was discontinued.

Mind you, touring attractions had started again, as part of the annual programme, way back in 1952, but rep continued to be the mainstay of the Alex, together with the pantomime. This was in spite of the Birmingham Rep being just down the road in Station Street. Eventually though, the problems that beset many touring theatres in the 1960s and 1970s took their toll on the Alex, and in 1968 the Birmingham City Council paid a miserly £85,000 for the theatre, which just about cleared the overdraft and the debenture holders. However, the Council did make a small annual grant to the theatre as well, which helped. Derek, though, who had taken over the running of the Alex when his father Leon died in 1937, was left with nothing other than a theatre to run which was in desperate need of investment. Despite all his worries, however, Derek was an unhappy man when the time came, on his sixty-fifth birthday, to retire from the theatre he loved. In his final curtain speech, he quoted the words spoken by David Garrick at his last performance: 'This is to me a very awful moment; it is no less than parting for ever with those from whom I have received the greatest kindness and favours and on the spot where that kindness and those favours were enjoyed.'

No man of the theatre could put it better than that.

And so, finally, to the Hippodrome which opened in October 1899 as the Tower of Varieties and Circus. This rather clumsy title went with an equally clumsy policy, and the theatre lasted less than a year. It reopened as the Tivoli Theatre of Varieties in August 1900 and stayed that way for a further three years, when it became the Hippodrome. Variety, early films, gramophone demonstrations and a policy for disabled people ('Invalids in bathchairs can be accommodated') kept it going for yet another seven years and then it changed hands again. Variety, musical comedy and revue were the next attractions, which worked well, until the beginning of the First World War. Once again there were problems, but the theatre pushed ahead with alterations and in 1917 it reopened for the fourth time in eighteen years advertising 'High Class Varieties and First Run Pictures'. Less than two years later, it closed a further time for yet more rebuilding, which must have caused many a raised eyebrow regarding the original quality of workmanship or architectural ability of the local professionals concerned. This time, though, the rebuilding was delayed for six years, when Moss' Empires took over and from 1925 until 1979 ran the theatre with varying degrees of success. The first thirty years of their tenure were highly prosperous, but gradually the malaise affecting all the big touring houses affected the Hippodrome too, so much so that for a time Moss' changed the name of the theatre to the 'Birmingham Theatre' in an effort to promote new interest, with wrestling, fashion shows and even Kung Fu taking place in the building to widen audience participation. This was all to no avail, and in 1979 the Birmingham City Council purchased the freehold and a new era began.

Again the theatre was closed for restoration and rebuilding – to the tune of £5 million – which enabled the theatre 'to house the largest opera and ballet productions, lavish West End musicals and top companies and stars across the broadest spectrum of live entertainment, thus enhancing its reputation as a major regional centre for the performing arts'. As you may have guessed, I was quoting from a Press handout, but what is written there is largely true and, in addition, the Sadler's Wells Ballet (now the Birmingham Royal Ballet) has moved its permanent home to the Hippodrome, and the Birmingham City Council has spent a further £4 million on the company's new facilities, with the Arts Council chipping in another £2 million.

It makes the Tower of Varieties and Circus seem like very small beer indeed, doesn't it?

EMBASSY THEATRE
Peterborough
KEY THEATRE
Peterborough

I regret to report that 'the Peterborough effect' on me was precisely nil. So much so, in fact, that for years I have been telling a story about an extra matinée that was mounted at the Embassy on a bank holiday Monday, which I have now discovered to be a load of old codswallop. When I came to write this part of the book, I looked up my diaries and discovered that we did not actually visit Peterborough on a bank holiday. We were there well into June and our Whit bank holiday had been celebrated at the Prince of Wales, Cardiff. There was no May Day bank holiday in those days (in spite of the Labour government) so I looked up August bank holiday (which was then at the beginning of the month) and discovered that we were visiting the Theatre Royal, Norwich on that date. *That's* where the extra matinée took place, so I will tell you the story when we reach that particular venue. A pity though. I mean, what can you say about Peterborough that they haven't already said about themselves? Absolutely nothing, as far as I can see.

The Embassy was built in 1937 as a cinema-cum-variety theatre and it closed as a theatre in the early 1960s, to become a cinema with 1,484 seats. This was a useful-sized house because local amateur musicals and the occasional professional pantomime could still use the theatre – until ABC Cinemas twinned the auditorium, and any further theatrical use was no longer possible.

Peterborough was not to be without its theatre, however. In 1973 a group of citizens, who had come together as the Peterborough Arts Theatre Trust, opened the Key Theatre. They had been helped in their scheme by both the local authority and the Arts Council, and six years later the Peterborough City Council became the proud owners of the small theatre – with just under 400 seats – which is pleasantly situated on the banks of the River Nene and which supports a varied programme of events, including tours, one-day concerts, pantomime and the inevitable local amateur dramatic societies, which have moved there from the old Embassy. Of course, being such a small house does mean that tours

visiting the theatre generally have to have a guarantee, but the management seem to be only too willing to oblige.

As I have mentioned on several occasions, the average touring show
visits a theatre on sharing terms, which can vary from sixty/forty per cent
to seventy/thirty per cent, according to the size of the production, the
capacity of the house and the drawing power of the attraction. The larger
percentage goes to the producing management who pay the salaries, travelling expenses, part of the printing, hire of equipment and costumes etc.,
plus the amortisation of their production costs. The theatre owners, who
keep all the bar and programme takings, pay out of their smaller share
the costs of the front-of-house and backstage staff, the electricity charges
(which can be considerable in these days of lighting designers), the clean-
ing and the upkeep of the theatre, as well as their own management
expenditure. The costs of the get-in and get-out are shared. Sometimes,
however, the theatre has to provide the touring manager with a minimum
guarantee against his percentage share, which can make it possible for a
more expensive show to visit the smaller (or dicier) houses, without losing
a fortune. This way, any fortune that is lost is generally borne by the local
council or, sometimes, by the Arts Council. Obviously, there is often
considerable argument as to whether or not a guarantee is necessary, with
the host manager taking a diametrically opposite view to his producing
counterpart. If you have the attraction, though, you always win – but with
the bricks and mortar generally arguing that if you are so certain of your
product, why do you want a guarantee in the first place? The answer is
simple: 'Because your theatre is too small' or 'because your audience is
notoriously fickle' or, less generally, 'because you are a cheating bastard
and I wouldn't trust you as far as I can throw you and want to see the
colour of your money first before I set foot in your tatty theatre.' Over
the years I have used all three arguments with considerable success. Or,
rather, Renée Stepham has – with far greater tact than I have suggested,
I hasten to add.

When we first visited Peterborough in 1950 we were so unknown there
was no way we could possibly demand a guarantee against our share. So
unknown, in fact, we were lucky to get a share at all. It's a wonder we
didn't have to pay the rent. Things were very different twenty-six years
later when we arrived with *Fringe Benefits* on our way to the Whitehall.
No less than three producing managements were involved – Duncan Weldon, Ray Cooney and me. We got our guarantee all right, but with only
3,192 people able to see the play during the entire week that is not
altogether surprising. What *is* surprising is that the amount was great
enough to cover the overheads of three separate managers and I wouldn't
mind betting it wasn't . . .

THEATRE ROYAL
Bath

When I first visited this glorious Georgian theatre in Beaufort Square, in the week commencing Monday 19th June, 1950, the theatre was showing signs of becoming threadbare, which is not altogether surprising when you consider that it was built in 1805. Designed by George Dance and supervised by the city architect John Palmer, the Theatre Royal was the successor to the Little Theatre in Orchard Street, which had seen the beginnings of Sarah Siddons' career and which was one of the first provincial theatres to be granted a Royal Patent in 1768. The title of Theatre Royal was transferred to the new theatre when it opened with Shakespeare's *Richard III*. You might be forgiven for supposing this to have been a success, but you would be wrong. Although the majority of the company were professional, the leading man was a 'gentleman' amateur, who suffered from first-night nerves, forgot his lines and was greeted with singularly unBath-like opprobrium. I imagine he would, indeed, have given his kingdom for a horse that night.

In spite of this opening hiccup, the theatre prospered – and was visited, amongst others, by William Charles Macready, Edmund Kean, the Duke of Clarence's mistress, Mrs Jordan, and the ever-popular Sarah Siddons, then launched into her phenomenally successful career. These happy times lasted for about twenty years, but began to decline when the Prince Regent decided to go to Brighton to absorb the ozone rather than to Bath to take the waters, and ended in disaster when the theatre was practically gutted by fire on Good Friday 1862. The poor manager at the time was one James Henry Chute who was not properly insured, but he decided to battle on, regardless. A competition was held to decide on the design, which was won by a local architect C. J. Phipps – and this was to be his very first theatre commission. It was but the precursor of many to come.

The theatre reopened less than a year after the fire in March 1863, and once more William Shakespeare was the chosen playwright with a production of *A Midsummer Night's Dream*. Continuity of policy was maintained some 119 years later, when the refurbished Theatre Royal was reopened yet again with the National Theatre's offering of the same play, but it is very doubtful that any of the original audience were around to make comparisons, in spite of the health-giving properties of the famous spa waters. Indeed, it is open to question if they would have done much better, even if they had followed the Prince Regent and staked their all on ozone. What is certain, though, is that Mr Phipps' designs for the Theatre Royals in Bath and Brighton have given great pleasure and joy to many theatre-goers for nearly a century and a half. But forget the spa and the seaside, and relax and build up your energies in the ambience of the theatres instead.

By the time we arrived in Bath the Theatre Royal, as I have mentioned, was looking decidedly the worse for wear and audiences were distinctly fickle. The Maddox family had taken over the management of the theatre in 1938; Reg, the father, had died and his widow, Nellie, and son, Frank, ran the place. The very week we arrived we read the following gloomy forebodings in the programme, which hardly filled us with optimism:

> As most patrons know, during these past few weeks, and in the future, the Management are endeavouring to bring as many top-flight stars of stage, screen and radio to Bath as possible. This can only be achieved of course, if the support given to the Theatre is both regular and encouraging . . . yet still there are far too few 'regular' theatre supporters, and people who make permanent bookings, to justify all the very best productions risking Bath on their tour sheet . . . There are many towns which have completely lost their theatres through lack of support and in most of these cases these buildings have been obliged to close and sell their interests . . . It is therefore every theatre lover's duty to see that the Theatre in his own midst does not suffer this most dreadful fate.

It was Frank Maddox's custom to walk round the dressing-rooms before the curtain went up on a Monday night and invite the cast to a post-performance drink in the Circle bar while, at the same time, handing out a programme to each member of the company. You can imagine the joy with which we read his managerial message, especially as the curtain rose to a pretty thin house, that confirmed his pessimistic prognostications. Even the drink in the bar after the show was more like a wake than a celebration, and we were definitely depressed. Fortunately, the notice in the *Bath and Wilts Chronicle and Herald* was infinitely more uplifting – '*Reluctant Heroes* ONE LONG LAUGH' – so we did persuade a few non-regulars to attend, but it was, without doubt, a struggle at the old Theatre Royal. As it was for many years.

Then came the metamorphosis. In the 1970s the Theatre Royal slipped out of the Maddox grasp and changed hands on several occasions, like an ill-judged slip catch. Finally, in 1979, local businessman Jeremy Fry bought the property and turned it over to a Charitable Trust, which was then forced to close the theatre as it was in danger of collapse; particularly the backstage area, for the stage itself was supported by rotting pit props, and the ancient wooden grid (from which you 'fly' the scenery, suspended in the old days on hemp 'lines', that is, ropes) was literally falling to pieces. So much so that chunks of wood fell on the heads of the Kent Opera Company (now, too, defunct – like most of the Theatre Royal's decaying equipment), who had to perform in front of the house tabs (the curtains) for safety's sake! Clearly, a great deal of money needed to be spent on restoration.

This came from a variety of sources, with considerable help from the Arts Council and the local authorities, while members of the public were extremely generous, too. Unfortunately, the first estimates to restore the theatre to its erstwhile glory were wildly in excess of the money raised, but a white knight, again in the shape of a property developer, was at hand. His name was Laurie Marsh, and I had just finished working with him at Cooney-Marsh Ltd, before joining MENCAP as that charity's secretary-general. (If you want to know all about that, may I refer you to my last book, *Farce About Face*, also published by Hodder & Stoughton, which I guarantee will fill in all the missing details. May I also refer you to the quotes: 'A doughty fighter, and a refreshing book,' *Daily Express*; 'A proud story,' *Sunday Telegraph*; and 'Fascinating,' J. C. Trewin. There. The plug is now over and we return to our white knight.)

I do not know if Laurie Marsh did anything to ruffle a few feathers in Bath, but in view of his heroic efforts to squeeze a quart out of a pint pot, I find the total absence of his name in the current theatre literature concerning the restoration to be incomprehensible. 'Thanks to the skills of Donald Armstrong and Carl Toms, the architect and designer who oversaw the restoration, the auditorium is once more a credit to C. J. Phipps, the famous theatre architect who was its original creator.' So runs the blurb for the 'Appeal Phase II' – 'Financing the Future', but no mention, you will notice, of Mr Marsh. You have to go back to a local Press report in June 1981 to discover that:

Bath's Theatre Royal has slashed more than £1 million off a £3½ million renovation bill by forming its own construction company. The scheme revealed at an open day today is believed to be the first of its kind in the country, and is the idea of theatre and cinema restorer Laurie Marsh . . . Theatre chairman, Jeremy Fry, one of the construction company's unpaid directors said: 'Since we announced plans for the theatre, costs have spiralled from £2 million to £3½ million. We felt it unrealistic to expect to raise such a sum, and had to find a fresh way forward. We met Laurie Marsh and with his help we've created a highly professional organisation.

So professional, in fact, that they now omit Laurie's name altogether from the paeans of praise heaped on all the other contributors. There's something odd, somewhere.

When I returned to the theatre in 1988 for our four-month season of *Dry Rot* at the Lyric Theatre, Shaftesbury Avenue, we opened out of town for two weeks at the Theatre Royal, Bath. It was a very pleasant fortnight in a lovely city and a lovely theatre, and it was equally pleasant to be appearing once again in a play with my wife, Elspet Gray. Elspet was housed in a delightful dressing-room backstage at the Theatre Royal, bearing the name of its benefactor. Guess who? Yes, you are right in one. Laurie Marsh. And he even had to pay for that privilege. About £25,000, I believe.

'"Curiouser and curiouser!" cried Alice.'

Our next two dates on tour, at the Royal Court Theatre, Liverpool and the Theatre Royal, Nottingham, have been already dealt with, so we now take a further trip overleaf and to the seaside . . .

THE LITTLE THEATRE
Bournemouth
alias PALACE COURT THEATRE
alias THE PLAYHOUSE
alas THE WESSEX CHRISTIAN CENTRE

I have played at this delightful little theatre in two of its past disguises. But I must confess – which is apposite – that I have never set foot in it since it assumed a religious role. When I first went there, it was to the Palace Court Theatre in July 1950. The summer season had started and we were greeted with headlines such as 'They laughed until they cried' and the theatre was *full*. '"O frabjous day! Calooh! Callay!" He chortled in his joy.'

I next visited the theatre twenty-five years later in 1975, when we played a summer season – from 30th June to 20th September – with a piece called *A Bit Between the Teeth*, by Michael Pertwee but based on an idea of mine. By then the theatre was the Playhouse but it was still comfortably full for the entire three months we were there.

But here is the story of the theatre. The Bournemouth Dramatic and Orchestral Club, an amateur group, had delusions of grandeur and decided to build a theatre of their own. So they borrowed plans from two similar clubs at the Oxford Theatre and the Bristol Little Theatre, and handed them over to two local architects, a Mr Seal and a Mr Hardy, who I feel must also have had a squint at Edward Stone's plans for the Whitehall, because the theatre, especially the front-of-house façade, is remarkably similar to its London counterpart. Even the opening dates were similar. The Whitehall was opened on 29th September, 1930 and the Little Theatre began nine months later (could it have been a gestation period?) on 15th June, 1931. However, the productions were different. Showing at the Whitehall was the highly professional Walter Hackett's *The Way to Treat a Woman*, starring Marion Lorne, which ran for 263 performances, while the amateurs, now known as the Bournemouth Little Theatre Club, were even more ambitious, presenting *The Merry Wives of Windsor* and *Berkeley Square* – each of which ran for four performances.

From then on, the Little Theatre continued to present its amateur productions, but supplemented its income for the remaining weeks of the year with seasons of repertory and tours. Resources were stretched to the limit and in order to make it easier to track down, particularly for visitors, the name of the theatre was changed to match the hotel next door – the Palace Court – and so it battled on.

By the 1960s audiences had dropped alarmingly and, in spite of support from the Bournemouth Borough Council and the Arts Council, the bank was anxious to have definite plans as to how the overdraft was to be repaid. There was no alternative other than to 'dispose of the property' and eventually in 1970 the Club sold the theatre to a board member, Louis Michaels. I have already mentioned on page 134, that by the time Louis Michaels died he had acquired the Theatre Royal, Brighton; the Richmond-on-the-Green Theatre; the Haymarket and the Strand Theatres in London, but the Palace Court, Bournemouth was the beginning of his interest in the theatre. It was also through his partnership with Duncan Weldon in the producing management of Triumph Theatre Productions Ltd that I came to be at the Playhouse, Bournemouth, in the summer of 1975. Not only had Louis renamed the theatre yet again, but he and Duncan were co-presenters with me of *A Bit Between the Teeth* during that happy, sunny, summer season when I actually swam in the English Channel.

After Louis Michaels' death, the theatre was sold to a church group, and the building's name was changed for a fourth time to the Wessex Christian Centre. The Theatres Trust and the Theatres Advisory Council tried to stop the change of use from a theatre to a revivalist hall, but all to no avail. Not altogether surprising really. A case of *nam homo proponit, sed Deus disponit.*

Yes, you were right. 'Man proposes but God disposes.' It just sounds more impressive in Latin, that's all.

GRAND THEATRE
Swansea

We arrived at the Grand Theatre, Swansea, on Monday 17th July, 1950, to find chaos. Apparently the electrician had drunk more than was good for him on the previous Saturday night – had been sacked and proceeded to avenge himself by smashing up the switchboard with a five-pound hammer. So there we were: two sets, eleven actors and actresses, a few advance bookings but *no* lights. But, as always seemed to happen in those days, a good Samaritan was there to give us a hand – this time in the person of Archie Pipe. He'd looked after the lighting for a number of amateur shows and offered his services, which were gratefully received. He slaved away all day trying to create some order out of chaos and at 7.30 up went the curtain on a stage lit in what can best be described as Stygian gloom. But that Swansea audience is one of the warmest in Britain. They peered through the murk and laughed and laughed. Perhaps they were all miners and found our lighting positively dazzling! At any rate, Archie Pipe decided to stay in the business and eventually became a big success in America – in the production side of religious programmes. Lead kindly light . . .

I wrote this in the first part of my autobiography, *My Farce From My Elbow* but I have never told the sequel to the story, which took place the next time I visited the theatre, some twenty-three years later, with the post-London tour of *Don't Just Lie There, Say Something*.

I was being interviewed by the local *South Wales Evening Post* on the Tuesday after the opening night of Michael Pertwee's very funny farce about two politicians – one venal and the other the soul of rectitude. Moray Watson was the philanderer. I was the virtuous one. It was a glorious day and we were sitting outside, enjoying the sunshine and the views of Rotherslade Bay, and I certainly wasn't attempting to be either virtuous or politic when I commented on the brightness of the scene and compared it unfavourably with the continuing gloom and inadequate facilities backstage at the Grand. I went on to complain that the local

159

council – which had taken over the lease of the theatre some four years earlier – had recently spent about £40,000 on the front-of-house, but absolutely nothing on conditions backstage, which were primitive and plain filthy to say the least. The anonymous *Evening Post Reporter* duly recorded my comments, which brought forth strenuous replies from the leader of the Swansea City Council, as well as from Ronnie Williams, one half of the Welsh comedy duo Ryan and Ronnie. Mr Williams even went so far as to state he and his partner 'went to Swansea to entertain the public – not to stay at the Hilton'. As we had broken all house records entertaining the public during our week at the Grand, this was too good an opportunity to miss, and I wrote the following letter to the *Evening Post*, which was published in full. I think it tells this sorry theatrical tale rather well:

Sir,

Having set the cat among the pigeons regarding backstage conditions at the Grand Theatre, I thought I should also set the record straight regarding any misapprehensions which may have arisen.

Last Friday, Ronnie Williams enquired whether or not I desired to work in conditions more suitable to the Hilton than the Grand. If working in the Hilton means you do not have to go to the Gents' through an old workshop-cum-paintshop, past a miniature horse trough which serves as the laundry and then into a lean-to outhouse, freezing cold and more reminiscent of wartime R A F ablutions than 1973 peacetime loos – then, yes, I would prefer the Hilton.

If rooms at the Hilton do not have windows nine feet off the ground, barred to stop anyone getting in or out – jammed shut so that it is impossible to open them to get a breath of fresh air – then this would seem to be another plus for the hotel.

Some of the dressing-rooms at the Grand even have three-inch nails and screws driven into the walls to act as coat hooks. Splendid for tearing expensive suits and dresses – but hardly suitable, I feel, for the idle rich at the Hilton.

Perhaps my mentioning that most Civic Theatres nowadays have a shower-bath provoked comparison with the Hilton? Lest this should be considered an extravagance, let me remind Mr Williams that in these permissive days actors and actresses are exposing more of themselves than their faces and hands, with the consequence that body make-up has to be worn. Frankly, it is very difficult to wash off, with one buttock balanced on the basin!

Mr Williams refers to it as 'our' Grand. You have every right to be proud of 'your' Grand in terms of the warm-hearted and generous audience – surely among the best in the country; in terms of the splendid auditorium and the fact that the civic authorities cared enough to come to the rescue of the theatre four years ago; in terms of your Theatre Club, which has recently raised £1,000 to put in a new counter-weight system and in terms of your dedicated and hard-working theatre staff and management.

But if you want the best shows to come regularly to 'your' theatre, you must realise that actors *have* become used to reasonable working conditions. Why not make Swansea an automatic choice for the choosiest – so that the theatre will flourish and grow and not become a fill-in touring date or occasionally be acceptable to the loyal artists who live in the area?

For very little money miracles could be wrought backstage. Your superb audiences deserve the best. They will get it, if the Grand becomes a Civic Theatre of which you can be proud, front *and* back.

Thank you for the use of this space. And please convey my grateful thanks to all those who made our box office record possible last week.

Yours etc.,

Brian Rix

I think you will agree that I sounded more like a politician there, didn't I? And I am happy to report that the Swansea City Council eventually bought the freehold of the property and between 1986 and 1989 spent over £7 million on the Grand, which is difficult to describe as 'very little money'. The theatre now has an entirely new front-of-house but, best of all, an entirely new *and* Hiltonesque backstage. Don't just lie there, *say* something paid off after all, wouldn't you say?

PALACE PIER THEATRE
Brighton

Although we had already played the Dolphin, Brighton, it seemed to be a good idea to revisit the town since the school holidays were in full swing and the *Sussex Daily News* reported that we were, indeed, 'ideal holiday entertainment'. By now I had signed the contract to go to the Whitehall, but we had to wait for Wally Patch to return to the cast before this was possible. In the meantime, Sgt Bell was played by the author of *Reluctant Heroes*, Colin Morris, and a jolly good job he made of it, too – although he and I did not always see eye to eye over how far I could go with the funny business. Marking time with my foot jammed firmly in a bucket, pressed up against the wall, was one particular moment I relished and I was inclined, shall we say, to milk this to my heart's content. As Colin was watching this, ready to shout 'Are you going far, Gregory?' and 'Say something, son, if it's only goodbye!', laughs in themselves, you can perhaps understand his impatience as I banged and clattered away with gay abandon. The schoolkids loved it. But then, so did I.

The Palace Pier Theatre opened in 1901. When we were there it was owned by the Brighton Marine Palace and Pier Co. which advertised, amongst its attractions, 'The Palace Players' who played daily (except Fridays) in the Deck Café from three-fifteen to four-forty-five p.m., and 'Dancing at the Pier Head' nightly from seven-fifteen to ten-fifteen p.m. In spite of this cornucopia of delights, the Palace Pier had to struggle to survive. Its last season presented 'The Golden Years of Music Hall' with Walter Landau, Bob and Alf Pearson, Marjorie Manners, Don Smoothey and Sandy ('can you hear me, mother?') Powell heading the bill. Then it was all over. A fierce storm in 1973 dislodged a barge, which was moored to a nearby landing stage, and drove it into the pier, which was badly damaged. Even though the pier soon re-opened and came under new management in 1984, the theatre remained closed, and was demolished in 1986. Well, I mean, could anything survive with its groynes and stanchions wrenched? I know I couldn't.

THEATRE ROYAL
Norwich

Now is my chance to tell the story I felt sure took place in Peterborough. But it didn't – it was in Norwich. For some unknown reason, the owner of the Theatre Royal, Jack Gladwin, decided to slip in an extra matinée on the August bank holiday Monday. This meant a very hurried get-in and set-up which, if wet, might have been worthwhile. It wasn't wet. In fact it was scorching and a disconsolate manager came round to see me minutes before the curtain went up and reported that only seven people were in front. Seven! It was hard to imagine anything worse. Clad in thick army uniforms and greatcoats, with a temperature outside pushing into the nineties, we contemplated the idea of the matinée with total dismay. I then had a bright idea. 'Why not ask them if they would like a free cup of tea, instead of watching us boil, and see if they can come later in the week,' I suggested. The manager agreed it was a jolly good wheeze, went on-stage, parted the front-of-house tabs and stepped forward to polite applause. 'Ladies and gentlemen,' he began, quite incorrectly, for there wasn't a man in the audience, just seven old ladies, 'ladies and gentlemen, would you care for a cup of tea?' Before he could blurt out the rest of the bargain, the Trojan women had chorused 'yes'. He then propositioned them further. To no avail. They were going to enjoy the cup that cheers *and* have a bit of a giggle into the bargain, and nothing would change their collective mind. We played the matinée. The memory of that lonely experience has stayed with me over the years. I just located it in the wrong town, that's all.

Mind you, we nearly missed the next evening's show anyway, which would have kept the number of performances down to the standard eight. The entire company hired a boat and went on to the Broads for the day. Halfway through the afternoon one of our members dropped a rope into the water. Sheets aren't they called, in nautical terms? Anyway, this rope became entangled around the blade of the propeller and our engine spluttered to a coughing halt. We were marooned in the middle of Wroxham Broad, literally without a paddle, slowly floating into the reeds, where we became stuck fast. Panic set in. We were miles from Norwich and the hour of curtain-up time was fast approaching. We shouted and hollered to any passing boat and finally one family stopped, listened to our tale of woe and offered to tow us back to base. We accepted with gratitude but didn't realise how slow such a journey would be. Time was ticking away and, back at the Theatre Royal, the stage management, who had declined to come on the outing, were beginning to wonder at the eerie hush which pervaded the dressing-rooms. Never had they heard such a deafening silence – which was to continue long after the half. The same manager who had brought the glum tidings about the size of our Monday matinée audience was informed and began to think it was a carefully organised plot by us to get our own back and was planning all manner of contractual penalties, as well as yet another speech of apology and explanation in front of the curtain, to an audience that would certainly be larger than seven. His homework was in vain. At the five, the entire cast of eleven screeched up to the stage door in the only two cars owned by members of the company, mine and Dermot Walsh's, leapt out, dashed into the theatre, threw on their costumes, clattered down to the stage and spot on time the curtain went up, leaving a very disappointed manager, who had been relishing visions of draconian fines which would have compensated the theatre for its losses, suffered as a result of the previous day's extra empty matinée. He was furious.

By the way, for the uninitiated, 'the half' is thirty-five minutes before the curtain goes up and 'the five' is ten minutes before the rise. 'The quarter' leaves twenty minutes to go, while 'beginners' is exactly five minutes to the off. 'Prompt side' (P.S.) is always actors' left and 'O.P.' (opposite prompt or off prompt) is always actors' right, even if the prompt corner is on the right of the stage, rather than in the usual position on the left. Just thought you should know.

As to the Theatre Royal, Norwich itself, it was built in 1936 by the Odeon group of cinemas and taken over by the Essoldo chain soon after. It was totally modernised in 1970, retaining its Odeon décor, and finally sold by Essoldo to the Norwich District Council, which created the Theatre Royal Norwich Trust, and this Trust runs the theatre to this day. Since my first visit in those cinematic 1950s I have only visited the theatre in its new guise twice. Once in 1971 with *Six of Rix* – one-hour versions of Vernon Sylvaine's farces, rewritten by Michael Pertwee, and presented, on tour, in pairs as a double bill, with BBC Television recording the productions in front of an invited audience at the Opera House, Manchester, the Grand Theatre, Leeds and the Theatre Royal, Norwich; and once in 1975 with *A Bit Between the Teeth*. Considering my forebears came from East Anglia, I seem to have toured there on very few occasions. Perhaps *that's* what is meant by a prophet in his own country. No wonder the family moved to Hull.

We were now very definitely 'busking till ready' which, in layman's terms, means marking time. No, I'm wrong. That is in H M Service terms, but as *Reluctant Heroes* was an army farce, perhaps the latter expression would be more appropriate. What I am trying to say is that we were filling in till the return of Wally Patch to our company and until that awful little farce, *The Dish Ran Away*, had worked out its notice at the Whitehall. It must have received the worst reviews of the decade when it opened earlier in the summer, business was terrible and that is the only reason the Whitehall management had bothered to take H. J. Barlow's advice and contact me. But I wasn't proud – just grateful!

We were off to the seaside yet again – but, then, August used to be a good month for our resorts. Till the package tours, that is. Or until we arrived . . .

VICTORIA PAVILION
Ilfracombe

I have a photograph of the Victoria Pavilion, New Concert Hall and Pleasure Grounds, Ilfracombe, on a programme, taken shortly after the Second World War. It is more reminiscent of the wartime era, than peacetime, for it manages to look like buildings huddled under the Rock of Gibraltar. One glance at the contents of the programme, however, and you are quickly disabused. 'You must see YE OLDE MANOR FARM with its Haunted Room AT CHAMBERCOMBE' reads one advert. 'FOR A REAL THRILL come for a trip in the fast Speed Boats WHOOPEE ROCKET & SPRAY' reads another. No, I'm wrong again. Those ads could have been penned and displayed with equal facility in Gib, come to think of it. I once went into a caff there which was offering on the menu 'Turboot' and 'Château Brian'. I thought they were being personal.

The Victoria Pavilion was woefully inadequate in terms of space, and once more good old demurrage came into play, for we had to leave most of Act III – the barn set – back at the station because there simply wasn't room for it on the cramped stage of the theatre. In those days, the Pavilion was run by Parkin's Entertainments Ltd, who were probably more interested in providing their customers with 'The Holiday of your life, away from all restrictions, at PARKIN'S LUXURY HOLIDAY CAMP, PLEMONT, JERSEY' than an evening of laughter at the Victoria Pavilion, Ilfracombe – for that was the first message to greet you on the front of the programme, immediately under the picture of the North Devon Rock. They even advertised 'Matinées if Wet', so you knew that if the weather was reasonably fine, business would be considerably reduced. It was. Both fine and reduced. But we survived and we were looking forward to the Whitehall so the slight indifference displayed by Ilfracombe was of little consequence.

Things are very different today, though. To begin with, the North Devon District Council now owns the Victoria Pavilion. Originally built in 1888 as a Crystal Palace-type structure and known locally as 'the cucumber frame', the Council completely refurbished the theatre in 1970, adding two wings to create proper spaces for sets and performers. Now the main theatre has about 600 seats, with two studios attached. In the summer, the main auditorium houses a holiday attraction, but at all times the complex is used for 'community' theatre, which is very popular. Regrettably, I have never been back to see this transformation – but it's good to know that a theatre *can* be enlarged and be successful. 'Small is beautiful' seems to be the catch-phrase of the theatre these days.

Now we were on the home straight. We had to do one final week on tour, so that Wally Patch could run himself in after fourteen weeks' absence. He was restored to us like a dying man in the desert, parched and starving from shortage of laughter. Within minutes his confidence was back, and again he was the bawling, bullying – but lovable – Sgt Bell, only a few days away from a triumphant return to the West End stage. I am happy to say that the rest of the cast didn't do too badly, either. But first we had to contend with what was known as 'a difficult get-in' – in other words a stinker of a date at the Royal Opera House, Leicester.

ROYAL OPERA HOUSE
Leicester

Designed by C. J. Phipps in 1877 and then booked 'in conjunction' with Howard and Wyndham, with its managing director the ever-present Prince Littler, the Opera House had a terrible reputation for lousy business and soon after our final week on tour it closed, much to the relief of all the artists who had ever suffered there, and was later pulled down. You could well be forgiven for thinking that would be the end of theatre in this city, but it wasn't. Far from it, in fact, for Leicester is now in the forefront of all regional theatre. A group of academics, led by Professor Philip Collins, and a group of local citizens, led by Councillor (now Sir) Mark Henig came together and raised both the money and the Phoenix Theatre, which opened in 1963 with 270 seats.

All went well, despite the opening around the same time of the then flagship of regional reps – the Nottingham Playhouse, in Leicester's rival city – and the Leicester Theatre Trust (for that is what had been formed) decided to go for broke. The Haymarket Theatre was built, and by 1973 Leicester could boast three auditoria: the Haymarket Main House and Studio, with the Phoenix as a young people's theatre. Furthermore, they thrived and, even today with all the problems of freezes and squeezes they still exist. The West End, too, has reason to rejoice at the Haymarket's success. Amongst successful transfers have been the second productions of *My Fair Lady*, *Oklahoma!* and *Me and My Girl*. I wouldn't have minded having a bob or two in *those*, I can tell you.

And so, we moved to the Whitehall. We opened on 12th September, 1950 and ran for 1,610 performances. It was to be four years before I toured again, and even then it was only for three weeks in the pre-London tour of *Dry Rot*. But between 1950 and 1954 I was responsible for presenting no less than ninety-five weeks on the road; and it went on from there. 'A year, a month, a week, a natural day . . .'

Curtain

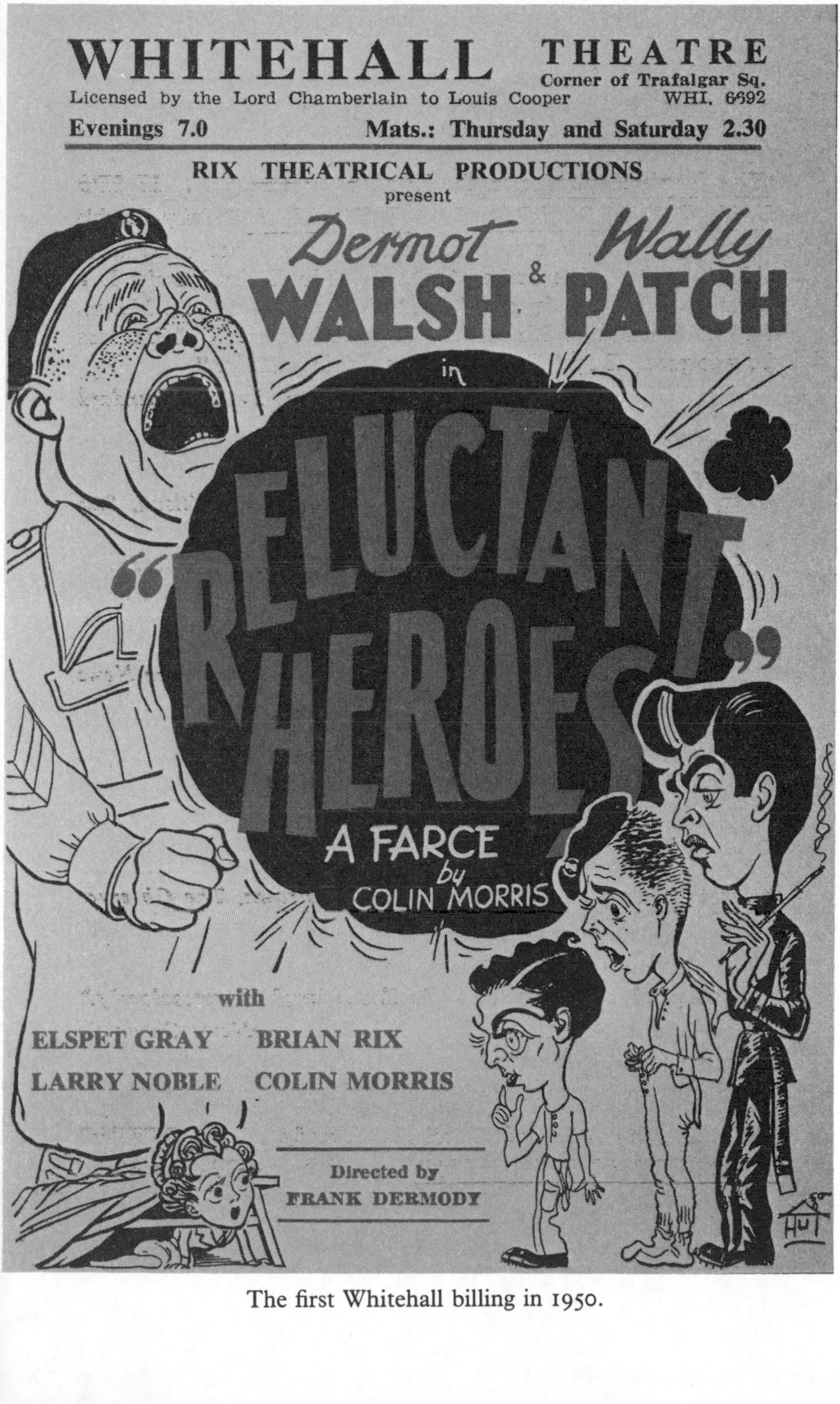

The first Whitehall billing in 1950.

"RELUCTANT HEROES"

" ......In two minutes I want ter see yer as yer mothers bore yer - If yer mothers stood the shock, the medical officer can......"

IN TWO MINUTES **YOU** WILL BE ROARING AT "RELUCTANT HEROES"- *The Farce with a 1,000 LAUGHS!*

INTERLUDE
'Hobson's Choice'

I have the fond impression that instead of schlepping round the country myself for the next twenty-odd years, I managed to persuade other actors to perform that chore for me. Mind you, many did not think of it in those terms. A regular round of golf each morning, a regular round of drinks each lunchtime, a regular social round each night and a regular round sum each week seemed to be all some actors desired, and I certainly didn't argue. The plays I sent out were, in the main, successful – so everyone was happy.

As I say, I have that fond impression. The reality was somewhat different. It really was 'Hobson's Choice' as far as I was concerned. I actually spent 123 weeks on tour myself – there really was no alternative – with a further 49 weeks away from home during summer and pantomime seasons, making a total of 172 weeks altogether. Meanwhile my task force of actors achieved over 180 weeks on tour, with a similar number of weeks to mine in summer seasons. So, in spite of apparently endless runs in the West End, much time was indeed spent in the provinces or, as is now the fashionable term, the regions. But regions or provinces, it all meant you were out in the sticks and – to prove it – turn to the complete set of date sheets at the end of this book – if any proof will be necessary when you have read on . . .

John Slater was my most willing touring actor, usually after he had first completed a successful run of the play in London. He used to tour with great gusto, mainly – I think – because his wife, Betty, generally went with him and seemed to encourage his regular visits to the golf course. She was also around to attend to his every creature comfort, and Johnnie was nothing if not sybaritic. The weekly change of scenery and theatre and audience was for him an actual pleasure. He also made some very good friends in those early days, too. Actors like Ray Cooney and Andrew Sachs were often with him. You will know Ray as a most successful farce actor/author, as well as the principal shareholder in the Playhouse Theatre, while Andy Sachs reached the pinnacle of his fame as the hard-pressed Manuel in *Fawlty Towers*, but he had, in fact, been noticed many times for his performances at the Whitehall and the Garrick. John Slater himself was already well known as television's storyteller, before he took over the role of Sgt Bell in *Reluctant Heroes* from Wally Patch in 1952. He then went on to create the bookie, Alf Tubbe, in John Chapman's *Dry Rot* – before touring the production while it was still running at the Whitehall, with Leo Franklyn now in the part, and ended up, before his untimely death, as Sgt Stone in that long-running police epic, *Z-Cars*. Before then, however, he had already toured for me again in *Simple Spymen* (another John Chapman farce) and *One For The Pot*, by Ray Cooney and Tony Hilton. Indeed, in that production he opened on 6th July, 1964 at the New Theatre, Cardiff and his first question to 'The Stroller' in the *South Wales Echo* was 'When are you going to have a motorway?' The rest of the company had attended the good old-fashioned train-call and had arrived in Cardiff in less than half the time it had taken Johnnie in his stately vintage Rolls, with the illuminated bird on top, which the police used to mistake for the Royal insignia. Mind you, such delays can still happen today when the wind blows and the Severn Bridge is falling down. Or seems to be, anyway. Johnnie was a lovely feller, and he always gave his audiences their money's worth. Even though his heart trouble got steadily worse throughout the years I never knew him to miss a performance.

So what were those plays and where did they tour? First, there was Colin Morris' *Reluctant Heroes*, which just toured and toured, even when still running at the Whitehall. It completed a further eighty-one weeks on the road in all, not counting the twenty weeks we had spent running round the country trying to end up in the West End. Then came John Chapman's *Dry Rot*, with a total of thirty-six touring weeks, followed by Michael Pertwee's *A Bit Between the Teeth*, with thirty-four weeks on tour and every single one played by me. Others which I sent out were *The Long March* (a second production of Colin Morris' *Desert Rats*, originally presented by Henry Sherek at the Adelphi Theatre), which only completed eight weeks, but never again came back into the West End; *Tell the Marines*, by Roland and Michael Pertwee, which also did eight weeks, but never saw the West End then, or later, for it was an attempt to recreate *Reluctant Heroes* and, unfortunately it was then out of date; *Simple Spymen* did fifteen weeks, while a farce I had originally presented on BBC Television, *You, Too, Can Have a Body*, was co-presented by me with Tom Arnold, and did an eight-week pre-London tour before coming to the Victoria Palace with Bill Maynard and Bill Kerr taking over the parts originally played on telly by Basil Lord and me. This 'new' farce, full of old-fashioned knockabout, was by a then builder's clerk, Fred Robinson. After this, though, Fred became a full-time writer, with an enormously successful television series to his credit, *The Larkins*, starring Peggy Mount and David Kossof. Like the original director of *Body*, Henry Kendall, Fred is no longer with us, but a piece of repartee between these two is worth recording. Fred's play had been first produced by some Hackney

Boy Scouts, from whence Fred hailed, and he was somewhat over-fond of quoting that production to an increasingly irate Harry, as Henry Kendall was known: ''Ere, 'Arry, I gotta n'idea,' said Fred.

'If it's one of those from that *dreadful* Girl Guides' production of yours,' replied 'Arry in his nasal, aristocratic voice, 'you can stick it up as far as your woggle.'

'No, 'Arry, no! It worked a treat for the Boy Scarts!'

'It is only too clear, my dear Fred,' responded the elegant, drawling 'Arry, 'that in the past you have had the benefit of a genius director, in the shape of Brown Owl, whilst I am but a humble thespian who has spent the best part of fifty years honing my art. However, I have seen and handled more cock in my life than you have had hot dinners, and your farce is the biggest cock of all. Kindly let me play with it as I will.'

One For The Pot only needed two weeks on tour at the Devonshire Park, Eastbourne and the Theatre Royal, Brighton before starting at the Whitehall – but John Slater did a further eighteen weeks in 1964. I, on the other hand, was present throughout the pre-London and post-London tours of *Chase Me Comrade!* – Ray Cooney's first solo effort – which did four weeks' pre and ten weeks' post. The first half of the post-London effort was shared with *Bang, Bang, Beirut!* (written by Ray Cooney and Tony Hilton as their follow-up to *One For The Pot*), which was my first crude attempt at repertoire, with Dickie Henderson playing the lead in *Beirut*, while I performed the same duty in *Comrade*. It was not a success. We visited the Opera House, Manchester (for two weeks); the Royal Court, Liverpool; the Theatre Royal, Glasgow and the King's Theatre, Edinburgh, with me playing one half of the week and Dickie the other. The cast for both remained roughly the same but – unfortunately – the business did not. Dickie was better known for his variety and cabaret act, as well as his TV situation comedy series – while I was a man of the Theatre. They came to see me, and forewent the pleasure of viewing Dickie – in droves. Being Dickie, a real pro, he was very good about it, but both of us were desperately disappointed, and when I came to do my repertoire in earnest at the Garrick theatre, but a few months later, Dickie saw the red light ahead and opted out. Quite rightly, as it turned out, for the Great British Public was totally confused and believed that each play I presented was on for a limited run only, and supported each accordingly. *Bang, Bang, Beirut!* – tactfully retitled *Stand By Your Bedouin* – was the first to bite the dust, followed closely by *Uproar in the House*, by Anthony Marriott and Alastair Foot, with *Let Sleeping Wives Lie* bringing up the rear – a very fortunate position for its authors, Harold Brooke and Kay Bannerman, for, when I had to drop the other two, it went on solo for another two years at the Garrick, with a ten-week tour thrown in at the end, as well as an opening summer season at the new Playhouse Theatre, Weston-super-Mare, with me playing my old part for four weeks and then

Leslie Crowther taking over his old part for a further six weeks. This allowed me to go on holiday and, at the same time, prepare for the next production at the Garrick Theatre, *She's Done It Again*, by Michael Pertwee, based on the play *Nap Hand*, by Vernon Sylvaine and Guy Bolton. This, too, toured for three weeks before coming into London in October 1969, but being a comparative failure, toured for a further eleven weeks in the autumn of 1970.

Six of Rix came next, which was an unbridled success. As I have already mentioned, these were cut-down Vernon Sylvaine farces, rewritten by Michael Pertwee and recorded as double bills on tour for BBC Television, but with all the additional perks, for the actors, of two salaries (both BBC and theatre), with me being able to add on my management fees from the Beeb, as well – not forgetting the sizeable profit from the guarantees I received from the theatres on this lengthy eight-week tour. Lengthy, by the way, because we had to keep returning to rehearse in London for the next two plays, so the whole exercise took well over four months. Four happy and productive months, I must add, and surely the forerunner of all the shows which the BBC now has to buy in from freelance programme makers. I only wish I was able to do it now. The profits would be even greater!

Don't Just Lie There, Say Something!, by Michael Pertwee, did four weeks before we took it to the Garrick Theatre, where it ran for nearly two years, surmounting black-outs, power cuts and the beginnings of the three-day week, and then toured for a further five weeks in 1973, before we turned it into a film. I was there, all the time, I hasten to add. Around that time, in 1972, I also presented Leslie Crowther and Dilys Watling on a tour of the new Harold Brooke and Kay Bannerman farce, *She Was Only An Admiral's Daughter* but, in spite of a twelve-week tour and that memorable title, it never saw the bright lights of the West End. A pity, for both Leslie and Dilys were very funny.

By 1974 I had concluded my deal with Duncan Weldon and Louis Michaels, which agreed that touring was as important a part of the scene as the West End. This meant that my next two productions – *A Bit Between the Teeth* by Michael Pertwee, based on an idea of mine, and *Fringe Benefits* by Donald Churchill and Peter Yeldham (rewritten considerably by Ray Cooney) – spent a total of thirty-three and seventeen weeks on the road respectively. Can you wonder I gave it all up on 8th January, 1977? If you add in the ten-week pantomime season at the New Theatre, Cardiff in 1973/4, when *Robinson Crusoe* was almost totally becalmed and marooned by Ted Heath's three-day week, a summer season of *A Bit Between the Teeth* at Louis Michaels' Playhouse Theatre in Bournemouth, from 30th June to 20th September, 1975, a further four weeks' pantomime at the Congress, Eastbourne in 1975 and a final eight-week season of *Fringe Benefits* at the Devonshire Park, Eastbourne in

1976, you may begin to understand why I felt that Hermione Gingold's quip, of being 'forced to tour', was beginning to apply to me, also. It was definitely time for a change. And that is when I gave it all up. I never toured again until September 1988. And then it was only for two weeks at the Theatre Royal, Bath on our way to the Lyric Theatre, Shaftesbury Avenue, with the revival of *Dry Rot*. That was only for a four-month season, as well. I had learned my lesson the hard way. But on this last occasion at least I had my wife, Elspet Gray, with me. That made it a lot more jolly, I can tell you. Well, most of the time, anyway . . .

I have now visited some forty-three theatres, in the majority of which I played, at one time or another. Yet to come are another fifty-two – and I am happy to say that thirty-two of these are extant. I am less happy to say that the remaining twenty are as dead as a dodo – or presenting bingo, which is pretty well the same thing. At least both words end in 'o' – which could be taken to be naught for your comfort – if you are a theatre-goer, that is. So – bouquets for those which have battled on – wreaths for the less fortunate. Let them be 'Larded with sweet flowers; which bewept to the grave did go . . .'

Act V beginners, please.

ACT V

STREATHAM HILL THEATRE

Tel.: Tulse Hill 1277.   Box Office open 10 a.m. to 8-30 p.m.

Week commencing MONDAY, 21st MAY, 1951
EVENINGS at 7-30
Matinees: Wednesday & Saturday at 2-30

John C. Mather and W. H. Williams
(on behalf of Chartres Productions Ltd.) present

HOLLYWOOD'S MASTER OF THRILLS!
IN PERSON

BELA LUGOSI
AND FULL WEST END COMPANY

IN

DRACULA

THE FANTASTIC STORY OF A VAMPIRE
by HAMILTON DEANE and J.L. BALDERSTON
ADAPTED FROM THE NOVEL
BY BRAM STOKER

BEAUTY AT THE MERCY OF A MONSTER!

DIRECTED BY
RICHARD EASTHAM

'Out of Order'

Taking our cue from Ophelia at the end of the Interlude, let us begin by taking a quick look at those theatres which have closed, for one reason or another. I know there are those among you who hate lists, so perhaps you could shut your eyes, think of a more theatrical England and bear with me – for it would seem to be a fruitless exercise to go into great detail about any theatre which is no longer in existence. However, I will try and colour this rather sad cavalcade and perhaps we should spend a little longer on those theatres which have a tiny hope of reopening. Let's make a start with the outer-London circuit.

Alas, the majority of these are dead, or clinging on to life with a somewhat tenuous grip. They only came on to my date sheet (or, rather, Renée Stepham's date sheet, for she was booking the tours) after the Whitehall run, in July, August and September 1954. I had two companies on the road then, both doing the same play, while I had a holiday and prepared for the next production – *Dry Rot*. A happy occasion – for the spondulicks rolled in, without my having to do anything but invite skin cancer by lying in the boiling sun in the South of France. Fortunately for my solar keratosis, such idleness was of short duration, and it was back to the rehearsal room and the Whitehall before you could even acquire a reasonable tan – and an evening trip to north-west London to see *Heroes* at the Hippodrome, Golders Green. As this is still intact, but now used for orchestral concerts by the B B C, it could – in theory – be returned to its theatrical use which, in 1954, was very welcome, for we played to huge business and I sat as a member of the audience, in a packed house, and thoroughly enjoyed myself.

The Hippodrome, designed by Bertie Crewe, had originally opened as a music hall in 1913, becoming a 'straight' theatre some ten years later. With the Streatham Hill Theatre (*Heroes*' next port of call) and the Lewisham Hippodrome (now demolished) it formed a splendid near-London triumvirate of theatres which could be visited, most profitably, either before or after the West End or – quite often – on both occasions. The Streatham Hill theatre still exists, but has been a Mecca property since 1962, housing wrestling (when that was popular) and, of course, bingo. Two of Frank Matcham's protégés, W. G. R. Sprague and W. H. Barton designed this theatre which opened in 1929 with Sir Charles Cochran's revue *Wake Up and Dream!*. I realise 'Cockie' was not knighted until 1948, but I thought it would be a pleasant gesture to dub him some fifteen years earlier, out of respect for his showbiz pzazz.

The now demolished Empire, Chiswick, followed Streatham on the date sheet, and there is little to report on that, except that in spite of having been a popular music hall it was *not* a Moss' Empire. Neither was another Frank Matcham design – the Empire, Hackney, *Heroes*' next port of call, although it had once been a Stoll Moss, and at least this theatre has now been restored to live entertainment again, after a twenty-five-year stint as a Mecca bingo hall. It was rescued by the Hackney Empire Preservation Trust in 1987, when it reopened with a variety bill, headed by Roy Hudd, who said 'it felt as if it had never been closed'. It now houses all manner of entertainment: one night stands, alternative comedy, pantomime, children's theatre – even the Royal National Theatre had a ten-night run there with *Ma Rainey's Black Bottom*. Bouquets for all involved here, I think.

There was one last Empire to go, as far as we were concerned – literally last, as it turned out – that which existed in Wood Green. For a brief time it gasped some oxygen into its breathless lungs by becoming a television studio, but eventually even that nebuliser packed up and the building was demolished, leaving but a fragment of the façade for future archaeologists to discover, as yet another building collapsed in a heap of dust and rubble. That's why so many of our beautiful theatres are but elegiac words and fading photographs.

Ah well! The next one is certainly an exception.

The Richmond Theatre when it was the Royal
Hippodrome and Theatre in 1919.

RICHMOND THEATRE
The Green
Richmond-upon-Thames

I say – 'certainly an exception' for, like its neighbour the Wimbledon Theatre, it opened its doors again in 1991, beautifully restored and refurbished. Mind you, it was always planned to rebuild and refurbish the place (at least it was planned in the recent past) but, unfortunately, fate stepped in and pre-empted the issue.

In April 1989 the theatre had to close rather hurriedly because the ceiling was about to fall in and this left the Richmond Theatre Trust (the charity formed to run the building) with the unenviable task of begging for money with nothing practical to show for it. However, the owners of the lease, Richmond Theatre Ltd, agreed to donate their lease interest to the Theatre Trust and the Richmond Council guaranteed the loan to actually carry out the restoration. Nevertheless, the Trust had to go into the highways and byways to raise other much needed capital – and this they have done with much vigour and great success. But then, that is not altogether surprising, for the theatre was built in 1899 and is considered by many to be the most beautiful and perfectly preserved of all Frank Matcham's theatres. Even so, it has had a fairly chequered history, for it would seem that many Richmond and nearby residents often preferred the ten-mile trip to the West End to see a show, rather than fall out of their front doors into the welcoming entrance vestibule of the Richmond Theatre, which is as near as dammit to that which saw the first performance on 18th September, 1899, of *As You Like It*, with Ben Greet and Dorothea Baird playing Touchstone and Rosalind. Old Sir Henry was once again present in some form or another, for Miss Baird was his daughter-in-law, married to his eldest son, H. B. Irving.

The theatre was then called the Royal Hippodrome, but changed its name to the Prince of Wales some four years later, when George Dance acquired the building. He kept this second name until 1909, when he decided to call it the Richmond Hippodrome and Theatre. This must have been a ploy to unload the property on to the London Theatre of Varieties Ltd, of which George Dance was a director, for almost immediately the theatre was leased to another company, Richmond Varieties Ltd and there is no sign of Mr Dance (later Sir George) being a director of *that*. In spite of a change of owner in 1915, when it was bought by a prominent local business man, Joseph Mears, it continued with the same name until 1924, when it became the Richmond Theatre, and that it has remained ever since, even though it has changed hands on a number of further occasions. I have already referred to Louis Michaels, who acquired the lease in 1973. This continued until his death in 1981, and beyond, but in 1986 it was taken over by the Trust, with the willing help of the leaseholder, Richmond Theatre Ltd, the London Borough of Richmond-upon-Thames, and the actual freeholder, Arnewood Estates Ltd.

So now you know . . .

As for me, I only played the theatre once, for two weeks, with *A Bit Between the Teeth*. I loved it. Not because business was particularly good, but simply because the theatre was but a mere three miles away from my home in Roehampton. I never played it when we moved to Barnes, all of one mile further away and now I've moved to Wimbledon (and have retired anyway), I don't suppose I ever will. Nor, I must confess, have I visited it very often, as a member of the audience. Like all local residents, I seem to find it easier to drive into the West End or south of the river to the National. Did I hear a cry of 'shame' from the balcony? I wouldn't be surprised.

That seems to cover all the outer London theatres which appeared on my date sheets. Of course, there were many more which did not. Now – risking your anger – I will list some of the provincial theatres which have closed since the days either I, or one of my companies, played them. Not to be irritating, I assure you, but just to keep the record straight: the Lyceum, Newport; the Pleasure Gardens, Folkestone; the Grand, Halifax; the Palace, Ramsgate; the 'old' Marlowe, Canterbury (the 'new', converted from a Gaumont Cinema, opened in 1985); the Hippodrome, Aldershot; the Prince's, Bradford – all have been demolished.

Bingo has claimed the Hippodrome, Ipswich; the Garrick, Southport and the Hippodrome, Coventry – but let me pause a moment to tell a little story about the last three. Actually, one of them will develop into quite a long story, for it is the tale of Duncan Weldon and Triumph Theatre Productions – not really about the Garrick at all.

GARRICK THEATRE
Southport

When Duncan C. Weldon (his billing as the chairman and managing director of Triumph Theatre Productions Ltd) was a lad of thirteen or fourteen, it was believed he would take over his father's photographic business in Southport, but he had other ideas. He was mad on the theatre and got himself a job as the call-boy at the Garrick, which had been opened in 1932 by Sir John Martin Harvey. His first week coincided with John Slater's visit to the theatre in *Dry Rot*, with Ray Cooney and Andrew Sachs also in the cast. It was the week commencing 15th October, 1956, just before the Garrick was turned into a cinema – bingo came nine years later – and Johnnie had recently left the Whitehall production (after two years playing the bookie, Alf Tubbe, which Leo Franklyn took over for a further two years), and was now taking the play round the country on a highly successful sixteen-week tour, before returning to the world of television. Duncan Weldon not only used to make sure all the actors were on stage on cue, but he also indulged in his intended future career by photographing John and other members of the cast, as well as running errands for all and sundry, with gay abandon – and I use the word 'gay' in its original sense. He was a busy young man – but he was hooked! The theatre, not the camera, was for him.

By the time he was nineteen Duncan was running two repertory companies, one at St Anne's-on-Sea and the other at St Helen's – where the Rugby League team comes from, and where Frank Matcham's old Theatre Royal was reconstructed in 1964, leaving only the stage as designed by him, and renamed the Pilkington Theatre, because it is now owned by the glass company. For a short time Duncan was in partnership with David Kossof, but in 1969 he teamed up with Paul Elliott (who, in turn, had been in partnership with *Dixon of Dock Green* actor, Peter Byrne, as E&B Productions) and together they presented many provincial tours, their first being a revival of *No, No, Nanette*. The late lamented Peter Bridge – then one of London's most prolific managers, as Alan Ayckbourn's first producer, as well as the impresario behind many large-cast classic revivals, which toured either before or after their West End runs – was particularly helpful to the fledgling producers. Renée Stepham was around, too, doing most of the bookings. Paul Elliott then met Louis Michaels, who was pretty big in the rag trade at the time, as well as being involved in the theatre as an 'angel' (in other words, an investor), Duncan was brought into the picture, as was actor Richard Todd, and Triumph Theatre Productions Ltd was born.

Their first production was not actually on tour, but at the Strand Theatre, for a season of yet another revival of J. B. Priestley's *When We Are Married*. After that, though, the touring started in earnest, and 'Triumph' became the premier management in that particular field. Eventually, 'personality clashes' resulted in the break-up of the union, and Paul Elliott went off on his own. It is pleasant to report, however, that Duncan and Paul have remained friends through all these vicissitudes, and today Elliott presents many of the successful pantomimes previously staged by 'Triumph' – with his own thrown in for good measure, of course.

I came on the scene in 1974, with *A Bit Between the Teeth*, when I joined forces, in a manner of speaking, with Duncan. I then went on to the Congress Theatre, Eastbourne with *Babes in the Wood*, one of Triumph's pantomimes, and finished with *Fringe Benefits*, which was a co-production between Brian Rix Enterprises, Triumph Theatre Productions Ltd and Ray Cooney Productions Ltd. All that effort to produce a play which, while not exactly a mouse, hardly qualified as an elephant and had me on the road for seventeen weeks, in addition to the Whitehall run. After that, it was oblivion for me as an actor for twelve years, until the revival of *Dry Rot*, during which time I was severally a director of Cooney-Marsh Theatres Ltd, secretary-general of MENCAP and, finally, chairman of that same august charity. I have worked for Duncan once more though, as the director of the Cannon and Ball tour of *A Bit Between the Teeth* (retitled *You'll Do For Me!*), which took place in 1989.

As for Duncan, he is now possibly the most prolific and powerful of all theatrical producers in the West End, although not the most financially successful. He himself would accord that accolade to Cameron Mackintosh, responsible for so many of the smash-hit musicals for which this country has recently become famous, but Duncan's output is both catholic and popular – with the added bonus of presenting many plays at the beautiful Haymarket Theatre (acquired by Louis Michaels before he died), as well as being the power behind the throne, for a short time, of the Peter Hall Company. Sir Peter and he had a little local difficulty at the beginning of their operation together, when Sir P had just left the National Theatre, but then everything was satisfactorily resolved and the three-year partnership flourished – to everyone's benefit, particularly that of all theatregoers. After Louis Michaels died, Duncan was without a rich partner for a little time, apart from a brief flirtation with the Apollo Leisure Group, but then a *seriously* rich one came along in the shape of New Yorker, Jerome Minskoff, and together they made a formidable team, with – at one time – no less than five West End theatres at their beck and call. Then Jerry Minskoff withdrew and Duncan, since then, has soldiered on with singular success, under the banner of Duncan C. Weldon Productions Ltd. A long way from making tea at the Garrick Theatre, Southport for Johnnie Slater and running errands for members of the *Dry Rot* Number One tour. But that is the very stuff of theatre – and exactly why people fall for its seductive charms.

One final story about Duncan Weldon. His first 'classy' tour was the well-known Scottish play, with Paul Daneman and Dorothy Tutin playing Lord and Lady M. He obtained an Arts Council guarantee against loss for £96,000 – a great deal of money in those days – but such was the unexpected success of the tour that he only needed to ask for £2,000 to meet his losses when it was all over. To his amazement, the letter of response from the Arts Council did not congratulate him on his good husbandry – that £94,000 was still in the kitty – but reprimanded him instead, saying that he should have budgeted more accurately, not applied for such a big grant in the first place, so that the money would have been available earlier, to be lost by some other, less careful, management. As far as I know, Duncan has never been offered a deal of a similar nature since. All his really big losses (and profits) have been in the commercial sector. Most other managements seem to keep theirs for the Arts Council. The losses, anyway.

SOUTHPORT. GARRICK THEATRE.

HIPPODROME
Coventry

The Coventry Hippodrome is built on the site of two previous theatres bearing the same name. This version opened in 1937, but in 1980 went over to bingo. It is a large theatre, which used to book plays only occasionally in the old days, concentrating on musicals or variety instead. Nevertheless, sometimes a popular play would visit the Hippodrome and all would be well. This was certainly the case when we played the theatre for two weeks in 1964, with *Chase Me Comrade!*, which was on its way to the Whitehall. It wasn't that the farce was then well known or popular, but the Whitehall company *was*, and we broke the theatre record for any play ever presented in Coventry, up to that time. It was splendid, but perhaps the most exciting part of it, from my point of view, was the pit orchestra. Until then, I had played in theatres where trios and quartets scraped out well-known musical airs as the audience straggled in before the show, brought everyone to their feet for a lacklustre, squeaky National Anthem moments before the curtain rose, played to empty seats during the intervals, as people escaped to the bars and, finally, decanted the theatre with wholly inappropriate hurry music, at the very end. One night, after Wolfit had given his all in *King Lear*, staggered through the parted tabs, clutched on to the right-hand curtain as though exhausted, bowed low in all humility to his appreciative audience, and stepped back into the backstage gloom, the pit trio immediately struck up an unusually spirited rendition of 'For he's going to marry Yum-Yum – Yum-Yum' from *The Mikado*. I need hardly add that they did not do it at the next performance.

The Coventry Hippodrome Orchestra was somewhat different, however. To begin with, it was a proper band. No less than twelve players (of varying ability) graced the pit and thumped and trumpeted their way through many a bouncy number, all taken at maximum volume and the fastest possible gallop. It was marvellous! We, the actors, used to be on the stage minutes before our appointed beginners call, simply to get the adrenalin stirred up by such old favourites as 'Basin St Blues' and 'Tiger Rag', as well as the more conventional *The Student Prince* and *Good Night*

Vienna. Eric Maschwitz was responsible for the lyrics in this musical and used to tell a lovely story against himself about another Hippodrome, this one in south-east London. 'One night,' he said, 'I happened to be passing the Hippodrome and saw that my musical was playing there, so popped in and asked the manager how *Good Night Vienna* was doing in Lewisham. Came the reply: 'About as well as *Good Night Lewisham* would do in Vienna.'

But we enjoyed it in *our* Hippodrome, I can tell you.

It was also 'Good Night Doncaster, Derby, Northampton, Plymouth, Wilmslow and Morecambe' to theatres that we had known in those respective towns, being the Grand, the Hippodrome, the New, the Palace, the Rex and the Winter Gardens. All are now disused, for one reason or another, although others have sometimes arisen to take their place. Nevertheless, hundreds of theatres, both variety and straight, have closed since the Second World War and something under fifty have been built, or converted, to fill the gaps. You can perhaps now begin to see why the Theatres Trust was formed to fight rearguard actions for those which remain. But it is an uphill battle. You would be amazed how devious planning committees and property developers can be, if they put their minds to it.

On second thoughts, perhaps you wouldn't be amazed after all.

Only in my latter years did I visit any of the new theatres, but perhaps that is not altogether surprising because: (a) they weren't built in the early part of my touring days and (b) older actors like me were nervous of visiting these newfangled houses anyway. I mean, why hadn't they been there before? Would there be an audience and, if so, was the capacity big enough to pay the bills and, anyway, what about your percentage? Would there be a sizeable guarantee? Isn't there something rather demeaning about playing a modern civic theatre in a garden city or at the seaside, instead of good old Phipps and Matcham velvet and plush in good old industrial towns? And so on – nevertheless, I did play a few. Here goes . . .

THE PLAYHOUSE
Weston-super-Mare

The longest time I have spent in any new theatre is at the Playhouse, Weston-super-Mare, so I had better begin here. I think it was Renée Stepham who approached me during the post-London tour which she had booked for *Let Sleeping Wives Lie* and asked me if I would like to open this new theatre before going back to the Garrick Theatre with *She's Done It Again*. As our first night was in the early autumn, this suited me down to the ground, for it meant I could keep the cast busy and together, before rehearsals began for the new production. There was only one snag. I wanted a holiday at our house in Spain, and the first two weeks of rehearsal coincided with the last two weeks of the Weston season, so there would have been no break for me at all. A solution was easily found, however. Leslie Crowther, who had left the cast to go into pantomime and a new T V series, had been succeeded by Simon Merrick. Simon, however, could easily take over my part, for the two characters were virtually inter-changeable, and Leslie was happy to come back for a limited summer season, so it all worked out splendidly. Simon and I did the first four weeks, then Simon took over from me, Leslie came back – and I went off on hols. No problem at all. In fact, I can remember no real problems during that entire tour or season.

It was very successful and very happy and very eventful. The Americans landed on the moon during my four-week stint and I was asked to stand by to play cricket for Somerset at about the same time. In those days, they were strapped for men – and as I had my cricket bag with me, and the match was in Weston, the team-manager-cum-secretary-cum-everything-else, Bill Andrews, popped into my dressing-room and suggested I might be able to help. I could, and I would – but I didn't. At the last minute a real pro came along, and my dreams of being a county cricketer, albeit for the wrong county, came to naught. Ah well, you can't have everything – but Somerset came to regret my omission. They were bottom of the Championship that year. Serve them jolly well right!

The Playhouse is a delightful little theatre. In those days it seated a few more than the Whitehall – 672 – and was built to take the place of the previous theatre that had been destroyed by fire in 1964. The backstage facilities were particularly pleasant, which showed that, at long last, actors were being considered at the original planning stage. They were certainly good enough to attract two other big names for the next two summer seasons, which I presented. First, Dickie Henderson in *Stand By Your Bedouin* and then Bob Monkhouse in *She's Done It Again*, which saw the emergence of a new young comedy actor, one David Jason. When I went to see the play, I was amazed how clearly Bob was prepared to take a back seat in the laughter stakes and leave it all to David. When I remarked on this generosity after the show, Bob simply shrugged and said, 'If you can't beat 'em, join 'em.' Which must be the most pragmatic remark I have ever heard from any 'star' in my life. You can tell Bob has never been an actor-manager.

FUTURIST
Scarborough

Scarborough is perhaps best known, nowadays, for Alan Ayckbourn's Stephen Joseph Theatre and for the fact that he premières all his phenomenally successful plays there. Its first theatre, however, was the Theatre Royal, which opened in 1767 and closed in the year I was born, 1924. Not that this has any relevance, but it adds a little local colour, that's all, for I drew my first breath not too many miles away in Cottingham, just outside Hull, and one of my earliest theatrical memories is being taken to see *Merrie England*, which opened the huge Open Air Theatre, seating 7,500, situated in the Manor Gardens in Scarborough. It was a breath-taking occasion, for the stage alone was seventy-five yards wide and thirty yards deep, with royal barges sailing up and down the lake and bonfires burning on the natural hills surrounding the amphitheatre. All great stuff but, alas, time marched on, and after a disastrous summer in 1968, when *West Side Story* was rained off pretty well every night, the authorities felt it more prudent to close, rather than battle with the notoriously fickle English elements.

The Royal Opera House, opened in 1878 as Mr Charles Adam's Grand Circus, has also bent to the winds of change and now only shows films. The Floral Hall, built by the local council in 1910, was demolished and a bowling centre has taken its place. The Spa Grand Hall and the Spa Theatre still exist, but most of the council's eggs seem destined in the near future to go into the Futurist's basket, which they acquired in 1985 and then leased to Apollo Leisure, being 'one of Britain's major summer season venues', according to the brochure. Well, if it's not already, it soon will be, for the council plan to spend over £1 million on the building over the next few years, 'to repair and up-grade the Theatre to make it the best on the East Coast'. All this, for a building that started life in 1909, when Will Catlin opened his New Arcadia to house his Pierrots. Over the years various cinemas and theatres were constructed on neighbouring sites, but in 1958 this general mish-mash was brought together by Robert Luff, especially for his Black and White Minstrel Show, and combined as the

Futurist. That is why I can place it in the post-war category of theatres to be opened since 1945. It's not the easiest of venues for a farce, I can tell you, and *A Bit Between the Teeth* felt distinctly lonely, out of season in this 2,155 seater. But we would have been worse off at the Open Air venue, so who's complaining.

Incidentally, in 1733 a doctor expounded the virtues of immersing the human body in seawater and Scarborough became the first seaside resort to adopt this 'healthy and pleasurable attraction'. In view of all the recent shock-horror stories about our coastal waters and the effluent therein, I wonder what that same quack would say now? Recommend people to go to the theatre instead, I hope. At least 'no smoking' is the order of the day there, thank goodness, so the environment is reasonably healthy and we can only trust there is a pleasurable attraction on the stage. It seems there are problems in this direction, however, at our next resort of call. According to a report in the *Stage*, theatres in the Torbay area are finding it more and more difficult to attract audiences. I imagine most of them are stuck in those endless holiday traffic jams on the M4 and M5 – never mind the Exeter by-pass. Perhaps it would be easier to unload the G. H. Lucking scenery vans in some convenient lay-bys, put up the sets and give the performances there. They would have done that in the old days, believe you me – with Ken Tynan on hand to offer his notices.

Catlin's Perrots in 1921.

PRINCESS THEATRE
Torquay

Without question, this is a genuine, one hundred per cent, post-war theatre, opening in 1961. Actually, in spite of its size – 1,514 seats – it gives the impression of being somewhat short of space, particularly backstage, but as we were comfortably full, with a conference in full swing in Torbay, I was travel-stained but happy. The Princess has a rival just down the road, in the shape of the Festival Hall, Paignton – which opened in 1967. If the Princess was designed with restricted space backstage, the Festival Hall was not designed as a theatre at all. It had a similar number of seats to its opposite number, but 1,000 of those 1,500 seats were on the flat, which made it very difficult for the audience to get a good view of the Black and White Minstrel Show which opened that first summer season. Max Bygraves could be clearly seen, however, in Torquay, which brought forth unfavourable comparisons (about the theatres, not the shows) and the authorities hurriedly had to rake the flat floor of the Festival Hall so that the following season *Snow White on Ice* at the Festival, and Val Doonican at the Princess, started off on an even keel or, should I say, an angled one. The theatres have been battling it out ever since and, strangely enough, only Tommy Cooper, Cilla Black, Jimmy Cricket, Little and Large and Cannon and Ball seem to have crossed the floor from one theatre to another in the last twenty-five years. About the same numbers who crossed the floor and formed the original SDP Party, and were present in Torquay at the Princess Theatre on the last occasion I appeared there. But this time it was for MENCAP and the Community Care Campaigners, trying to enlist the Party's support for our cause. That was in 1985. At least the theatre is still there, even if the Party is not.

Apart from those three post-war theatres at the seaside, I have only played three new theatres inland, and as they *are* new and my visits have been somewhat few and far between, I will lump them all together, beginning in that Venice of the North – Billingham – and then travelling south.

FORUM
Billingham
GORDON CRAIG THEATRE
Stevenage
WYVERN THEATRE
Swindon

In the paperback version of *Farce About Face*, I wrote, 'I believe ICI and Shell are largely responsible for what must be the greatest square-footage of paved canine lavatory in the world. The Entertainments Centre, housing the theatre, is an island entirely surrounded by dogs' droppings. Or so it was in my day.' For those of you who have never had cause to set slippery foot in the place, I was describing, of course, Billingham, and the Entertainments Centre houses the Forum, seating 643 without an orchestra – fifty less, if music be the food of love – along with a swimming pool, an ice rink, indoor cricket nets, squash courts and other sports facilities. Those Teessiders in pursuit of these particular forms of happiness have been in luck since the community centre was built in 1968. What they did before that, God alone knows.

I have only appeared there once, in *Fringe Benefits*, from Friday 20th February, 1976 to Saturday 6th March. In the same year, you understand. It was not one of my lengthy London runs. In fact, it was about as far from London as it is possible to be in England – 257 miles to be precise – and distance certainly did not lend enchantment. In truth, I don't think I have ever been so miserable in all my life, but it is only right and proper that I explain why.

It was all Duncan Weldon's fault. You may recall that Duncan was one of a triumvirate of managers presenting this particular play, Ray Cooney and myself being the other two, but when it came to the touring scene, Duncan was indisputably the gaffer. That is why we produced at Billingham, why we opened on a Friday night and why we stayed there for a further two weeks, rewriting, rerehearsing and preparing the play for the rest of the tour and its eventual West End presentation. You see, Duncan had a deal with Billingham, which suited everyone down to the ground, for he was able to get his productions on the road for a fraction of the costs normally encountered. With the aid of a little cash injection from the managers down south, Billingham built the set, bought the furniture, prepared the posters and provided an audience which was as responsive and warm-hearted as only a northern audience can be. After that, Billingham paid itself back by collecting a royalty every week and, by way of a bonus, a share of the profits – always assuming there were any, of course. It suited everyone – all except me, that is – for on that first Friday night I found myself shaking and aching more and more as the performance proceeded. When it was over, I repaired back to my hotel room, excusing myself from the first night post-mortem supper (a thing I had never done before), flopped into a freezing bed and took my temperature. It was pushing 104° Fahrenheit which, even in Centigrade terms, is very warm indeed. I was, as they say up there, 'proper poorly'.

Proper poorly or not, it was over to the Forum in the morning for notes and a discussion as to how the play had gone, a little light rehearsing, a little light lunch and then two shows, it being a Saturday. Sunday was off, which allowed me to nurse my 'flu (for that was my affliction) with tender loving care being administered by the hotel porter, a particularly good example of a retired army P T instructor, a believer in fresh air and exercise, and with all the nursing finesse of a muscle-bound gorilla. Nevertheless, I survived, but had far from recovered when it came to yet further rehearsals on the Monday morning, and these were now pretty intense, for a great deal had still to be done to the play. That was the end of my treatment – if hot Bovril with hunks of white bread floating in it and the windows flung wide open could be described as such, and I had to soldier on as best I could. The result was a laryngitis which accompanied me for most of the tour, as well as what I believe is known as a 'toxic temperature'; in other words my temperature rose alarmingly every night at the beginning of Act II, and I felt simply dreadful. Does that explain why I was so unhappy in Billingham? I do hope so, for it had nothing to do with the local population, I assure you. They were kindness itself, even my P T instructor Florence Nightingale but, if you have to be ill, avoid touring at all times, especially in the Far North in February. Avoid touring at all times anyway – or travel with your own nurse . . .

The Gordon Craig Theatre in Stevenage was another Duncan Weldon date and, like the Forum, is part of a large leisure centre which was opened in 1976 by the Duke of Edinburgh. This time, however, we played there at the end of a tour, instead of the beginning. It was the last week of *A Bit Between the Teeth* before I went to the Congress, Eastbourne (again for Duncan) with *Babes in the Wood*. What an extraordinary way to earn a living!

The Gordon Craig is named after Ellen Terry's son, Edward, who was born in the old village of Stevenage in 1872. When he was fifteen, however, he chose to change his name, keeping Edward, after his father, adding Henry after Irving, Gordon after his godmother and Craig after his sister, Edy. She, in turn, had already renamed herself Edith Geraldine Ailsa Craig, for she rather fancied that lump of rock off the Ayrshire coast, so – by this rather circuitous route – Gordon Craig came into being. Gordon

Craig is perhaps best remembered as a stage designer, and for one of his books, *On the Art of the Theatre*, which – together with his articles on theatre and design – had a great influence on his contemporaries. However, at the time, he was equally well known for his highly publicised affair with the American dancer, Isadora Duncan, as well as for his other innumerable 'liaisons dangereuses' – possibly in excess of the total number who can sit in the theatre named after him, 507. The centre, too, boasts that it has 'indoor courts for ball games of all sorts'. It is likely that Gordon Craig found outdoor ones just as convenient, too.

The Wyvern was at it, if such a thing is possible, before the Gordon Craig, opening in September 1971. The theatre, holding 658, is part of the civic centre in Swindon, and represents something of a triumph for the local borough council, for other nearby authorities allowed dust to gather on their similar plans, but Swindon forged ahead with a centre that includes shops, a pub and a post office. Whether or not there are by-laws pertaining to the local dog population, I am not in a position to say, but I hope the local planners paid a visit to Billingham first, before completing their designs for pedestrian alleys, little irregularly paved squares, ramps and bridges; otherwise those semi-mature trees they also planned to plant will have been kicked down by now . . .

In a book of this nature, it is perhaps inevitable that a touch of the 'good old days' permeates the atmosphere, especially in recording the enormous surge of theatre building which took place in Victorian–Edwardian times, and the great circuits which came into being as a result – culminating in those of Stoll Moss and Howard and Wyndham. The majority of the buildings remaining are now in the hands of local authorities (or trusts set up by them), but one circuit does still remain or, rather, has come into being during the last dozen years or so. This is the Apollo Leisure Group, to which I have referred already in connection with Duncan Weldon, as well as mentioning their theatres in Liverpool, Manchester and Scarborough. Now to tell the rest of their story, for I am about to revisit two more of their theatres, although they were *not* theirs in my time, if you see what I mean . . .

NEW THEATRE
(now APOLLO THEATRE)
Oxford

I visited the New Theatre, Oxford for the first time with the pre-London tour of *Dry Rot* in 1954, and then ten years later with *Chase Me Comrade!*, *en route* again to the Whitehall. Both occasions were sell-out successes, but that did not stop me complaining about the huge ninety-six-sheet which faced busy George Street, and which was changed on the Saturday morning before our last two performances, advertising some totally different show for the following week. I think it was the Festival Ballet during *Comrade*. Any casual passer-by could be excused for being completely confused about which attraction was, in fact, appearing at the New that evening. Many might have preferred the actual offering, while many others may have innocently bought tickets for the ballet, and caught me prancing round in ballet tights instead. Which I did, in that particular play. The then managing director, John Dorrill (son of Stanley Dorrill, who was the managing director on my first visit), explained that the local bill-posting firm refused to turn out to change the bills on Saturday nights, so – instead of waiting till the crack of dawn on Monday mornings – the incumbent show was saddled with some quite extraneous title for the whole of a busy Saturday, and could well suffer as a consequence. It was the same story as his father told ten years earlier, and this ridiculous habit continued on all the other six visits I (or one of my tours) paid to the theatre. I can only hope that the new management has found a more amenable bill-poster. Oh, and by the way, a ninety-six-sheet is a means of describing a theatrical bill. You have playbills, daybills, hanging cards, double crowns, quad crowns, four-sheets, eight-sheets, sixteen-sheets, forty-eight-sheets and ninety-six-sheets. You can see that a ninety-six-sheet is pretty big. Room for me to complain, anyway.

The Dorrills had been connected with the New ever since Charles Dorrill became the managing director of the theatre in 1908, after fire damage to the old theatre – originally built in 1886 – had necessitated extensive rebuilding. It was Charles' son Stanley who demolished the New and rebuilt it again in 1933 and Stanley's son John who eventually had to sell the theatre to Howard and Wyndham in 1972. They too, as we know, fell on hard times and in 1977 the New was sold to Paul Gregg, the managing director of Apollo Leisure, and the first of this group's chain of theatres was thus acquired. Since then Apollo has taken over the two theatres in Scarborough and Liverpool, as well as the Apollo Theatre, the Palace and the Opera House, Manchester, the Apollo Victoria, London, the Playhouse Theatre, Edinburgh and, our next port of call, the Bristol Hippodrome. In the main, drama is not suited to Apollo's large auditoria, and they are generally filled by concerts, opera, ballet, one night stands, pantomime and so on, but the buildings *are* being used, and refurbished, as theatres, and that is what matters.

HIPPODROME
Bristol

The Oxford capacity is 1,826 whilst that at Bristol is even larger, 1,975. A lot of bums on seats and it is exhilarating when they are all in place, enjoying themselves and not shuffling around too much. They were certainly squirming with laughter on the occasions I played there, with the pre-London tours of *Dry Rot* in 1954 and *Chase Me Comrade!* in 1966, as well as the post-London offering of *A Bit Between the Teeth* some eleven years later still. I wonder how many were conscious that they were perched in Frank Matcham's last major work, undertaken in 1912 for Oswald Stoll as a West Country version of the London Hippodrome, although it was designed with a conventional auditorium as opposed to the Hippodrome's amphitheatre. It did, however, include the provision of a water tank, every bit as big as the one in London, and which was used to the full on the Hippodrome's first night, 12th December, 1912, for an attraction which had already played at the London Hippodrome. *Sands o' Dee* was a Victorian melodrama culminating in an 'amazing water spectacle in which enormous waves break across the Seashore and Horses dive into 100,000 gallons of water to the rescue of Mary, the Heroine.' But, inevitably, the use of the water tank declined as did the popularity of melodrama, and as the spectacle afforded by the cinema took its place. However, the Bristol Hippodrome contributed to this also, in a roundabout way, for shortly after the First World War a young local lad joined the backstage staff as a call-boy. His name was Archibald Leach, but you know him better as Cary Grant. I was once filming in the same studios as him, Shepperton, when he was over here making *The Grass is Greener*, and that easy charm of his was even apparent across a steamy, busy canteen at lunchtime. They had something, those old Hollywood stars.

The Hippodrome, Bristol, continued to have something for everyone for many years, too, but major problems began to develop in the late 1960s when Stoll Moss (who had assumed the management of the theatre) were forced to close for many weeks at a time, simply because they found difficulty in booking the right attractions, and there was even talk of permanent closure. However, the company rid themselves of all their other out-of-town theatres to concentrate on the Hippodrome as their sole regional flagship, with the result that the 1980s brought forth many very attractive shows, such as Danny La Rue in *Aladdin*, the English National Opera, a revival of *Annie Get Your Gun*, the Welsh National Opera and the Sadler's Wells Royal Ballet, when the box office staff were most surprised by a woman who called to ask for a refund on her tickets as 'Val Doonican is no longer in the show.' About as difficult to make head or tail of another woman who was told that there were only single seats left for a particular performance and replied that it would be all right, as long as they were together; or the little girl who enquired if the ballet would be in colour or black and white. Perhaps such remarks make it easier to understand why box office staff are sometimes, shall we say, a tinge irascible.

In spite of the apparent turnaround in their fortunes, Stoll Moss decided to sell the Hippodrome and in 1984 the property was acquired by the Apollo Leisure Group and the successful years continued, with a great deal of money being spent on improvements, too. I wonder what has happened to the bathroom which was part of the Number One dressing-room? That was a very unusual feature of the theatre, as I recall. For years I moaned at various managements about the lack of bathing facilities for actors, but Bristol was not guilty of such an omission. At least, not for the leading artist. One thing is certain, though. If I go down in history for nothing else, I shall go down as the man who insisted on (and achieved) the installation of no less than four shower-baths in four separate theatres, two in London and two in the sticks.

I have no idea of the backstage conditions at that other Bristol venue, the Theatre Royal, for, I regret to say, I have never had the privilege of appearing at this historical and beautiful playhouse. I do know, however, that J. H. Chute, the lessee of this theatre from 1853–78, had to connect the building's water supply at his own expense because the sanitation was so bad, and because the owner didn't care. Little chance of a shower-bath there, by the sound of it.

Not exactly my idea of good, clean fun, I must say.

There now only remains one other theatre not in local authority hands which I, personally, have visited at one time or another. I will deal with that next, and then go on to the public-sector properties which, I am delighted to say, are most encouraging in their provision of shower-baths. Maybe they are beginning to recognise that we are not such smelly 'rogues, vagabonds, sturdy beggars and vagrants' after all.

THEATRE ROYAL
Hanley

In 1841, on the site of an old coal mine winding-house, a certain Mr Elphinstone raised the curtain for the very first time on the potteries' own Theatre Royal at Hanley. Enlarged in 1841, partially reconstructed in 1894, restored after a small fire in 1934, it suffered a very large fire in 1949 and was virtually destroyed. The Sadler's Wells Ballet happened to be at the theatre on that particular date, too, and the box office enquiries (not that there was a proper box office left) were of a very simple and direct nature on this occasion: 'Can we have our money back, please?' The enquirers got it, and also another theatre two years later in which to spend it once more, on Émile Littler's production of *Annie Get Your Gun*.

It was after that time I had cause to visit the theatre, on my way to the Whitehall with *Simple Spymen*. It was the week following the production at the New Theatre in Hull and 24th February, 1958 was our first night. The snow still lay all around, but – just like the theatre-goers of Hull – those in the potteries used tractors and chains and shovels and salt to make their way to the theatre, and the place was packed for every single performance. And yet . . . and yet . . . Already the rumours abounded that the theatre was about to go over to bingo. Seeing the business, we could hardly credit such pessimistic talk, but the Jeremiahs were right and within three years Mecca converted the stalls area and reopened the Theatre Royal for bingo and as a social club. It carried on like that for nearly twenty years but, in 1980, Mecca closed the theatre altogether. Fortunately some local citizens, with greater hope than certainty, formed the Theatre Royal Restoration Trust, and I will now let the chairman, Charles Deacon, of what is now the Theatre Royal Hanley P L C, write for himself:

In these days of increasing variety of choice in leisure activities, with hi-fi, video cassettes, satellites and other assorted wizardry to stimulate the idle palate, the decision to reopen a major 1,400-seat-plus theatre, dark for more than twenty years and derelict for two years, in an area unaccustomed in that time to the habit of traditional theatre-going, might be regarded by some as a task unsuited to the faint-hearted. To seek to implement that decision with no financial support from any government or local government body, without grant or subsidy, might even be regarded as foolhardy.

To achieve in a period of two years, not only the reopening and restoration of that theatre, but also successfully to mount and tour major theatrical productions based in that theatre may fairly be judged as the stuff of which dreams are made, and thus be discounted as impossible.

But miracles can be the product of belief and, in the final analysis, it has been belief which has transformed dreams into reality – belief aided and abetted by a blend of professional expertise, commercial reality and sheer determination.

When the full story of the rebirth and development of the Theatre Royal, Hanley is chronicled by individuals far better equipped than I to do so, I believe that the achievement deserves to be seen as little short of miraculous.

The word 'miraculous' would seem to indicate the work of a supernatural agency but, in fact, a small earthbound army of volunteers has made all this possible, led by Charles Deacon, as well as the director of the theatre John Jones. Mr Jones was an erstwhile tax inspector before seeking a worthwhile retirement activity. He seems to have found it – and is still able to get blood out of a stone. I wonder if he operated in my tax district, come to think of it? I must ask him some time.

DEVONSHIRE PARK THEATRE
Eastbourne
CONGRESS
Eastbourne

Though totally dissimilar in nature these two theatres in Eastbourne are owned by the local authority. There was a time when Triumph Theatre Productions had a lease on the Devonshire Park, and during their tenancy I appeared there in a short summer season of *Fringe Benefits*. I also appeared in Eastbourne for the same management in *Babes in the Wood* at the Congress, although Triumph did not have a lease on that building, too.

Originally designed by H. Curry in 1884, with further reconstruction work by Frank Matcham in 1903, the Devonshire Park is a pleasant seaside theatre, holding just under a thousand patrons, who can take a quick look at the well-known Eastbourne tennis courts as they approach the theatre. Or take a long look, if they prefer, for sometimes the tournaments are of a very high standard. The Davis Cup was being contested when I was last there in 1976. Or, rather, the European Zone part of the contest. I can't recall who was playing who when I first visited the theatre in July 1961 and, as a matter of fact, I was not quite certain who was playing who, as far as I was concerned, either. You see, the play was *One For The Pot* in which I played four identical brothers. It was very complicated so I will let Sir Harold Hobson (actually the knighthood came later) try and explain, in his review for *Pot* which appeared in *The Sunday Times*:

> The theatre must always astonish . . . This is exactly what Brian Rix does in *One For The Pot* at the Whitehall. Mr Rix astonishes simply by being in a different part of the stage from where you expect him. You know that man in the corner is Mr Rix. You have heard him speak. You have seen his face. You would recognise his clothes anywhere. Well, you are wrong. It isn't Mr Rix. It was Mr Rix once; in fact, only a couple of seconds ago. But it isn't Mr Rix any longer. Mr Rix is indeed at this moment entering through a door at the back of the stage, in a place where you had not the slightest idea he would be.

And, I must admit, neither had *I* at the Devonshire Park. You see, the stage is very shallow, so the set was hard up against the back wall, which meant that instead of running round the stage, as I changed from one brother to the next, I had to gallop out of the nearest exit into the dressing-room corridor, race along the corridor – cutting a swath through any unfortunate passers-by – come tearing in at the furthest entrance to the stage, screech up to my point of entry and rejoin the frolics convulsing a happily confused audience. It was *very* exhausting. At all times, in fact, but particularly so in Eastbourne.

The Congress opened in 1963 and was deemed to be a suitable venue for *She's Done It Again* – primarily, I suspect, because it was October and there was a huge political party conference going on in the Winter Gardens at the time. Renée Stepham was dead right in choosing the venue. As she predicted, the delegates – sated with verbal diarrhoea and dogma – avoided the evening fringe meetings like the plague and flocked to enjoy an honest bit of Whitehall farce, as opposed to their more usual kind back in Westminster. Nevertheless, the Congress is hardly an ideal situation for a play, for it is described as a 'civic, multi-purpose hall/theatre. 1,678 seats in two tiers.' Need I say more?

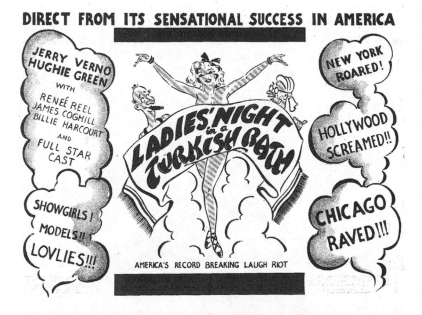

Not one of my productions. Surprisingly a few years later Eastbourne banned *No Sex Please, We're British*. Obviously the watch committee was more lenient to American productions.

PAVILION
Bournemouth

O h, I do like to be beside the seaside – but now I am running out of excuses to stay there, except for one final visit to Bournemouth, which followed Eastbourne with *She's Done It Again*. This time, though, instead of the intimate little Playhouse, we were rattling round the vastness of the Pavilion stage, with its 1929 architecture, its forty-foot opening, its forty-two-foot depth, its enormous wing space, its two-tiered 1,518-seat auditorium and all its adjacent Terraces and Ballroom and Ocean and Viking Rooms etc., etc. After the Congress, it was just like home from home. Nowadays, of course, the Bournemouth International Centre has been added to the general mish-mash, but even in 1963 the Pavilion was big enough to house a medium-sized conference – and us as well. Thank God, otherwise business might have been awful. As it was, it was splendid. I told you Renée Stepham knew her stuff.

NEW THEATRE
Cardiff

As we have just played a return date, or at least revisited the same town, if not the same theatre, let us move inland and westward to Cardiff and do the same there with the New Theatre. You will no doubt recall that this was the theatre preferred by the local authority to the Prince of Wales, when the Council decided to go into showbiz, and so I had cause to be there a number of times. The first time I was at the New was with a week of *Chase Me Comrade!* in December 1966 – whilst my fourth visit encompassed ten damp, miserable, Prime Minister Heath three-day weeks of *Robinson Crusoe*. I actually played the New seven times in all, and I must say I grew to like the theatre – well, certainly the audience – very much indeed. They are a warm-hearted lot in Welsh Wales.

On 10th December, 1906 a Mr Robert Redford opened the New Theatre with a production of *Twelfth Night* given by Sir Herbert Beerbohm Tree and His Majesty's Theatre Company from London. As Mr Redford had already run the New Theatre Royal in Cardiff for eight years, and had been the business manager for the D'Oyly Carte Opera Company for some fifteen years before that, I think it extremely unlikely that he went on to make his name in Hollywood. But you never know, in these days of face-lifts and hormone replacements. However, one thing *is* certain, Robert Redford could do no wrong in those early years at the New.

Beerbohm Tree returned several times. Sir Johnston Forbes-Robertson gave his farewell performance of *Hamlet* there, with George Bernard Shaw in front as a critic. Anna Pavlova danced at the New with the Imperial Russian Ballet and, like Tree, was so delighted with her reception that she gave a repeat performance a few months after her initial success. The D'Oyly Carte Company and the Carl Rosa Opera Company were frequently at the New, as were a number of George Edwardes and Charles Frohman musicals. The Divine Sarah graced the stage and Robert Redford probably made himself a hostage to fortune by showing D. W. Griffiths' famous film *A Birth of a Nation* in 1917. He did add a full stage orchestra, though, possibly to remind the audience that there is nothing like a 'live' performance.

After the First World War business declined, as it did in so many other theatres, but especially so at the New for there was renewed competition from the Theatre Royal, by now renamed the Prince of Wales, and the Empire just down the road, quite apart from the cinemas. For Robert Redford, now a widower and in his seventies, the struggle became too much and he left the running of the New to his two sons, who rapidly lost interest. In 1935 they leased the ailing theatre to the one and only Prince Littler – who also controlled the Prince of Wales.

The dynamic, thirty-four-year-old impresario soon restored the New to its former glory, albeit with twice-nightly variety. All through the war the top names appeared on the bill and it was a veritable Who's Who of the music-hall world – or what was left of it. But then, who wouldn't work for Mr Littler? He virtually controlled about fifty theatres, many of them in London, and it would have taken a brave man or woman, who relied on appearing in those theatres, to ignore him. In 1956, even Robert Redford's grandsons succumbed and sold the freehold to the Godfather, in the shape of the chairman of Stoll Theatres Corporation, and Cardiff – theatrically – belonged to Mr Littler. It did not last long. By the early 1960s, both theatres were in rapid decline. Littler had unloaded the Prince of Wales in 1957 and by 1961 he was trying to knock down the New to make way for offices. He lost his battle, and Cardiff City Council slapped a preservation order on the building, preventing its use for anything other than theatrical purposes and Littler had no option other than to sell to Mecca. The spectre of bingo put fire in the belly of many a Cardiff theatre-lover and the New Theatre Society was formed which forced the Cardiff Council to act yet again and the New was leased from Mecca. Within five years the Council had purchased the theatre outright.

Martin Williams, another dynamic young impresario, appeared on the scene – alas to die within a few years – and under his guidance the theatre was redeveloped and an exciting programme of attractions was made available to the Cardiff public with the Welsh National Opera, perhaps understandably, topping the list. The New Theatre went from strength to strength, and in 1985 a new general manager was appointed, this time on the distaff side – Judi Richards. She saw the theatre through a £3 million refurbishment and in 1988 *A Chorus of Disapproval* – the play, not the audience reaction – greeted the spectacular new New Theatre. Old Robert Redford – and I dare say his younger namesake – would have been delighted.

Until the advent of the Severn Bridge, access and egress to and from Cardiff was never easy – particularly if you had to travel to a date in the North of England. That is where I now propose to go, for it will save a great deal of leaping about and afford you, the reader, with a simpler route to follow than many we had to suffer, as the weeks on tour mounted and additional dates were tacked on with reckless abandon, just to keep the whole operation going. Or a ludicrous journey was undertaken, simply because a generous guarantee was on offer. None of this panic planning for you. Then, finally, I will dive over the water to Ireland, both North and South, and record the theatres I have never seen, but which were visited by my companies in the past. I do hope that meets with your approval. So let us take the long journey north, yet again, and assemble overleaf.

EMPIRE
Sunderland

As I have already mentioned – see page 82 – the coming together of Edward Moss and Richard Thornton actually happened in the Theatre Royal, Sunderland. Dicky Thornton had started his professional career as a busker on Marsden seafront, just a mile or two away from his home town South Shields, where he was eventually able to take over a tatty, disreputable music hall, which he then transformed into a well-run, profitable business. Such was his success that he was soon wealthy enough to move to the larger town of Sunderland, where he established control of both the Avenue Theatre and Opera House, as well as the Theatre Royal – the latter in partnership with Edward Moss. Both these theatres are sadly now no more.

The end of Thornton's fruitful partnership with Stoll and Moss, however, came when Thornton built the Empire, Sunderland – then called the Empire Palace. An association with Moss' Empires did continue though, booking artists in conjunction with his erstwhile partners, who were both on the stage with him at the final curtain of the opening night in 1907, when the newly established music hall was launched by Vesta Tilley at the top of the bill. The theatre continued to enjoy considerable success for the next twenty years, but then the decline caused by the coming of the cinema affected the Empire and it was hard going. There was a revival of interest, of course, during the Second World War, but after that it was downhill all the way, with the good folk of the North-east infinitely preferring the joys of television to the tawdry strip shows, which had become the music hall's staple diet.

Then in 1960 an amazing thing happened, for the Sunderland Corporation took the unprecedented step of buying the freehold, restoring the theatre and opening it again as a Number One touring date, under civic control. Since that reopening, the Empire has been refurbished and re-equipped twice, with the result that it is now fully computerised, with a state-of-the-art sound system, all mod cons both back and front, completely new seating and carpeting throughout, and a capacity of over 2,000 when all standing room is taken, although 1,900 can sit in considerable comfort, at all times. Would that all local authorities were as far-sighted as the one in Sunderland and that all other Trustees had such imagination.

I have only played the theatre once, in the week commencing 2nd November, 1970, with the post-London tour of *She's Done It Again*, although *Reluctant Heroes* visited the Empire in its struggling days in 1954. I was not a popular man on that Monday 2nd November for, at that time, I was the president of the Lord's Taverners and, as such, was expected to attend the President's Ball in the Great Room at London's Grosvenor House. The Ball was then, as it is now, the main fund-raising fixture in the whole Taverner's calendar and the president is, quite naturally, a *sine qua non*. I was nearly 300 miles away at the time and no argument or cajoling could persuade the Empire to give up a packed first night, or the Taverners to engage a fast aircraft or other alternative speedy transport for me. The memory of the icy conversations which went on between me and all concerned has coloured my views on the good burghers of Sunderland ever since. Actually, though, it wasn't their fault in any shape or form. In the world of the theatre, if you sign a contract, then that is it – and if it's not, then it jolly well ought to be.

Once though, I did manage to drive 150 miles after a show to attend a charity ball in London, and I arrived there just in time to introduce the cabaret at midnight. It was when I was in *Robinson Crusoe* at the New Theatre in Cardiff, and the Friends of Normansfield, of which I am chairman, were holding their annual ball at the Dorchester. To complicate matters further, I arranged this particular 'do' year after year in every detail, persuading my friends to perform in the cabaret, selling programme advertising and dozens of tickets, chasing up tombola and raffle prizes, as well as undertaking the unpopular chore of arranging the table plan – with all the enemies you can make doing *that*. 1974 was no exception and, in spite of being in Cardiff, I was still responsible for the eventual success of the evening, although I received much valuable support from my general manager, Gilbert Harrison, who remained in London. There was one additional hazard to this enterprise, however, in 1974. I was awaiting the hearing of a speeding charge, levelled at me on my way to Cardiff, and there was no way I was going to add any further risk of losing my licence by racing along the M4 to London. A good fairy, in the unlikely sixteen stone shape of a Cardiff police sergeant from the driving pool, and a Rugby flank forward to boot, volunteered to perform this risky drive and, even though he would have no further protection once outside Cardiff's city limits, he was prepared to take the chance. I think it was because I was the proud owner of a Jaguar xj12 at the time and he wanted to test that splendid engine to the utmost. He succeeded! With me bucketing about in the back of the car, trying to change out of my absurd pantomime walk-down costume into my D J, with the further difficulties of removing my make-up without any water, and comb my hair without any mirror, he careered along the motorway like a man possessed. Including the run-in from Heathrow, where the M4 thoughtfully narrows down to two lanes, and through the West End traffic to Park Lane, the journey took exactly two hours from door to door, with my sergeant friend cool, calm and collected throughout, driving with exemplary skill and exactitude. I am only grateful that the Thames Valley Police were not particularly vigilant that evening and would hope that my driver passed his Inspector's exams, which he was about to take the following week. If ever a man deserved promotion, it was he – in my books anyway. They might have had different ideas, though, back in the Thames Valley Constabulary, if he'd been caught. They certainly did when my case came to court. I was fined £30 and my licence endorsed. I suspect my friend would have lost his job, or his stripes, at the very least. Assuming Cardiff police take any notice of Maidenhead police, that is. Which I doubt.

Come to think of it, I wonder if my splendid chauffeur could have made that long haul from Sunderland in time? I wouldn't mind betting on it.

CIVIC THEATRE
Darlington

Duncan Weldon had an arrangement with Darlington, as well as Billingham, which is why we came to the town in April 1975 with *A Bit Between the Teeth*. I viewed the prospect with the utmost horror. All I knew about the town was that it was something to do with the origins of our railway system – and hence the huge extension of touring in the nineteenth century – and that the Stockton and Darlington Railway began it all in 1825. I imagined the town to be grimy from all that smoke, and the buildings to consist mainly of engine sheds and signal boxes. How wrong can you be? The town (and the people) turned out to be clean, attractive and very proud of the Civic Theatre. Furthermore, they loved us and there were only two seats unpaid for in the entire fortnight we were there – and those were the comps for the local Press on the first night. Unfortunately the capacity of the theatre was pretty small – 601 seats – but we still played to 9,614 paying customers in sixteen performances, which is not to be sneezed at in any circumstance.

Of course, this limited capacity has made it difficult for the theatre to operate without considerable financial support, but recently 300 more seats have been added, after the council shelled out a further £1.4 million to make this, and other improvements, possible. Now the theatre is one of the four remaining sizeable dates in the North-east. Mark you, Darlington, until comparatively recent times, had never been in the forefront of theatrical enterprise, mainly because of a strong Victorian Quaker influence. Before the first Theatre Royal was built in 1865 a stern injunction was issued to all employees of Henry Pease & Co. exhorting them 'never to go within the doors of the theatre for we know full well how too often our evening classes are neglected, and the theatre preferred at whatever sacrifice, even to pawning the Sunday clothes and so becoming unable to attend a place of worship, and we know how ruinous both to character and health this dissipation has proved to many around us.' Clearly, this did not carry as much weight as might have been expected, for a replacement Theatre Royal was opened in 1881, only to be burned down and rebuilt in 1887. This lasted as a theatre until 1936, when it was ousted by a cinema.

Much to everyone's surprise, a second large theatre was opened in 1907 by the son of a wealthy Italian merchant, Signor Rino Pepi. Eschewing his father's business, Signor Pepi had become a successful quick-change artiste on the Continent – a form of entertainment not unlike that thrust upon us with such regularity on the television nowadays: the impressionist – but had gone into management in England, opening the Tivoli in Barrow in 1902. He then moved on to the Palace, Carlisle and ended up in Darlington, where he built the New Hippodrome and Palace Theatre of Varieties. The price of admission ranged from twopence in the gallery to a shilling in the circle, or a penny or two more to go in by the 'early doors' to ensure good seats, while a box for four cost half a guinea – in other words, 52½p. But then wages were around £1 per week for unskilled labour and income tax was a shilling in the pound, so everything is relative.

The Hippodrome flourished, as did Signor Pepi's other houses, to which he added one more in Middlesbrough and a fifth in Bishop Auckland. Eventually, though, his business all boiled down to the Hippodrome and by the time Pepi died in 1927 things were beginning to slide and although the theatre enjoyed some odd moments of success, particularly during the Second World War, it closed in 1956.

The revival came about quicker than most people believed possible, thanks to the endeavours of the local Darlington Amateur Operatic Society. Lacking a home, now that the Hippodrome was closed, the Society formed Darlington Civic Theatre Ltd, a non-profit-making company, which received a grant of £1,150 a year for four years from the local council. The Society cleaned up the Hippodrome and reopened the theatre in 1958 with a production of *White Horse Inn*. By 1964 the council had bought the theatre and two years later they assumed full responsibility for the entire operation. Alterations were made to the building, reducing the seating to 601 but in spite of this small capacity the theatre, existing on a diet of touring companies and local amateur groups, continued to struggle.

In 1972 Peter Tod, aged twenty-four, was appointed as the youngest theatre director in the country at that time and the theatre was transformed. Peter struck a deal with Duncan Weldon and Paul Elliott, then still together as Triumph Theatre Productions, which ensured a stream of good touring productions or shows that were on their way to London, and the annual audience went up from twenty per cent to eighty-four per cent. Now, under the current theatre director, Brian Goddard, it has increased further to ninety-five per cent, hence the need for those 300 extra seats which, no doubt, will be constantly full.

In comparison, our house record looks very small beer, I'm afraid, but in these days of deficits and the constant struggle for so many theatres and companies to survive, it makes heart-warming reading for us all.

Let us now move a little further south, to a theatre I never visited in my youth, for it was strictly out of bounds when I was at Bootham School, York. A great pity, really, but Bootham wasn't a Friends' School for nothing. The odd thing is that we had a flourishing amateur dramatic group – along with the girls from the Mount School – but visits to the wicked professional theatre were strictly off limits. I wonder if the pupils can go now? It is only a few hundred yards away, down through Bootham Bar and close to the Minster. A very pleasant evening's stroll – and a *very* pleasant theatre, too.

THEATRE ROYAL
York

Like the Civic Theatre, Darlington, this is another 'house' which reduced its seating capacity, in 1967. Currently able to hold 950 (the previous auditorium seated 1,300), its ability to house the larger opera and ballet productions has gone. However, it performs a valuable and comfortable civic theatre function, as befits a City Council enterprise. The theatre does not have a regular touring policy, for repertory and young people's theatre is the staple fare. However, from time to time, touring companies visit the Theatre Royal, and it has been my luck to have been in one of those on three occasions, for it is a very attractive house in which to work.

Originally built in 1765, it was reconstructed about sixty years later. A new Gothic piazza was added in 1835, a new façade in 1880 and a new auditorium in 1902. In 1967 a new foyer was built, the auditorium was reduced and excellent restaurant and bar facilities were added, as well as the dressing-rooms, workshops and other backstage facilities being modernised. Part of the back wall of the stage is inviolate, however, for it is the original stonework of an erstwhile adjacent medieval nunnery, and this reduces the depth on that right-hand side of the stage a little, but nothing can be done about it. On the other hand, it does give the visiting actor something to dramatise. Practically every theatre will claim a ghost. None has ever been claimed by York, if you will pardon the ghastly pun, but when you pass that wall after the show is over and only the working lights are on, casting shadows everywhere, you hurry by with a chill running up and down your spine, I promise you.

I suppose the rules drawn up by Bootham in York and Henry Pease & Co. in Darlington were right, after all: 'Never go within the walls of a theatre.' If I'd gone backstage as a schoolboy and seen that shadowy wall, I think I would have died from fright. I nearly did as an adult, as it was . . .

ALHAMBRA THEATRE
Bradford

We really are among those dark Satanic mills now, or rather, so one is led to believe. I will grant you that my dressing-room was rather warm on the three occasions I had to visit the Alhambra Theatre, but even that has now been rectified, I am told. Otherwise, Bradford – like Darlington – is a surprise to us all, especially the delightful theatre. Originally opened in 1914 by Francis Laidler – who became known as the 'King of Pantomime' – it soon proved a rival to the Bradford Empire, which was operated by the ever-present Moss' Empires. As a result of a truce agreed between the two companies, Moss' and Laidler's Yorkshire Theatres Ltd, Moss' Empires became the booking agents for the Alhambra – an arrangement which lasted forty years, until the theatre was put up for sale by Laidler's widow, Gwladys. (The 'w' is correct, by the way, for it was a stage name she affected, together with her first husband's surname, Stanley, when she played Prince Charming in the Alhambra's 1921/22 *Cinderella*. She changed her surname again, however, by becoming Laidler's second wife in 1926.) When Laidler died in January 1955, Gwladys was described as the most influential woman in the provincial theatre, for she now controlled her late husband's 'houses' – including the Bradford Prince's, the Leeds Theatre Royal and the Keighley Hippodrome, as well as the Alhambra. Only the latter now remains.

Originally, the Bradford City Council turned down the chance to buy the Alhambra, but seven eventful years later, when the Bradford Alhambra Company had gone into voluntary liquidation, the Council changed its mind and bought the theatre for £78,900 – promptly leasing it back to a newly formed Bradford Alhambra Company, with Rowland Hill as the managing director. He had been at the Alhambra since 1922, with *both* companies of the same name. *Plus ça change* . . .

Over the next six years, however, Rowland Hill managed to make a profit for the Council of £8,782. Then, in 1971, business began to slip into the red once more and, in less than three years, the Bradford Alhambra Company was finally wound up, and the Council took over the theatre completely. By 1986 they had concluded successful negotiations with the EEC, and the Common Market contributed £2.1 million towards a total of £8.2 million spent by the local authority on the theatre. It is now a superb venue, still reflecting the original design of its architects Messrs Chadwick and Watson, who wished to provide a contrast to those nearby grimy, looming mills by creating a building that was based on its original namesake, the Alhambra in Granada. The three domes still shine forth as a credit to all who have made this possible. They are proudly proclaimed to be the 'Domes of Delight', and are aptly named indeed.

When I was a lad living in Yorkshire, I occasionally used to see the adverts for Bradford and Leeds pantomimes, which seemed to stretch, if not into eternity, at least until the late spring. Even so, attractions other than variety and pantomime did occasionally grace the Alhambra stage, particularly in the early days. Actor-managers such as Sir John Martin-Harvey, Matheson Lang and Sir Frank Benson dramatically leavened the bread, but it is doubtful if Bradford saw them in their full pomp and glory. Indeed, Sir Frank was nearly seventy when he last visited the town and although he was becoming increasingly absent-minded his athleticism defied his years. So much so that at one memorable performance of *The Merchant of Venice*, in which he played Shylock, Sir Frank thought he was playing Henry V instead. In this latter role, the ageing, athletic knight would, as it were, pole vault over a wall into 'Once more unto the breach, dear friends, once more' but, to save money, this same piece of wall was used in *The Merchant* for 'Act I Scene III – Venice. A Public Place' and on this particular night at the Alhambra, the audience were astounded to see Shylock making his first entrance by using his staff to straddle the wall, realise his mistake, accept his applause and then get on with the scene, somewhat puffed but still resonant – ' "Three thousand ducats," phew! phew! "well", phew!!'

In my childhood there were no less than five theatres still operating in Bradford: the Alhambra itself, the aforementioned Moss' Empire, the Palace, the Prince's and the Theatre Royal. It was while he was appearing at the Royal that the prince of actor-managers, Sir Henry Irving, died. The ominous date was Friday 13th October, 1905, and Irving had just played Becket and spoken those immortal last words: 'Into thy Hands, O Lord, into thy Hands!' Under two hours later, he had joined Thomas à Becket in the hereafter.

Sir Henry died penniless, on the road, just like any other old character actor might have done. The autumn tour, which was to make him a little money, was less than two weeks old, starting the week before in Sheffield.

LYCEUM THEATRE
Sheffield

I have never played the Lyceum, although Johnnie Slater was there a number of times in *Reluctant Heroes*, *Dry Rot* and *One For The Pot*, so I can claim a tenuous connection. In view of this, it seems right and proper I should pay the Lyceum a cursory visit – quite apart from the fact that it was Irving's last full week in the theatre, before his death in Bradford. The date sheet is just in reverse order, that's all. Incidentally, Sir Henry's repertoire contained *The Merchant of Venice*, *Becket*, *The Bells* and *Louis XI* – a somewhat different diet of drama than that which I sent to this country's sixth-largest city – but tastes change; so much so in fact, that in the mid-1960s the Lyceum closed and became yet another bingo hall. Now, amazingly, it has been rescued and is a theatre once again.

Originally built as the City Theatre in 1893, it changed completely four years later when it was redesigned by W. G. R. Sprague. Sprague, you may recall, was a disciple of Frank Matcham's, designing no less than eight beautiful London theatres – including the Albery, Wyndham's, the Globe, the Aldwych and the Strand. The Lyceum is his only remaining work outside London. After it went over to bingo, the Lyceum Theatre Trust was formed to campaign for the reopening of the theatre but, at first, things went against them. To begin with, the city's theatrical needs appeared to have been met with the building of the thrust-stage Crucible in 1971. A very good policy of repertory was introduced and, of course, in more recent days the Crucible has become extremely well known for housing the televised snooker championships. All seemed lost as far as the Lyceum was concerned, especially as at the beginning of the 1980s permission was granted for a new owner of the theatre to turn it into a pop venue.

Then came a change of heart. The City Council joined forces with the Lyceum Theatre Trust and a great overall scheme for Tudor Square (which houses the Crucible, the Lyceum, the Ruskin Museum) came into being with plans for a new art gallery and international hotel. By 1989 work had begun on the splendid restoration of the Lyceum. This design work was undertaken by the same architects who created the Crucible – the Renton Howard Wood Levin Partnership – and it was of the highest standard. The late Mr Sprague would have been delighted. So would the late Sir Henry for, eighty-five years after his last performance there as Shylock, the Lyceum reopened its doors with a theatrical gala week, and the first night was a splendid affair. I know – for I was there – and the theatre interior is quite one of the most beautiful I have ever seen. Now it provides a complementary touring date to its neighbouring theatres in Yorkshire and will certainly continue to thrive. Unhappily its success has adversely affected business at the Crucible. Plans are afoot to ensure the programmes for the two theatres are as contrasting as possible.

Incidentally, the whole operation to restore the Lyceum cost around £12 million – £5 million from the Council, £2 million from the voluntary sector and £5 million from the EEC. With the £2 million-plus the Common Market gave to the Alhambra in Bradford, it would appear that 'where there's muck there's brass' still applies – except Bradford and Sheffield seemed awfully clean and pleasant when I visited them. You will simply have to go and see for yourselves. And do go to the theatres while you're up there. You will be delighted.

GRAND THEATRE
Wolverhampton

I have only played the Grand on three occasions – in the opening week of *Stand By Your Bedouin*, which was on its way to start the season of repertoire at the Garrick Theatre in February 1967, and then later with *She's Done It Again* and *Fringe Benefits*. On six other occasions I sent my productions there, but I was not present in the flesh, so to speak. I can't say I was sorry, because in those days the theatre was getting tattier and tattier, with mounds of rubbish piled up at the stage door when you arrived on the Monday, all left over from the previous Saturday's two performances and get-out. It was very unattractive.

I am happy to report that all has now changed, and the theatre is run impeccably. One million pounds was spent on it in 1983 by the Council and an enthusiastic group of Friends, to make it once again a theatre of which the Black Country patrons can be proud, just as they were when it opened in 1894 – the same year which saw the closure of the old Theatre Royal. Since those days the Grand has followed a similar pattern to practically every provincial theatre still open to the public, culminating in its purchase by the local authority in 1969. Even that, though, did not stop the slide into near bankruptcy, and by 1980 the theatre was forced to close. Most people assumed at the time that it would not be long before the bulldozers were on the site – but they were wrong and, thanks to an expert campaign conducted by the local Theatre Club and the foresight of the Wolverhampton Council, C. J. Phipps' splendid design was saved and refurbished to the highest standards. No longer do touring actors dread the date and no longer is it necessary to sit on the wooden chairs in the dressing-rooms because you are nervous of the insect life which thrives in the upholstered variety. In the bad old days there was no way you could have a rest between shows. You just had to keep on your feet or go for a walk round the block. As that took you to the railway station, there wasn't much mileage in that, either.

From 1936 to 1966, the Grand housed repertory, provided by our old friend from the Alexandra Theatre, Birmingham – Derek Salberg. Many famous actors and actresses cut their artistic teeth here, including Kenneth More, Leonard Rossiter, Peggy Mount, Peter Vaughan and John Barron. I could name some more – but would hate to be accused again of publishing lists and I refuse to end with the cliché 'to name but a few'.

Talking of Salberg, I can't quite recall which theatre I was visiting to see the final try-out of *One For The Pot*. It was certainly a Salberg Company, though, and it could have been either the one at the Alex in Brum or the one at the Grand in Wolves. That, I am glad to say, is immaterial. The year was 1960 and I was driving up the newly opened sixty-eight-mile stretch of the M1 to see the play, accompanied by its future director Henry Kendall. You have already met Harry as the irate director of *You, Too, Can Have A Body*, when he had his spat with the author of that piece, Fred Robinson, and you may have gathered that he was a camp old fellow with a mordant wit. I was very proud of my fast cars in those days and, as there was no speed limit on the motorway, I was determined to show Harry my Facel Vega's paces – for it was a brute of a French car with a 7½-litre Chrysler engine, which meant it went like 'shit off a shovel'. That was Harry's description of its performance, I hasten to add. As we approached 145 mph I noticed, too, that he was turning slightly ashen – not to say green – which surprised me, for he had been a brave First World War fighter pilot – trained by no less a luminary than Ben Travers (although Ben was still a few years away from the Aldwych) and awarded the A F C – so I remarked that it must be as nothing compared to such derring-do in the sky. Harry soon put matters into perspective: 'Utter bollocks, dear boy, I have never been as fast as this before, even in a vertical dive in a Sopwith Pup.'

Mr Macready as King Richard III, 1822.

THEATRE ROYAL
Bury St Edmunds

So we arrive at the last theatre, and probably one of the oldest, in which I have appeared and certainly one of the most attractive. Built in 1819 as the New Theatre, it is a superb example of a Georgian playhouse designed by the architect William Wilkins, whose father – another William and an architect, too – created the Norwich circuit, including the Theatre Royal at Norwich and the theatres at Yarmouth, Colchester, Ipswich and Cambridge. It is believed that the younger Wilkins incorporated many of the features he had included in the competition for designing the new Drury Lane theatre in 1811, which he failed to win. (Although he did go on to design the National Gallery and University College, London which are still here today.) The Theatre Royal is a remarkable work, especially when you consider that the theatre became a beer-barrel store for its owners, brewers Greene King, from the late 1920s to the mid 1960s, and was only restored as a result of pressure, led by the local Amateur Operatic Society, headed by Air Vice-Marshal Stanley Vincent, and other worthies. But I am jumping ahead.

The Norwich Company was one of the oldest and most respected of all the circuit companies and only played at the best theatres in the region. The New Theatre, Bury St Edmunds was one of these, and a large and varied repertoire of plays was on show during the weeks the theatre was open, annually in October and November, when the Great Fair attracted all the local farmers and their families to a giant celebration of the end of harvesting, and their ability to sell farm produce for a sound profit. There was no shortage of money, for members of the gentry had come to live in Bury St Edmunds, too, so the company could charge high prices (for those days) and do well for its proprietors, as well as keeping the actors in low-paid but regular work. Success also meant that one of the greatest actors of the day, William Charles Macready, was attracted to join the company at the theatre and in November 1828 he performed a repertoire of no less than five plays, including *Macbeth*, *Othello* and a stage adaptation of Walter Scott's *Rob Roy*. Not bad for someone who had already played eighteen provincial theatres in that year, with a similar repertoire, as well as Paris for seven weeks and Drury Lane for four. Macready went on to complete his exhausting schedule with a further six weeks on tour, before the end of the year – and even at Christmas-tide, he was at Ipswich. No wonder the famous 'Macready pause' came into being. He must have been trying to remember where he was.

Actually, that is not as silly as it sounds. When you have been in a play for a long time, it is very easy to 'go to sleep' during the performance, and then 'wake up' wondering where the heck you are. Not the name of the town, of course, but exactly where you are in the play. 'Have I said that' or 'did I cut that' creates panic in your brain and it is then that you can dry and emulate Ronnie Shiner with 'we know the bloody line, but who the hell says it.' No joke, I can assure you, because it has happened to me on numerous occasions, especially when dreaming of the supper I might be having after the show, or the late-night film on television which could accompany it, or the day's work ahead on the morrow etc., etc. The distractions are endless, especially when you are giving your 1,475th performance – or what have you – and many a 'Macready pause' has been given by many a long-run actor, simply trying to collect his thoughts. I hasten to add that when I use the words 'actor' or 'his', I mean them in an androgynous sense; actresses are just as prone to the 'pause' as their male counterparts. Even more so, if they have left a baby at home.

The coming of the railways affected Bury St Edmunds, and the actors therein, just as it did the rest of the country. From being an important provincial centre, Bury St Edmunds became a sleepy county town, and the theatre suffered accordingly. Mind you, the malaise was country-wide. In 1826, the leader in *The Times* commented: 'The state of theatrical property in England is wretched beyond description. Many of the large towns which supported a theatre three or four months in the year do not now encourage even a week's acting and in many places where the theatres are open, the performers are starving.' And so, in 1843, the New Theatre closed for what would now be known as 'major refurbishment'.

It reopened two years later as the Theatre Royal, but unhappily that didn't seem to make much difference, and after a further fifty-eight years it closed yet again. Though not before it had staged the very first performance, on Leap Year's Day, 29th February, 1892, of *Charley's Aunt* by Brandon Thomas, with W. S. Penley playing the part which was to bring both men fame and fortune when the 'farcical comedy' opened at the Royalty Theatre in London some ten months later. This must have been one of the modern theatre's first try-outs of a farce. Years later, I always followed this same principle – in a repertory company at Windsor or Guildford or Folkestone or Birmingham or Wolverhampton; the only difference was that I had to pay the original try-out theatre an ongoing royalty. Bury St Edmunds got nothing – although seventy-five years after that first night an occasional actor-manager, George Baker (better known as TV's Inspector Wexford) presented an anniversary production of *Charley's Aunt*, with John Moffat as Fancourt Babberley, and a cheque came winging from the Brandon Thomas estate in celebration. The sum? – £100. I'm not sure if such munificence was repeated for the more recent centenary production. After twenty-five years of inflation it would have been worth having.

Better seating and electric lighting were included in the 1906 alterations – three years after the venue had closed – but still the theatre was unable to attract a regular and devoted following. In 1920, the brewers Greene King bought the place and tried to run it as of yore, but to no avail, and in 1925 it became a barrel store. Then came the miracle of the Air Vice-Marshal and his amateur operatic friends, and the theatre has never looked back since its opening forty years after its conversion to a cooper's cellar. Greene King have gone even further with their generosity, however, and now a 999-year lease has been granted to the National Trust, while an Arts Council Incentive Funding Award has been won by the theatre, in excess of £100,000, so the future seems set fair for many interesting productions to continue visiting Bury St Edmunds – including those by Hull Truck and Cheek by Jowl. A bit different from *Charley's Aunt* maybe – but it's all good theatre, and that is what matters.

One final story. Terry Alexander and I were appearing at the Theatre Royal in February 1976 with *Fringe Benefits*. Because the seating capacity is so small – 333 seats – we had been given a substantial guarantee, which was necessary, even though every seat was full for every performance. On the Thursday night we had just started the second act when there was a commotion behind us and the manager, flushed and excited, came rushing on to the stage, commanded the play to stop and the audience (plus the actors) to file out into the street. Everybody was dumbfounded, but he explained that there had been a bomb warning and the security forces were on their way, so would we please scarper. We needed no second bidding, and on a cold winter's night we all found ourselves crammed on to the pavement, audience and actors alike, outside the front-of-house. Eventually, the security forces arrived. One policeman in a panda car, the other on a bicycle – complete with bicycle clips. No sophisticated equipment, no dogs, no nothing. But our security forces *did* look round, shining torches under seats and in dark corners, and eventually announced themselves satisfied that all was well. Tentatively, we returned – with many a surreptitious glance at any suspicious-looking object – and enquired if the audience would like us to continue. Just like the reaction of *The Watch on the Rhine* audience, after that wartime fracas at the

Aldwych Theatre, there came an overwhelming shout of 'yes'. We continued, and I guarantee that *Fringe Benefits* has never had bigger laughs, before or since. There's nowt like trouble at t'mill to unite folk, tha' knows.

THE ROYAL SHAKESPEARE
THEATRE
Stratford-upon-Avon
or, as it used to be called,
THE SHAKESPEARE MEMORIAL
THEATRE

I wish I could claim to have played this date with memorable success, as part of the annual Shakespearian cycle of plays. Alas, the truth is far more mundane. I have *never* graced those hallowed boards (or even disgraced them), but a company of mine did visit the theatre in February 1955, with *Reluctant Heroes*. It wasn't even the Number One tour of the play (either Bert Brownlow or Robin Wentworth was playing Sgt Bell, the seventh and eighth takeover respectively), but I must report that we played to enormous business. In those days, the theatre used to allow midwinter visitors to fill-in before the season proper began, and I honestly believe the local audience were so relieved to have something other than a diet of Shakespeare, they would come to anything – especially something which made them laugh – and *Heroes* certainly did that. So, there we are – an unexpected triumph, as you might say.

The original Memorial Theatre was built in 1879, thanks to the generosity of a local brewer, Charles Edward Flower, who presented the newly formed governors with the riverside site on which the theatre was eventually to be built. He then headed the national appeal, and when this was unsuccessful, contributed most of the necessary £20,000 himself – and his family has continued its interest ever since. Initially, the 'season' could hardly be described as such, for it lasted but a week in the middle of summer, but 'star visitors' – like Ellen Terry and Beerbohm Tree – used to appear in Shakespearian roles which they nominated themselves and the audiences were happy. Then along came the first of the famous directors of the theatre, Frank Benson, who extended the season to two months, with tours going out between times.

In 1925 the company was granted a Royal Charter, and actually made a profit for the first time, but less than twelve months later the theatre was almost completely destroyed by fire, and yet another theatrical phoenix had to arise from the ashes of what had been, unfortunately, a Victorian monstrosity of a building (so much so, in fact, that Bernard Shaw sent the governors a telegram of congratulation when it was burned to the ground). In 1932 true congratulations were in order, for the present theatre – a warm, pleasant building – opened on the date considered to be Shakespeare's birthday, 23rd April. Along with the new theatre came a new style of production, with directors such as B. Iden Payne, Komisarjevsky and Robert Atkins (later to run Regent's Park) at the helm, while Donald Wolfit was able to watch Randle Ayrton's monumental *King Lear*, which provided him with so much insight into the character, once he came to undertake the role himself. Forsaking his beloved Birmingham Repertory Company, which he had founded in 1913, Sir Barry Jackson took over as artistic director in 1946, and saw the company through all the post-war difficulties with vision and application. It was he who gave the first major opportunities to director Peter Brook and actor Paul Scofield. Then it was Anthony Quayle's turn, after the theatre had been altered and improved in 1950, who was joined by Glen Byam Shaw in 1953 and succeeded by him in 1957.

In 1960 Peter Hall assumed the mantle, and a London base at the Aldwych Theatre was added, moving to the Barbican in 1982. Trevor Nunn became the artistic director in 1968, followed by Terry Hands some eighteen years later, when the Swan Theatre at Stratford opened. Today Adrian Noble is in overall charge, supported by Michael Attenborough, faithful old David Brierley as general manager and, now, Jonathan Pope – who was a drama officer at the Arts Council – as the administrator. Genista McIntosh had held that job for a short time, but then moved to the Royal National Theatre to succeed David Aukin as that theatre's executive director. David, himself, moved to Channel 4 Television as the head of drama. A veritable La Ronde, as you can see. Both Michael and Genista were serving on the Arts Council Drama Panel when they were appointed, with Jonathan Pope as an officer, and I was both proud and pleased for them all, for, as I have mentioned, I was the Panel's chairman at the time. Well, I still am, actually – which makes it all the more embarrassing when the Royal Shakespeare Company falls on hard times, which it seems to do with fairly monotonous regularity. Hopefully, its substantially increased grant in 1991 from the Arts Council will make all that unpleasantness a thing of the past.

Even so, I doubt if the RSC would like to go back to the week-long summer festival of 1879. And I trust all concerned do not take that first production as a comment on their work over the years. Its title? *Much Ado About Nothing.*

FESTIVAL THEATRE
Malvern

In a way, I suppose I have played the Festival Theatre, for I went there in the autumn of 1989 to sell my last book, *Farce About Face*. Actually, it was the twenty-fifth anniversary of the Malvern Theatre Association – the supporters' organisation, which provides the majority of the 'staff' for the theatre on a voluntary basis – and it was a great 'do'. Drinks and a jolly good supper, plus the chance to reminisce to an interested, captive audience made for a good evening, as far as I was concerned. What is more, I sold quite a lot of books, too.

In fact, though, this is another of those theatres only visited by one of my companies. Two, to be precise: *Tell the Marines* (by Roland and Michael Pertwee) in June 1953 and *Reluctant Heroes* for the Christmas fortnight, 1954/5 – with either Mr Brownlow or Mr Wentworth losing their voices as Sgt Bell. In *Tell the Marines*, Wally Patch, having left *Heroes* for a time, was losing his, as yet another sergeant, in the Pertwee army farce. No wonder burly, thickset actors were glad when National Service was over. They could go back to playing quieter-spoken detective-sergeants instead. Theatrical E N T (ear, nose and throat) specialists, like John Musgrove and Norman Punt, nearly went out of business.

The Festival Theatre began life as the Malvern Assembly Rooms in 1885, with an all-purpose 'concert hall and theatre' and seating for '700 persons', accommodated on a flat floor in the auditorium. Frank Benson was one of those who visited the place, from his Stratford-upon-Avon Memorial Theatre, and there were many other tours as well, plus the popular 'flying matinées'. Amateur productions, though, were the staple diet during the majority of the year.

Then in 1927 the Malvern Urban District Council purchased the Assembly Rooms and, despite local opposition, set about transforming the building. But first, they had the good sense to interest none other than Sir Barry Jackson, who lent his support to the alterations which were to take place. The stalls were raked, a circle added, and many other changes made. But – guess what – the dressing-rooms were untouched; poky cells,

227

with a larger room for the chorus, and these were left as such until after the Second World War, when their improvement brought an outcry from local ratepayers, resentful that a comparatively modest sum was to be spent on the so-called comfort of actors. It always seems to be a battle, wherever you are.

Sir Barry Jackson introduced the first Malvern Drama Festival in 1929 – it lasted a fortnight and was dedicated to Bernard Shaw. *The Apple Cart, Back to Methuselah, Heartbreak House* and *Caesar and Cleopatra* were the productions, headed by Cedric Hardwicke and Edith Evans, with members of the Birmingham Rep to play all the parts unclaimed by the stars. The Festival grew and many other works were included, other than those by Shaw. Indeed, in the ten years up to the outbreak of war in 1939, there were sixty-five plays presented, by some forty-odd authors – but with G B S having pride of place, as it were.

After the war was over, things were not quite so well organised and the theatre virtually became a cinema, with only occasional stage shows, including my two productions, to remind people of its past. But in 1977 the Festival was revived and has gone from strength to strength, with a resident amateur company, the Malvern Theatre Players, keeping interest going when other attractions are not readily available. It's almost like the old days, when the amateur really was the backbone of English drama. I'm glad it's not too popular an idea, though, in the rest of the country. Actors' salaries are low enough already, without having to compete with their acting unpaid opposite numbers in any great profusion. We've come a long way in the last 500 years. But not far enough, some would think . . .

PALACE THEATRE
Westcliff-on-Sea

Before we take our fleeting voyage across the Irish Sea to look at the touring venues with a touch of the blarney, it's time to put a tentative last toe in the North Sea from the beach at Westcliff, hard by Southend. Actually, the Palace was another of those theatres visited by *Reluctant Heroes* on its final tour, but for the life of me I cannot understand why we chose to go there on 17th January, 1955. I don't suppose we chose it at all, really. Just accepted the date because it was the middle of the pantomime season and all that Renée Stepham could manage for us. But it does seem a bit unlikely, all the same.

Originally called Raymond's New Palace, it has been altered and improved on several occasions since it opened in 1912, including a change of name. It was last refurbished in 1988 and now alternates between a resident repertory company and the occasional touring show. As far as I am concerned, its main claim to fame is that Ray Cooney has tried out two or three of his farces there – and I think he only did that because his mum and dad lived next door in Southend-on-Sea. These plays were *Move Over Mrs Markham* (with co-author, John Chapman) in 1969, *There Goes the Bride* in 1970 and *Why Not Stay for Breakfast?* in 1973. He doesn't seem to have been back for some time, does he? And I cannot recall that his parents ever moved. But there we are. I seem to remember that Johnnie Slater's in-laws lived close by, too – and that seems to be that. Hardly a wildly exciting note on which to end my tour of the British mainland theatres – but at least I am being honest. Let's go to Ireland forthwith.

GRAND OPERA HOUSE *Belfast*
OPERA HOUSE *Cork*
OLYMPIA *Dublin*
GAIETY *Dublin*

I wish I could report that I have enjoyed appearing in Dublin's fair city, or Cork or Belfast for that matter. I fear such a claim would not be the truth and, indeed, I have never visited Cork in my life. I have been to Belfast on a number of occasions, though, on behalf of M E N C A P and I once visited Dublin on a similar mission – to speak to parents of mentally handicapped children and adults – but I chose a somewhat difficult day. It was the occasion of hunger-striker Bobby Sands' funeral and it made the reception of an Englishman, albeit in a good cause, rather – shall we say – polite.

It was *Reluctant Heroes* which visited Belfast, Cork and Dublin first, with *Dry Rot* venturing back to both the north and south of the great divide with a week in each capital, leaving out Cork, nearly four years later. I think it fair to say that the latter farce, about bookmaking and horse-switching, went down better with our Irish friends and relations than *Heroes*, with its British Army theme. Actually, I am amazed that they were prepared to show *Heroes* in the first place, although things were a bit quieter in December 1954, and the spirit of Christmas was in the air. Nevertheless, all was not sweetness and light and David Drummond, who has provided the pictures for this book, but was then an actor working for me, reports:

> In Belfast, after an incident at Omagh barracks, a tight lock was kept on the rifles and blank ammunition in the play. The next date was Cork, where the military uniformed nature of the piece was scarcely appropriate for the anniversary of the British troops sacking the town and commemorated in a special monster edition of *The Kerryman*.

But, as always, Renée Stepham was carrying out her job to keep the tour going, and it is never very easy to book dates around Christmas-tide, as you can imagine, with all those pantomimes. Nevertheless, what with the cost of transporting a two-set play – *Reluctant Heroes* – and the unsuitability of the theme, we might have been better to keep the scenery in demurrage at Liverpool docks.

The Grand Opera House in Belfast is the last of Frank Matcham's theatres we will visit on our grand tour. He designed it in 1895 and it is described in *Curtains!!!* as 'the best surviving example in the U K of the Oriental style applied to theatre architecture – largely Indian in character'. Seven years after we were there with *Heroes* the theatre was sold to Odeon Cinemas, but was subsequently bombed and closed. It reopened in 1980, after complete restoration overseen by the architect Robert McKinstry and supported by the Arts Council of Northern Ireland, and was then available again as a major touring venue, with just over a thousand seats. Perhaps a little small for the biggest opera and dance companies, but they all seemed to visit the theatre nevertheless. Alas, the theatre is no longer available for *any* company, having been bombed yet again at the beginning of the 1991 panto season. When I rang Renée Stepham to check this she came out with a classic theatrical *non sequitur*: 'Oh yes, terrible,' she said, 'but at least it was the day before the get-in.'

This tale of woe continues south of the border for the original Opera House my company visited in Cork was destroyed by fire in 1955, but ten years after that it was rebuilt as the result of a board of Trustees from the business community raising the necessary funds. But life since then has not been easy, even though the Trustees own the theatre on behalf of the people of the city, and many and great have been the financial crises of the Opera House, in spite of a regular audience occupancy of somewhere in the region of seventy per cent. The Corporation are being asked to grant-aid the theatre to the tune of £1.25 million over the next five years for, apart from an operating budget, the building is in need of extensive renovation after twenty-five years of shuffling on seats, walking on carpets, going to the loos and propping up the bars. It's amazing what even seventy per cent can do in the way of wear and tear . . .

The Olympia, Dublin is perhaps best known for the number of times it has changed its name, rather than as a house for 'straight' drama – if *Reluctant Heroes* qualifies for such an accolade. First built in 1855, and then several times after that, it was opened as the Monster Saloon Music Hall. It then became the Star of Erin Music Hall and, after that (and more sedately) the Empire Palace. For good measure, it was also known as Dan Lowry's. In 1897 it was rebuilt yet again as the Olympia and has stayed that way ever since, although not without difficulty. The proscenium arch collapsed in 1974, dragging down much of the auditorium with it, including all the plasterwork. However, there was a very successful fundraising campaign and it wasn't long before the Olympia once more opened its doors to in-house productions, touring shows and pantomimes, watched, when full, by 1,300 people. The name 'Olympia' makes it sound bigger, somehow, but I imagine the size is about right for a city the size of Dublin, even though Dubliners do love their theatre, along with their cockles and mussels! alive, alive, oh!

The Gaiety, Dublin is a little more used to 'straight' drama, although the original Letters Patent granted to the theatre in 1871 allowed the founders 'therein at all times to act, represent or perform any interlude, tragedy, comedy, prelude, opera, burletta, play, farce or pantomime'. A pretty catholic choice, I think you will agree, which is perhaps appropriate for this Irish capital.

The list of famous artistes visiting the theatre over the years is formidable indeed, but before the turn of the century all the great names seem to have been there, including Irving, Edwin Booth, Beerbohm Tree, Frank Benson, Wilson Barrett, Sarah Bernhardt, Lillie Langtry and Ellen Terry just to be going on with, and it seems ironical that in the early days all the works of those great Irish playwrights, W. B. Yeats and George Bernard Shaw were only performed at the Gaiety by English companies. On the other hand, the founder of the great English theatre-lighting organisation, Strand Electric (now the Rank-Strand Electric & Engineering Co. Ltd), was but a humble Dublin-born electrician at the Gaiety, but went to London to start his stage-lighting service and found the streets were indeed paved with gold.

For a little time, from 1936, the theatre changed its policy to one of presenting vaudeville, and marked the occasion by engaging Sir Harry Lauder. However, the Second World War and Irish neutrality caused many a booking difficulty for the Maurice Ellimann Group who had acquired the theatre, and from then on Irish-based companies had the task of keeping the theatre open. The extremely creative partnership of Hilton Edwards and Michael MacLiammoir (who had founded Dublin's Gate Theatre several years earlier) now presented seasons at the Gaiety, while one of the finest Shakespearian actors of his generation – so 'tis said – Anew McMaster, also made many appearances there. With the 1950s came a number of seasons under the guidance of Cyril Cusack, but in 1955 the theatre closed for a time to be reconstructed and then reopened with a special celebratory programme, which included pretty well all the great Irish names then extant, including the Dublin theatrical companies – the Abbey, the Gate, the Longford Players, Cyril Cusack's Company, Anew McMaster's Company and the Illsley-McCabe Company. A splendid list indeed.

Since then, the Gaiety has been run by the late Eamonn Andrews' production company, but has now returned to its original owners, who continue the policy originally laid down in the Letters Patent – being all things to all men, it seems. No wonder the Gaiety is affectionately known as the Grand Old Lady of South King Street. A fitting tribute to C. J.

Phipps who designed this theatre in his heyday, and his design has changed little over the last 130 years.

Matcham and Phipps. There will never be such a pair of theatre architects again, simply because the building boom is over, never to return. Indeed, it is arguable that the West Yorkshire Playhouse will be the last theatre to be purpose-built in this country until the next millennium, so I do hope you have enjoyed this largely personal visit to our theatrical heritage. We must be constantly vigilant in our scrutiny of any developments which could threaten the removal of any more of our beautiful and historic theatres and also constantly supportive of our theatrical companies on tour, if they merit such attention. Thank God, many of them do and now I shall describe, briefly, some of those still out on the road. I am only glad it isn't one of mine – but I am equally glad that so many actors *are* prepared to live out of a suitcase for weeks and months on end. Without them – and the managements, of course – our provincial theatre – sorry, *regional* theatre – would surely perish.

So, to the After-piece. More appropriate, don't you think, than the more pompous-sounding Epilogue? Then my tour de farce is o'er . . .

Slow curtain.

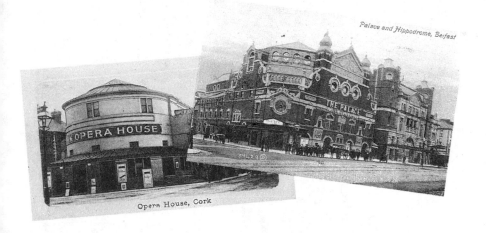

Palace and Hippodrome, Belfast

Opera House, Cork

AFTER-PIECE

PALACE THEATRE

SHAFTESBURY AVENUE　　　　**LONDON, W.I**

With Millie 15.3/40

LEE EPHRAIM

PRESENTS

IN

"UNDER YOUR HAT"

6D.

Cicely Courtneidge and Jack Hulbert in *Under Your
Hat* of which, from 1938 to 1940, they gave 512
performances and then many more on tour.

'Will Any Gentleman?'

The answer to the question, *Will Any Gentleman?* (the very funny 1950 farce by Vernon Sylvaine), as it applies to touring and actor-managers, is most certainly 'yes'. The nadir had been reached when Donald Wolfit put away his make-up box, and the classical actor on the road, in his own productions and with his own company, was no more. Many believed there would be no resurrection. Happily such Jeremiahs were wrong.

The Arts Council of Great Britain has come in for a great deal of stick over the years, some of it deserved, most of it not. Touring productions, however, and the new generation of actor-managers owe the Arts Council – particularly Jack Phipps, until 1992 the Director of Touring – a considerable debt of gratitude, for all those I am about to name, apart from Kenneth Branagh and Renaissance, have received considerable support in their endeavours to get their companies on the road. Furthermore, the Touring Department backs many other clients, and has been largely instrumental in influencing local authorities to take over their ailing theatres, restore them with the latest technical improvements and make them available to the community throughout the day, as opposed to the old-fashioned sacrosanct hours of seven p.m. to eleven p.m. When I was appearing in *Reluctant Heroes*, my one-time RAF drill sergeant came to see the play and, like the rest of the audience, roared with laughter. He came round afterwards and in his Bow Bells' cockney confided that he didn't know he could enjoy himself in the 'featre'. He thought it was like going to church. Thank God (as this seems appropriate) the Arts Council has helped break down such reverential treatment.

The leader of this renewed interest in touring is undoubtedly Ian McKellen, who on more than one occasion has been the head of a company, either as an actor or as the manager as well. He was first seen in this capacity with Prospect Productions in the Edinburgh Festival, and the subsequent tour of *Edward II* and *Richard II* in 1968. In these productions he was paired with Timothy West, who also eventually became an actor-manager, unhappily overseeing the demise of Prospect Productions when it finally kicked the bucket as the Old Vic Company in 1981. However, one of the early members of Prospect (founded at the Oxford Playhouse in 1961 by Elizabeth Sweeting and Iain Mackintosh) was director Richard Cottrell, who, in 1969, went on to be the first director of the Cambridge Theatre Company, backed by the Cambridge City Council, the Arts Theatre Trust and the Arts Council, and who was dedicated to appearing at both the Arts Theatre in that university town, as well as touring. One of Richard Cottrell's first recruits was a fellow Cambridge graduate, Ian McKellen who, in 1970, appeared in *The Recruiting Officer* and *Chips With Everything* and two years later joined forces with another actor, Edward Petherbridge, to found the Actors' Company – also dedicated to touring as part of its overall policy, with Richard Cottrell and the Cambridge Theatre Company offering general support, as well as acting as midwife at the birth of this fledgling group. I remember I tried to help them come into the Garrick Theatre when I was going on tour with a different kind of classic – *Don't Just Lie There, Say Something* – but the boss of the theatre, John Hallett, wouldn't hear of it, dismissing the Actors' Company as beginners and presenting the kind of play which would drive audiences away. How wrong can you get!

Ian McKellen then went to the Royal Shakespeare Company, and helped revive the community touring of towns and villages without theatres, a task now undertaken by the RSC with a 500-seat mobile auditorium. In 1986 he led a National Theatre company to Paris and Chicago and in 1990 he took off on a world tour as Richard III, in company with Brian Cox as King Lear. Included in this RNT tour, lasting for eight months, were such dates as Tokyo, Paris, Madrid, Cairo, Prague, Bucharest and Moscow, with Cardiff, Belfast, Edinburgh, Leeds and Nottingham visited in the UK to preserve some sort of balance. In an interview he gave to Peter Lewis for *The Sunday Times* he was quoted as to his 'attitude to giving up a year of his life to the tour': 'I don't see it as giving anything up. What else would I rather do with a year of my life? Nothing.' Clearly, Ian McKellen believed it to be all well worthwhile. And so it was – and *is*, for no doubt he will go on and on. Whether the productions were quite as riveting as they should have been is open to question, but it was still a splendid enterprise.

So, three cheers for Sir Ian McKellen – knighted for all his efforts in the 1991 New Year's Honours. And there are others on this roving role of honour, apart from him, beginning with David Conville (he received an OBE somewhat earlier) who actually worked for me in 1956 when John Slater took out *Dry Rot*. David describes his first encounter with me thus: 'I toured for you after a strenuous argument in your Whitehall dressing-room when you offered me £18. After many crocodile tears (on both our parts), we settled for £20!' This incredible generosity on my behalf must have enabled him to put together enough capital to become an actor-manager himself only three years later, when he sent out a tour of *Not in the Book* – a play by the film censor, Arthur Watkyn – with Jack Hulbert playing the leading part. The fact that he engaged Jack Hulbert shows a forgiving nature on the part of David. Prior to being Jack's boss, David had toured with him in *The Reluctant Debutante* by Willie Douglas-Home. At the Grand, Leeds on the first night, David was summoned to the prognathous actor's Number One dressing-room. Expecting a pat on the back for his seemingly brilliant performance, David was greeted by, 'Oh, it's you.'

'Yes, Mr Hulbert.'

'You know that laugh you got just after your first entrance?'

'Yes, Mr Hulbert.'

'Well, D O N' T.'

David then went on to form the New Shakespeare Company in 1962, which has presented the yearly summer season in Regent's Park ever since, but has also toured extensively overseas, particularly in Asia and the Middle East. David is now the chairman. In the early days as the Artistic Director, however, David struggled to keep the Shakespearian flag flying in the U K, and his first tour in 1964, the Shakespearian Quatercentenary Year, was decidedly eccentric – both in venues visited and distances travelled: Opera House, Belfast; Rosehill Theatre, Cumberland; Hippodrome, Birmingham; New, Hull; Civic, Darlington; Gulbenkian Foundation, Lisbon and Oporto; the Middle Temple, London; New, Oxford and Theatre Royal, Norwich. You can't blame Jack Phipps for any of that. It was seven years before the Arts Council set up its Touring Department.

Clearly, 'Compass Theatre' must come next, for it was founded by no less a figure than Sir Anthony Quayle. Never afforded the recognition he should have received for his nine years' work as Artistic Director of the Shakespeare Memorial Theatre in Stratford, starting in 1948, he had to wait for his knighthood until Compass was launched, only four years before his sad death from cancer. But Compass still exists today, led by another actor-manager, Tim Pigott-Smith, and – with the odd hiccup – continues to battle on, with courage and conviction.

Tony Quayle began thinking about forming his new touring company when he was working for Triumph Theatre Productions and 'because so much depends on famous stars from film and television and doesn't build the name of the company, which is really what I believe in'. So, he set about raising the money to launch the company, with some from the Arts Council, Prudential Assurance and Rank Xerox. The rest was his own, for he sold his yacht, *Jenny Rose* (the first names of his daughters), kept the compass and named his company after the only tangible asset he had left from his favourite pastime – sailing. He persuaded the irreplaceable Roy Kinnear to join him, plus Joyce Redman, in David Garrick's *The Clandestine Marriage* and they were off, boxing the compass. What is more, they were successful.

239

Now, alas, the skipper is no longer on board – but with Tim Pigott-Smith at the helm, supported by a trusty crew, I'll warrant that Compass will be sailing for many more years yet to come.

Yet another company paying homage to Shakespeare in its title comes next – the English Shakespeare Company. Launched in 1986 by actor (now actor-manager) Michael Pennington and director (now director-manager) Michael Bogdanov, its express purpose was to answer the 'need for high-quality popular productions of Shakespeare to tour the larger theatres of the United Kingdom'. They went further than this, of course, and soon were off round the world to favour Japan, America, Australia and Germany with their spectacular productions – 'the Henrys' (*Henry IV, Part I, Henry IV, Part II* and *Henry V*) and *The Wars of the Roses*, when they enlarged the cycle of plays with *Henry VI* and *Richard III*. It was a massive and overwhelming achievement and won them numerous awards. They have now added many overseas countries to their tour list, but have also kept their promise to bring 'high-quality' productions to many a city in the UK – nineteen to be precise, with seasons at the Old Vic in London chucked in for good measure and, more recently, a further thirty weeks touring in the UK, twenty-seven weeks overseas and fourteen weeks in London. Who said theatrical entrepreneurs were finished? Not me, I'll be bound.

Of course, apart from the RSC with its largescale and community-based touring, and the revival of the Royal National Theatre's interest, there are numerous medium and smallscale touring companies operating around Britain, many of them with actor-managers or director-managers in charge and many, also, supported by the Arts Council of Great Britain. There are so many, in fact, that it would be quite impossible or invidious to single any one of them out, and that is why I have concentrated on the better-known companies or artistes. I apologise to those who will be hurt by my omission, especially if you have been 'promoted' to star status while this book is in production – but 'twas ever thus. I will finish, therefore, with a young actor-manager who rivalled me in his precocity. I became an actor-manager at the age of twenty-four, bringing my first production to London at the age of twenty-six. He became an actor-manager *and* brought his first production to London at the same age – twenty-six – so he could be seen as quicker than me. Some might say 'more talented'. Some might well be right. His name, of course, is Kenneth Branagh.

The Renaissance Theatre Company was launched in 1987 by actors Kenneth Branagh and David Parfitt, with an eighteen-month programme of classical and modern work. The first production was Branagh's own play, *Public Enemy*, which opened at the Lyric, Hammersmith and this was followed by *Life of Napoleon* by John Sessions, at the Riverside Studios, eventually transferring to the Albery Theatre in St Martin's Lane. *Twelfth Night* was next, with Richard Briers playing Malvolio, and then came *Much Ado About Nothing*, *As You Like It* and *Hamlet*; I saw the latter one stiflingly hot night at the Theatre Royal, Newcastle. The Arts Council were there mob-handed and Renaissance put us all in the circle. As I am sure you know hot air rises, and over four hours we wilted somewhat. Were Messrs Branagh and Parfitt trying to remind us that we had never given them a grant? Mark you, I am not certain, to date, if they have even asked for one and, quite frankly, they seem to do so well, I am not absolutely positive it is necessary. What with their award-winning film of *Henry V* and their immensely successful 1990 tour of *A Midsummer Night's Dream* and *King Lear*, perhaps they should be giving *us* money. I saw *Lear* at the Edinburgh Festival, with Richard Briers in the title role, and found it different, but no more earth-shattering, I fear, than Brian Cox in the National's touring version.

Which makes for an extremely interesting comparison.

Here, then, was the Royal National, with all its great reputation and greater subsidy, failing to make any of this head start obvious when compared with the totally unsubsidised, but well-sponsored Renaissance. To make this comparison even more poignant, in my view neither production touched the hem of Donald Wolfit's version – funded only by Donald and his friends all those years ago in 1942 – but, then, I was a small part of that tour, and could be accused of bias. To refute this, however, let me quote a letter in the *Daily Telegraph* of the time, from that great showman, Sir Charles B. Cochran: 'The war has given us the finest native Shakespearian performance of the twentieth century unaided by C E M A or any other outside assistance or encouragement. I refer to the King Lear of Donald Wolfit.'

It's my fault, I'm afraid. I shouldn't have made comparisons in the first place. Comparisons are odious and, without doubt, the arguments will rage as long as the theatre exists. Let's face it, how can we ever be sure?

'When we are born we cry that we are come to this great stage of fools.'

So quoth Lear. I don't know about you, but I'm jolly glad I came along – even though I am fast nearing the years when 'I am a very foolish, fond old man.' Some approach the stage and become great artistes and impresarios; some become rich beyond belief; some have honours heaped upon them, whilst some become old actor-laddies with penury never far away, eking a living as best they can. Whatever station in life we achieve, you can be sure that old Will Shakespeare wasn't far from the truth. It is indeed a 'great stage of fools'.

In the old days, those same penniless actor-laddies used to keep their sticks of Leichner make-up in discarded cigar boxes. One such actor was striding down the Strand in the vicinity of Charing Cross Station with the Havana box tucked underneath his arm. A thespian colleague approached, raised his hat in greeting, glanced at his friend's package and said: 'Ah! Cigars! I see you have hit the big time at last, dear boy.' Came a weary shake of the head and the disconsolate reply: 'Big time be buggered, old man. I'm *touring*.'

Who knows? Perhaps you saw that particular thespian at your local theatre. It could have been any one of us.

It could have been me . . .

Final curtain.

CURTAIN CALLS

THE PLAYERS

(In order of year of birth and from the early sixteenth century – when companies of players were in the service of the Court – to the end of the twentieth century, when they most definitely were not.)

James BURBAGE (*c*.1530–97) Like Stewart Cruikshank of Howard and Wyndham, over 300 years later, he was a joiner by trade but, unlike Mr Cruikshank, Mr Burbage started as an actor with the Earl of Leicester's Men about 1572. In 1576 he had constructed England's first ever building solely devoted to the presentation of plays, but was always troubled by lack of money. He had two sons: Cuthbert (*c*.1566–1636), who eventually built the Globe at Bankside, Southwark, and Richard (*c*.1567–1619), who became the first great Shakespearian actor, playing the original performances of *Hamlet, Lear, Othello, Richard III* etc. at his brother's theatre. As Richard had been trained as an actor by his father (as had Shakespeare), he seems to be an excellent example of the advantages of nepotism in the theatrical profession. When times are hard, it is generally easier to rely on family support than any other.

William SHAKESPEARE (1564–1616) An actor, who occasionally wrote some plays and poems. You may have heard of him. Also known as Francis Bacon, John Fletcher, Philip Massinger, Christopher Marlowe, the sixth Earl of Derby – oh yes – and the seventeenth Earl of Oxford.

Edward ALLEYN (1566–1666) Founder of Dulwich College after he retired as a highly successful actor. In 1583 was a member of the Earl of Worcester's Men, and then the principal actor of the Admiral's Men from around 1587. In 1592 he had the good sense to marry the stepdaughter of Philip Henslowe, who owned the Rose, the Fortune and the Hope playhouses, thus becoming the part-owner of his stepfather-in-law's enterprises. Who says nepotism doesn't pay?

William KEMPE (?–1603) Elizabethan clown and the original 'Dogberry' in *Much Ado About Nothing*. He was a member of the Earl of Leicester's company on its visit to Holland in 1585–6, and was with the Chamberlain's Men from 1594–1600. In 1602 he morris-danced from London to Norwich, probably because he hadn't married into a rich family and needed the money – or possibly, posthumously, to enter the *Guinness Book of Records*. His feat would have fitted happily alongside all those other hard earned but seemingly pointless events.

Christopher BEESTON (*c*.1570–1638) Began as a member of Strange's Men, then Chamberlain's Men and, in 1602, Worcester's Men. Then moved into management with the 'Cockpit' in Drury Lane. He also trained young actors under the name of 'Beeston's Boys', who continued under his son, William. Many of these youngsters went on to make their names in Restoration theatre.

Richard PERKINS (*c.*1585–1650) A member of the Queen's Men, and one of the most popular players of his time. Apparently an extremely versatile actor, with no nepotistic claims on anyone.

Richard SHARPE (*c.*1602–32) Excellent actor with the King's Men. Was originally a boy actor playing women's roles, specialising in hoity-toity young maidens. As already recounted, owed the actor-manager Henry Condell 41s. 10d. for stockings, which was a lot of loot in those days, especially as the latter put up the money (along with fellow actor-manager, John Heminge) for printing the first complete works of Shakespeare – all thirty-six plays, that is. For the price of Richard Sharpe's debt you could buy two copies of the compendium and still have 1s. 10d. change. Now, that's what I call a bargain.

Michael MOHUN (*c.*1620–84) One of the leading men of Thomas Killigrew's company, when it took over the Theatre Royal, Drury Lane in 1662. Was a boy actor under Beeston, playing adult parts by the time of the Civil War, which is just as well, for he became a major in the royalist army. At the Restoration, he returned to the stage and had much success. So did Mr Killigrew. He became Master of the King's Revels, which was an appointment made by the Lord Chamberlain to enable the office-holder to supervise and pay for Court hoolies.

Thomas BETTERTON (*c.*1635–1710) Described as 'the greatest figure of the Restoration stage', he broke with the management of the Theatre Royal, Drury Lane and reopened the theatre in Lincoln's Inn Fields with the first performance of Congreve's *Love for Love*. He and his wife, Mary Sanderson, were much admired by their contemporaries, particularly for their kindness to lesser mortals struggling to climb the theatrical ladder, including one Miss Anne Bracegirdle, of whom more in a minute.

Mary KNEPP (?–1677) One of the first actresses on the English stage, and a major source of Pepys' backstage gossip. Also popular for her witty delivery of Prologues and Epilogues. She originally spelt her name 'Knipp', but changed it, no doubt, because of the popularity of cockney rhyming slang. 'Knipp and tuck' could well have cast doubts on her undoubted respectability.

Nell GWYNN (1650–87) One of the best-loved actresses of her day, which owed more to her undoubted charm and *joie de vivre* than to her acting. Originally a seller of oranges at Drury Lane, she made her first appearance on stage at the age of fifteen – her last, some four years later. Much in demand as a speaker of Prologues and Epilogues, and by Charles II – which was as good a reason as any to seek early retirement.

Elizabeth BARRY (1658–1713) First really outstanding Restoration actress, playing opposite Thomas Betterton for many years. As an actress she was a slow starter and matured late. Not so in her private life, which was riddled with scandals from beginning to end.

Anne BRACEGIRDLE (*c.*1663–1748) Unlike Mrs Barry, Mrs Bracegirdle's private life was impeccable, and she continued to be one of the best-loved actresses on the English stage until she retired at the height of her fame in 1707, leaving the field wide open for Anne Oldfield. Both Barry and Bracegirdle had the benefit of coming from the Thomas Betterton stable. Two of the best. They just mounted and took their jumps in diametrically opposing styles.

Robert WILKS (1665–1732) Gifted actor, especially in comedy. Spent some time in Ireland. Managed Drury Lane with Doggett, but his rotten temper meant that many actors moved to the Lincoln's Inn Fields theatre simply to get away from him.

Thomas DOGGETT (*c*.1670–1721) Began his career as an actor in the provinces, then came to London, establishing a reputation for low comedy – an early proto-type of the Whitehall Theatre farces some 250 years later. Joint manager of Drury Lane with Cibber and Wilks until he resigned in protest at the granting of a share in the Theatre Royal Patent to Barton Booth. When George I came to the throne, he launched the Doggett Coat and Badge for Thames watermen in celebration – still rowing strong today.

Colley CIBBER (1671–1757) Actor, manager and writer. Went on stage in 1690 against his parents' wishes, and was an excellent comedian. Became an uninspiring (and uninspired) Poet Laureate. His eldest son was part of an unusual ménage à trois, and his daughter shocked the world by dressing as a man. Cibber himself spent a great deal of his time worrying about other things, though, particularly trying to keep the peace at Drury Lane between Doggett, Wilks and himself. It all fell apart when Booth came along, and Doggett left in protest at his political views. No doubt Colley penned some doggerel in punning retribution.

Barton BOOTH (1681–1733) Like his partner-to-be, Colley Cibber, Booth went on the stage against his family's wishes, for he, too, had all the advantages of a good education. Spent two seasons in Dublin, and then toured the English provinces. In 1700 was engaged by Betterton and proved a fine tragic actor. Became manager of Drury Lane with Cibber and Wilks. In later years married Hester Santlow, a successful actress and dancer with money. Some people said that's why he married her. They could be right at that.

Anne OLDFIELD (1683–1730) A very popular actress and successor to Anne Bracegirdle. First persuaded to go on the stage by the renowned Restoration playwright, George Farquhar, she was at her best in comedy and by a strange coincidence is buried in Westminster Abbey near the greatest Restoration play-wright, William Congreve. 'Alack he's gone the way of all flesh.'

James QUIN (1693–1766) It is necessary to mention Quin, for he was the last of the 'declaimers', rather than a genuine actor and he was superseded by David Garrick, with whom he was in constant rivalry until his dying day, failing to understand the new naturalistic playing of the younger (and better) performer.

Lacy RYAN (1694–1760) Great actor, who played the lead in classics at Covent Garden when Garrick was at Drury Lane. It's said Garrick went to see his Richard III to mock, but was astonished by the genius of a man with little training and a distinctly unkempt appearance. Sounds for all the world as though Mr Ryan would have been quite at home amongst many of the modern acting fraternity.

Henry GIFFARD (1694–1772) Principally known for giving David Garrick his first job at the unlicensed Goodman's Fields theatre in Whitechapel. All London flocked to Whitechapel to see the new star, and the manager of Drury Lane, Charles Fleetwood, had to bite on the bullet and do a deal to take Mr and Mrs Giffard to the Theatre Royal, along with the newly discovered great actor. It may not be nepotism – but it is certainly a close relative – opportunism.

Charles MACKLIN (*c*.1700–97) An Irish actor who was renowned for his playing the Jew, Shylock. Considered by many to be too natural, he moved between the provinces and London, never having the success he deserved. Always in litigation – and in the shadow of Garrick.

Peg WOFFINGTON (*c*.1714–60) Born in Dublin, daughter of a bricklayer. At ten, was with a children's company. Famous for her breeches part of Sir Harry Wildair, which she first played at Smock Alley in her native city in 1740. An excellent character actress, she was always fighting with fellow actresses, once stabbing George Ann Bellamy (who was actually a potential rival to another actress, Mrs Cibber), whom she chased off the stage. Peg was considered to be one of the most beautiful women of her day, with a voice like a corncrake. Obviously this did not deter Garrick, for he was her lover for quite some time. Perhaps Miss Woffington kept her hands over his ears. In 1757, she was taken ill towards the end of *As You Like It* and spent her last three years doing 'good works' – although many would have said her stage career could be counted as such.

Lewis HALLAM (1714–56) Well worth mentioning, for he took his first company of twelve to America in 1752, which really was the beginning of good American theatre.

David GARRICK (1717–79) One of the great actors, and a man who changed many things, including the style of acting. He was also one of the few performers who had little need of the provinces, and as well as having a fiery temper, was considered vain and snobbish by many, preferring to spend his out-of-season time at the homes of his noble friends, rather than on tour. Mind you, if they had started country-house cricket by then, who shall blame him? From 1747 he became manager of Drury Lane, and while there had to put up with two riots: one caused by his abolishing half-price ticket concessions and the other by his rather tactless casting of some French dancers just before the outbreak of yet another war with France. Xenophobia and jingoism were all part of the British character, even then – as Garrick found out to his cost. His farewell performance was on 10th June, 1776. He retired to Hampton, where he died, and is buried in Westminster Abbey. Nearby lie two of his successors as leaders of the acting profession – John Henderson and Henry Irving – but an actress, Anne Oldfield, was there first.

Roger KEMBLE (1721–1802) A strolling actor-manager, who had been a barber until he was thirty, he and his actress wife begat one of the most famous families in the English theatrical firmament and others have written biographies which describe their multifarious activities. The father, Roger, toured his own company all over England with his twelve children making up much of it. His eldest daughter was Sarah Siddons. His eldest son, John Philip Kemble (1757–1823), was manager of London's patent houses and suffered the riots of 1808 at Covent Garden when he put up the price of admission to try and cover his losses caused by a disastrous fire. His famous sister, too, had lost a great deal of money as a result of this Covent Garden conflagration. John was responsible for many spectacular shows and effects, and did much to improve the reputation of actors. Stephen (1758–1822) was born as his mother came off stage and no doubt she was late for her next entrance. He grew to such a size that he was able to play Falstaff without padding. He was the manager of a provincial company, a theatre in Edinburgh and a company in Ireland, and briefly ran Drury Lane. Charles (1775–1854) retired from acting after twenty-five years because of bad hearing, and became Examiner of Plays. His daughter, by his wife Theresa, was Fanny. She rescued Charles from bankruptcy with performances at Covent Garden, and went on to become a star in America. There are still Kembles around, even now. One of them, Vivian, directed the first TV series of *An Invitation to Remember*, which I originally dreamt up as *Theatre Knights and Dames* – interviewing famous actors and actresses – and which still benefits MENCAP to this very day.

George Anne BELLAMY (*c.*1727–88) She had a somewhat bizarre beginning, being the daughter of Lord Tyrawley by a certain Miss Seal, a Quakeress who eloped with him and then married a sea captain, whose name was Bellamy. That explains how George Anne gathered her surname, but her Christian names were the result of a hard-of-hearing vicar misinterpreting 'Georgina'. She was very beautiful and received much attention, marrying twice, once bigamously, and was always involved in scandal, including being stabbed by Peg Woffington. Was a leading lady with Garrick, but as her beauty faded so did her popularity, and by 1785 she had to have a benefit at Covent Garden. To make ends meet, she was probably the first actress to indulge in the 'kiss-and-tell' method. The highly coloured version of her life was published, warts and all, in the same year as her benefit. Next time you read such a lurid story concerning a latterday name, remember it is a habit which goes back over 200 years. There is nothing new under the sun.

Ned SHUTER (1728–76) Great comic actor, who first appeared at Richmond in 1744, and was still playing at Covent Garden the year he died.

Henry MOSSOP (1729–74) Irish actor. Came to Drury Lane from Ireland, and became an ally to Garrick in his rivalry with Barry, taking over many of the parts originally played by James Quin. His desire to play young lovers on stage led to ridicule and he blamed this on Garrick. In 1761 he set up the Smock Alley Theatre in Dublin, but this, his gambling and his excessive lifestyle ruined him. He was a proud man, and in the end had lost all his friends and died of starvation in a Chelsea garret.

Tom KING (1730–1804) One of the most famous members of Garrick's Drury Lane company. At seventeen he was a strolling player with Ned Shuter. First appeared at Drury Lane in 1748. A high comedian, coming to prominence for his performance as Lord Ogleby in *The Clandestine Marriage*, he made a great deal of money but lost it gambling and in unfortunate theatrical ventures. If he did not exactly die of starvation, he certainly died a poor man.

William SMITH (1730–1819) English actor known as 'Gentleman Smith'. Sent down from Cambridge. Alternated roles with Garrick, and kept John Philip Kemble at bay until his retirement. Hunting- and racing-mad and proud that he'd never acted in a farce, he sounds the most appalling snob. Well, he would to me, wouldn't he? Never acted in a farce!! What is the world coming to?

Tate WILKINSON (1739–1803) Actor and theatre manager. Worked with Shuter, then Garrick, and known for his satirical impersonations of other actors. Ran the York circuit for thirty years, which included Hull – but this was a little before my time. Wrote his *Memoirs* and a second autobiography, *Wandering Patentee*. Gilbert and Sullivan could have written a song about this, but chose a wandering minstrel instead. Dorothy Jordan, a famous comedy actress, was much involved in her early days with Wilkinson's company, and he is again to the fore in her biography.

John BRUNTON (1741–1822) Now here's a fascinating riddle. What Drury Lane grocer played Hamlet in 1774, just down the road at Covent Garden? Then went on to appear with the Norwich and Bath stock companies, eventually becoming manager of the Norwich circuit? Oh! You've been peeking. Yes, it was John Brunton. Three of his children went into the business. Ann (1768–1808) first appeared at Bath, aged fifteen, ending up in America where she was very popular. John (1775–1849) acted at Lincoln aged eighteen, moving to London and Covent Garden when he was twenty-five and then managed several provincial theatres. Louisa (1779–1860) began at Covent Garden in 1803, getting many laughs in light comedy, but retired in 1807 to marry the first Earl of Craven. From then on life was a load of laughs, with a difference.

Tour de Farce

John HENDERSON (1747–85) Here is another riddle. What apprentice jeweller and silversmith was turned down as an actor by Garrick's brother, George, for a job at Drury Lane because his voice and appearance were so poor, owing to near-starvation, and then went on to receive a letter of recommendation from Garrick himself, so that he was able to gain employment at the Theatre Royal, Bath? Who then put on weight so that he was a triumphant 'Falstaff' and was particularly successful with Sarah Siddons in Edinburgh? Furthermore, who died young and was buried near his mentor, Garrick, in Westminster Abbey? The answer is, of course, John Henderson. The wonder is that his comparatively limited career should have merited such an honour. If you know the answer to that, please tell me. Was it sheer talent?

Sarah SIDDONS (1755–1831) Eldest daughter of Roger Kemble, she became the greatest tragedienne on the English stage. At eighteen married William Siddons who was touring with her father's company. Became a success in London at the second attempt, after many seasons in the provinces, including a stint with Tate Wilkinson on the York circuit. She first retired at the age of fifty-seven but made a comeback to support her younger brother Charles some seven years later. It was a disaster. The huge dramatic talent was but a memory – William Charles Macready describing it as 'the last flicker of a dying flame'. How often she must have heard the words from *As You Like It*: 'He that wants money, means, and content is without three good friends.' She did not heed them.

Elizabeth FARREN (1759–1829) Daughter of strolling players, with whom she appeared from the outset. First appeared in London in 1777, and soon became very popular, particularly playing fine ladies. In the end she metamorphosed, becoming one herself by marrying the Earl of Derby in 1797. That was a Derby Day and a half. Well, a Derby Night, anyway.

Dorothy JORDAN (1761–1816) A marvellous comedy actress. Spent many years on the York circuit, and toured all over the country, as well as being a firm favourite at Drury Lane. Often at the centre of scandal and frequently made pregnant, generally – but not exclusively – by the Duke of Clarence, later William IV, who sired ten of her innumerable children. A good-hearted and obliging soul (as must be pretty obvious), she heard that her former boss, the York-based actor-manager, Tate Wilkinson, was involved in a crippling accident, so she decided to play at his benefit in Leeds, while on her way to take up an engagement in Edinburgh. Tate was obviously thrilled at the news of such an attraction being present, but on the day of the benefit, Dorothy had still not turned up. A combination of her pregnancy and a number of delays meant that she did not arrive until a couple of hours before the show. But it was too late. Tate had already postponed the performance, in fear of not having his star. Dorothy was furious – she faced a £500 contractual fine if she arrived in Edinburgh late – and insisted on being paid by Tate if he wished her to perform on the next Wednesday. He gave her ten guineas and she presented *Sir Harry Wildair*. Obviously time was not as pressing as she first led Tate to believe, because she also managed to fit in a few days at Harrogate before moving on to Edinburgh, and she still wasn't late there, either.

An interesting aside to this tale is the reaction of the 'precise Ladies of Leeds' to the sight of a heavily pregnant woman playing the part of a man. They were deeply shocked. Not that a pregnant woman on stage was anything new. Mrs Siddons played Cleone while eight months pregnant, which included 'raving over her murdered child', and Dorothy Jordan herself had given birth to her first child while touring with Tate Wilkinson – though not, I gather, until the show was over.

The working relationship between Tate and Dorothy demonstrates the way in which the stock and touring companies operated. They were, to a great degree, 'family' businesses. Dorothy's mother had been Tate Wilkinson's first Desdemona in Dublin and one of her aunts was still with him. When Dorothy herself arrived from Ireland, now with her mother, brother and sister to support, Tate gave her a very lenient audition, and she too joined the company, spending three years trudging on foot from town to town, across the rugged Yorkshire countryside, huddled behind the company's wagon. In Sheffield she was nearly killed by a falling drop scene and roller, and in almost every town the company visited they would play a benefit for one or other of the actors. It was a hard school. Gradually, though, Dorothy built up a reputation, particularly in 'tomboy' roles, and moved up the pecking order until she became a leading player. Of course, not everything in the garden was rosy. As Dorothy advanced, another leading player, one Mrs Smith, began to feel threatened. So much so that although she, too, was in the family way, she refused to take time off and the day after she had her baby, she walked eighteen miles to Sheffield. Hardly surprisingly, she put herself out of action for the next three months. But Mrs Smith did not give up her battle against Mrs Jordan so easily. Dorothy had just had a baby too and so, in Hull, Mrs Smith and friends began to spread rumours about the young actress's character and reputation. But they had not bargained on Dorothy's popularity with the audiences, the rumour-mongering backfired, and next season Dorothy found herself in competition with another actress. It was 1783 and Mrs Ward was just as jealous as Mrs Smith. She arranged for her friends in the company to hiss at Dorothy and to make disparaging comments as she went on stage. Once again they did not bargain on Mrs Jordan's rapport with the audience. Dorothy went on stage fighting back tears, and her fans wanted to know what was wrong. She told them and Mrs Ward's practice was stopped – literally by public demand.

Charles MATTHEWS (1776–1835) Possibly the first of what is now a modern-day phenomenon – an impersonator – particularly the number we see (or hear, in *Spitting Image*) on television. He conceived another idea still popular today, that of the one-man show, which he toured for many years around the provinces, as well as in London and New York. It was on his return from one of his American trips that he died in Liverpool, where he had once managed the Adelphi. He had never 'died' there before, always being remarkably popular.

John LISTON (1776–1846) I must mention him, simply because he was a huge success in farce and was the first comic actor to be paid more than his more serious contemporaries. Actually, he too wanted to play Hamlet or some such other part, but his audience wouldn't let him. Where have I heard that before?

Edmund KEAN (1787–1833) The first of the great tragedians whose private life, from beginning to end, was as dramatic as any of the great characters he portrayed at the height of his fame and fortune – and a fortune it was, for he earned over £10,000 a season at Drury Lane, and could well afford great houses and the cost of sending his younger son, Charles, to Eton – the elder, Howard, having died of malnutrition in Kean's struggling days. Unfortunately, as the years went by, more and more of this fortune was frittered away on drink – as was the talent – but he must have been a formidable actor. His Shylock, with which he electrified a half-empty, snow-bound Drury Lane, was described by William Hazlitt thus: 'His style of acting is, if we may use the expression, more significant, more pregnant with meaning, more varied and alive in every part, than any we have almost ever witnessed.' He collapsed in his son's arms whilst playing Othello (Charles was Iago) at Covent Garden and died some seven weeks later, on 15th May, 1833. He was refused burial at Westminster Abbey because of his lifestyle, but the parish church at Richmond-upon-Thames was more charitably minded. He rests there – if 'rests' is an appropriate word for such an untamed spirit.

William Charles MACREADY (1793–1873) Likened to Kean, inasmuch as he too was a fine tragedian – although both men were totally different, in style and personality. Mr Hazlitt again pronounced judgement: 'He has talent and a magnificent voice, but he is, I fear, too improving an actor to be a man of genius. That little ill-looking vagabond Kean never improved in anything. On some plays he could not, and in others he would not.' The son of a provincial actor-manager, Macready made his first appearance as Romeo in Birmingham in 1810. He then toured the provinces, playing with Sarah Siddons in Newcastle in 1812. First appeared in London, at Covent Garden, in 1816, and there and in the provinces he continued, until by 1819 he was being spoken of as Kean's rival. For a time he went into management in Bristol and Bath, but eventually he was manager of both of London's patent theatres (against whose monopoly he fought), where he was an artistic rather than a financial success. Had numerous friends and enemies, and brought many changes to acting and texts – restoring the works of Shakespeare to their erstwhile glory. However, he hankered after a comfortable retirement and realised he would have to tour to line the coffers. This he did in the provinces, in Paris and America, with great success – except for becoming involved in the New York Astor Place riot (twenty-two people died) over his disparaging remarks regarding the American actor Edwin Forrest – and having the doubtful distinction of a dead sheep being thrown at him whilst he was on-stage. Although greatly upset by the whole tragic incident, Macready spent the next two years touring the English provinces and finally left the theatre in February 1851, having played Macbeth at Drury Lane, and lived a further twenty-two years in that centre of excellence for retired gentlefolk – Cheltenham. A Macready pause, indeed.

Tyrone POWER (1795–1841) An Irish actor, son of a strolling player, he began acting in 1815, playing light comedy in the provinces and minor London theatres until 1826 when he turned his attention, not unnaturally, to Irish characters – generally comic – at both patent theatres. This made him very popular. Returning from America, he drowned when the SS *President* went down. He had four daughters and four sons: Sir William Power, a distinguished soldier whose grandson was Sir Tyrone Guthrie; Maurice Power, an unsuccessful actor; Frederick, a wealthy civil engineer – one of whose projects was the Trans-Caucasian Railway; and Harold Power whose son, Tyrone (1869–1931) was also an actor in America, appearing in London with Tree and Irving, and his great-grandson was yet another Tyrone, the third, a film star, whom I saw in London at the Coliseum in 1950, just after I had opened at the Whitehall in *Reluctant Heroes*. Tyrone III was also in a service comedy, about the US Navy, *Mister Roberts*. It must have cost a fortune to produce – but it didn't get as many laughs as ours. Now the line continues, for Tyrone IV is a busy stage and film actor in America. More power to his elbow – and I can hear the groans already.

Junius Brutus BOOTH (1796–1852) Lumbered with those Republican names by his father, Junius Brutus went on the stage when he was seventeen, by touring the provinces. Eventually he ended up at Covent Garden, playing Richard III, and began to model himself on the man he was to rival, Edmund Kean. Indeed, there came a time at Drury Lane when the audiences could hardly tell the difference, which was just as well, because Kean was somewhat erratic as to his number of appearances. In 1821 J B left his wife and ran off with a flower-seller to America, where he remained – except for two fleeting visits to Drury Lane – for the rest of his successful days. He was, unfortunately, mentally unstable and passed this to his immediate progeny and beyond. Indeed, a grandson shot himself and his wife in a London hotel, whilst a son, Edwin Thomas, suffered severe depression but overcame this to become a great American actor and one of the first to win European acclaim, once alternating Othello and Iago with Irving (at the latter's request), at the Lyceum in London. Another son was John Wilkes Booth who shot Abraham Lincoln at Ford's Theatre in Washington on 14th April, 1865, leading to that wicked cartoon caption – 'Apart from that, Mrs Lincoln, did you enjoy the play?'

Benjamin WEBSTER (1797–1882) Actor, manager and dramatist, from theatrical stock. Started as a dancer in the provinces and then at Drury Lane. Moved to broad comedy, and in 1837 became lessee of the Haymarket, where he stayed for sixteen years, and in 1844 he took over the Adelphi as well. His grandson, Benjamin (1864–1947), first appeared with Hare and Kendal, then with Irving, and in 1839 he went to the States and stayed till his death. His wife, May Whitty (1865–1948), first appeared at the Court Theatre in 1881 and went on to have a distinguished career on both sides of the Atlantic, and is particularly remembered for her film performances. She was the second actress to be created a Dame of the British Empire, in 1918, for her work in the First World War – Dame Edith Lyttelton being the first. Daughter Margaret, too, had a distinguished career, particularly in America with her productions of Shakespeare.

John Baldwin BUCKSTONE (1802–79) An actor and dramatist, he was extremely popular, appearing in his own plays (he wrote over 200 – mainly melo-dramas and farces), generally at the Haymarket Theatre, which he is said to haunt, even to this very day. In the 1950s we live young actors used to haunt the Buckstone Club, which was 'dead' opposite the Haymarket stage door in Suffolk Street. Names like Stanley Baker, Dickie Henderson, Dennis Price, Nigel Green and John Gregson come swirling out of the past from those gay, abandoned days. I hope their spirits are now joined with John Buckstone in one long round of entertainment – possibly golf. They deserve to enjoy themselves.

Samuel PHELPS (1804–78) Actor and manager. Originally a journalist and an amateur actor, he then toured the provinces for a number of years, particularly the York circuit, before gaining the attention of Macready, though first appearing at the Haymarket in a variety of Shakespearian leads, then moving to Covent Garden. His greatest claim to fame, however, is that when the Patent Theatre monopoly was abolished in 1843, he took over the Sadler's Wells Theatre and from that year until 1862 staged many fine productions of Shakespeare. He then retired from management, but continued acting till the end. He was a hard-working and courageous actor-manager, who succeeded by sheer grit and determination.

TERRY A famous family of actors, indeed. The dynasty began when Benjamin (1818–96), who was the son of a Portsmouth innkeeper, married Sarah Ballard (1819–92), the daughter of a Scottish builder, and they proceeded to produce no less than eleven children, whilst earning a living as reasonably successful strolling players. Although two of the children died in infancy, six of the remaining nine went 'into the business' – one of the sons literally, for he took up a management role in the burgeoning theatre world. Their eldest daughter, Kate (1844–1924), was on stage as a child and went to London at the age of eight to be with Charles Kean's company. She seemed to be heading for a brilliant career, via Bristol and

London, when she suddenly hiccupped to a halt by marrying a Mr Arthur Lewis, a wealthy linen-draper. They produced four daughters, the eldest of whom (another Kate) was to become the mother of Val and John Gielgud, whilst a further daughter, Mabel, had a long and successful career when she returned to the theatre after her husband died in the First World War. However, without doubt, it was Ben and Sarah's second daughter, Ellen (1847–1928) who was the star in the Terry firmament beginning, like her elder sister Kate, when she joined Charles Kean as a child to appear in *The Winter's Tale* at the Princess's Theatre. Both Queen Victoria and Prince Albert were in front on that very first night and *The Times* commented on her 'vivacious precocity that proves her a worthy relative of her sister'. Such a notice was but a harbinger of things to come, and from then on her career appeared to be without let or hindrance, culminating in her long association with Henry Irving's Lyceum Company, from 1878 to 1902, and her continuing splendid work for yet another twenty-three years – mainly touring and lecturing in America and Australia – which reached a climax, when she retired in 1925, with her appointment as a Dame of the British Empire. She married three times, but her children, Edy and Teddy, were fathered by an architect, Edward Godwin. However, the children called themselves 'Craig', after the island off the Scottish coast, Ailsa Craig, and Teddy changed his first name, too, to Gordon – and that is how the designer, Gordon Craig, came into being. Finally, Ellen's younger sisters – Marion and Florence – were reasonably successful actresses whilst her youngest brother, Fred, became a well-known romantic actor, marrying Julia Neilson, and both their children (Dennis and Phyllis Neilson-Terry) became actors, too. I think I mentioned nepotism at the beginning of these biogs, didn't I? If not, I certainly should now, for there are many dynasties yet to come.

Dion BOUCICAULT (1822–90) Actor and dramatist, of Irish extraction, in spite of his name, Dionysius Lardner Boursiquot. He was a prolific author, responsible for over 150 plays, in many of which he acted himself. From 1901 to 1915 all the current crop were produced under the management of Charles Frohman at the Duke of York's Theatre in St Martin's Lane. In the fairly recent past, his comedy *The Shaughraun* was revived with great success at the National Theatre, whilst my wife, Elspet Gray and daughter, Louisa Rix, appeared together as mother and daughter a year or two earlier in the Stratford East production of *The Streets of London*. In spite of being a load of old malarkey, my withers were well and truly wrung. Both were good evenings in the theatre, and you can't ask for more than that.

Charles CALVERT (1828–79) Well worth mentioning, for he was an English actor-manager who concentrated his efforts in the provinces, particularly in Manchester, where he first ran the Theatre Royal in 1859 and then the Prince's Theatre from 1864. His work was much admired by discerning critics of the day for productions of Shakespeare and other works. In 1856 he married Adelaide Biddles who had appeared with Charles Kean at the age of six. She appeared in leading parts for her husband with great success, and after his death continued to tour. All eight children went on stage but only one son, Louis, gained much recognition, appearing for nearly all the London managements.

John Laurence TOOLE (1830–1906) When I first went into the theatre, it was still customary for many leading actors to make certain speeches, generally on tour, and always in repertory, to let the audience know what was on next week. One such actor, particularly well known for his end-of-performance speeches, was John Laurence Toole. Both an actor and a theatre manager, he was the son of a toastmaster, apprenticed to a wine merchant, had amateur success and then joined Dillon's company in Dublin in 1852 as a low comedian. In 1854 he was briefly in

London but then returned to the provinces until 1856. He was at the Adelphi for nine years, and toured with Irving. In 1879 he took over the Charing Cross Theatre (eventually renaming it Toole's Theatre), setting up an excellent stock company with which he toured the provinces in summer, thereby earning a good name and loads of money. He left the stage in 1895, crippled by gout, but was always a very popular man, best known for farce – and his speeches.

Sarah THORNE (1837–99) Actress and theatre manager who ran the stock company at the Theatre Royal, Margate, where many future stars, including Dame Irene and Violet Vanbrugh and Harley Granville-Barker, learned the ropes. She opened her Drama School in 1885, charging £20 for three months' training and £30 for six months'. The pupils boarded at her house, attended classes and did walk-on parts for her company. None of your restricted entry in those days. Her father was Richard Samuel Thorne, another provincial actor-manager.

Sir Charles WYNDHAM (1837–1919) One of England's most distinguished actor-managers. First trained as a doctor in Dublin, and was a keen amateur actor, before becoming a professional with his first appearance at the Royalty Theatre, London in 1862. Some months later he went back to medicine, joining in the American Civil War as a surgeon in the Confederate Army. He then tried the New York stage with little luck and returned to Manchester in a farce he himself had written. In 1869 he took his own company to America, but his first big London success was in 1874 with a play called *Brighton*, which he presented at the Criterion. He leased this theatre, and then built the New Theatre (now the Albery) and Wyndham's. His second wife was Mary Moore (1862–1931) – herself a widow of the playwright James Albery – who became his leading lady, and after his death took over the management. Indeed, the story is told that it was Mary Moore who raised the capital from the City, in the first place, for the New and Wyndham's. Her son from her first marriage, Bronson, and Charles' son from his first marriage, Howard, took over the theatres with considerable success. The Albery line continued until the 1980s, when Ian Albery resigned as the managing director of Maybox, the company which had taken over the Wyndham group. His father, Sir Donald, had run the theatres before him, and his father, Sir Bronson, was also knighted for his services to the theatre.

Sir Henry IRVING (John Henry Brodribb, 1838–1905) Actor-manager who dominated the London stage for thirty years, and the first British actor to be knighted, in 1895. He made his first appearance aged eighteen at the Lyceum, Sunderland, and for the next nine years he worked in provincial stock companies. His first work in London was as a play-as-cast actor and assistant stage manager for Dion Boucicault at the St James's Theatre (extraordinary – that was my first job description there, too), but he finally made his name overnight, 11th September, 1871 in *The Bells* for H. L. Bateman's company at the Lyceum. In 1878 he became manager of the Lyceum, and around him he gathered the best in every field. At one time he is reputed to have employed more people than the entire Royal National Theatre today. He died penniless in a hotel foyer in Bradford, having given his last performance as Becket at the Theatre Royal in that city. His ashes are buried in Westminster Abbey. Both his sons were actors; the elder, H. B. (Henry Brodribb), learned the ropes in the provinces and then revived many of his father's roles in England and America, but was never as good. The younger, Laurence, was drowned when the *Empress of Ireland* sank in a collision with a Norwegian collier during fog in the St Lawrence. He had begun to build a decent reputation, but he was obviously not a lucky man. He went on tour with Benson when he was twenty, but left when a bullet narrowly missed his heart during an accident with a pistol. Another Laurence Irving made his name in the theatre, however, and that was H. B.'s son, who went on to become a very well-known designer, as well as writing the definitive work in 1952 about his grandfather: *Henry Irving: The Actor and His World*.

Dame Genevieve (Lucy) WARD (1838–1922) The first actress to be created a Dame of the British Empire (for acting) was, in fact, American by birth, although probably better known in England. Her debut as an actress was in 1873 playing Lady Macbeth in Manchester, having been an opera singer but losing her singing voice in Cuba after a bout of diphtheria – and lucky, indeed, not to lose her life. In 1879 she produced her own play, *Forget-Me-Not*, opposite a young Johnston Forbes-Robertson, which she then toured all over the world. In 1891 she joined Irving, but from 1900 on was seen less and less, although she did appear with Sir Frank Benson and at the Old Vic, shortly before she died. She received her D B E just in time, too – in 1921.

Sir Squire BANCROFT (1841–1926) and Marie BANCROFT (née Marie Effie Wilton, 1839–1921) Together they made many changes in the style of acting and to the plays themselves, thus helping to raise the status of the profession. Through the Bancrofts, drawing-room comedy became extremely popular and stage decor embraced the idea of the 'box set', with real doors and windows. Marie was the daughter of provincial actors (she was Fleance in Macready's final provincial tour of *Macbeth*), and in 1865 she set up her own company. Squire Bancroft made his first theatrical appearance in 1861 for Birmingham stock, spent four years touring and then met Marie. She invited him to join the company at the newly named Prince of Wales's Theatre (where the Scala used to stand) – from then on things never looked back, and two years later they married. Their domestic comedies were particularly popular, and in 1880 they moved to the Haymarket. They retired in 1885 and only gave occasional performances after that, contenting themselves with a spot of writing. I thoroughly endorse this way of becoming a happy and contented senior citizen.

William KENDAL (1843–1917) Actor-manager who made his first appearance on stage in 1861. He played the provinces for some years and was a member of the Glasgow stock company. In 1866 he went to the Haymarket for John Buckstone, and there he met Madge Robertson (1848–1935) and their two careers became insepar-able, Miss Robertson becoming Mrs Kendal for marital and professional purposes. She was the twenty-second child of an actor-manager and was on stage from an early age, making a name for herself before her marriage. The Kendals toured all over England and, with John Hare, managed the St James's Theatre, playing the leading parts in many fine productions. They retired in 1908, but unlike the Bancrofts did not enjoy such a long life together, for William died in 1917, whilst Madge went on until she was eighty-seven. In 1926 she was made a Dame and died nine years later. The couple were held up as an ideal, both on stage and off, and their companies provided excellent training for many young actors.

Sir John HARE (1844–1921) Actor-manager who made his first appearance in Liverpool in 1864 and in London one year later at the Prince of Wales Theatre. Went into management at the Court Theatre in 1875, then joined Kendal in running the St James's for a further eight years, finally moving to the newly built Garrick Theatre for another six. I moved there from the Whitehall in 1966 and it was then I was told the story of how W. S. Gilbert had the theatre built for Hare, but the contractors kept finding water, having struck an underground river. Gilbert said he was in two minds – whether to finish building the theatre or to let out the fishing rights. Be that as it may, it's a pleasant theatre in which to work, and no doubt John Hare found it so, too. He subsequently went to New York with Pinero's *The Notorious Mrs Ebbsmith*, then returned to England to tour some of his past successes. He began to make his farewell performances in the year he was knighted, 1907, and finally retired in 1911.

Sarah BERNHARDT (1845–1923) French actress who was adored everywhere, and certainly appeared everywhere. She is accredited with being one of the finest actresses of all time, and even in her old age, with one leg amputated and speaking in a foreign tongue (except in France), she could still fill a theatre anywhere – including the Adelphi in Liverpool, where French is scarcely the native language. The Divine Sarah had a habit of fainting at parties if she was bored, which was the least of her eccentricities.

Wilson BARRETT (1847–1904) English actor-manager and writer who had few equals in 'virtuous' melodrama. He took over the management of the Princess's Theatre in 1881, and stayed for five years, producing *The Lights of London*, which ran for 228 performances and then toured the world. With this and other plays, including *The Silver King* and his own work, *The Sign of the Cross*, he made a fortune, but it was the latter play which excited clergymen to preach many a sermon and help fill all his touring dates. Nothing like having God to do your P R.

William TERRISS (1847–97) Whereas one crazed actor murdered Abraham Lincoln *inside* a theatre, another murdered William Terriss *outside* one – the Adelphi, where Terriss had been appearing with great success in a series of melodramas with no plot as lurid as his own end. So popular was he, in fact, that he was known as 'No. 1, Adelphi Terriss'. A sailor in his younger days, he had tried the theatre once, but was not successful and emigrated with his actress wife, Anne Fellowes, to the Falkland Islands, where he reared sheep. There his daughter, Ellaline, was born in 1871 and went on to achieve great success in the theatre, marrying Sir Seymour Hicks along the way, in a very long life – being a hundred years old when she died. Her father, unhappily, had his life somewhat foreshortened, but it was a happy one, for he was the kindest of men, and was greatly loved and admired.

Osmond TEARLE (1852–1901) Made his debut at Liverpool in 1869. Played Hamlet at Warrington in 1871. After six years in the provinces he came to London, soon forming his own company, which he toured constantly, often with his brother Edmund. He visited New York, and then alternated between the two countries. In 1888 he organised a Shakespeare company which appeared at Stratford, and this was a fine training ground. His last appearance was in 1901 in Carlisle, a week before he died. His son, Sir Godfrey (1884–1953) took over this company until in 1906 he appeared in London. He continued to tour, however, and had a long career on the London stage and in films. I remember my mother returning from London in 1938 with a programme of his then latest success – Commander Ferrers in *The Flashing Stream*. My mother thought he was wonderful. One critic, though, dismissed his performance by saying that in 'the last scenes the nervous breakdown failed to move'. But it was my mother, and other mothers, too, who were right in the end, for the play was a great success, both in London and New York. In 1932 Godfrey Tearle became the first president of Equity, and was knighted in 1951, two years before he died. He left most of his estate to the actress Jill Bennett – who later committed suicide.

Lillie LANGTRY (1852–1929) Actress daughter of the Dean of Jersey, her maiden name (she did have one) was le Breton. At twenty-two she married a member of the Diplomatic Service, Edward Langtry, and became a prominent member of London society and an intimate friend of Edward VII, then the Prince of Wales. Indeed, the story is told that her house on Kingston Hill had the only gate leading from its garden directly into Richmond Park. According to the tale, this allowed easy access for the Prince when he was out riding. I will refrain from any *double entendre*. Mrs Langtry made her acting debut in 1881 under the Bancrofts, causing a sensation more because of her position and looks, rather than her acting ability. She formed her own company, playing in London and touring the USA and the English provinces. It is because of this latter activity that she warrants a place in this history of touring. For no other.

Sir Herbert Draper Beerbohm TREE (1853–1917) Actor-manager. Was intended to be a grain merchant, like his father, but began to be known in amateur productions and in 1878 he turned pro. From 1887 to 1917 he managed variously the Comedy, the Haymarket and Her Majesty's Theatre, the latter which he built and which housed his sumptuous Shakespearian productions, although it cannot be said that Tree was a great Shakespearian actor. Indeed, his Hamlet was described by W. S. Gilbert as 'funny without being vulgar' and 'he did not always know Shakespeare's lines,' whilst his production of *The Tempest* was likened to a Christmas pantomime. But the audiences loved him, although his greatest success was as Svengali in a modern work, *Trilby* by Paul Potter, adapted from George Du Maurier's novel, which never failed to draw the crowds and provided him with the money to build Her Majesty's. He did his share of touring the provinces, was founder of the now Royal Academy of Dramatic Art and was knighted in 1909. In 1883 he married Maud Holt (1863–1937), and she became his leading lady, continuing successfully after his death. Their eldest daughter, Viola, was also an excellent actress but did the most startling thing. In 1912 she married a dramatic critic, Alan Parsons. Knowing the slings and arrows Sir Herbert (as he liked to be called) had suffered at the hands of those gentlemen, the old boy must have needed all his well-known sense of fun *that* day.

Sir Johnston FORBES-ROBERTSON (1853–1937) Actor-manager who made his first stage appearance in 1874. He had always intended to be a painter (his father was an art critic), but when asked why he had gone on the stage, replied, 'six guineas a week, from [Samuel] Phelps'. He was certainly the finest Hamlet of his time, having a 'rich, melodious voice, with the tone of an organ'. Irving, after seeing his performance as the moody Dane, never played it again. Forbes-Robertson appeared at many London and provincial theatres, in both the classics and new works. In 1885 he made his first appearance in New York, having just completed an English tour, and in 1895 he took over the London Lyceum. He was knighted in 1913, the same week as he retired. It was an emotional last performance at Drury Lane and he stepped down off the stage to mingle with the audience to say his farewells. In 1961, when I beat the Aldwych Theatre record for the longest run of any farce team in any one theatre, at the Whitehall, I did better than that. I not only mingled with the audience, but I gave them champagne as well. What is more, champagne was a darn sight cheaper in Sir Johnston's day. In 1900 he married an American actress, Gertrude Elliot, who was his leading lady on many occasions. His younger brothers Ian, Norman, and Eric were also actors, but his daughter, Jean, became better known as a Forbes-Robertson than they.

Edward COMPTON (1854–1918) Son of an actor and actress, he ran the Compton Comedy Company, touring the provinces from 1881 to 1918. His wife was Virginia Frances Bateman (1853–1940), who had first appeared on stage at the age of twelve, and changed her name to Virginia Francis when she joined her parents' company, but then changed it back again. She became Edward's leading lady and ran the company after his death. Their children included the novelist, Sir Compton Mackenzie (the knighthood and the occupation came later) and Fay Compton, who became known as the 'actress who was never out of work'. Television addicts will remember her as Aunt Ann in *The Forsyte Saga*. She died in 1978, having been appointed a CBE three years earlier.

Sir Arthur Wing PINERO (1855–1934) Left school, aged ten, being apprenticed to a law firm. To while away the time he took to amateur theatricals but eventually chucked law to become an actor in a stock company in Edinburgh. He was an actor for ten years, but always wished to be a writer and that is where his success lay, his first play *Two Hundred A Year* being performed in 1877 at the Globe. He is probably best remembered by the general public for his Court Theatre farces, *The Magistrate*, *The Schoolmistress* and *Dandy Dick* – but he is best remembered by me as the 'father' of modern British farce, and for his cartoon by Sir Alfred Munnings which hangs in the loo at the Garrick Club. All his plays are listed thereon. It makes very impressive reading when you are adjusting your dress.

Violet MELNOTTE (1856–1935) Actress and theatre manager. First appeared in London with (Sir) Charles Wyndham in 1880, but wished to go into management. From 1885 she got her wish, and ran the Avenue (now the Playhouse) and the Comedy Theatres. She was the first to build a theatre in the slum street which was St Martin's Lane. Originally named the Trafalgar Square Theatre, it became the Duke of York's and it was not long before the New Theatre (the Albery) followed. She loved litigation, as well as producing plays with one set and eight characters, which rather limited her choice. She lived most of her life in the Hotel Metropole, Brighton, and the Piccadilly Hotel, London, presenting a succession of flops at her erstwhile slum property. Capital Radio rebuilt it in the 1970s and it is now very upmarket.

Sir Ben GREET (1857–1936) Actor-manager who began with Sarah Thorne in Margate. He rivalled Sir Frank Benson in bringing Shakespeare to the masses via his tours both here and in America, and he was fond of giving open-air performances, too. His touring companies gave many actors their first break on both sides of the Atlantic, and for his hard-working, practical contribution to the theatre, he was knighted in 1929.

Sir George ALEXANDER (1858–1918) Actor-manager who, like so many, began as an amateur. In 1879 he was appearing at Nottingham, and then spent the next two years touring the provinces. He was with Irving at the Lyceum during the 1880s, and in 1890 took over the management of the St James's Theatre, where he stayed as a highly successful actor-manager until he died. His policy was to present plays by English dramatists, and this was very popular. In his twenty-seven years at the St James's he produced sixty-two full-length plays and nineteen one-acters. His major successes were Oscar Wilde's *Lady Windermere's Fan* and *The Importance of Being Earnest*, whilst his playing of the two leading characters in *The Prisoner of Zenda* brought the smart West End flocking to this lovely theatre, now sadly demolished. He was knighted in 1911, dying some seven years later, some say from consumption, others from diabetes. Whatever the cause, it was pretty final.

Sir George DANCE (1858–1932) Not an actor, but must be mentioned as one of the most successful theatre managers of his day, at one time having as many as two dozen companies on tour, all at the same time. He was also a successful author and songwriter, who wrote libretti for musical plays, as well as being financially behind many West End theatres. In 1924 he gave £30,000 towards the reconstruction of the Old Vic. No one could say such open-handed generosity earned him his knighthood. He had received that the year before.

Sir Charles HAWTREY (1858–1923) Actor-manager, and one of the finest light comedians around, specialising in the English man-about-town. He first appeared under the prosaic name of Bankes in 1881, but soon reverted to his real name and went into management. He had many successes but was not good with money, and was often in financial difficulties. He always wore a moustache and maintained that on the one occasion he didn't, the play was a flop. He was knighted in 1922, but lived less than a year to enjoy it. His family once owned the Prime Minister's country residence, Chequers.

Sir Frank BENSON (1858–1939) Actor-manager who started off at the top of the tree, and if he did not exactly slide down to the bottom, he had many a struggle to maintain his position at the fork. He first came to the notice of the great and the good, including Irving and Ellen Terry, for his production of *Agamemnon* whilst he was still at Oxford. In the same year he won the three-mile race in the inter-university sports in record time, and from then on he was always known for his love of the classics and his abiding passion for sport. Then it was a successful amateur production in London of *Romeo and Juliet*, when he was grabbed by Irving to play Paris in the same play at the Lyceum. He was twenty-four years old. The following year, with the aid of his father's money, he was able to take over a stranded theatre company – and so began his long association with Shakespeare and touring, for he produced all the Bard's works except *Titus Andronicus* and *Troilus and Cressida*. He also presented numerous London seasons, beginning in 1889–90, and was an important part of the Stratford Festival, too – he was so popular, the town would turn out to welcome him at the station – thus becoming a national institution, for generations of schoolchildren gained such knowledge as they had about Shakespeare from the F. R. Benson Company. The only actor to be knighted in a theatre (in 1916, which nearly went wrong – a story I recounted earlier), Benson married Constance Featherstonhaugh in 1886, their son Eric being killed in the First World War, and she played leading parts with her husband for many years. In 1933 he was knocked down by a boy on a bicycle and was unable to work again. Having now a struggle to make ends meet, he was granted a meagre Civil List pension and died in 1939. In his life he had been treated somewhat condescendingly by the critics (rather as his natural successor, Donald Wolfit, was to be) but at his death the doyen of theatre critics, James Agate, wrote: 'About Benson in his heyday I cannot and will not be dispassionate. He gave what, to a young playgoer, seemed tremendous things . . . most modern actors lack – presence, a profile befitting a Roman coin, voice, and virility to make you believe that Orlando overthrew more than his enemies.'

Lewis WALLER (1860–1915) Actor-manager and outstanding romantic actor, with a magnificent voice described as 'ringing through the theatre like a bell'. His first appearance, after amateur experience, was in 1883 with Toole. One of the early matinée idols, performances were held up by the yelling and hand-clapping and foot-stamping which went on when he first appeared, from his female admirers. The modern phenomenon witnessed at pop concerts is nothing new. Not altogether surprisingly, he was at his best in romantic parts, and first went into management at the Haymarket. His wife Florence West (1862–1913) appeared in many of his successes.

Cyril MAUDE (1861–1951) Actor-manager who began his career in America, appearing in good old *East Lynne* at Denver, Colorado in 1884. His first big success in London was in 1887 at the Grand Theatre, Islington. In 1896 he took over the Haymarket, one year after Lewis Waller, and with Frederick Harrison he had enormous success. His leading lady was his wife, Winifred Emery. He was the manager of the Playhouse when it was destroyed when part of Charing Cross Station collapsed on it, which is a highly original way of bringing the house down. This did not halt the success of his career, however, although his train might have been a little delayed that day.

Sir John MARTIN-HARVEY (1863–1944) Another popular actor-manager who had to rely on touring to keep the bank manager happy, particularly with *The Only Way*, which was an adaptation of Charles Dickens' novel, *A Tale of Two Cities*. In this, Martin-Harvey played Sydney Carton, having first done so in 1899 when he went into management at the Lyceum when Sir Henry Irving was away. He continued in this part, off and on, until five years before he died, for he was still appearing as Sydney Carton at the age of seventy-six – his last performance being at Newcastle-upon-Tyne in 1939. Now that's what I call being typecast. And it was all the wife's fault, for she it was who suggested he began his career as an actor-manager with that particular play. Mind you, she supported him as his leading lady for many years, so she must have been pretty sick of it too.

Dame Marie TEMPEST (*née* Mary Susan Etherington, 1864–1942) Began her career as a singer in the provinces and made her London debut in 1885. For a further fourteen years she continued to perform in musical comedy and light opera, but in 1899 she appeared as some of her theatrical predecessors, Nell Gwynn, Peg Woffington and Becky Sharp, in *The Marriage of Kitty* for Charles Frohman at the Duke of York's Theatre. She then continued to act in modern comedies, being the original Judith Bliss in Noël Coward's *Hay Fever*, with appearances in *Mr Pim Passes By*, *The First Mrs Fraser* and *Theatre Royal* adding to her West End successes, her last one being Dora Randolph in Dodie Smith's *Dear Octopus*. She tried again to rehearse a new play in 1942 but found her memory was gone and the words eluded her. A sad ending, for she died six months later. She was made a Dame in 1937 for her services to the stage, which were described by Eric Johns after her death. He was not particularly charitable: 'She had perfected a number of technical tricks that never failed to conjure laughs out of an author's flimsiest lines. People who flocked to see Marie Tempest did not care a jot for the play. All they wanted was to enjoy her sparkling performances.' Well, I can't see anything wrong in that, can you? At least play-goers flocked . . .

Mrs Patrick CAMPBELL (*née* Beatrice Tanner, 1865–1940) The first men in Mrs Pat's life all had money troubles. Her grandfather ran through two fortunes, leaving nothing to her father, John, whilst her first husband, Patrick Campbell, chased all round the world to make a living, but ended up being killed in the Boer War. With two children to support (her son, too, was killed in the First World War) she turned to the only profession which seemed to offer her any chance of making money, for she had been a great success in amateur theatricals, and first appeared as a professional at the Alexandra Theatre, Liverpool in 1888. She then toured with Ben Greet, appearing for him in London at the Vaudeville Theatre in 1890. She had to wait only three years for success, which she attained whilst playing Paula in Pinero's *The Second Mrs Tanqueray* for George Alexander at the St James's Theatre. She soon was one of the outstanding actresses of the day, popular in America also, and becoming an actress-manager in 1899. Had a long professional association with Forbes-Robertson, and with authors J. M. Barrie and George Bernard Shaw. Rumours about those associations being something other than professional abounded, and her liaison with G B S is still the subject of much speculation, even to this very day. I cannot think why. She was mad about little dogs, too, which led to the story of her failing to be recognised by a cabbie at the height of her fame. She was furious – and he was, too, because she flung the exact fare at him – threepence – as she stalked towards her destination. ''Ere missus,' bawled the cabbie, 'your little dog has just pissed in my cab.' Mrs Pat drew herself up to her full height. 'Pissed in your cab? Pissed in your cab! *I* pissed in your cab!' In her heyday, Mrs Pat played Mélisande in Maeterlinck's *Pelléas et Mélisande*. Ten years later she tried it again, this time in French and with Sarah Bernhardt playing Pelléas – Martin-Harvey having played the part originally. A Dublin critic wrote, 'Both (ladies) are old enough to know better.' By this time Mrs Pat's beauty was beginning to fade and, according to one waspish New Yorker, she gradually became 'fat and yellow', dying in 1940 and 'going down like a battleship firing on her rescuers', according to a friend. With friends like those, who needs enemies?

Violet VANBRUGH (1867–1942) Made her first appearance in 1886 at Toole's theatre, and in 1888 joined Sarah Thorne's company at Margate. Later went with the Kendals to America, then joined Irving at the Lyceum. In 1894 she married Arthur Bourchier (1863–1927) and was his leading lady at the Royalty and when he took over the Garrick Theatre for six years in 1900. Both were very popular. Her sister Irene (1872–1949) was also trained by Sarah Thorne, first appearing in 1888. She then worked with pretty well everyone, including Tree, Alexander and Hare – being particularly successful as the interpreter of Pinero's heroines. She was an actress of great charm. In 1941 she was created a Dame. Her elder sister got nothing – except a great deal of adulation.

Henry V. ESMOND (1869–1922) Actor-manager and dramatist. Went on stage in 1885 and gained experience on tour. Appeared in London in 1889, and from the turn of the century toured his own plays with great success and his wife, Eva Moore, playing opposite him.

Sir Seymour HICKS (1871–1949) Actor-manager and dramatist – already mentioned as the son-in-law of William Terriss. Began as a walk-on in 1887, and was with the Kendals in England and America. He was an unusual hybrid, being the top of the bill in the music halls, and also a star in musical comedy and straight plays. He organised the first entertainers to perform in France in both wars, receiving the Legion of Honour from the French in 1931 and being knighted in 1935. Married, as you know, to Ellaline Terriss, who appeared with him often.

Oscar ASCHE (1871–1936) Actor-manager-playwright of Scandinavian descent, born in Australia. First appeared with Benson in 1893, who engaged him because Asche said he was a first-class wicket-keeper. Was a huge success, with his wife Lily Brayton, at the Adelphi Theatre in *The Taming of the Shrew* which they turned into broad, knockabout farce. With tours thrown in, they played this version over 1,500 times. His biggest success, though, was his own work – he wrote both book and lyrics, *Chu-Chin-Chow*. It ran at His Majesty's for 2,283 performances, from 1916 to 1921, creating a long-running record for those days which was not beaten until *The Mousetrap* came along. I only managed 1,610 with *Reluctant Heroes*.

Dame Lillian BRAITHWAITE (1873–1948) Started in amateur shows in Natal, South Africa, but then became a professional actress, working with Frank Benson, Julia Neilson and George Alexander. Was in the original production of Coward's *The Vortex* in 1924 and, twenty years on, in her seventy-first year, showed considerable stamina by appearing in *Arsenic and Old Lace*, which ran for 1,337 performances at the Strand during the Second World War, and in which she played the eccentric Abby Brewster. I saw her. She was wonderful. What is more, she was created a Dame during the run, in 1943. She deserved it, simply for making people laugh.

Sir Nigel PLAYFAIR (1874–1934) Actor, producer and manager who gained experience with amateur groups. In 1902 he first appeared with Benson. Was in Shaw's plays at the Court, and with Tree at Her Majesty's. His most important contribution to the theatre, however, was running the Lyric Theatre, Hammersmith from 1918 to 1932. Everybody who was anybody (or about to become anybody) appeared there and for this he was knighted in 1928. His was a unique contribution to the theatre between the wars.

Sir Lewis CASSON (1875–1969) Actor, and married to Dame Sybil Thorndike. First professional performance was in 1903. After the First World War he returned to the stage and, in conjunction with his wife, produced seasons at the Holborn Empire and the Little Theatre. For some years was mainly concerned with production, though continuing to act, from time to time, touring South Africa and Australia, often with Dame Sybil. During the Second World War husband and wife worked tirelessly for both C E M A and E N S A, specialising in tours of the mining towns. Dame Sybil received her D B E in 1931; Sir Lewis had to wait a further fourteen years for his K. But he deserved it, and went on working right up to 1966, when the two of them appeared in a revival of *Arsenic and Old Lace*. By then the old boy was ninety-one years old. For once he outran his indefatigable wife. She gave up when she was only eighty-seven.

Harvey GRANVILLE-BARKER (1877–1946) Playwright, actor and producer. First performed with the Stage Society in 1900. The Barker–Vedrenne management at the Court (1904–7) was one of the highlights of the period. With his wife he went to the Savoy in 1912, where their productions again set new standards. Probably his best-known play is *The Voysey Inheritance*, which he wrote in 1905, but which is still regularly revived today.

Matheson LANG (1879–1948) Actor-manager and playwright, seen often in the provinces. Was best known for his performance as Wu Li Chang in *Mr Wu* which toured the world with great success. When I was a boy people still talked in awe about this, and his subsequent productions (which included some of his own writing) of *The Wandering Jew*, *The Chinese Bungalow* and *Jew Suss*. I think they would talk in a different tone today.

Harcourt WILLIAMS (1880–1957) Actor and producer, first appeared in Belfast with Benson and then in London in 1900. Worked with Kate Rorke, Ellen Terry, H. B. Irving and George Alexander. From 1929–34 was the producer at the Old Vic, causing a great stir with his innovations.

Dame Sybil THORNDIKE, C H (1882–1976) We have already met Dame Sybil as Sir Lewis Casson's wife, which may have given a glimpse of her career. She started with Ben Greet, touring the provinces and the United States, and was leading lady for several seasons at Miss Horniman's Manchester Rep. It was at the beginning of her contract with Miss Horniman, in Belfast, that she met her future husband. They were to be together for a further sixty-one years, and it was during her time in Manchester that their three children were born. All went into the theatre and, indeed, I appeared with daughter, Ann Casson, when she played Regan in *King Lear* and Olivia in *Twelfth Night* for Wolfit in 1942. From 1914–18, Sybil Thorndike was at the Old Vic, where she established her reputation. After the war, the Cassons went into management at the New (Albery) Theatre and it was here that she created the part especially written for her by Shaw – *Saint Joan* – which must surely have been the highlight of her formidable career, although she was to be seen to great effect in the legendary Old Vic season headed by Laurence Olivier and Ralph Richardson at the New towards the end of the Second World War and after. She was created a Dame of the Order of the British

Empire in 1931 and a Companion of Honour in 1970. A critic once wrote of her: 'Miss Thorndike will be a great actress so long as she learns to keep her hands beneath her shoulders.' She never did, and she became a great actress all the same. Which all goes to prove how wrong some critics can be.

Robert ATKINS, CBE (1886–1972) Spent most of his career in the service of Shakespeare. After training at the Royal Academy of Dramatic Art, Tree hired him for Her Majesty's in 1906. He then toured with Martin-Harvey, Forbes-Robertson and Frank Benson. In later years he took his own Shakespeare company on tour, founded the Bankside Players, was producer at the Stratford-upon-Avon Memorial Theatre and organised the Open Air Theatre in Regent's Park. Often impersonated for his plummy vowels, but always with affection. He was made a CBE. The K eluded him. Perhaps it was those vowels . . .

Dame Gladys COOPER (1888–1971) Actress-manager and producer who, if for no other reason, deserves a place in this book for being the only woman between the wars – apart from Lilian Baylis – to run a West End theatre, the Playhouse, which she controlled from 1917 to 1931. And it is arguable as to whether or not Lilian Baylis operated in the West End, as such. But Gladys Cooper deserves a place in this book for her acting also – and for the fact that she was Robert Morley's mother-in-law from 1940 until she died thirty-one years later, a Dame of the British Empire, awarded her in 1967. She had three careers in fact: an actress who appeared in four of Somerset Maugham's most celebrated plays – *Home and Beauty*, *The Sacred Flame*, *The Letter* and *The Painted Veil*, plus revivals of *My Lady's Dress*, *The Second Mrs Tanqueray* and *Magda*; a producer, who presented these plays, as well as many others. That's two careers – but she then became a Holly-wood film star and lived in Tinsel City for thirty years, appearing in such successes as *Separate Tables* and *My Fair Lady*. That's three careers. Not bad for someone who began life as a child photographic model and whose first job was the name part in Seymour Hick's tour of *Bluebell in Fairyland*. I wonder if she did believe in fairies? I shouldn't be surprised. After all, her life had a fairytale quality about it.

Dame Edith EVANS (1888–1976) There are not many actors who become known for their way of speaking two words. Robertson Hare was one, with 'Oh, calamity!' whilst Edith Evans was the other with 'A handbag?' Bunny Hare was also known for losing his trousers. As far as I am aware, Dame Edith clung on to hers. She also clung on to an awesome reputation as the actress who was never out of work, appearing last at the Phoenix Theatre only two years before her death, at the ripe old age of eighty-six – which means she gave up one year younger than her illustrious contemporary, Dame Sybil. Dame Edith first made a name for herself as an amateur, and then, in 1913, played Cressida at Stratford-upon-Avon. She toured with Ellen Terry, followed by a succession of West End productions, becoming a firm favourite of the critics. It was in 1924, though, that she achieved her first major success as Mrs Millamant in *The Way of the World* at the Lyric, Hammersmith. A season at the Old Vic followed and she was on the road to becoming the distinguished actress perhaps best known for her performance as Lady Bracknell in the 1939 revival of *The Importance of Being Earnest*. During the war she toured extensively overseas for ENSA and was made a Dame for this work, just after the war was over, in 1946. She continued to appear in the West End, the Old Vic, the RSC, the National, on tour, in films and on television until old age and infirmity took their toll. John Gielgud described her as 'the finest actress of our time' and I, for one, will not argue with that.

Owen NARES (1888–1943) One of the most popular matinée idols in London. Indeed, I can remember my mother breathing his name with a certain degree of adulation. In 1923 he took over the management of the St James's Theatre (where I made my first London appearance) and just before his sudden death at the age of fifty-five he had given two memorable performances as Robert Carson in *Robert's Wife*, opposite Edith Evans and as Maxim de Winter in *Rebecca* – the part which pushed Laurence Olivier to Hollywood stardom.

Sir Cedric HARDWICKE (1893–1964) Made his first appearance as an actor in 1912 for Tree while at the Academy of Dramatic Art. In 1913 he joined Benson's company, but then came the First World War and Hardwicke was not seen again for another eight years, for he was the last officer to be demobbed from France. He went straight to Birmingham Rep and began to establish himself, particularly with his performance of Churdles Ash in *The Farmer's Wife*, which transferred to the West End, and as Caesar in *Caesar and Cleopatra*, which did likewise. By now more and more interesting work was coming his way, particularly his appearances at the Malvern Festival, and in 1934 he was knighted for his services to the theatre. In 1936 he went to New York and then on to Hollywood, where he stayed at the request of the British Government during the war, so it is said, for propaganda purposes. In 1944 he returned to England and toured for E N S A in his old success, *Yellow Sands*, before appearing as Sir Toby Belch in *Twelfth Night* with the Old Vic. Then it was back to appearances on Broadway, and touring the summer theatres around the States, his last success being 556 performances at the Shubert Theatre of *A Majority of One*, beginning in 1959. Sir Cedric died in New York in 1964.

Ivor NOVELLO (1893–1951) Actor-manager, dramatist, composer and one of the most successful in all departments, to boot. Even after he served a short term of imprisonment in the Second World War for petrol offences (it was strictly rationed), he was greeted back to *The Dancing Years* at the Adelphi Theatre as if he, personally, had just won the war. In a roundabout way he had – or at least contributed considerably, for his productions kept a wartime Britain happy – as did his composition, 'Keep The Home Fires Burning', in the First World War. The list of his credits is very long indeed, including *Glamorous Night*, *Careless Rapture*, *Perchance to Dream*, *King's Rhapsody* and *Gay's The Word* for Cicely Courtneidge, although the current coinage of the word might well have made that title more appropriate for Mr Novello himself. He died shortly after a performance of *King's Rhapsody*, no doubt with the usual tumultuous reception ringing in his ears, for he was undoubtedly the biggest box-office attraction of his time, and toured extensively to the delight of his audience of myriad millions. Sadly, his work now seems strangely dated. It is extraordinary how quickly tastes change and for those of us who bridge the gap 'twixt then and now, it provides an object lesson in our attempts to assess the quality of those great stars of yesteryear. In truth, they must have been very different.

Dame Cicely COURTNEIDGE (1893–1980) and Jack HULBERT (1892–1978) I have coupled these two together, for in British audiences' minds they were as inseparable as salt and pepper or roast beef and Yorkshire pud. Cis was the daughter of a well-known impresario, Robert Courtneidge, and at the age of eight she was appearing for him as one of the fairies in *A Midsummer Night's Dream*. He believed in nepotism and engaged her for a number of productions until, in 1913, she met Jack. The production was *The Pearl Girl* and her future husband had been engaged by her father straight from the Cambridge Footlights. From then on they continued to work for Cis' dad, until they married in 1916. Alas, things began to go wrong, and nepotism was of little help, for Robert Courtneidge was in debt, Jack had to go into the army and Cicely couldn't get herself arrested. It was then she tried her hand at music hall and began to realise that she was, in fact, a comedienne. Jack was demobbed, and continued in the 'legitimate' theatre, but they hated being apart and in 1923 they launched themselves at the Little Theatre in *Little Revue Starts Here*. That was the beginning of their enormously successful partnership, including films and plays, as well as revues and musicals, which continued – with the odd break – for fifty-three years. She was made a Commander of the Order of the British Empire in 1951 and elevated to Dame in 1972; Jack remained just plain Mr Hulbert. His brother Claude – also a comic actor – was even plainer, but funny with it.

Sir Noël COWARD (1899–1972) Actor, dramatist, director, composer and the self-styled 'Master'. First appeared at the age of twelve as Prince Mussel in a children's fairy play, *The Goldfish*, and last appeared, aged seventy, in *Suite in Three Keys*. I do not believe the first piece was his own work, but the last was – like pretty well everything else in between. A legend in his own life, he sometimes had to struggle to remain at the very top of the entertainment tree, but he never let it show and was always able to present an urbane and untroubled countenance to his critics. He was knighted only three years before his death, for a lifetime's gift to the world of music and laughter and tears.

Sir Tyrone GUTHRIE (1900–71) An actor who rapidly became a director. First appeared in 1924 at the Oxford Playhouse, but less than two years after that he was directing the Scottish National Players. He then moved to the Festival Theatre, Cambridge, and in 1931 came his first London production, *The Anatomist*, at the Westminster Theatre. He was on his way. Then followed Priestley's *Dangerous Corner* and the Old Vic–Sadler's Wells. He was producer there in 1933 and 1936, and Administrator from 1939–45. His work continued and there is no doubt that he was one of the most influential theatrical figures of the mid-1900s. He was knighted in 1961, which must have given a smug sense of satisfaction to his old adversary, Sir Donald. Wolfit had received the tap on the shoulder four years earlier, giving him, no doubt, a justifiable sense of superiority.

Sir Donald WOLFIT, CBE (1902–68) Born in Newark as Donald Woolfitt, he changed his name when the printers kept spelling it incorrectly on programmes and bills. I cannot believe that you need to know anything more about my first boss but, lest you do, he started as a walk-on at York in 1920. Then toured with Fred Terry and made his first London appearance in *The Wandering Jew* in 1924. With the Old Vic from 1929–30. Toured Canada in 1931–2. At Stratford in 1936, then formed his own touring company in 1937. The rest is anything but silence.

Sir Ralph RICHARDSON (1902–83) This remarkable, idiosyncratic actor's story must be familiar to all theatre-goers who have taken an interest in such people over the recent past. To recite his works would take another book, and this has already been written. However, I think I should mention that he began his career with another well-known touring actor-manager, out of the F. R. Benson stable – Charles Doran. Doran even exceeded the number of plays toured at any one time by Wolfit and when Richardson joined him, he was rehearsing seven plays (all Shakespeare) in only three weeks, and preparing to rehearse another three whilst on tour, to add to the repertoire. It was a hard school – and Richardson had, indeed, to learn the hard way. But he did, as we all know, to our considerable gain. He is perhaps most renowned for accepting Tyrone Guthrie's offer to lead the Old Vic Company in their end-of-war great days from 1944. Ralphie (as he was known) had the good sense to ask for Laurence Olivier to join him as co-leading actor, as well as John Burrell as a co-director. The rest is history. As befits the original leader of the company, Richardson was knighted first, in January 1947 with Olivier following in the same year's Birthday Honours. Sir Ralph continued

266

to enchant his audiences with a wide variety of performances, including those conjured up by the avant-garde playwrights of the 1950s and 60s, with impeccable appearances on film, too. Loved his motorbike.

Sir John GIELGUD, CH (b.1904) Actor and director. Like his two colleagues, Sir Ralph and Sir Larry, it is impossible to list all the great man's achievements, or to recount all the myriad stories which surround his patrician personality. Can we just say that we who are alive today are lucky to have seen the works of such a trio, including those of this grand-nephew of Ellen Terry.

Sir Laurence (Lord) OLIVIER, OM (1907–89) As Baron Olivier of Brighton he was the first Peer of the British Theatre, and deservedly so. Actor-manager, producer, director and founding father of the National Theatre. Loved sticking on false noses . . . Well, why not?

Dame Peggy ASHCROFT (1907–91) By sheer coincidence, born in the same year as Olivier. She, too, takes her place quite effortlessly in this pantheon of our mid- to late-twentieth-century theatrical gods, more than upholding the consummate abilities of the distaff side.

Sir Bernard (Lord) MILES, CBE (1907–91) 1907 must have been a vintage year for theatrical babies. Here we have the second Peer of the theatre (Baron Miles of Blackfriars) born in the same year as his illustrious companion, Lord Olivier. Mind you, Bernard's work was of a totally different nature, encompassing variety, as well as all the traditional actor's stock-in-trade on stage, film and television. However, like Olivier, he began a theatre – the Mermaid at Puddle Dock – but, unlike Olivier, it was not started with any idea in mind of being a National Theatre, requiring an Act of Parliament to bring it to fruition, but simply at the request of the then Lord Mayor of London, who asked Bernard and Josephine Miles to transfer their own little theatre from their house in St John's Wood to the Royal Exchange for the Coronation festivities. Bernard enjoyed the experience so much, he and his wife decided to settle in the City and, with the help of the City Fathers, opened the Mermaid in 1959. It flourished – but then came the time when much-needed work had to be undertaken and additional accommodation provided. The Mermaid had building permission for a nearby plot and with this they were able to negotiate a deal with the developers to spread the work into the Mermaid. Alas, the money provided was not sufficient to complete the task to everyone's satisfaction, the City's interests seemed to be more involved in the Barbican Centre, and after struggling on for a few years, Lord Miles, as he had then become, decided to call it a day and retire. But we shall always remember his Long John Silver and that amazing parrot. Christmas will never be the same without him or it.

Sir Michael REDGRAVE, CBE (1908–85) Although he is listed in *Who's Who in the Theatre* as 'actor, author, director, manager', I think Sir Michael's activities on the production line were strictly limited. However, he was an actor of considerable stature and sired (with a little help from his good lady, Rachel Kempson), a not inconsiderable family of actors, which has now extended unto the third generation. For that alone he deserved his knighthood, which he received in 1959.

Robert MORLEY, CBE (1908–92) Born the same year as Sir Michael and, like him, no major activity on the management side, that I can see. Just one of the most outrageously funny actors of the last generation or two, never making any other attempt than to be Robert Morley, at which he was supreme. A highly amusing author, as well, and, by all accounts, a highly amusing father, too. For providing much laughter, Robert was awarded the CBE way back in 1957. He seemed to be forgotten after that. I can't think why.

Sir John CLEMENTS, CBE (1910–88) Probably the longest-serving actor-manager of the mid-twentieth century, spanning the years from before the Second World War to long after. He first ventured into this arcane world (although there are no mysteries when things go wrong) in 1935, when he took over the Intimate, Palmers Green. During the war, he was heavily engaged in ENSA activities, but still managed to appear in several West End productions, including a revival of Coward's *Private Lives*, with his delightful wife, Kay Hammond, playing Amanda to his Elyot Chase. He leased the St James's Theatre, just after the war, for a season and then went into the Old Vic company as an 'ordinary' actor. In 1949 he was back in management again, with *The Beaux' Stratagem* at the Phoenix and then moved over to the New (Albery) Theatre in *Man and Superman*. In both these plays, and others, he was again partnered by Kay Hammond, who was unhappily forced to retire from the stage because of ill health. But Clements battled on, eventually taking over the mantle elegantly laid down by Olivier, as the director of the Chichester Festival Theatre. He was knighted in 1968, left Chichester, and was last in the West End in a very big success at the Haymarket, *The Case in Question*. Once his wife died, he was rarely seen again.

Sir Michael HORDERN, CBE (b.1911) Famous as a fulminating old fogey, as an actor and a fanatical fisherman, but – as a civilian – Michael Hordern is the most courteous of men with a unique personality which puts him into the same rather quirky league as Ralph Richardson. He is as at home in the classics as he is in a modern work, such as David Mercer's *Flint*, which I so enjoyed when I saw it at the Criterion Theatre in 1970. He has done his turn at the RSC, at the Old Vic, the National and Stratford East and was knighted for his excellence as an actor in 1984. Fishing was not even mentioned in the citation – but it could well have been.

Alec CLUNES (1912–70) Like Sir John Clements, Alec Clunes kept the actor-manager flag flying for a long time, founding the Arts Theatre Group of Actors in 1942, whose home was the little theatre in Great Newport Street, just a stone's throw from the Ambassadors' and St Martin's Theatres, which have successively housed *The Mousetrap*. Not that he was in the same commercial league as that particular production, but in the eight years he was at the Arts he produced over 150 plays, appearing in some and directing others. A famous critic, Ivor Brown, called it a 'pocket National Theatre'. After leaving the Arts Theatre, he occasionally returned to actor-management, but died quite young, which put a premature stop to any further plans he might have had.

Sir Anthony QUAYLE, CBE (1913–89) Another great freewheeling spirit in the theatre, especially as an actor-manager on two separate occasions. First appearing at the long-lost 'Q' Theatre in 1931, he went west a year later to be in *Richard of Bordeaux* at the New (Albery) Theatre, with John Gielgud making a huge success of the title part. A spell at the Old Vic followed, then New York in *The Country Wife* and back with the Old Vic to Elsinore, going on to Egypt and the Continent. A gunner during the war – reaching the rank of major – in 1948 he became the actor-manager-director running the Shakespeare Memorial Theatre at Stratford-upon-Avon and stayed until the end of 1956. Then he became a freelance actor once again. Much work on film and in the theatre followed, but Tony still hankered after running his own 'classical' touring company, and in 1984 his wish was fulfilled and Compass Theatre Company came into being. It is still going strong (and described elsewhere in this book), even though Sir Anthony – he was knighted in 1985 – is sadly no longer around to lead it. He died from cancer in 1990.

Sir Alec GUINNESS, CBE (b.1914) Neither an actor-manager nor a touring actor, but I felt I must include Sir Alec – knighted in 1959 – for he is so familiar to so many, for his performances on film (the Ealing Comedies, *The Bridge on the River Kwai*, *Star Wars* – to mention but a few) and for George Smiley in John Le Carré's great spy stories on television. If ever a man has been able to capitalise on a scarcity of hair, it is Sir Alec. Perruquiers and producers alike have reason to bless his chameleon-like talent.

Paul SCOFIELD, C B E (b.1922) Although never an actor-manager, no theatrical book would be complete without mention of this prodigiously talented actor. Unfortunately, as I was working in the theatre every night, too, it was impossible for me to see his stunning performances in the 1950s and 60s, but I did catch him as the homosexual hairdresser in Charles Dyer's *Staircase*, which was in the R S C Aldwych Theatre repertoire in 1966. It was then I felt the pangs of envy for perhaps the first and last time – and then quietly got on with my own preparations for a repertoire of plays at the Garrick. I just wish one of those had presented the same opportunities as *Staircase*, that's all.

Donald SINDEN, C B E (b.1923) Moves from tragedy to comedy and back to farce with equal facility. R S C, Chichester, Ray Cooney, films, television, his mentors are many and varied. Has done his share of touring, too. One of the bastions of the Garrick Club and the author of three autobiographies. That's how multifarious his activities have been.

Sir Brian (Lord) RIX, C B E (b.1924) 'Damn fine chap and my dad. Oh yes, and the third theatrical peer – Baron Rix of Whitehall and Hornsea, too.' So wrote my son, Jonathan. Modesty forbids that I contradict him.

Walter PLINGE (b. in desperation) Little to say about him either, for he never existed. Used as a *nom de guerre* in the old days when a leading actor was doubling in a smaller part or the manager was not quite certain who was going to turn up and had to put a name on the bill to make up the numbers. Not a member of Equity.

Now we come to those who are still actor-managers, to this very day:

Ray COONEY (b.1932) Started his acting career as a child actor in *The Song of Norway* but in spite of this has grown into a pleasant human being. His great break came when he joined the tour of *Dry Rot* I was sending out with John Slater. He and Tony Hilton (who was playing my old part) teamed up to write scripts for John's television programme, an advertising feature called *Slater's Bazaar*. Having been bitten by the writing bug, the two of them continued and wrote one of the most successful farces I ever did – *One For The Pot*. Ray and Tony then scripted a film for me and a further farce, *Stand By Your Bedouin*, which went on at the Garrick. Prior to that, Ray – alone – had written another smash hit for the Whitehall, *Chase Me Comrade!* And so it went on, a stream of farces coming from Ray's typewriter, including two with John Chapman, *Not Now, Darling* and *Move Over Mrs Markham*. For a time he went into management with Laurie Marsh, but returned to his love of writing, directing and acting, as well as founding the Theatre of Comedy. Is now the proud owner (with others) of the Playhouse – presenting his latest farce – *It Runs in the Family*. His last-but-one farce, *Run For Your Wife* has been a phenomenal success all over the world. Ray cannot resist popping in to act whenever the opportunity arises. His favourite bit of business is expressing consternation by running on the spot. Well, that's what it looks like to me, anyway. It is known as 'the Cooney school of acting'.

Edward PETHERBRIDGE (b.1936) All the right classical background for an actor who was the co-founder of the Actors' Company in 1972, having been at the Old Vic, the Royal Court, the Regent's Park Open Air Theatre and the Mermaid, before going into management with Ian McKellen. Since then has continued in similar vein, being a member of the R S C since 1978 and co-director of the McKellen-Petherbridge Group at the National Theatre from 1984–6. One of his recreations is 'theatre history'. I hope he finds this book of interest.

Sir Ian McKELLEN (b.1939) Like his erstwhile partner, Edward Petherbridge, Ian McKellen has impeccable references when it comes to being a classical actor. An Hon. Fellow of St Catherine's College, Cambridge; President of the Marlowe Society before that; one-time member of the Council of Equity; Visiting Professor of Contemporary Theatre at St Catherine's College, Oxford; appearances at the Belgrade Theatre, Coventry and the Nottingham Playhouse in their heyday; Clarence Derwent Award; National Theatre; Old Vic; Chichester Festival – the list is endless. Can you wonder he was anxious to have a company of his own. Since those Actors' Company days, McKellen has gone from strength to strength, collecting umpteen acting awards from all over the globe. Heaven knows what heights he will scale next.

Michael PENNINGTON (b.1943) Not too dissimilar a background to Ian McKellen before becoming co-director of the English Shakespeare Company with Michael Bogdanov in 1986. Cambridge, R S C, Royal Court, National Theatre, all show on his cv – with some stunning performances to go with them. The wonder is that less people go in for actor-management than might be apparent from their backgrounds. It's obvious it needs a particular single-mindedness – and all three of the current classical lot certainly have that, as, I am sure, do the last two – the babies of the bunch.

Tim PIGOTT-SMITH (b.1946) The man who has succeeded Sir Anthony Quayle as the leader of the Compass Theatre Company is perhaps best known for a television performance, that of Captain Merrick in *Jewel in the Crown*, but his theatre background is as strewn with good works as that of his peers. Bristol Old Vic, Nottingham Playhouse, the R S C, the Lyric, Hammersmith, the Royal National Theatre, B A F T A Best Actor Award, Edinburgh Fringe First Award, all these – and more – qualify him to be the current artistic director of Compass. Tony must have been delighted.

Kenneth BRANAGH (b.1961) There is more about young Branagh in the book – but he has come a long way in a very short time, as well as getting married to a talented young actress, Emma Thompson. He first made his mark in *Another Country* at the Queen's Theatre, but there was little let or hindrance before he went on to other equally good and noticeable work. The apogee of his career to date must surely be the forming of the Renaissance Theatre Company with David Parfitt, although Mr Parfitt seems to have sublimated his acting ambitions to the cause of management at the moment, but I am sure we will hear more of him. Together, these two, plus a stockbroker, Stephen Evans, formed Renaissance Films Plc and with their very first effort, in 1988, produced a smash hit, *Henry V*, with Branagh both directing and playing the name part. The film collected a number of awards, and people have been only too anxious to compare Branagh with Olivier. Such comparisons are pointless, for the two men are totally dissimilar in appearance and approach – or rather were, when Olivier was alive. But it's jolly good to know there is a young actor-manager prepared to take risks, just like Olivier, and also that there are a number of like-minded actor-managers today, all floating about the place at the same time. We may not be quite back to the turn of the century as regards numbers – but we are getting there.

Old Thespis would have been very pleased . . .

Acknowledgments

Would all the following take a bow please, for being so helpful in the preparation of this book — supplying me with information, brochures, programmes, books and reminiscences, in generous profusion. I am most grateful.

David Aukin (Royal National Theatre) Geoffrey Axworthy (Prince of Wales Theatre, Cardiff) Ivor Barnes (King's Theatre, Southsea) Elyot Beaumont (Howard and Wyndham) Andrew Blackwood (Arts Theatre of Cambridge) John Botteley (Grand Theatre, Wolverhampton) Jean Bullwinkle, OBE (Arts Council of Great Britain) Luis Candal, Anthony Hardman (Pavilion, Bournemouth) Ian Carpendale (Futurist, Scarborough) Tony Clayton, Pam Langfield (Key Theatre, Peterborough) Julia Clotworthy-Bird (Theatre Royal, Bath) David Conville, OBE (New Shakespeare Company) John Cornwell (Lyceum Theatre, Sheffield) John Curtin (Festival Theatre, Malvern) Tony Docherty (Hippodrome, Bristol) James Donald (His Majesty's Theatre, Aberdeen) Michael Eakin (Hexagon Theatre, Reading) Sue Evans (English Shakespeare Company) J. Farquharson (Theatre Royal, Exeter) Norman Fenner (Richmond Theatre Trust Ltd) Julian Forrester (Compass Theatre Ltd) Dr Levi Fox (Shakespeare Birthday Trust) Brian Goddard, Steve Luck (Darlington Civic Theatre) Vanessa Hart (Torbay Theatres – Princess, Torquay; Festival, Paignton) Russell Hills, Michael Lister, Judi Richards (New Theatre, Hull) Jackie Hinde (Apollo Theatre, Oxford) David Jackson (Theatre Royal, Glasgow) John Jones (Theatre Royal, Hanley) Andrew Leigh (Old Vic, London) Mike Lyas (Wimbledon Theatre) Iain Mackintosh (Theatre Projects Services Ltd) Laurie Marsh (Laurie Marsh Consultants Ltd) John Martin (Alhambra Theatre, Bradford) Professor Ronnie Mulryne (University of Warwick) Fred O'Donovan (Gaiety Theatre, Dublin) Peggy Parnell (Pavilion, Torquay) Jack Phipps (Arts Council of Great Britain) Roger Redfarn (Theatre Royal, Plymouth) Robert Scott (Manchester Theatres Ltd) David Shinwell (Fairfield Halls, Croydon) Sam Shrouder (Apollo Leisure UK Ltd) Betty Slater (John Slater's memorabilia) Warren Smith (Grand Theatre and Opera House, Leeds) Roger Spence (Royal Lyceum Theatre, Edinburgh) Brenda Thomas (Stoll Moss Ltd) Peter Tod (Hippodrome, Birmingham) Anne Travers (Theatre Royal, Brighton) Alan Twelftree (Empire, Sunderland) Stephen Walton (Theatre Royal, Bury St Edmunds) Derek Webster (Theatre Royal, Newcastle) Duncan Weldon, Peter Wilkins (Triumph Theatre Productions Ltd) James Williams (Cambridge Theatre Company)

Having taken those individual calls, I must now go on to the bibliography and ask all those authors who have provided me with such pleasure in the reading of their works, and whose background information has been invaluable, to step forward to receive their share of the applause. Any direct quote has been acknowledged in the text.

Joss Ackland, *I Must Be In There Somewhere* (London 1989)   Natalie Anglesey, *Palace Theatre, Manchester* (Manchester 1981)   Michael Baker, *The Rise of the Victorian Actor* (London 1978)   Squire Bancroft, *The Bancrofts* (London 1909) L. Carson (Ed.), *The Stage Year Book* (London 1908 and 1912)   John Cottrell, *Laurence Olivier* (London 1975)   T. W. Craik, Clifford Leech, Lois Potter (Ed.), *The Revels History of Drama in English, Volumes I to VII* (London 1975–83) Harvey Crane, *Playbill* (Plymouth 1980)   Michael Denison, *Double Act* (London 1985) F. Donaldson, *The Actor Managers* (London 1970)   Aubrey Dyas, *Adventure in Repertory* (Northampton 1948)   John Elsom, *Theatre Outside London* (London 1971)   J. O. Halliwell-Phillips (Ed.), *Letters of the Kings of England* (London 1818)   Alan Hankinson, *The Blue Box* (Keswick 1983)   Phyllis Hartnoll (Ed.), *The Oxford Companion to the Theatre* (London 1957)   J. L. Hodgkinson and Rex Pogson, *The Early Manchester Theatre* (London 1960)   Peter Holdsworth, *Domes of Delight* (Bradford 1989) Richard Huggett, *Binkie Beaumont* (London 1989) Laurence Irving, *Henry Irving* (London 1951)   William Kelly (Ed.), *Notices Illustrative of the Drama and Other Popular Amusements, extracted from the Chamberlain's accounts and other manuscripts of the Borough of Leicester* (London 1865)   Robert King, *North Shields Theatres* (Gateshead 1948)   Iain Mackintosh, *Pit, Boxes and Gallery* (National Trust 1976)   Jack Mitchley and Peter Spalding, *Five Thousand Years of Theatre* (London, 1982)   Malcolm Morley, *Margate and its Theatres* (London 1966) Sheridan Morley, *The Great Stage Stars* (London 1986)   Timmie Morrison, *A Theatre for the People* (Clevedon 1983)   Garry O'Connor, *Ralph Richardson* (London 1982)   John Parker (Ed.), *Who's Who in the Theatre* (London 1952) Hesketh Pearson, *The Last Actor Managers* (London 1950)   Belville S. Penley, *The Bath Stage* (London 1892)   Cecil Price, *The English Theatre in Wales* (Cardiff 1948)   Proscenium Publications, *Theatre Royal, Newcastle-upon-Tyne* (Clifton 1988)   Brian Rix, *My Farce From My Elbow* (London 1975)   Brian Rix, *Farce About Face* (London 1989)   Christopher Robinson, *A History of the Bristol Hippodrome* (Bristol 1982)   George Rowell and Anthony Jackson, *The Repertory Movement: A History of Regional Theatre in Britain* (Cambridge 1984)   Derek Salberg, *My Love Affair With a Theatre* (Luton 1978)   Michael Sanderson, *From Irving to Olivier* (London 1984)   Donald Sinden, *Laughter in the Second Act* (London 1985)   Donald Sinden, *A Touch of the Memoirs* (London 1982)   Bill Slinn, *The History of the Birmingham Hippodrome* (Norwich 1983)   Anthony Swainson, O B E (Ed.), *Theatrical Digs* (Lord's Taverners 1987)   J. C. Trewin, *The Pomping Folk* (London 1968)   Glynne Wickham, *A History of the Theatre* (London 1985) Donald Wolfit, *First Interval* (London 1954)

DATE SHEET

Donald Wolfit Tour 1942

Week commencing

24 August	Prince of Wales, Cardiff
31 August	Pavilion, Torquay
7 September	Theatre Royal, Exeter
14 September	Coliseum, Harrow
21 September	Arts Theatre, Cambridge
28 September	New, Hull
5 October	Opera House, Manchester
12 October	Royal Court, Liverpool
19 October	Grand, Leeds
26 October	Theatre Royal, Glasgow
2 November	King's, Edinburgh
9 November	Theatre Royal, Newcastle
16 November	Theatre Royal, Nottingham
7 December	Grand, Croydon

Followed by a six-week E N S A Tour of *Twelfth Night*, February/March 1943 and a further six-week E N S A Tour of *Suspect*, February/March/April 1944.

'Reluctant Heroes' Tour 1950

Week commencing

27 March	White Rock Pavilion, Hastings
3 April	Wimbledon Theatre
10 April	Dolphin, Brighton
17 April	Stoke Newington (cancelled)
24 April	Winter Gardens, Blackpool
1 May	Pavilion, Torquay
8 May	Palace, Plymouth (twice nightly)
15 May	New, Hull
22 May	King's, Southsea
29 May	Prince of Wales, Cardiff
5 June	Theatre Royal, Birmingham
12 June	Embassy, Peterborough
19 June	Theatre Royal, Bath
26 June	Royal Court, Liverpool
3 July	Theatre Royal, Nottingham
10 July	Palace Court, Bournemouth
17 July	Grand, Swansea
24 July	week out
31 July	Palace Pier, Brighton
7 August	Theatre Royal, Norwich
14 August	Victoria Pavilion, Ilfracombe
21 August	week out
28 August	week out
4 September	Opera House, Leicester

'The Long March' Tour 1953

Week commencing

9 March	New, Hull
16 March	Theatre Royal, Bath
23 March	Lyceum, Newport
30 March	Wimbledon Theatre
6 April	Pleasure Gardens, Folkestone
13 April	King's, Southsea
20 April	Arts Theatre, Cambridge
27 April	Pavilion, Torquay

'Tell the Marines' Tour 1953

Week commencing

4 May	Theatre Royal, Bath
11 May	Prince of Wales, Cardiff
18 May	Theatre Royal, Nottingham
25 May	Grand, Doncaster
1 June	Festival, Malvern
8 June	King's, Southsea
15 June	Palace Pier, Brighton
22 June	Grand, Halifax

'Reluctant Heroes' Tour 1954 (with John Slater)

Week commencing

29 March	Alexandra, Birmingham
5 April	Pavilion, Bournemouth
12 April	Hippodrome, Bristol
19 April	Opera House, Manchester
26 April	Hippodrome, Coventry
3 May	Grand, Leeds
10 May	Royal Court, Liverpool
17 May	King's, Edinburgh
24 May	King's, Glasgow
31 May	Theatre Royal, Newcastle
7 June	Grand, Blackpool
14 June	Theatre Royal, Nottingham
21 June	New, Oxford
28 June	Theatre Royal, Brighton

There was then a pause. *Reluctant Heroes* finished its run at the Whitehall and two tours went out – one headed by John Slater again – and the other by an actor who had been playing Sgt Bell at the end of the run, Antony Baird. The audiences still packed all the dates.

Week commencing

19 July	King's, Southsea
26 July	Hippodrome, Golders Green and Pleasure Gardens, Folkestone
2 August	Palace Pier, Brighton and Streatham
9 August	New, Oxford and Empire, Chiswick
16 August	Richmond Theatre and P O W, Cardiff
23 August	Empire, Hackney and Palace, Ramsgate
30 August	Marlowe, Canterbury and Coliseum, Harrow
6 September	Empire, Wood Green and Regal, St Leonard's
13 September	Devonshire Park, Eastbourne only
20 September	Theatre Royal, Norwich and Hippodrome, Aldershot. This latter company then toured B A O R Germany

John Slater had now left the company and the U K tour continued with Bert Brownlow and/ or Robin Wentworth playing Sgt Bell.

Week commencing

4 October	Theatre Royal, Hanley
11 October	Hippodrome, Derby
18 October	Lyceum, Sheffield
25 October	Prince's, Bradford
1 November	Grand, Wolverhampton
8 November	Memorial, Stratford-upon-Avon
15 November	Empire, Sunderland
22 November	Palace, Leicester
29 November	Opera House, Belfast
6 December	Opera House, Cork
13 December	Olympia, Dublin
20 December	week out
27 December	Festival, Malvern
3 January 1955	ditto
10 January	Prince of Wales, Cardiff
17 January	Palace, Westcliff
24 January	New, Cambridge
31 January	Coliseum, Harrow
7 February	Garrick, Southport
14 February	New, Hull
21 February	New, Northampton
28 February	Theatre Royal, Norwich
7 March	Lyceum, Newport
14 March	Palace, Plymouth
21 March	Theatre Royal, Bath
28 March	Hippodrome, Ipswich (twice nightly)
4 April	Streatham Hill Theatre
11 April	week out
18 April	Empire, Swansea
25 April	Winter Gardens, Morecambe

Then came a further break, and a new tour of *Reluctant Heroes* was launched later in the year. Meanwhile, the army farce was enjoying a record-breaking run of almost four years, touring and playing seasons all round Australia and New Zealand, and there had also been the record-breaking British film of the play in 1952/3. It was quite a property!

'Reluctant Heroes' Autumn Tour 1955

Week commencing

5 September	New, Oxford
12 September	Theatre Royal, Birmingham
19 September	Theatre Royal, Nottingham
26 September	King's, Southsea
3 October	Theatre Royal, Newcastle
10 October	Lyceum, Sheffield
17 October	His Majesty's, Aberdeen
24 October	King's, Glasgow
31 October	Hippodrome, Derby
7 November	Grand, Wolverhampton
14 November	Royal Court, Liverpool
21 November	Grand, Blackpool
28 November	Empire, Chiswick
5 December	Hippodrome, Bristol

And that was the end of the *Reluctant Heroes* tours. However, over the next sixteen years I presented it three more times on BBC Television and, on each occasion, picked up remarkable viewing figures.

'Dry Rot' pre-London Tour 1954

Week commencing

9 August	New, Oxford
16 August	Theatre Royal, Nottingham
23 August	Pleasure Gardens, Folkestone

After two years at the Whitehall, John Slater left the cast and took the play on tour in 1956 as follows:

Week commencing

27 August	Theatre Royal, Brighton
3 September	Hippodrome, Coventry
10 September	Devonshire Park, Eastbourne
17 September	Pavilion, Bournemouth
24 September	Theatre Royal, Nottingham
1 October	Royal Court, Liverpool
8 October	Grand, Leeds
15 October	Garrick, Southport
22 October	Theatre Royal, Birmingham
29 October	Opera House, Manchester
5 November	Theatre Royal, Hanley
12 November	King's, Glasgow
19 November	His Majesty's, Aberdeen
26 November	Lyceum, Sheffield
3 December	Theatre Royal, Newcastle
10 December	Grand, Wolverhampton

That was the end of a very successful tour, whilst the play still merrily went on its way at the Whitehall. When the run finished in 1958, another tour was mounted, with dates which follow.

'Dry Rot' Tour 1958

Week commencing

10 March	Alexandra, Birmingham
17 March	Streatham Hill Theatre
24 March	Hippodrome, Golders Green
31 March	Grand, Wolverhampton
7 April	New, Hull
14 April	Lyceum, Sheffield
21 April	Alhambra, Bradford
28 April	Theatre Royal, Bath
5 May	Prince of Wales, Cardiff
12 May	Palace, Plymouth
19 May	King's, Southsea
26 May	Theatre Royal, Brighton
2 June	Hippodrome, Bristol
9 June	New, Oxford
16 June	Opera House, Belfast
23 June	Gaiety, Dublin
30 June	Hippodrome, Coventry

Meanwhile, at the beginning of 1958, *Simple Spymen* had done its pre-London tour, as now listed:

Week commencing

17 February	New, Hull
24 February	Theatre Royal, Hanley
3 March	Prince of Wales, Cardiff
10 March	Alexandra, Birmingham

'You, Too, Can Have A Body', pre-London Tour 1958 (with Bill Maynard & Bill Kerr)

Week commencing

24 March	Theatre Royal, Brighton
31 March	Streatham Hill Theatre
7 April	Hippodrome, Golders Green
14 April	Grand, Wolverhampton
21 April	New, Hull
28 April	Palace, Manchester
5 May	Hippodrome, Coventry
12 May	Theatre Royal, Nottingham

'One For The Pot' pre-London Tour 1961

Week commencing

17 July	Devonshire Park, Eastbourne
24 July	Theatre Royal, Brighton

'Simple Spymen' post-London Tour 1961
(with John Slater and Andrew Sachs)

Week commencing

7 August	Theatre Royal, Brighton
14 August	King's, Southsea
21 August	New, Oxford
28 August	Hippodrome, Bristol
4 September	Grand, Leeds
11 September	Opera House, Manchester
18 September	Hippodrome, Coventry
25 September	Grand, Wolverhampton
2 October	Streatham Hill Theatre
9 October	Hippodrome, Golders Green
16 October	Theatre Royal, Exeter
23 October	Pavilion, Bournemouth
30 October	Theatre Royal, Nottingham
6 November	Royal Court, Liverpool
13 November	Grand, Stockton

'Simple Spymen' 1961 Tour

20 November	Theatre Royal, Glasgow
27 November	King's, Edinburgh
6 December	Theatre Royal, Newcastle
13 December	Memorial, Stratford-upon-Avon

'Chase Me Comrade!' pre-London Tour 1964

Week commencing

15 June	Hippodrome, Coventry
22 June	Hippodrome, Coventry
29 June	New, Oxford
6 July	Theatre Royal, Brighton

'One For The Pot' Tour 1964
(with John Slater and John Clegg)

Week commencing

6 July	New, Cardiff
13 July	Hippodrome, Coventry
20 July	New, Oxford
27 July	Theatre Royal, Brighton
3 August	King's, Southsea
10 August	King's, Southsea
17 August	Wimbledon Theatre
24 August	Arts, Cambridge
31 August	Grand, Wolverhampton
7 September	Lyceum, Sheffield
14 September	Royal Court, Liverpool
21 September	New, Hull
28 September	Grand, Leeds
5 October	Theatre Royal, Nottingham
12 October	Pavilion, Bournemouth
19 October	Theatre Royal, Newcastle
26 October	Grand, Blackpool
2 November	Opera House, Manchester

'Chase Me Comrade!' post-London Season 1966

Season started

27 June	Winter Gardens, Morecambe and ran until 10 September

'Chase Me Comrade!' and 'Stand By Your Bedouin' Tour 1966

Following the season in Morecambe, I arranged a short repertoire tour of *Chase Me Comrade!*, with me playing the lead, for half the week and *Stand By Your Bedouin*, with Dickie Henderson topping the bill, for the other. These are the dates:

Week commencing

3 October	Opera House, Manchester
10 October	Opera House, Manchester
17 October	Royal Court, Liverpool
24 October	King's, Glasgow
31 October	King's, Edinburgh

Then I reverted to one play only – *Chase Me Comrade!* – for the rest of that 1966 tour:

Week commencing

7 November	Theatre Royal, Newcastle
14 November	Grand, Leeds
21 November	Alexandra, Birmingham
28 November	Hippodrome, Bristol
5 December	New, Cardiff

'Stand By Your Bedouin' pre-London Tour 1967

Week commencing

20 February	Grand, Wolverhampton
27 February	New, Hull
6 March	Alexandra, Birmingham

'Let Sleeping Wives Lie' post-London Tour 1969

Week commencing

7 April	Royal Court, Liverpool
14 April	Alexandra, Birmingham
21 April	Grand, Leeds
28 April	New, Hull
5 May	Opera House, Manchester
12 May	King's, Edinburgh
19 May	Theatre Royal, Newcastle
26 May	Hippodrome, Coventry
2 June	Pavilion, Bournemouth
9 June	Theatre Royal, Brighton
7 July	Playhouse, Weston-super-Mare

for a ten-week summer season.

'She's Done It Again' pre-London Tour 1969

Week commencing

22 September	Alexandra, Birmingham
29 September	Opera House, Manchester
6 October	Royal Court, Liverpool

'She's Done It Again' post-London Tour 1970

Week commencing

14 September	King's, Edinburgh
21 September	King's, Glasgow
28 September	New, Hull
5 October	Congress, Eastbourne
12 October	Pavilion, Bournemouth
19 October	New, Cardiff
26 October	Theatre Royal, Nottingham
2 November	Empire, Sunderland
9 November	Theatre Royal, York
16 November	Gaumont, Shrewsbury
23 November	Grand, Wolverhampton

'Six of Rix' Tour 1971

Week commencing

1 March	Opera House, Manchester
8 March	Alexandra, Birmingham
5 April	New, Cardiff
12 April	Grand, Leeds
10 May	Theatre Royal, Norwich
17 May	Theatre Royal, Nottingham
24 May	Alhambra, Bradford
31 May	King's, Southsea

'Don't Just Lie There, Say Something' pre-London Tour 1971

Week commencing

16 August	Alexandra, Birmingham
23 August	Theatre Royal, Brighton
30 August	Theatre Royal, Brighton
6 September	King's, Southsea

'Don't Just Lie There, Say Something' post-London Tour 1973

Week commencing

5 March	Theatre Royal, Nottingham
12 March	New, Cardiff
19 March	Grand, Swansea
26 March	Pavilion, Bournemouth
2 April	Rex, Wilmslow

'She Was Only An Admiral's Daughter' Tour 1972 (with Leslie Crowther and Dilys Watling)

Week commencing

14 August	King's, Southsea
21 August	King's, Southsea
28 August	Theatre Royal, Brighton
4 September	Theatre Royal, Brighton
11 September	Wimbledon Theatre
18 September	Alexandra Theatre, Birmingham
25 September	New, Hull
2 October	Royal Court, Liverpool
9 October	week out
16 October	Grand, Leeds
23 October	Hippodrome, Bristol
30 October	Opera House, Manchester
6 November	Theatre Royal, Nottingham

'A Bit Between the Teeth' pre-London Tour 1974

10 July to 24 August, Cape Town, East London, Pretoria, Johannesburg, Durban, and week commencing 2 September the Theatre Royal, Brighton.

'A Bit Between the Teeth' post-London Tour 1975

Week commencing

3 February	Lyceum, Edinburgh
10 February	Grand, Leeds
17 February	King's, Glasgow
24 February	Theatre Royal, Bury St Edmunds
3 March	Theatre Royal, March
10 March	King's, Southsea
17 March	Wimbledon Theatre
24 March	Ashcroft, Croydon
31 March	Richmond Theatre
7 April	Richmond Theatre
14 April	Civic, Darlington
21 April	Civic, Darlington
28 April	Theatre Royal, Bath
5 May	New, Oxford
12 May	Wyvern, Swindon
19 May	Theatre Royal, Nottingham

From 30 June to 20 September, Playhouse, Bournemouth.

Week commencing

22 September	Futurist, Scarborough
29 September	Princess, Torquay
6 October	Hippodrome, Bristol
13 October	Theatre Royal, Newcastle
20 October	Alhambra, Bradford
27 October	Theatre Royal, Norwich
3 November	Royal Court, Liverpool
10 November	New, Cardiff
17 November	Key, Peterborough
24 November	week out
1 December	Gordon Craig, Stevenage

'*Fringe Benefits*' pre-London Tour 1976

Week commencing

27 February	Forum, Billingham
1 March	Forum, Billingham
8 March	Theatre Royal, York
15 March	Theatre Royal, St Helens
22 March	Theatre Royal, Newcastle
29 March	Theatre Royal, Bury St Edmunds
5 April	Grand, Leeds
12 April	week out
19 April	King's, Southsea
26 April	Rex, Wilmslow
3 May	Grand, Wolverhampton
10 May	Tameside, Ashton-under-Lyme
17 May	New, Hull

A short break, and then . . .

14 June	Pavilion, Bournemouth
21 June	Ashcroft, Croydon

28 June to 21 August a short summer season at the Devonshire Park, Eastbourne, followed by the production moving to the Whitehall Theatre.

INDEX

INDEX

Figures in **bold** refer to
entries in *Curtain Calls*

Abbey Theatre, Dublin, 39,
 232
Ackland, Joss, 5
Actors' Company, 4, 238
Adelphi Theatre,
 Edinburgh, 74; Glasgow,
 30; London, 76, 172
Advance Players'
 Association Ltd, 99
Agate, James, 86
Aladdin, 199
Albert, Prince Consort, 96
Albery Theatre, London,
 217, 240
Aldwych Theatre, London,
 24, 65, 76, 145, 217, 220,
 224, 226
Alexander, Sir George, 33,
 36, **259**
Alexander, Terry, 223
Alexandra Theatre,
 Birmingham, 3, 128, 147,
 148–9, 219, 220; Stoke
 Newington, 125, 126,
 133; Widnes, 3
Alhambra Theatre,
 Bradford, 215–16, 218
Alleyn, Edward, **245**
Ambassador's Theatre,
 London, 4
Amphitheatre, Liverpool,
 30
Andrews, Eamonn, 232
Anew McMaster's
 Company, 232
Anne, HRH The Princess
 Royal, 90
Annie Get Your Gun, 199,
 200
Apollo Leisure Group, 84,
 90, 91, 94, 185, 190, 195,
 197, 199
Apollo Theatre, London,
 76, 134; Oxford, 197
Apollo Victoria Theatre,
 London, 197
Apple Cart, The (Shaw), 228
Appleby, 'Tommy', 89
Ardwick Hippodrome, 90
Arms and the Man (Shaw),
 119
Armstrong, Donald, 155
Armstrong, William, 39
Arnewood Estates Ltd, 182
Arnold, Tom, 172

Arthur, Robert, 104, 105,
 108
Arts Council of Great
 Britain, 42, 90, 91, 94,
 119, 120, 139, 150, 151,
 152, 155, 158, 185, 223,
 226, 237–41
Arts Council of Northern
 Ireland, 231
Arts Theatre of Cambridge,
 42, 66–7
Arts Theatre Trust, 238
As You Like It
 (Shakespeare), 20, 119,
 181, 241
Asche, Oscar, 34, **262**
Ashcroft, Dame Peggy, 43,
 114, 125, **267**
Ashcroft Theatre, Croydon,
 73, 114
Ashton, Sir Frederick, 67
Ashwell, Lena, 36–7
Askey, Arthur, 89, 129
Associated Theatre
 Properties (London) Ltd,
 75, 76
Atkins, Robert, CBE, 40,
 226, **264**
Attenborough, Michael,
 226
Attenborough, Sir Richard,
 124
Avenue Theatre,
 Sunderland, 208
Ayckbourn, Alan, 183–4,
 190

Babes in the Wood, 184,
 194, 202
Back to Methuselah (Shaw),
 228
Baker, George, 223
Baker, Josephine, 118
Bancroft, Marie (née Marie
 Effie Wilton), **255–6**
Bancroft, Sir Squire, 25,
 256
Bang, Bang, Beirut! (later
 Stand By Your Bedouin),
 173
Banks, Leslie, 89
Banks, Monty, 119
Bannerman, Kay, 173, 174
Barlow, H. J., 147–8, 165
Barnes, Ivor, 146
Barnes, Richmond-
 upon-Thames, 182
Barnum, 90
Barrett, Wilson, 29, 34, 36,
 96–7, 131, 145, 232,
 257

Barrie, Sir James Matthew,
 43
Barry, Elizabeth, 16–17,
 246
Bartholomew, Freddie, 56
Barton, W. H., 180
Bath Company of
 Comedians, 20
Bath Players (the 'Brandy
 Company'), 18
Bayliss' Coliseum, Glasgow,
 99
'Beat the Clock', 111
Beaumont, Edward, 96, 97
Beaumont, Hugh 'Binkie',
 42, 43, 76
Beaumont, John, 76, 96,
 97, 128
Beaux' Stratagem, The
 (Farquhar), 20
Becket (Anouilh), 216, 217
Beecham, Sir Thomas, 59,
 89, 100
Beecham Opera Company,
 89
Beeston, Christopher, **245**
Beggar's Opera, The (Gay),
 20
Bellamy, George Anne,
 248–9
Bells, The, 73, 144, 217
Ben Hur, 88
Benson, Sir Frank, 3, 4, 29,
 31–4, 36, 37, 107, 108,
 131, 145, 216, 225, 227,
 232, **260**
Berkeley Square, 157
Bernhardt, Sarah, 83, 145,
 205, 232, **257**
Betterton, Thomas, **246**
Billingham, 192–5
Bird, William, 32
Birmingham Rep, 147, 149,
 226, 228
Birmingham Royal Ballet,
 150
Birmingham Theatre, 150
Birth of a Nation, The
 (film), 205
Bit Between the Teeth, A
 (*You'll Do for Me*), 100,
 102, 134, 145, 157, 158,
 164, 172, 174, 182, 184,
 191, 194, 198, 211;
 Tours, 286–7
Black, Alfred, 112
Black, George, 111, 112
Black, George, Jnr, 39, 112
Blackpool Tower Company
 Ltd, 136, 137
Blithe Spirit (Coward), 89
Bloom, Leslie, 125–8, 137

Blythe, Michael, 62–3
Bogdanov, Michael, 4, 240
Booth, Barton, **247**
Booth, Edwin, 232
Booth, Junius Brutus, **252–3**
Bootham School, York,
  213, 214
Boucicault, Dion, 30, **254**
Bournemouth Dramatic and
  Orchestral Club (later
  Bournemouth Little
  Theatre Club), 157
Bournemouth International
  Centre, 204
Bracegirdle, Anne, 16, **246**
Bradford Alhambra
  Company, 215
Bradford City Council,
  215–16
Braithwaite, Dame Lillian,
  29, **262**
Branagh, Kenneth, 4, 237,
  240, 241, **270**
Brandon-Thomas, Jevan,
  39, 131
Bridge, Peter, 4, 183–4
Bridlington, 52, 124, 127
Brierley, David, 226
Briers, Richard, 240, 241
Brighton Marine Palace and
  Pier Co., 162
Brighton Repertory
  Company, 133
British National Opera
  Company, 89, 100
Broadhead Variety Circuit,
  92
Brooke, Gustavus, 26
Brooke, Harold, 173, 174
Brownlow, Bert, 225, 227
Brunton, John, **249**
Buckstone, John Baldwin,
  253
Bulldog Drummond, 40
Bullwinkle, Jean, OBE,
  120
Burbage, Richard, 15, **245**
Bury St Edmunds Amateur
  Operatic Society, 221
Bygraves, Max, 192
Byrne, Peter, 183

Caesar and Cleopatra
  (Shaw), 228
Calvert, Charles, **254**
Cambridge, 16, 76, 221
Cambridge Arts Theatre
  Trust, 67
Cambridge Theatre
  Company, 4, 238
Cameron, Basil, 59, 129

Campbell, Mrs Patrick (née
  Beatrice Tanner), **261–2**
Cannon and Ball, 184, 192
Canterbury Tales, The (The
  Miller's Tale) (Chaucer),
  9–10
Cardiff, 49, 50, 51, 206
Carl Rosa Opera Company,
  205
Casson, Sir Lewis, 29, 119,
  146, **263**
Catlin, Will, 190
Cato (Addison), 20
CEMA (Council for the
  Encouragement of Music
  and Arts), 42, 46, 48,
  115, 117, 119, 120, 241
Century Theatre 'Blue
  Box', near Keswick, 37
Chaplin, Sir Charles, 88, 92
Chapman, John, 65, 172,
  229
Charing Cross Theatre,
  London, 31–2
Charles, HRH The Prince
  of Wales, 90
Charles I, 144
Charles B. Cochran Ltd, 76
Charles Doran
  Shakespearean Company,
  44
Charley's Aunt (Thomas),
  31, 222, 223
Chase Me Comrade!, 134,
  173, 186, 196, 198, 205;
  Tours, 282, 283
Cheek by Jowl, 223
Chips With Everything
  (Wesker), 238
Chorus of Disapproval, A.
  206
Chu Chin Chow, 34, 112
Churchill, Donald, 174
Chute, James Henry, 153,
  199
Cibber, Colley, 20, 103, **247**
Cinderella, 215
City Theatre, Glasgow, 30;
  Sheffield, 217
Civic Theatre, Darlington,
  211–12, 214, 239
Clandestine Marriage, The
  (Garrick), 33, 239
Cleaver, John, 124
Clements, Sir John, CBE,
  268
Cleopatra (ballet), 88
Clunes, Alec, **268**
Cochran, Sir Charles B.,
  180, 241
Coghill, Professor Neville,
  10

Cole, George, 95
Coliseum, London, 83, 84
Collingwood, Lester, 148–9
Comedy Theatre, London,
  148
Community Care
  Campaigners, 136, 192
Compass Theatre, 4,
  239–40
Compton, Edward, **258–9**
Compton Comedy
  Company, 36
Congress Theatre,
  Eastbourne, 174, 184,
  194, 200, 201, 204
Connaught Theatre,
  Worthing, 134
Conville, David, OBE, 111,
  238–9
Cooke, George, 27
Cooney, Ray, 152, 171–4,
  183, 193, 229, **269**
Cooney-Marsh Theatres
  Ltd, 155, 184
Cooper, Dame Gladys,
  264
Cooper, Joan, 145–6
Cooper, Tommy, 192
Corbett, Ronnie, 52–3
Corn is Green, The
  (Williams), 89
Corsican Brothers, The
  (Boucicault), 30
Corson, George, 96
Cottrell, Richard, 4, 238
Court Interluders, The, 12
Court Players, 39, 40, 130
Courtneidge, Cicely, 146,
  265–6
Coutts, William, 147, 148
Coutts Theatre,
  Birmingham, 147
Covent Garden (Royal
  Opera House), London,
  108
Coventry Hippodrome
  Orchestra, 186
Coventry Hock Tuesday
  Show, 15
Cowan, Joseph, 107, 108
Coward, Sir Noël, 43, 66,
  70, 89, 118, 146, **265**
Cox, Brian, 238, 241
Cox, Constance, 57
Craig, Gordon, 194–5
Crawford, Michael, 90
Crewe, Bertie, 179
Cricket, Jimmy, 192
Cross, Cecil (Hugh), 99,
  100–1
Crowther, Leslie, 51, 174,
  188

Croydon Repertory
  Company, 133
Crucible Theatre, Sheffield,
  217, 218
Cruikshank, A. Stewart,
  75, 76, 102, 128
Cruikshank, Dorothy, 76,
  96
Cruikshank, Stewart, Jnr,
  75, 76
Cummings, Constance, 89
Curtains!!!, 231
Curzon Hall, Birmingham,
  147
Cusack, Cyril, 232

Dan Lowry's, Dublin, 231
Dance, Sir George, 153,
  181, 182, **259**
Dancing Years, The, 89
Daniel Mayer C. Ltd, 76
Darlington Amateur
  Operatic Society, 212
Darlington Civil Theatre
  Ltd, 212
David Copperfield (film), 56
Day, Kenney, 127, 128
Day, William, 107
Deacon, Charles, 200–1
Dean, Basil, 42, 117
Dear Brutus (Barrie), 43
Dear Departed, The
  (Houghton), 40
Dear Octopus (Smith), 43
Delderfield, R. F., 147
Delfont, Bernard (later
  Lord), 128, 131–2, 136,
  137
Denham, Reginald, 118
Denise (Dumas), 108
Denison, Michael, 111
Denville, Alfred, MP, JP,
  39, 64–5
Denville Hall, Northwood,
  Middx, 65
Denville Stock Companies,
  64
Dermody, Frank, 124
Desert Rats (Morris), 172
Design for Living (Coward),
  22, 43
Devonshire Park,
  Eastbourne, 173, 174,
  202, 203
Diplomatic Baggage, 137
Dish Ran Away, The, 165
Dixon, Jack, 110
Dock Theatre, Devonport,
  24–5
Dock Theatre, Plymouth,
  139

Doggett, Thomas, **247**
Dolphin Theatre, Brighton,
  125–6, 133, 134, 162
Donald family, 76, 104, 105
Donald Wolfit's Company,
  86, 111; Tour, 273
Donat, Robert, 131
*Don't Just Lie There, Say
  Something!*, 134, 145,
  159, 174, 238; Tours, 285
Doonican, Val, 192, 199
Dorrill, John, 196–7
Double Act (Denison
  autobiography), 111
Double Dealer (Congreve),
  20
D'Oyly Carte Opera
  Company, 205
Dresser, The (Harwood), 5
Drummond, David, 230
Dry Rot, 30, 47, 156, 168,
  172, 175, 179, 183, 184,
  185, 196, 198, 217, 230,
  238; Tours, 279–80
du Maurier, Gerald, 33
Duke of Norfolk's Men, 14
Dumas, Alexandre, 108
Duncan, Isadora, 195
Duncan C. Weldon
  Productions Ltd, 185
Dunlop Street Theatre,
  Glasgow, 30

E&B Productions, 183
Edinburgh Festival, 237
Edward II, 237
Edwardes, George, 88, 96,
  205
Edwards, Hilton, 232
Elgar, Sir Edward, 59
Elliott, Paul, 183, 184, 212
Elliston, Robert, 29
Elphinstone, Mr (at
  Hanley), 200
Embassy Theatre,
  Peterborough, 151
Empire Palace, Dublin,
  231; Sunderland, 208
Empire Theatre,
  Birmingham, 80, 147;
  Bradford, 215, 216;
  Cardiff, 206; Chiswick,
  180; Edinburgh, 80;
  Hackney, 180; Hull, 80;
  Leeds, 80; Leicester, 83;
  Leicester Square,
  London, 83; Liverpool,
  80, 94; Newcastle, 80;
  Newport, 83;
  Nottingham, 83, 112;
  Sheffield, 80;

Sunderland, 208–9;
  Swansea, 83; Wood
  Green, 180
English National Opera, 84,
  199
English Shakespeare
  Company, 4, 240
ENSA (Entertainments
  National Service
  Association), 42, 44, 54,
  115, 117–20, 123, 125
Equity, 25, 98
Equity Contract for Tours
  and Season, 11
Esmond, Henry V., 31,
  262
Evans, Dame Edith, 3, 43,
  89, 228, **264**
Everyman Theatre,
  Liverpool, 94

Fairburn, Sir Andrew, 96
Fairfield Halls, Croydon,
  73, 114
Farce About Face (Rix),
  155, 193, 227
Farren, Elizabeth, **250**
Fawlty Towers (TV series),
  171
Festival Ballet, 196
Festival Hall, Paignton, 192
Festival Theatre,
  Cambridge, 39; Malvern,
  227–8
Ffrangcon-Davies, Dame
  Gwen, 43
Fielding, Harold, 90
Fields, Dame Gracie, 119,
  131
Filer, Roger, 84
First Interval (Wolfit
  autobiography), 33,
  102–3, 114–15, 117–18
First Leisure PLC, 136,
  137
Five Finger Exercise
  (Shaffer), 119
Flower, Charles Edward,
  225
Fly Away Peter, 129
Fol-de-Rols, 129
Fonteyn, Dame Margot, 67
Foot, Alastair, 173
Forbes-Robertson, Sir
  Johnston, 3, 29, 32, 34,
  104, 205, **258**
Formby, George, 119
Forsyth, Bruce, 112
Forum, Billingham, 193–4
Frankfort Gate Theatre,
  Plymouth, 139

Franklyn, Leo, 172, 183
Friends of Normansfield, 209
Fringe Benefits (Churchill and Yeldham), 92, 142, 145, 152, 174, 184, 193, 202, 219, 223–4; Tour, 288
Frohman, Charles, 205
Fry, Jeremy, 155–6
Fumed Oak (Coward), 118
Futurist Theatre, Scarborough, 190–1

Gaiety Theatre, Bootle, 53; Dublin, 232–3; Edinburgh (known as Moss's then Moss), 79; Hastings, 129; Manchester, 39
Galloping Major, The, 129
Garibaldi, Giuseppe, 107–8, 110
Garrick, David, 16, 26, 29, 149, 239, **248**
Garrick Theatre, London, 5, 32, 93, 134, 142, 145, 171, 173, 174, 219
Garrick Theatre, Southport, 182, 185, 188
Gate company, 232
Germaine, Mabel, 124
G. H. Lucking & Sons, 55, 191
Gielgud, Sir John, CH, 43, 59, 89, 118, **267**
Giffard, Henry, **247**
Gilbert, Walter, 105
Gillam, Melville, 134
Gingold, Hermione, 4, 44, 175
Gladwin, Jack, 163
Glimpses of Real Life (Paterson), 26
Globe Theatre, London, 217
Gloucester, Duke of (players of), 11
Goddard, Brian, 212
Gondolier Dancing Academy, 105
Goodbye Mr Chips (Hilton), 89
Good Night Vienna, 186–7
Gordon Craig Theatre, Stevenage, 194–5
Grand Opera House, Belfast, 231, 239; Harrogate, 39
Grand Theatre, Blackpool, 137; Doncaster, 187;

Halifax, 182; Plymouth, 140; Swansea, 159–61; Wolverhampton, 128, 219, 220
Grand Theatre and Opera House, Croydon, 73, 114; Leeds, 34, 53, 76, 95–8, 128, 164, 239
Grant, Cary, 198
Granville-Barker, Harvey, **263**
Grass is Greener, The, 198
Gray, Elspet (Lady Rix), 51, 52, 124, 156, 175
Gray, Roderick, 80
Gray, Terence, 39
Greater London Players, 133
Greene King, 221, 223
Greenwich Theatre, London, 64
Greet, Sir Ben, 29, 32, 181, **259**
Gregg, Paul, 197
Greyhound Theatre, Croydon, 133
Grime, Sir Harold, 136
Guinness, Sir Alec, CBE, 89, **268–9**
Gulbenkian Foundation, Lisbon, 239; Oporto, 239
Guthrie, Sir Tyrone, 44, 46, **266**
Gwynn, Nell, 16, 17, 26, **246**

Hackett, Walter, 157
Hackney Empire Preservation Trust, 180
Haddon, Peter, 131
Hall, Henry, 89
Hall, Sir Peter, 184, 226
Hallam, Lewis, **248**
Hallett, John, 239
Hamlet (Shakespeare), 20, 32, 54, 73, 88, 134, 205, 241
Hands, Terry, 226
Hanson, Harry, 39–40, 129
Harbord, Gordon, 125
Harding, James, 134
Hardwicke, Sir Cedric, 36, 37, 228, **265**
Hardy, Mr (architect), 157
Hare, Sir John, **256–7**
Harris, Sir Augustus, 108
Harrison, Gilbert, 209
Harrison, Sir Rex, 146
Hart, John, 97
Hartley, Basil, 53

Harvey, Sir John Martin, 183
Harwood, Ronald, 5
Hastings Municipal Orchestra, 129
Hawtrey, Sir Charles, 34, **260**
Haymarket Theatre, Leicester, 169, 184; London, 158
Heartbreak House (Shaw), 228
Hellman, Lillian, 24
Helpmann, Sir Robert, 67
Henderson, Dickie, 177, 189
Henderson, John, **250**
Henig, Councillor (now Sir) Mark, 168
Henry IV (pts I and II) (Shakespeare), 20, 240
Henry V (Shakespeare), 240, 241
Henry VI (Shakespeare), 240
Henry Pease & Co., Darlington, 211, 214
Her Majesty's Theatre, Aberdeen (later His Majesty's Theatre and Tivoli Theatre), 104
Her Majesty's Theatre, London, 108
Heston, Charlton, 108
Hicks, Sir Seymour, **262**
Hill, Rowland, 215
Hilton, Tony, 172, 173
Hippodrome, Aldershot, 182; Birmingham, 147, 149–50, 239; Bristol, 30, 83, 197, 198–9; Coventry, 182, 186–7; Derby, 187; Golders Green, London, 43, 179, 198; Ipswich, 182; London, 30, 83
His Majesty's Theatre, Aberdeen, 76, 104–5; London, 76
His Majesty's Theatre Company, 205
Hitchcock, Alfred, 65
H. M. Tennent Ltd, 22, 42, 43, 76
Hobson, Sir Harold, 202
Home and Beauty (Maugham), 89
Hordern, Sir Michael, CBE, **268**
Horne, Kenneth, 65
Hornsea Parish Hall (Floral Hall), 19, 56

Howard, J. B., 73, 74, 84
Howard and Wyndham
 Ltd, 3, 40, 57, 73–6, 78,
 79, 93, 96, 89, 93, 96, 97,
 99, 102, 104, 105, 108,
 125, 128, 168, 195, 197
Howard and Wyndham
 Tours Ltd, 75
Howe, George, 43
Howes, Bobby, 118
Hudd, Roy, 180
Huddersfield Rep, 39
Hulbert, Jack, 239, **265–6**
Hull, 10, 29, 57, 68–71,
 164
Hull Repertory Company,
 39, 70

*I Must Be In There
 Somewhere* (Ackland
 autobiography), 4
Iden, Rosalind (later Lady
 Wolfit), 48, 115
Illsley-McCabe Company,
 232
Imperial Theatre,
 Birmingham, 147
*Importance of Being Ernest,
 The* (Wilde), 43
Iron Chest, The, 21
Irving, H. B., 144, 181
Irving, Sir Henry, 3, 25,
 29–33, 57, 93, 97, 102,
 104, 134, 140, 144, 181,
 216, 217, 218, 232, **255–6**
Isabella, 144

Jack and the Beanstalk, 40
Jackson, Sir Barry, 39, 226,
 227, 228
Jackson, Gordon, 133
James, Jimmy, 89
Jason, David, 189
Jeans, Isabel, 89
Jerrold, Samuel, 23
Jewell, Jimmy, 89
Jones, John, 201
Jordan, Dorothy, 26, 153,
 250–1

Kanter, Ben, 131
Kaye, Danny, 89
Kean, Edmund, 11, 21–2,
 23, 134, 153, **251–2**
Kemble, Charles, 134
Kemble, Fanny, 130
Kemble, Roger, 27, **248**
Kemble family, 26, 106
Kempe, William, **245**

Kendal, Dame Madge, 27,
 57, 134
Kendal, William, 57, **256**
Kendall, Henry ('Harry'),
 4, 172, 173, 220
Kent Opera Company, 155
Kerr, Bill, 172
Key Theatre,
 Peterborough, 151–2
Keynes, John Maynard
 (Lord), 42, 66, 67, 117
King, Philip, 68
King, Tom, **249**
King Arthur's Round
 Table, Cumbria, 9
King Lear (Shakespeare), 5,
 44, 46, 48, 49, 58, 68, 86,
 102–3, 112, 114, 115,
 186, 226, 241
King's Men, 15
King's Rhapsody, 53
King's Theatre, Edinburgh,
 75, 102; Glasgow, 75,
 100; Hammersmith,
 London, 4, 131;
 Southsea, 144–6
Kinnear, Roy, 239
Kismet, 88
Knepp, Mary, **246**
Kossof, David, 172, 183

La Rue, Danny, 199
Laidler, Francis, 215
Laidler, Gwladys, 215
Land, David, 135
Landau, Walter, 162
Landport Hall,
 Portsmouth, 145
Lang, Matheson, 131, 216,
 263
Langtry, Lillie, 134, 232,
 257–8
Larkins, The (TV series),
 172
Lauder, Sir Harry, 88, 232
Laughter from the Whitehall,
 112
Laurel, Stan, 92
Laye, Evelyn, 146
Lee, Bernard, 133
Leicester Theatre Trust,
 168
Leigh, Vivien, 89
Leighton, Margaret, 89
Leno, Dan, 36, 80, 88, 140
Let Sleeping Wives Lie, 93,
 134, 142, 173, 288; Tour,
 284
Levene's Hall, Cardiff, 83
Levi Eshkol Memorial
 Forest, Israel, 98

Lewis, Peter, 238
Life of Napoleon (Sessions),
 240
Lillie, Beatrice, 118
Linnit and Dunfee Ltd, 76,
 125
Liston, John, **251**
Little Theatre, Bath, 153;
 Bournemouth, 157–8;
 Bristol, 157; Epsom, 133;
 Hull, 70, 71
Littler, Sir Emile, 200
Littler, Prince, 57, 75, 83,
 147, 168, 206
Livermore, Sir Harry, 93
Lloyd, Marie, 88, 140
Lloyd-Webber, Sir
 Andrew, 32, 135
Logan, Jimmy, 100
London Lyceum Company,
 73
London Museum Concert
 Hall, Birmingham, 147
London Palladium, 84, 112
London Theatre of
 Varieties Ltd, 181
Long March, The, 172;
 Tour, 275
Longford Players, 232
Look Back in Anger
 (Osborne), 119
Lord, Basil, 147, 172
Lord's Taverners, 52, 209
Lorne, Marion, 157
Loss, Joe, 89
Louis XI, 217
Love's Last Shift (Cibber),
 20
Loy, Myrna, 49
Luff, Robert, 190
Lyas, Michael, 132
Lyceum Theatre,
 Birmingham, 147, 148;
 Edinburgh see Royal
 Lyceum Theatre,
 Edinburgh; London, 31,
 97; Newport, 182;
 Sheffield, 76, 97, 128,
 217–18; Sunderland, 31
Lyceum Theatre Trust, 217
Lynn, Dame Vera, 119
Lyons Mail, The, 144
Lyric Theatre,
 Hammersmith, London,
 240; Shaftesbury Avenue,
 London, 47, 76, 156, 175

Ma Rainey's Black Bottom,
 180
McBean, Angus Rowland,
 95

Macbeth (Shakespeare), 107, 185, 221
McGill, Donald (originally Fraser Gould), 92
McIntosh, Genista, 226
McKellen, Sir Ian, 4, 237, 238, **270**
McKinstry, Robert, 231
Mackintosh, Cameron, 184
Mackintosh, Iain, 238
Macklin, Charles, **247**
MacLiammóir, Anew, 232
Macready, William Charles, 21, 26, 106–7, 153, 221–2, **252**
Maddermarket Theatre, Norwich, 49
Maddox, Frank, 154–5
Magic Cupboard, The, 127
Malvern Drama Festival, 228
Man For All Seasons, A (Bolt), 108
Manchester Apollo, 90, 92
Manchester Theatres Ltd, 90, 91
Manners, Marjorie, 162
Marlowe Theatre, Canterbury, 182
Marriott, Anthony, 173
Marsh, Laurie, 155, 156
Martin-Harvey, Sir John, 3, 34, 36, 104, 216, **260**
Maschwitz, Eric, 187
Matcham, Frank, 30, 62, 83, 94, 100, 104, 108, 112, 137, 144, 145, 180, 181, 183, 187, 198, 202, 217, 231, 233
Matthews, Charles, **251**
Matthews, Jessie, 119
Maude, Cyril, **260–1**
Maugham, W. Somerset, 89
Maurice Elliman Group, 232
Maynard, Bill, 172
Me and My Girl (Gay), 71
Mears, Joseph, 182
Melnotte, Violet, **259**
MENCAP, 47, 57, 95, 155, 184, 192, 230
Merchant of Venice, The (Shakespeare), 73, 216, 217
Merrick, Simon, 188
Merrie England, 190
Merry Wives of Windsor, The, 157
Metropole, Birmingham, 147; Camberwell Green, London, 131; Glasgow, 100

Meyer, Bertie A., 76
Michaels, Louis, 134, 158, 174, 182, 184
Middle Temple, London, 239
Midsummer Night's Dream, A (Shakespeare), 48, 62, 68, 69, 118, 153, 241
Miles, Sir Bernard, CBE (Lord), 113, **267**
Miller, Max, 89, 119
Minskoff, Jerome, 185
Mr Charles Adam's Grand Circus, Scarborough, 190
Mrs Fanny Rix and Her Bright Young Things, 29
Moffat, John, 223
Mohun, Michael, **246**
Monck, Nugent, 48, 49
Monkhouse, Bob, 189
Monster Saloon Music Hall, Dublin, 231
Moore, Eva, 31
More, Kenneth, 220
Morley, Robert, CBE, **267**
Morrell, Ralph, 141
Morris, Colin, 124, 162, 172
Moss, Edinburgh *see* Gaiety Theatre, Edinburgh
Moss, Sir Edward, 79, 80, 83, 84, 94, 111, 208
Moss Empires Ltd, 3, 83–4, 75, 83, 89, 111, 112, 147, 150, 208, 215
Mossop, Henry, **249**
Mount, Peggy, 172, 220
Mousetrap, The (Christie), 129
Move Over Mrs Markham (Cooney and Chapman), 229
Much Ado About Nothing (Shakespeare), 73, 102, 226, 241
Murdoch, Richard, 129
Musgrove, John, 227
Music Hall Artistes' Railway Assocation, 36
My Fair Lady, 168
My Farce from my Elbow (Rix), 47, 99, 100–1, 159
My Girl, 168
My Love Affair With a Theatre (Salberg), 148

NAAFI (Navy, Army and Air Force Institute), 117
Nap Hand, 174
Nares, Owen, 33, **264–5**
National Theatre, 113, 154, 182, 184

Neilson, Julia, 131
Neville, John, 92
New Arcadia, Scarborough, 190
New Coliseum Theatre, Harrow, 64–5
New Grand Theatre, Birmingham, 147; Margate, 33
New Hippodrome and Palace Theatre of Varieties, Darlington, 212
New Palace of Varieties, Plymouth, 140
New Prince of Wales Theatre, Liverpool, 94
New Queens Theatre, Manchester, 89
New Shakespeare Company, 239
New Theatre, Bury St Edmunds, 221, 222; Cardiff, 57, 172, 174, 205–7, 209; Hull, 68–71, 128, 142–3, 200, 239; Manchester, 88–9; Northampton, 187; Oxford, 196–7, 239
New Theatre Royal, Portsmouth, 145
New Theatre Society, 206
Newcastle Arts Centre, 110
Night Train to Munich (Hitchcock), 65
Night We Got the Bird, The (film), 65
No, No, Nanette, 183
Noble, Adrian, 226
Noble, Larry, 124, 140
Northampton Company, 40
Northern Stage Company, 110
Norwest Holst, 89, 90
Not in the Book (Watkyn), 239
Nothing Barred (Chapman), 65
Novello, Ivor, 53, 89, **265**
Nunn, Trevor, 226
Nye Chart, Ellen Elizabeth, 134
Nye Chart, Henry, 134

Odeon group of cinemas, 164, 231
Oklahoma!, 168
Old Vic company, 46, 119, 237

Old Vic Theatre, London, 44, 46, 104, 240
Oldfield, Anne, **247**
Olivier, Sir Laurence, OM (later Lord), 4, 44, 119, **267**
Olympia Theatre, Dublin, 231–2; London, 108
On Approval, 43
On the Art of the Theatre (Craig), 195
One For the Pot, 134, 172, 173, 202, 217, 220; Tours, 281, 282
Open Air Theatre, Scarborough, 190, 191
Open House, Cork, 231
Opera House, Harrogate, 118; Manchester, 86, 88, 89, 90, 164, 197; Sunderland, 208
Opera North, 97
Osborne, John, 119
O'Shea, Tessie, 89
Othello (Shakespeare), 21, 24, 25, 120, 221
Oxford Playhouse, 39, 238
Oxford Theatre, 157

Page, Tilsa, 63
Palace Court Theatre, Bournemouth, 157, 158
Palace Pier Theatre, Brighton, 162
Palace Players, The, 162
Palace Theatre, Bradford, 216; Carlisle, 212; Manchester, 88, 89–90, 197; Plymouth, 139, 140, 141, 187; Ramsgate, 182; Westcliff-on-Sea, 229
Palace Theatre Trust, 89, 90
Palmer, John, 153
Parfitt, David, 240, 241
Paris Cinema, Brighton, 133
Parkin's Entertainments Ltd, 166
Parnell, Val, 111, 147
Parnell, William, 107
Parthenon Music Hall, 82
Passing of the Third-Floor Black, The, 34
Patch, Wally, 65, 124–9, 133, 137–8, 162, 165, 167, 172, 227
Pavilion Theatre, Bournemouth, 204; Rhyl, 119; Torquay, 58–9, 125, 126, 129, 137

Pavlova, Anna, 205
Payne, B. Iden, 226
Peer Gynt (Ibsen), 119
Penley, W. S., 31, 222
Pennington, Michael, 240, **270**
Pepi, Rino, 212
Percy, Edward, 118
Perkins, Richard, **246**
Pertwee, Michael, 102, 145, 157, 159, 166, 172, 174, 227
Pertwee, Roland, 172, 227
Peter Hall Company, 184
Peterborough Arts Theatre Trust, 151
Petherbridge, Edward, 4, 238, **269–70**
Phelps, C. J., 60, 62, 73, 99, 107, 112, 145, 153, 154, 155, 168, 187, 219, 232–3
Phipps, Jack, 237, 239
Phoenix Theatre, Leicester, 168; London, 76
Piccadilly Hayride, 112
Pigott-Smith, Tim, 4, 239, 240, **270**
Pilkington Theatre, St Helens, Merseyside, 183
Pinero, Sir Arthur Wing, **259**
Play Parade (Coward), 89
Playbill (Crane), 22
Playfair, Sir Nigel, 29, **262–3**
Playhouse Theatre, Bournemouth, 157, 158, 174, 204; Cardiff, 57; Edinburgh, 197; Liverpool, 39, 94; Nottingham, 168; Weston-super-Mare, 173, 188–9
Pleasure Gardens Theatre, Folkestone, 182
'Plinge, Walter', **268**
Pope, Jonathan, 226
Portsmouth Orpheus Society, 144
Portsmouth Theatres Ltd, 145
Powell, Sandy, 50, 162
Power, Tyrone, 26, **252**
Present Laughter (Coward), 89
Prince Littler Consolidated Trust Co. Ltd, 76
Prince of Wales Theatre, Birmingham, 147, 149; Cardiff, 48, 53, 56, 57, 151, 205, 206; Richmond, Surrey, 181

Prince's Theatre, Bradford, 182, 215, 216; Portsmouth, 147
Princess Theatre, Torquay, 192
Princess's Theatre, London, 97
Private Secretary, The, 31
Prospect Productions, 237–8
Public Enemy (Branagh), 240
Punt, Norman, 227

Quayle, Sir Anthony, CBE, 4, 226, 239, **268**
Queen Street Theatre, Glasgow, 30
Queen's Room, Greenock, 79
Queen's Theatre, Dublin, 31
Quiet Week-End, 19
Quin, James, **247**

Radford, Basil, 18, 20, 65, 129, 133, 137, 140–1, 142
Radford, George, 124, 129
Ramsden, Dennis, 19
Rank-Strand Electric & Engineering Co. Ltd, 232
Ray, Ted, 89
Ray Cooney Productions Ltd, 184
Raymond's New Palace, Westcliff-upon-Sea, 229
Raynor, William E., 124
Rebecca (Du Maurier), 40, 43
Recruiting Officer, The (Farquhar), 238
Redfarn, Roger, 141
Redford, Robert, 205, 206
Redgrave, Sir Michael, CBE, 29, **267**
Redgrave, Vanessa, 146
Redman, Joyce, 239
Regent's Park, London, 226, 239
Reluctant Debutante, The (Douglas-Home), 239
Reluctant Heroes, 18, 40, 51, 59, 65, 112, 124–6, 129, 130, 131, 134, 136, 137, 140, 142, 143, 147, 154, 162, 165, 172, 179, 209, 217, 225, 227, 229, 230, 231, 237; Tours, 274, 276–8

Renaissance Theatre
Company, 4, 237, 240–1
Renton Howard Wood
Levin Partnership, 112,
218
Rice, Tim, 135
Richard II (Shakespeare),
237
Richard III (Shakespeare),
119, 153, 240
Richards, Judi, 206
Richardson, Sir Ralph, 44,
89, 119, **266–7**
Richmond Theatre, Surrey,
158, 181–2; Yorks, 18
Rippon, Geoffrey, 137
Riverside Studios, Lond,
240
Rix, Herbert (BR's father),
68, 70, 71, 124, 126
Rix, Sir Brian, CBE (Lord),
269
Rix, Elspet *see* Gray, Elspet
Rix, Fanny (BR's mother),
29, 68, 70, 100–1, 106,
115
Rix, Sheila (BR's sister),
95, 115
Rix Theatrical Productions,
124
Rob Roy (Scott), 221
Robert Arthur Theatre
Company, 105
Robert Arthur Theatres
Ltd, 108
Robertson, Mr and Mrs (of
Lincoln Circuit), 27
Robey, Sir George, 80, 88,
104, 140
Robinson, Fred, 172–3,
220
Robinson Crusoe, 174, 205,
209
Rogers, Anne, 63
*Romance of David Garrick,
The*, 57, 115
Romany Rye, The (Sims),
60
Rosehill Theatre,
Cumberland, 239
Rossiter, Leonard, 220
Royal Court Theatre,
Liverpool, 93–4, 156
Royal General Theatrical
Fund, 32
Royal Hippodrome,
Richmond, Surrey, 181
Royal Lyceum Theatre,
Edinburgh, 39, 73, 74,
83, 102
Royal Lyceum Theatre
Company, 102

Royal National Theatre
(RNT), 180, 226, 238,
240, 241
Royal Opera House,
Leicester, 167, 168;
Scarborough, 190
Royal Shakespeare
Company (RSC), 15, 110,
225, 226, 238, 240
Royal Shakespeare Theatre,
Stratford-upon-Avon,
225
Royal Society for Mentally
Handicapped Children
and Adults *see* MENCAP
Royalty Theatre, Glasgow,
74; London, 222
Rutley, Henry, 145
Ryan, Lacy, **247**

Sachs, Andrew, 171, 183
Sadler's Wells Ballet (later
Royal Ballet), 67, 150,
199, 200
Sadler's Wells Theatre,
London, 33
St James's Theatre,
London, 76, 86, 114–15,
117
Salberg, Derek, 148, 149,
219, 220
Sands o' Dee, 198
Santangelo, Peppino, 70,
71, 128, 143
Saunders, Sir Peter, 128–9
Scala Theatre, London, 86
Scarborough, 22, 50,
190–1, 195, 197
Scofield, Paul, CBE, 226,
269
Scott, Allan, 124
Scott, Robert, 90, 91
Scottish Opera, 100
Seagulls Over Sorrento, 112,
134, 147
Service, Robert, 68
Sessions, John, 240
Shaffer, Peter, 119
Shakespeare, William, 4,
14, 15, 17, 20, 32, 33, 34,
40, 46, 59, 92, 102, 117,
118, 119, 153, 225, 226,
240, 241, **245**
Shakespeare Memorial
Theatre,
Stratford-upon-Avon,
225–6, 227, 239
Sharpe, Richard, 17, **246**
Shaw, George Bernard,
205, 225, 228, 232
Shaw, Glen Byam, 226

*She Was Only An Admiral's
Daughter* (Brooke and
Bannerman), 174; Tour,
286
She's Done It Again, 93, 98,
142, 174, 188, 189, 203,
204, 209, 219; Tour, **284**
Sherek, Henry, 172
Shiner, Ronnie, 11, 133,
147, 222
Shuter, Ned, **249**
Siddons, Sarah, 21, 134,
139, 153, **250**
Sign of the Cross, The, 34
Simple Spymen, 57, 142,
172, 200; Tour, 281–2
Sinden, Donald, CBE, **269**
Six of Rix, 145, 164, 174;
Tour, 285
Slater, Betty, 171
Slater, John, 137, 171–2,
173, 183, 185, 217, 229,
238
Slater, Raymond, 90
Sleeping Partnership
(Horne), 65
Smith, William, **249**
Smoothey, Don, 162
Snow White on Ice, 192
Somerville, J. Baxter, 133,
134
South-Western Theatrical
Productions Ltd, 131
Spa Theatre, Bridlington,
40; Scarborough, 190
Sprague, W. G. R., 180,
217, 218
Squire, Ronald, 89
Stand By Your Bedouin,
142, 148, 173, 189, 219;
Tours, 283
Star of Erin Music Hall,
Cork, 231
Stepham, Renée, 128–9,
133, 137, 138, 152, 179,
184, 188, 203, 204, 229,
230, 231
Stephen Joseph Theatre,
Scarborough, 190
Stern, Ernst, 115, 117, 118
Stock, Nigel, 133
Stoll, Sir Oswald, 79, 80,
83, 84, 94, 111, 198, 208
Stoll Moss, 3, 57, 76, 83,
195, 198–9
Stoll Moss Theatres Ltd,
84
Stoll Theatres Corporation
Ltd, 73–5, 108, 206
Stone, Edward, 147, 157
Strand Theatre, London,
158, 184, 217

Streatham Hill Theatre, London, 179–80
Stross, David, 95
Student Prince, The, 186
Sullivan, Barry, 103
Suspect (Percy and Denham), 54, 118, 123
Swan Theatre, Stratford, London, 15, 226
Sweet Lavender, 40
Sweetest and Lowest, 4
Sweeting, Elizabeth, 238
Sylvaine, Vernon, 65, 145, 166, 174, 237

Take It From Here (stage adaptation of radio series), 112
Tamburlaine the Great, 44
Tameside Theatre, Ashton-under-Lyne, 91, 92
Tearle, Sir Godfrey, 33, 34, 36
Tearle, Osmond, **257**
Tell the Marines, 172, 227; Tour, **275**
Temperance Hall, Birmingham, 147
Tempest, Dame Marie, **261**
Tennent, H. M., 75–6
Terriss, Ellaline, 131
Terriss, William, **257**
Terry, Dame Ellen, 3, 73, 104, 145, 194, 225, 232
Terry, Fred, 131, 145
Terry family, **253–4**
Theatre and Opera House (Leeds) Ltd Company, 96
Theatre Royal, Barnsley, 3; Bath, 3, 153–6, 175; Birmingham, 147, 148, 149; Bradford, 97, 216; Brighton, 125, 133, 134–5, 154, 158, 173; Bristol, 199; Bury St Edmunds, 221–3; Cardiff, 57, 205, 206; Darlington, 211–12; Drury Lane, London, 33, 75, 84, 108, 117, 138, 221, 222; Edinburgh, 74, 75; Exeter, 60–2; Glasgow, 30, 31, 39, 74, 99–100; Hanley, 200–1; Hastings, 130; Haymarket London, 134; Hull, 22, 96–7; Ipswich, 30; Leeds, 40, 215; Liverpool, 30, 31;

Manchester, 31; Newcastle-upon-Tyne, 31, 106–9, 241; Norwich, 151, 163–4, 221, 239; Nottingham, 111–12, 156; Oxford, 31; Plymouth, 139–41; St Helens, 183; Scarborough, 190: Sunderland, 80, 208; Windsor, 64; Wolverhampton, 219; York, 213, 214
Theatre Royal Brighton Company, 133
Theatre Royal Norwich Trust, 164
Theatre Royal Restoration Trust, 200
Theatres Advisory Council, 137, 158
Theatres Trust, 158, 187
Theatrical Digs (Lord's Taverners), 52
There Goes the Bride, 229
Thespis, 8, 37
Third Finger Left Hand (film), 49
This Happy Breed (Coward), 89
This Is Your Life (TV series), 69
Thomas, Brandon, 222, 223
Thomas, Julius, 149
Thompson, Jimmy, 114
Thorndike, Dame Sybil, CH, 3, 89, 119, 146, **263–4**
Thorne, Ada, 96
Thorne, Sarah, **255**
Thornton, Mr (of Reading circuit), 144–5
Thornton, Richard, 80, 83, 208
Tilley, Vesta, 80, 88, 105, 208
Timon of Athens (Shakespeare), 44
Tivoli Theatre, Aberdeen, 104, 105; Barrow, 212
Tivoli Theatre of Varieties, Birmingham, 149
Tod, Peter, 212
Todd, Richard, 184
Toms, Carl, 155
Toole, John Laurence, 31–2, 33, **254**
Tower of Varieties and Circus, Birmingham, 149, 150
Travers, Ben, 65, 220
Treasure Island (Stevenson), 113

Tree, Sir Herbert Beerbohm, 29, 31, 36, 145, 205, 225, 232, **258**
Trewin, J. C., 141, 155
Trilby (Du Maurier), 36
Trinder, Tommy, 89, 112, 119
Triumph Theatre Productions Ltd, 4, 134, 158, 183, 184, 202, 212, 239
Tutin, Dorothy, 146, 185
Twelfth Night (Shakespeare), 20, 48, 58, 88, 115, 117, 118, 205, 240
Tynan, Kenneth, 4, 14, 44, 92, 120, 191
Tyne Theatre and Opera Company Ltd, 110
Tyne Theatre and Opera House, Newcastle-upon-Tyne, 74, 107–8, 110
Tyne Wear Theatre Company, 110

Uproar in the House (Marriott and Foot), 173
Ustinov, Sir Peter, 89

Val Parnell's Sunday Night at the London Palladium, 111
Vanbrugh, Dame Irene, 3, 145
Vanbrugh, Miss Violet, 145, **262**
Vaughan, Peter, 220
Victoria Palace Theatre, London, 172
Victoria Pavilion, Ilfracombe, 166–7
Victoria Theatre, Burnley, 46
Vincent, Air Vice-Marshal Stanley, 221

Wake Up and Dream! (Cochran), 180
Wall, Max, 89
Waller, Lewis, 33, **260**
Walsh, Dermot, 124, 125, 140, 164
Wandering Jew, The, 4
Ward, Dame Genevieve (Lucy), **256**
Wareing, Alfred, 39

Warner, Jack, 89
Warner, James, 129
Warriss, Ben, 89
Wars of the Roses, The, 240
Washbourne, Mona, 129–30
Watch on the Rhine, The (Hellman), 24, 223–4
Watkyn, Arthur, 239
Watling, Dilys, 174
Watson, Moray, 159
Way to Treat a Woman, The (Hackett), 157
Wayne, Naunton, 65
Webster, Benjamin, **253**
Welch, Andrew, 141
Weldon, Duncan C., 4, 134, 152, 158, 174, 182–5, 193, 194, 195, 211, 212
Welsh National Opera, 199, 206
Wentworth, Robin, 225, 227
Wessex Christian Centre, 158
West, Timothy, 237
West Side Story (Bernstein), 190
West Yorkshire Playhouse, 233
Westminster Theatre, 133
When We Are Married (Priestley), 184
White Horse Inn, 212
White Rock Pavilion, Hastings, 124–30

White Rose Players, 14, 39, 118
Whitehall Theatre, London, 5, 11, 19, 30–1, 32, 40, 71, 92, 112, 129, 134, 137, 138, 142, 145, 147, 148, 152, 157, 162, 165, 168, 171, 172, 173, 179, 183, 186, 189, 196, 200, 202, 238
Why Not Stay for Breakfast?, 229
Wigram, Lord, 43
Wilkins, William, 221
Wilkinson, Tate, **249**
Wilks, Robert, **246**
Will Any Gentleman? (Sylvaine), 237
Williams, Emlyn, 89
Williams, Harcourt, **263**
Williams, Martin, 206
Williams, Ronnie, 160
Wilson Barrett and Jevan Brandon-Thomas Company, 131
Wimbledon Theatre, 125, 126, 131–2, 181
Windmill Theatre, London, 47
Winter Gardens Theatre, Morecambe, 187
Winter Gardens Pavilion, Blackpool, 125, 126, 136
Without the Prince (King), 68
Woffington, Peg, **247–8**

Wolfit, Sir Donald, CBE, 4, 5, 14, 29, 40, 44, 46–9, 53, 54, 57, 58, 59, 64, 66, 68, 69, 73, 78, 86, 88, 89, 92, 95, 102–3, 104, 113, 114–15, 117–18, 120, 124, 137, 186, 226, 237, 241, **266**; Tour, 273
Wolfit, Lady *see* Iden, Rosalind
Worm's Eye View, 11, 130, 147
W. S. Cruikshank & Son, 75
Wyndham, Sir Charles, 3, 29, **255**
Wyndham, F. W. P., 73, 74, 75, 84
Wyndham's Theatre, London, 137, 217
Wynyard, Diana, 24
Wyvern Theatre, Swindon, 195

Yeldham, Peter, 174
York, 10, 12–13, 18, 21, 213, 214
Yorkshire Theatres Ltd, 215
You, Too, Can Have a Body, 172–3, 220; Tour, 281
You'll Do For Me! (previously *A Bit Between the Teeth*), 184
Young, Charles, 26